Oxford University Committee for Archaeology

Monograph No. 5

MEDIEVAL VILLAGES

A Review of Current Work

edited by Della Hooke

Oxford University Committee for Archaeology

1985

Oxford University Committee for Archaeology
Monograph No. 5

Published by the Oxford University Committee for Archaeology
Institute of Archaeology
Beaumont Street
Oxford

Distributed by Oxbow Books
10 St. Cross Rd, Oxford OX1 3TU

ISBN 0 947816 05 4

Typeset on a Monophoto Lasercomp at Oxford University Computing Service
Printed in Great Britain at the Alden Press, Oxford

Preface

This volume embodies many of the papers presented at a conference organized by Trevor Rowley for the Department for External Studies, the University of Oxford, in January 1982. It was obvious that many new ideas were circulating concerning the origin and development of the medieval village, although these were often the outcome of many years of experience and study of village problems by the individual participants. Written as individual conference papers, and representing work carried out in many different regions, some suggestions were in apparent conflict while others represented ideas which were still being explored by their authors but which had not yet reached a stage of conclusion. During the conference it was felt, however, that ideas were beginning to synthesize and to reach a stage where they might provide valuable pointers towards future research. Twelve of the fourteen speakers at the conference agreed to publish their work in this volume and the papers deal with a range of subject matter which includes study techniques and methods of settlement classification, as well as case studies examining the evidence for settlement evolution and the forces which contributed to it. A number of additional papers which were not presented at the conference have been included in order to extend the study to cover a wider area of Britain and to consider additional aspects of village development.

The first group of papers tends to concentrate upon some sources of evidence available for village study and techniques for utilizing them, the evidence ranging from the written and cartographic to that provided by the morphology of the settlements themselves. Several papers deal with more specific aspects of settlement study which are applicable to much of the country as a whole. Later papers explore village development within particular regions. As each paper deals with development over a considerable time-span no attempt has been made to place these contributions in any sort of chronological order—rather, the sequence is geographically arranged, commencing in the South-West and proceeding northwards. The final papers deal with research strategy (one, by example).

Throughout the volume several themes tend to recur—notably, village origins and the subsequent development of the fully fledged medieval 'village'. Settlement patterns have obviously been subject to constant change but there seem to have been periods at which this was more likely to occur. Numerous factors likely to cause change have been outlined and will hopefully stimulate further discussion upon this subject. Although the subject of the conference was 'The Medieval Village' it is hoped that the resultant volume will be of value in wider-ranging studies of settlement evolution and will convey to a wider audience some of the excitement and enthusiasm of what must have been one of the most successful archaeological conferences ever organized by the Department for External Studies at the University of Oxford.

Della Hooke

Contributors

Michael A. Aston, B.A. F.S.A.
  Staff Tutor in Archaeology, Department of Extramural Studies, University of Bristol,
  Wills Memorial Building, Queen's Road, Bristol BS8 1HR

Mary A. Atkin, B.A.
  Formerly Senior Lecturer in Geography, Preston Polytechnic;
  Fiddler's Cotes, Levens, Kendal, Cumbria LA8 8NX

David Austin, B.A. Dip.Arch.
  Archaeology Unit, Department of Geography, Saint David's University College,
  Lampeter, Dyfed SA48 7ED

C. James Bond, B.A. F.S.A.
  Department of Museum Services, Oxfordshire County Council,
  Oxfordshire County Museum, Fletcher's House, Woodstock OX7 1SN

Christopher C. Dyer, B.A. Ph.D.
  School of History, University of Birmingham, P.O. Box 363, Birmingham B15 2TT

David N. Hall, M.A. F.S.A.
  Fenland Field Officer, Cambridgeshire Archaeological Committee,
  c/o Department of Archaeology, Downing St., Cambridge CB2 3DZ

Paul D. A. Harvey, M.A. D.Phil.
  Professor of Medieval History, Department of History, University of Durham,
  43/46, North Bailey, Durham DH1 3EX

Della Hooke, B.A. Ph.D.
  Department of Geography, University of Birmingham, P.O. Box 363, Birmingham B15 2TT

John G. Hurst, M.A. F.S.A.
  English Heritage, Historic Buildings and Monuments Commission for England,
  Fortress House, 23 Savile Row, London W1X 2HE

Glanville R. J. Jones, M.A. F.S.A.
  Professor of Historical Geography, School of Geography, University of Leeds, Leeds LS2 9JT

Douglas G. Lockhart, B.A. Ph.D.
  Department of Geography, University of Keele, Keele, Staffordshire ST5 5BG

Richard K. Morris, B.A. B.Phil. F.S.A.
  Research Officer, Council for British Archaeology.
  Department of Archaeology, University of Leeds, Leeds LS2 9JT

Philip A. Rahtz, M.A. F.S.A.
  Professor of Archaeology, Department of Archaeology,
  University of York, Micklegate House, Micklegate, York YO1 1JZ

Brian K. Roberts, B.A. Ph.D.
  Department of Geography, University of Durham, Science Laboratories, South Road, Durham DH1 3LE

R. Trevor Rowley, B.A. M.Litt. F.S.A.
  Staff Tutor in Archaeology, Department for External Studies, University of Oxford,
  Rewley House, 3–7 Wellington Square, Oxford OX1 2JA

Peter H. Sawyer, M.A.
  Formerly Professor of Medieval History, University of Leeds; Viktoriagatan 18, 441 33 Alingsås, Sweden

Contents

The Medieval Village: Introduction

R. T. Rowley

One hundred years ago Frederic Seebohm produced his *English Village Communities* (London 1883). He used detailed local evidence from the parishes of Hitchin and Much Wymondley in Hertfordshire to discuss the origins of the open field system which he believed to be inextricably linked with the origins of the English village. This publication stimulated a debate on the nature and development of the English village which has continued at an increasingly multi-disciplinary level to the present day. Seebolm approached the problem as an economic historian with a legal training. Since then the other specialists, such as place-name historians, historical geographers and field archaeologists, have made a major contribution to our understanding of the problem. The papers incorporated in this volume reflect the diversity of approach, but although there are wide geographical variations apparent in the contributions there is an underlying consistency in a desire to understand the dynamics of rural settlement—an exasperatingly slippery concept!

During the past century there have been several significant shifts in attitudes towards the origins of the medieval village. Seebohm believed that the open field system and the institutions that were associated with it were essentially an amalgam of Roman and Germanic influences. He also believed that the surviving customs of Wales and Ireland appeared to have developed from Celtic pre-Roman roots. In subsequent arguments the role attributed to the Romans in creating the system was gradually diminished until it disappeared altogether and for many generations the conventional wisdom was that the English village and its associated field systems were the product of the Anglo-Saxon settlements of the fifth to seventh centuries. The belief was that Germanic settlers brought with them, into a largely uninhabited primeval wilderness, a fully fledged pattern of regular settlements surrounded by their open fields, which they created by reclaiming the woodland and draining the marsh. References to land reclamation during the early medieval period were taken to represent the very last phases of this activity.

During the 1950s and 60s the increasing archaeological evidence showed that the 'Anglo-Saxons versus the wilderness' theory just was not true. Apart from anything else, even the most superficial examination of the aerial photographic record showed ancient land management of the prehistoric and Romano-British periods on a scale which, even allowing for some reversion in the post-Roman hiatus, demolished the wilderness concept. So, as is frequently the case in such arguments, the pendulum swung dramatically in the other direction and continuity became the fashionable term. This was not continuity in the Seebohm sense, that is the survival of Romano-British institutions, although Professor Finberg did resurrect this with his work on Roman/Saxon Withington in Gloucestershire. It was the idea of continuity of occupation, on or close to Romano-British native settlements in particular, and the survival of territorial units such as estates into the medieval period.

More recently more sopisticated models, which are well represented in this volume, have emerged. The basis of these arguments is twofold. Firstly, that rural settlement is rarely static for very long and has to be seen as organic, capable of growing, shifting, shrinking and then disappearing altogether. Secondly, that the mature open field system and the regular nucleated villages that go with it appear to be created in the late Anglo-Saxon or early post-Norman Conquest period. There are of course enormous regional variations both in time and in form and these too are well represented in this volume.

The papers included in this volume are, as always, intended as interim statements or questions and it is my belief, and indeed hope, that this volume will have a life (or perhaps I should say half-life) of no more than five years. I do believe, however, that the preoccupation which underlies several of the contributions with origins of the medieval village, which some say is an obsession, is leading us to a much more realistic understanding of settlement dynamics. This approach promises to have important implications for earlier archaeological periods and appears to be pushing us towards the conclusion that at a relatively late date between 800 and 1200 there was throughout much of England a massive reorganization of the agrarian system, accompanied by a re-structuring of much, if not most, rural settlement. Such concepts may still be difficult for many of us to accept but ironically enough have long been in daily use with Scandinavian, German and French scholars for many years.

1. The Anglo-Norman Village

P. H. Sawyer

The sources for rural society in Anglo-Norman England have great limitations: they tend to conceal local variations and also exaggerate the changes caused by the Norman Conquest. The tenants named in Domesday Book before and after 1066 often had different status; sitting tenants were commonly named before but not afterwards. The English ancestry of many twelfth-century landowners is concealed by their Norman names. Domesday is an unsatisfactory guide to both the distribution and character of settlements and provides no information on the scale of nucleation. It does not consistently record rural or urban markets, many of which certainly existed long before they were granted charters. It also omits many rent-paying tenants and its evidence for both population and social structure is therefore suspect.

There was, of course, no such thing as the Anglo-Norman village. In the eleventh and twelfth centuries, as at other times, there were many forms of settlement ranging from nucleations of different shapes and sizes to highly dispersed communities. What is more, the pattern was not static; the size, shape and location of settlements was always liable to change. This obviously makes generalization hazardous. Our evidence is too incomplete to allow confident assertions about the character of settlements at any one time or even in any one area. Domesday Book, despite its 13,000 and more place-names, is a misleading guide to the distribution and character of settlements in the mid-eleventh century, and the other available evidence is far less comprehensive and systematic than that text. Surveys and charters were naturally compiled on behalf of lords and therefore present a seigneurial view. The men and women who lived on, and worked the land probably saw the commmunities to which they belonged in a very different light. The written evidence for the period 1086–1135 has been well covered by Lennard (1959). This very thorough and careful treatment of the available historical evidence is the indispensable guide for anyone, archaeologist, geographer or historian, interested in the history of settlement in the eleventh and twelfth centuries.

The archaeological evidence, although of the greatest value, is even less comprehensive and systematic than our written sources, and there is no equivalent of Lennard to act as guide. Only a handful of sites has been investigated at all thoroughly, and no medieval village has been completely excavated. The one that has been most thoroughly studied is, of course, Wharram Percy, but one of the most important results of more than 30 years work there has been to demonstrate that it is impossible to generalize about the development of even one settlement. The relationship between settlements inevitably remains a still deeper mystery.

The effort made in the Wharram Percy project to relate that settlement to the surrounding landscape has only served to underline the problems that have to be faced. Fieldwalking can certainly help us locate, and sometimes date, early settlements but the absence of occupational debris cannot be taken to prove the absence of earlier settlements in an area.

My aim in this introductory paper is to comment on some of the problems posed by the written evidence and to draw attention to a few of the factors that affected the history of rural settlement in the century and a half after the Norman Conquest. In doing so I hope to pose some questions that will certainly be discussed, and may perhaps be answered, by other contributors to this volume.

The obvious starting point is the event that put the Norman into Anglo-Norman England, the Norman Conquest. Great changes resulted but, as Stenton remarked, 'the structure of rural society was not seriously affected by the Norman settlement' (1971, 686). The changes that did occur in that century were as much the work of time as of the Conquest. There was in fact a great gulf between conquerors and conquered, not only politically and socially, but also linguistically, for the language spoken in the countryside remained English. It is true that in time French, or rather Anglo-Norman, did have a marked influence on the English language but that was the work of the thirteenth and fourteenth centuries, not the eleventh and twelfth. Unlike the Scandinavians, the Normans had little effect on field-names (Gelling 1978, 238). Long after 1066, the Norman conquerors found it difficult to communicate with the mass of the population and that was also true of most leading churchmen. Very few were like Samson, Abbot of Bury, who was able to preach in his native Norfolk dialect. At a lower social level the gulf is vividly revealed by a story told about Wulfric of Haslebury who cured a dumb man and taught him to speak both

English and French. This made the parish priest, Brihtric, very indignant 'All these years I have served you and today I have proved that it was for nothing. To a stranger, whose tongue it would have been enough to open, you have given the use of two languages, while to me, who am forced to remain dumb in the presence of the bishop and archdeacon, you have never imparted a word of French' (Mayr-Harting 1975, 344). In such circumstances it is perhaps not surprising that the invaders did little to disrupt the continuity of rural life once their conquest was complete.

The gulf between the Anglo-Norman aristocracy and the majority of the population is partly obscured by the change that occurred in personal nomenclature. The names used by the conquerors quickly became popular, first among the aristocracy and leading burgesses, later among the peasantry. A century after the Conquest, the names William, Robert, Richard, Ralph, Hugo and Walter were common in all parts of England (Reaney 1961) and it is often possible to show that the parents of a William or a Theobald had English or Anglo-Scandinavian names. It is therefore unsafe to assume that a man with a French name after the middle of the twelfth century had French ancestry. There were, at the same time, some native survivals and in thirteenth-century Yorkshire such names as Waltheof, Uhtræd and William son of Svannild occur (Sawyer 1973, 80).

It has often been asserted that one of the most significant changes wrought by the Normans was the imposition of a new but much less numerous aristocracy, a few of whom acquired vast estates. This change can perhaps be exaggerated. The English had been familiar with very large landowners before the Conquest, not only the Earls but also men like Wulfric Spot, who bequeathed land in 80 places scattered through 12 counties, (Sawyer 1978a, xvii) or Mærlswein, who held land in Yorkshire, Lincolnshire, Gloucestershire, Somerset, Devon and Cornwall (von Feilitzen 1937, 326).

Men who held land in several counties could not, of course, manage it themselves; they had to rely on stewards or agents. The duties of a steward or reeve are described in an English text of the eleventh century known as *Gerefa* (Liebermann 1903, 453–5). Landowners could also let land at farm (Lennard 1959, 105–41) but a more common solution, before as well as after the Conquest, was to have subtenants. At least some of the people named in Domesday Book as pre-Conquest landowners were tenants and the compilers of Domesday Book do not seem to have been concerned always to name the lords from whom the land was held. The explanation may be that it was unnecessary to name them because they were, in fact, the *antecessores* into whose shoes the Norman lords had stepped. Domesday names pre-Conquest holders of land not in order to prove title to land as much as to define the land

in question. Local people would perfectly well know what was meant by the land of Archil or Wulfmær and there was no need to describe the bounds and appurtenances in more detail. We do, however, sometimes learn the name of the pre-Conquest overlord when a dispute is recorded. A good example is the claim made by Robert of Stafford against Earl Alan to land at Billingborough in Lincolnshire that had been held by Carle. This claim was rejected because Carle had held it from Ralf the Staller, who was Earl Alan's *antecessor*, but the Domesday description of Billingborough gives no hint that Ralf had any interest in the place (Domesday Book 1, 348, 377b). It is obviously impossible to determine the full extent of such subtenancies but there are indications that they were common. The fact that Fyach is not recorded as holding any land in Lincolnshire although he is listed among those who had full rights as landowners in the county (Domesday Book 1, 337) suggests that he retained no demesne there and, similarly, extensive subtenancies may explain why the Bishop of Dorchester held so little land in Lincolnshire before the Conquest. We may furthermore suspect, but cannot prove, that Ulf Fenisc, who held land in many counties and was succeeded almost everywhere by Gilbert of Ghent, had Tonna as a subtenant in Lincolnshire, Northamptonshire and Oxfordshire. This is suggested by the fact that Ulf is listed among those who had full land-owning rights in Lincolnshire while Tonna is not (Domesday Book 1, 337).

In describing the situation in 1086 Domesday Book further exaggerates the changes that had occurred by concentrating on the tenants-in-chief and their main subtenants. In many entries it mentions inferior tenants but does not bother to name them and some Domesday satellites (that is texts that are independently derived from the material gathered while making Domesday Book) reveal some subtenants whose existence is concealed by Domesday Book itself (Sawyer 1960, 12–13). Some of these men were newcomers from the Continent but many were of native descent. In Yorkshire, for example, although by the end of the twelfth century most landowners had continental names, many of those whose ancestry can be traced back to the first half of the century can be seen to have had English or Anglo-Scandinavian ancestors. Thus, Theobald of Dishforth, who lived in the middle of the century, was the son of Wulgeat (Clay 1963, 279), while his contemporary Adam of Giggleswick was the son of Meldred (Clay 1963, 41). A particularly interesting case is Adam, who appears in 1166, who was the son of Norman, grandson of Uhtræd and the great grand-son of a pre-Conquest tenant called Alwine. Adam held land that had been Alwine's but had been split between two fees, Percy and Meschin (Clay 1963, 243–5), and the essential continuity is therefore obscured by feudal geography. Many landowners may well have been of continental ancestry, but at least some of these families included English wives (Stenton 1944).

Subtenants like Theobald of Dishforth and Adam son of Norman played a key role in local affairs, attending the courts of hundreds or wapentakes and also, perhaps, the shire, as well as the honorial courts of their feudal lords. Many of them had scattered holdings but it appears from the evidence of charters that they tended to maintain particularly close associations with the area in which they lived and it was there that they were especially active. We can observe them witnessing the charters of their neighbours, marrying members of local families, making benefactions to the local churches and sometimes appointing their relatives as priests. They also made gifts to local religious communities, especially to nunneries. Speaking the same language as their less well-born and well-endowed neighbours, these men dominated their own villages, cultivating their demesnes and holding manorial courts. It was these men who played a crucial role in maintaining the continuity of English rural society.

Another neglected, but important group in Anglo-Norman village society were the *censarii*, the rent-paying tenants who were in at least some places completely omitted from Domesday Book. It is only the chance survival of two surveys of the estates of Burton Abbey from the early twelfth century that makes it possible to show how misleading Domesday can be. It has been claimed that these *censarii* in the surveys were a new group that had developed since 1086, and that there had been a great population increase, but, as John Walmsey demonstrated (1968), detailed comparison of the three texts clearly shows that this explanation cannot be maintained. The following table, compiled by Walmsey, speaks for itself. Survey B was compiled in 1114 and Survey A about 12 years later.

We may suspect that similar omissions were made elsewhere, but not everywhere. The equivalent groups appear to have been recorded, for example, in East Anglia and Lincolnshire.

There is no need to emphasize the inadequacy of Domesday Book as a source for the study of settlement (Sawyer 1978b, 136–41). This is made very clear by the lists of eleventh-century churches in Kent which include 160 places that are not named in Domesday Book, many of them in the Weald which according to Domesday was almost devoid of habitation. We lack such convenient controls elsewhere but there are many indications that other areas that are blank on the map of Domesday settlements were, in fact, well settled (Darby 1977, 15–26). This makes one a little doubtful about the scale of the expansion of settlement that is commonly supposed to have occurred in the twelfth century. There were, of course, some areas in which such expansion is well evidenced, notably the Fens and in Yorkshire, but in many areas one may suspect that what appears to be expansion of the cultivated area and an increase in the number of settlements is, in effect, largely a trick of our sources.

Just as one name could be used to describe a large estate with many settlements in it, so too what appear to be 'village' names may well refer not to nucleations but to dispersed settlements. The development of nucleations, nucleated settlements and their associated common fields has been fully discussed at a recent Oxford conference (Rowley 1981) and will certainly be an important topic here and I will therefore do no more than underline the danger of assuming that the places named in Domesday Book were nucleated settlements. Neither demesne farming nor co-aration necessarily implies the existence of nucleated settlements.

Dispersed settlements obviously functioned as communities. The evidence for much communal

Table 1.1   Burton abbey estates in the early twelfth century

Manor	Villani			Censarii		Others			Totals		
	DB	B	A	B	A	DB	B	A	DB	B	A
Burton	9	11	6	12	9	–	36	27	9	59	42
Branston	5	8	5	9	10	3	4	4	8	21	19
Stretton	8	18	16	9	9	2	5	7	10	32	32
Wetmore	6	9	6	14	15	–	4	8	6	27	29
Abbots Bromley	1	5	–	6	15	2	1	–	3	12	15
Leigh	10	12	12	8	9	1	1	1	11	21	22
Mickleover	20	18	19	10	9	10	5	5	30	33	33
Littleover	–	18	14	8	8	–	6	7	–	32	29
Findern	–	–	–	8	13	–	7	6	–	15	19
Potlock	–	–	–	1	6	–	–	–	–	1	6
Stapenhill	12	7	6	9	9	–	8	10	12	24	25
Winshill	10	11	10	16	18	–	11	2	10	38	30
Appleby	8	16	15	9	7	–	2	–	8	27	22
	89	133	109	119	137	18	90	77	107	342	323

activity, for example in by-laws, is late, but there are earlier indications, including the custom of making communal presentments and the existence of tithings. The most obvious manifestation of a community was, of course, the church. A few churches may have been built by a group of peasants, but most were constructed by lords. And this raises the question of why villages with several lords often have only one church. The answer which will be given by Richard Morris later in this volume is quite simply that some communities may originally have had more than one church, but that the number was reduced deliberately in the eleventh or twelfth centuries.

Finally, in this very short review of some of the factors affecting our interpretation of the evidence for settlements in the eleventh and twelfth centuries, I should like to draw attention to the importance of local markets. Their number and significance at that time has been somewhat obscured by our sources. There is indeed a temptation, to which many scholars succumb, to treat the market charters that were granted in large numbers in the thirteenth and fourteenth centuries as evidence for a vast expansion of markets. There are however many indications that markets, or rather *congregationes gentium*, were a widespread feature of

rural life in pre-Conquest England (Sawyer 1981). They were often held at churches on Sundays and our sources are silent because these assemblies were not owned by anyone, they did not yield either toll or stallage. Long before the Norman Conquest, English kings tried to regulate this trade and limit buying and selling to royal markets, but they failed. The Normans brought alien ideas and began to impose tolls where none had been paid before but in time the royal prerogative was asserted and all markets then required royal licence, either by charter or the recognition of prescriptive right. Local exchanges between producers must always have been important and we may suspect that the rapid success of some new town foundations in the twelfth century was largely due to the existence in those places of 'pre-markets'. It was in these assemblies that peasants and their lords sold their surplus produce and were able to buy the specialized wares that they needed and could afford.

The pattern of rural life in Anglo-Norman England was therefore rather more complicated than sometimes appears in our sources and, as I emphasized at the beginning of this paper we must take care not to allow the limitations of our evidence to delude us into assuming uniformity.

References

Clay, C. T. 1963: *Early Yorkshire Charters* Vol. 11, The Percy Fee (Wakefield, Yorkshire Archaeological Society).

Darby, H. C. 1977: *Domesday Book* (Cambridge, Cambridge University Press).

Domesday Book, Record Commission 1783.

Gelling, M. 1978: *Signposts to the Past* (London, Dent).

Lennard, R. V. 1959: *Rural England 1086–1135* (Oxford, Clarendon Press).

Liebermann, F. 1903: *Die Gesetze der Angelsachsen* Vol. 1, (Halle, Niemeyer).

Mayr-Harting, H. 1975: Functions of a twelfth-century recluse. *History* 60, 337–52.

Reaney, P. H. 1961: *A Dictionary of British Surnames* (London, Routledge and Kegan Paul).

Rowley, T. (editor) 1981: *The Origins of Open-Field Agriculture* (London, Croom Helm).

Sawyer, P. H. 1960: Evesham A Domesday text. *Miscellany I* (Worcester, Worcestershire Historical Society) 3–36.

Sawyer, P. H. 1973: Baldersby, Borup and Bruges: the rise of northern Europe *University of Leeds Review* 16, 75–96.

Sawyer, P. H. 1978a: *Charters of Burton Abbey* (London, British Academy).

Sawyer, P. H. 1978b: *From Roman Britain to Norman England* (London, Methuen).

Sawyer, P. H. 1981: Fairs and markets in early medieval England. In Skyum-Nielsen, N. and Lund, N. (editors). 1981, 153–68.

Skyum-Nielsen, N. and Lund, N. (editors) 1981: *Danish Medieval History New Currents* (Copenhagen, Museum Tusculanum Press).

Stenton, F. M. 1944: English families and the Norman Conquest. *Transactions of the Royal Historical Society* 4th series, 26, 325–34.

Stenton, F. M. 1971: *Anglo-Saxon England* 3rd edition (Oxford, Oxford University Press).

von Feilitzen, O. 1937: *The Pre-Conquest Personal Names of Domesday Book*. Nomina Germanica No. 3 (Uppsala, Almquist and Wiksells Boktryckeri).

Walmsey, J. F. R. 1968: The 'censarii' of Burton Abbey and the Domesday population. *North Staffordshire Journal of Field Studies* 8, 73–80.

2. Village Patterns and Forms: some Models for Discussion

B. K. Roberts

Surviving plans form one of the sources available for the study of medieval villages: a proportion of these have indisputable medieval antecedents. Retrogressive analysis is a well-established technique but to produce the most results several scales of study are necessary. Four models demonstrate varied scales of analysis: the first defines the essential spatial relationships present within plans; the second demonstrates a system of classification designed to order the vast range of plan-types of the real world; while the third attempts to integrate in one diagram some of the interrelationships between changing plans and changing patterns, leading towards questions concerning the processes generating morphological and spatial change or stability. A final model returns to classification and, starting with the threshold between dispersion and nucleation, shows that the plan-types defined in the main classification can be seen as points on a continuum of development. Such broad pictures, based on landscape evidence, provide frameworks for detailed studies.

'Besides their diversity in function and density, . . . settlements . . . . display great variety of form . . . the present pattern has developed through a long period of time, i.e. through rather more than a thousand years. It is the geographical record of its own evolution. Traditional forms, inexplicable by present conditions, survive side by side with modern forms everywhere.' (Conzen 1949, 76)

This paper is ultimately concerned with two fundamental questions concerning villages; can village plans, the physical parts of settlements, be used as a source of evidence to throw some light on their evolution, and what processes account for the varied characteristics of villages now present in the landscape? At the outset, however, it must be stressed that scholars working on 'the medieval village' are concerned with three fundamental objectives, the reconstruction of the physical structures, the reconstruction of the organizational and economic arrangements, and the reconstruction of the social conditions of the inhabitants. Each of these can of course be studied independently; thus the work of the Toronto school, associated with J. A. Raftis (1957), is particularly concerned with the third of these aspects, excluding the first, and treating the second as a context. In practice most work adopts one aspect as a focus, a theme, in the context of which complex interrelationships can be described and examined. These interrelationships and our perception and description of cause-effect linkages within them constitute explanations of defined problems.

All such studies draw upon three categories of sources; documents, including maps and place-name studies; archaeological excavations, the scientific destruction of physical remains; and the evidence of landscapes, the physical survivals of the past within the present. This paper deals mainly with landscape evidence and its use for reconstructing and understanding the physical structures of villages—not necessarily medieval villages—for time is a seamless robe, the matrix within which things exist and processes operate. The viewpoint adopted was succinctly encapsulated by Conzen when he wrote that settlement 'is the geographical record of its own evolution'. Nevertheless, this is no narrow perspective, for it is concerned with a theme which focusses upon the morphological evidence provided by village plans, which are ultimately reflections of organizational arrangements and social and economic conditions. We have a situation, common in both archaeology and science, in which the thing itself is evidence for the processes which have moulded it. Thus, the sequences of logical analysis applied in considering villages are essentially similar to those used when examining the architectural history of a great church (Rodwell 1981) or the character of soils within a local region (Clarke 1971; Curtis *et al.* 1976); analysis and explanation must be preceded by careful description, the recording of the observations, and classification, to place the particular case in a wider context, and case-studies are in themselves both the foundation of more general hypotheses and the means of criticising and reconstructing these same hypotheses.

Scale, Classification and Terminology

Questions concerning scales of enquiry touch upon a highly productive area of tension: on the one hand investigations may focus upon the character, development and origins of a particular village, while on the other such studies present a real challenge to seek a wider perspective, at a local, regional or national scale.

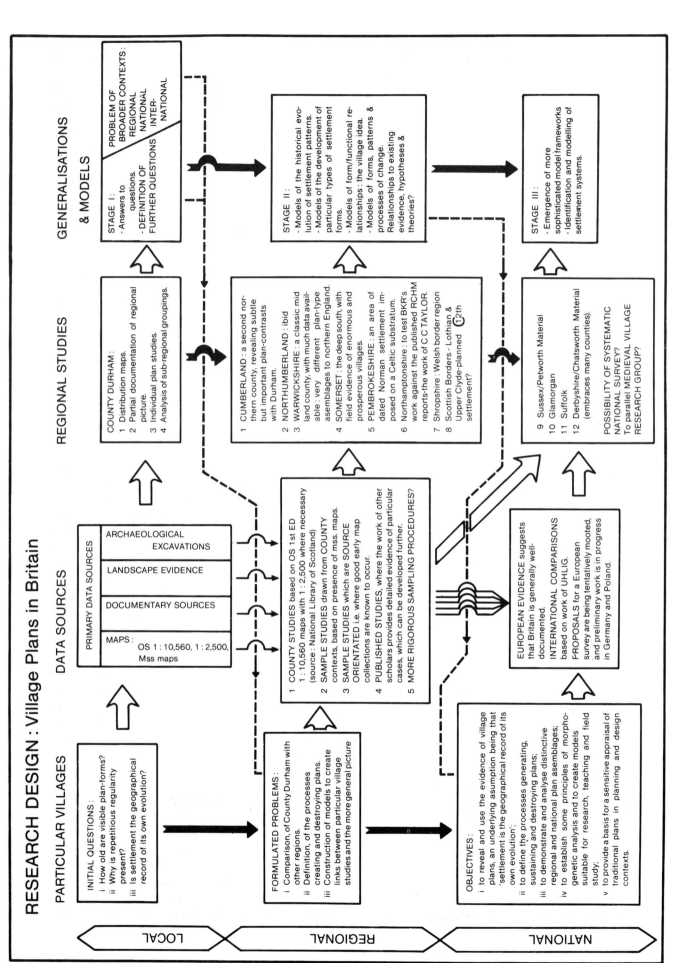

Fig. 2.1 *Research design: village plans in Britain*

Whatsoever questions, training, objectives and attitudes are being taken to our evidence (assuming that our evidence could indeed be independent of these) a point is reached when the language used to decribe the particular characteristics of a single place must be tested in the context of other localities for the purposes of comparison or contrast, and the scale tensions find expression in the need to create a terminology and classify the features observed. The terms used and the classifications adopted are, as David Harvey notes, the means 'by which we impose some sort of order upon the vast flow of information from the real world, and the word-symbols applied to characterize basic observations in the field or the document reflect, very much, the state of the discipline' (1969, 326–7). This affects, in turn, the ultimate value of comparisons and contrasts. In moving collectively from the stage of mere description towards an understanding of process, scholars must have some unanimity concerning the meaning of terms they use.

Beresford pinpointed another key problem when he wrote 'since historians have learned much in the last thirty years (he was writing in 1958; 126) from geographers' essays in classification it may be well to point out that some systems have too easily assumed that the pattern of fields and houses on the modern map is *ipso facto* medieval'. He, of course, went on to demonstrate how much of the contemporary scene *can* be medieval, but his essential point remains valid. This fundamental caveat has important repercussions for those using landscape evidence: we cannot just look at the medieval village. The post-medieval past is a filter which must be carefully evaluated and morphogenetic analysis must be retrogressive, working backwards from the known to the unknown (Baker 1968). In the absence of medieval maps Paul Harvey was constrained to use the earliest he had, an estate map of 1767, as a framework around which to carefully assemble an argument based upon medieval documents and create his 'conjectural plan' for the Oxfordshire village of Cuxham in the period 1279–1349 (1965, 122, 172–3). Thus, the models examined below relate to a continuum of settlement evolution: no simplistic retrogressive projections of the type Beresford warned against are involved.

The geographical analysis of medieval villages at any scale demands two things; first, an attempt to define what was present, an exercise in seeking evidence, in reconstruction and in description and, second, an attempt to establish what changes were taking place. Only then can causal links be examined and explanations sought. In essence the first part of this exercise involves assessing what proportion of the visible elements within a given pattern could be medieval, a procedure necessarily dependent upon particular studies of individual settlements (Ravensdale 1974, 121–50; Sheppard 1976; Wade-Martins 1975). Working with imperfect evidence makes the reconstruction of processes of change within a spatial as well as a temporal dimension impossible (Roberts 1982a). Nevertheless, the fact that so many local, regional and national patterns of change have been identified, in enclosure movements, population trends, village depopulations and social trends, does give some hope, although there will always be thresholds beyond which deficiencies in the evidence prevent the definition of meaningful patterns. The author's own work on the distribution of moated sites is a pointer to the problems; while it is possible to suggest that some spatial variations result from differences *between* estates, differences between portions of the *same* estate also occur (Roberts 1976–7), and even these tentative conclusions rest on the assumption that the particular administrative contexts which *might* have produced the observed differences were in existence long enough for them to have indeed been causal factors! In such contexts deductive models, ultimately drawing upon post-medieval data, can provide one framework within which to evaluate the less voluminous and less tractable evidence from earlier periods.

Figure 2.1 is a diagram showing the present author's research design: it deliberately lays emphasis upon scale changes as a factor in stimulating enquiry; it moves from personally generated initial questions towards discipline-orientated problems and eventually broader objectives; and it recognizes the place of models as means of summarizing arguments, stating generalizations, and as stimuli for further enquiry. The research design in no way represents an attempt to create a scheme for the study of the 'medieval village' which might be universally acceptable; it represents one solution, the author's solution, to the problems raised in treating *one* of the three fundamental objectives defined in the first paragraph of this paper. Nevertheless there is a challenge here: our research designs must achieve a measure of convergence in both language and objectives if we are to move beyond idiosyncratic appraisals by individual scholars. This, for the author, was one of the most important and interesting possibilities emerging from the 1981 Oxford conference on *The Medieval Village*, the stimulus for the present volume.

Sources and Comparisons

In a number of published studies, cited in the footnotes to this paper, the author has demonstrated how map sources, together with other documentary evidence and field investigation, can be used to demonstrate the character and diversity of village plans and to pose and, in part at least, answer some of the questions concerning their distribution and development. In this,

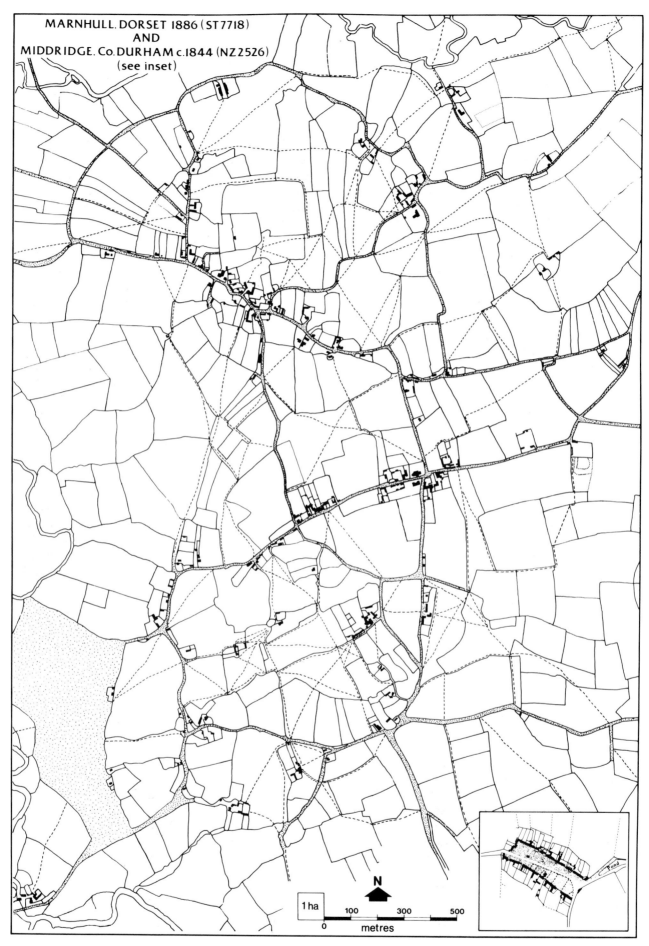

MARNHULL. DORSET 1886 (ST 7718)
AND
MIDDRIDGE. Co. DURHAM c.1844 (NZ 2526)
(see inset)

N

1 ha

0   100   300   500

metres

Pond

Fig. 2.2 Marnhull, Dorset, 1886 (ST 7718) and Middridge, County Durham c. 1844 (NZ 2526)

leads given by Thorpe in 1951 and Beresford in 1958 were followed. Nineteenth-century Ordnance Survey maps provide the basis for all such work—universally available surveys, following rigorously applied conventions and at standard scales. These can then be supplemented with earlier map sources, widely available in the early nineteenth century and second half of the eighteenth century, but becoming only sporadically available, in biased samples associated with great estates, as one moves towards the late sixteenth century. True medieval maps are rare indeed (Harvey 1980). These studies do three things:

i)   they reveal a rich harvest of village types, all of which are solutions to essentially the same organizational problem, that of providing a home-base for a community of farmers raising grain crops and producing some stock;

ii) they reveal the presence of both stability and change within the village, suggesting the presence of diverse processes;

iii) they demonstrate the need to classify and compare; for while initial analyses show identical plan-types appearing in widely separated regions, further study hints at the presence of well-marked regional contrasts, both in the character of overall patterns and in the composition of the individual plans of which these are made (Roberts 1980).

In themselves, however, such studies tell us nothing of the medieval scene, for it is essential that any conclusions concerning early periods should be based upon proven relationships between the documented plan-types and their medieval antecendents. The author believes that he has done this in County Durham and work in Yorkshire, Cambridgeshire, Northamptonshire, Oxfordshire and East Anglia has produced either similar arguments or modification, qualification or dispute (Roberts 1972, 1977, 1982b; Sheppard 1966, 1974, 1976; Taylor 1977; Harvey 1978; Wade-Martins 1975; see also Lockhart 1980).

The models presented here have been chosen to illustrate several aspects of the study of villages, particularly, the morphology of the individual settlement, the problems of classification and comparison and the processes of change affecting both forms and patterns of rural settlements. They range from simple to complex. One of the problems of presenting arguments in print is that the number of illustrative cases put before the reader is necessarily limited and although there are indeed disadvantages in twelve or so figures illustrating two or three dozen village plans, they do have the advantage of being an instant introduction to the volume of the evidence and the diversity and similarity to be found. Fig. 2.2, of the villages of Marnhall, Dorset and Middridge, County Durham, is one illustration selected from many possibilities: it reveals the great scale variations found

between places which may be called villages, contrasts in the degrees of plan simplicity or complexity, and provides a challenge to explain such diversity.[1]

MODEL 1: The Basic Village

The first model to be discussed looks, and is, exceedingly simple (Fig. 2.3), but is designed to raise questions concerning the normal spatial relationships within hamlet or village clusters, and the terminology which can be applied to the basic plan elements; it also touches questions of village genesis. Nevertheless, it is not in any sense restricted in application to any single time-period: living examples of this layout can be found throughout northern Europe, and indeed beyond (Erixon 1961; Uhlig 1961; Helmfrid 1972; Myhre 1973; Rönneseth 1975; Fenton 1978; Dodgshon 1980). It is a type commonly seen on seventeenth-century maps (Northumberland County History Committee, 1893, 1, 256; 1935, 14, 184, 280) and provides one way of integrating both archaeological and documentary evidence concerning the Anglo-Saxon village (Roberts 1981a, 160–1). It ignores the layers of landscape development which must be present in many parts of Britain, and it is not designed to examine the complex questions of continuity; indeed, in no small measure it draws upon discoveries made upon settlement margins. The value of this model lies in the questions which it stimulates. In essence, it divides a simple nucleated settlement into a series of points (the houses), lines (the boundaries) and areas (the types of land use), and this statement touches two vital thresholds; firstly, the problem of defining single farmsteads, hamlets and true villages, a line of discussion which will not be pursued

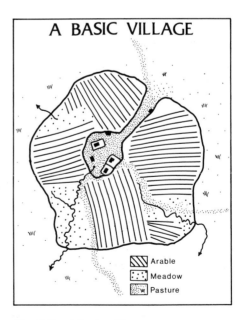

Fig. 2.3 A basic village

further, and second, it touches the threshold between nucleation and dispersion, for variants of this layout occur where farmsteads lie at a distance from each other, while sharing the same arable and meadow areas: for instance, they could lie on the periphery of the main enclosure, adjacent to the rough grazing land. The latter raises many interesting questions and recent explorations suggest that townships lacking both a nucleated settlement or traces of a depopulated nucleation are sufficiently common not to be in any way exceptional, occurring, nevertheless, within regions otherwise dominated by nucleated settlements. This is a topic for future work (Roberts 1982b; see also Uhlig 1961, 296–301).

The model can be analysed in terms of both areas and boundaries: there is an inner area of land where houses can be put. This is not, initially, a village green, although it embraces, in part, a similar function, and a true integral green, where commonable beasts can be grazed and lawful games played, can be regarded as the formalized residuum of this space. Its primary function is that of land where dwelling houses and associated outbuildings could be legally erected, and it should be noted that the positioning of those structures shown in this model is deliberate; they can sit either on the open land without a surrounding individual enclosure, or on the space and be separately enclosed, or peripheral to the space, abutting the boundary, and be either enclosed or not. These varied locations, it can be argued, represent very different relationships to the inner space and to the functional and legal characteristics it may posses. Fenton, writing of the Northern Isles, documents something of such arrangements (Fenton 1978, 18–39), but a search of the readily available by-laws concerning villages reveals surprisingly little concerning this *settlement land* (Miller and Hatcher 1978, 87–8). Rowland Parker raises fascinating questions when be cites a sixteenth-century by-law ruling for Foxton, Cambridgeshire; 'No one shall carry away the common dung made in the street unless for every two cart-loads of dung he shall carry back one load of stones into the roads of Foxton', and even this retains elements of ambiguity, for the street may not be the village street (Parker 1976, 108).

The presence of dung is a reminder of one use of the settlement land, as the focus of routeways, not least the outgang, rake, or driftway, the cattle-track leading from the village to the rough grazings. In practice it can be difficult to differentiate between these three elements, settlement land, driftway and rough grazings, but they are different and in more formalized arrangements would be the subject of separate rules of usage. It is not the purpose of this paper to consider the character of the arable and hay-meadow land or the unimproved pastures in detail, but it is worth noting that hay-meadow, dunged and improved, could precede the arable use of a given site and that, as Fenton hints, the relationship between such directly productive land and the settlement land need by no means be a simple one (Fenton 1978, 24–5). The accumulation of phosphate-rich debris, dung and organic waste, in and around the settlement could create a situation in which the land's productive potential could be realized, with the settlement land of one period becoming a crop production core in the next. The settlement-site shifts recognized by Wade-Martins in East Anglia could well have this factor as a part-cause, particulary if the communities concerned were not producing garden crops. If garden crops were produced, beans, leeks, cabbages, onions and flax, then this could be a factor tying a settlement to the enhanced soils of the settlement lands (Wade-Martins 1975; Finberg 1972, 420–2).[2]

The key boundaries shown in the model are of tremendous practical importance: between the dwelling area and the improved lands a boundary is essential and this will normally be both stock-proof and permanent, and the same can be said of those boundaries between the driftway and the cropland. While these are certainly not immutable they create fixation lines within the evolving plan and their maintenance will normally be a communal obligation, in distinction to the fences around an individual farmstead. The Laws of Ine, AD 690, made this contrast quite clear (Finberg 1972, 416). The boundaries between improved land and rough grazings are equally essential—to protect hay and arable crops from the depredations of deer and domestic stock, but in an expanding settlement this outer perimeter emerges as a frontier line, subject to movement; it may, of course, also retreat.

This discussion contains both explicit and implicit questions for those scholars concerned with the medieval village. The arrangements, both morphological and organizational, found within more complex villages are associated with formalizations of the structures described. This formalization may either take place at one fell swoop, as in the creation of a planned village, or it may appear in a piecemeal and often incomplete manner, or it may involve complex processes of evolution and reorganization at many stages in the life-history of a single settlement. The model can, of course, only represent one, much-simplified, antecedent village type, but the questions it raises are of fundamental importance in generating more sophisticated models. In effect, the larger the settlement the more complex are the rules needed to provide an operational framework for the good of the whole community and although questions concerning the ultimate origins of by-laws and the settlements to which they relate are not easily resolved because of the problem of evidence, this is no reason why they should not be asked (Ault 1972, 18–19).

VILLAGE PLAN-ELEMENTS

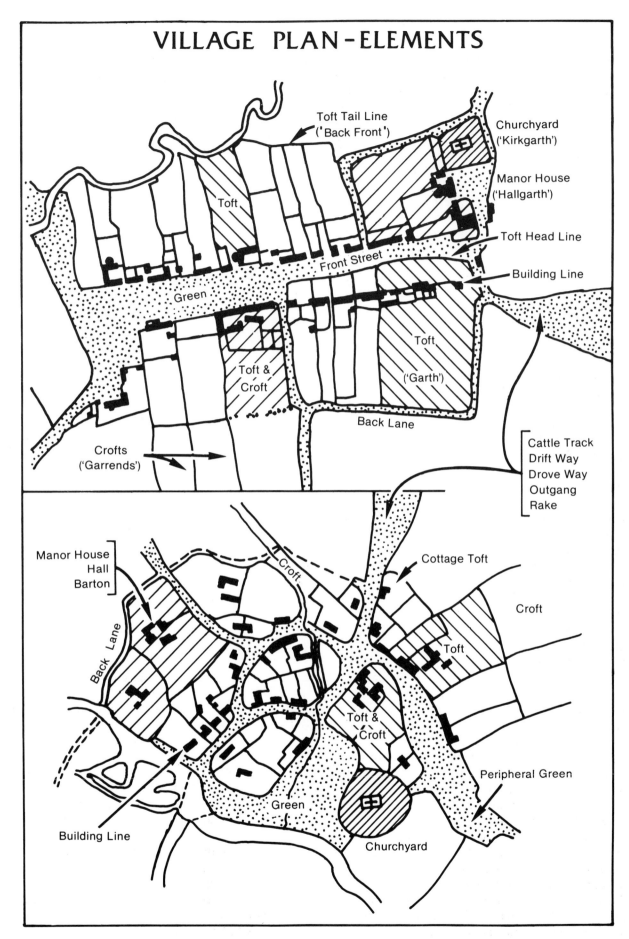

Fig. 2.4 Village plan-elements

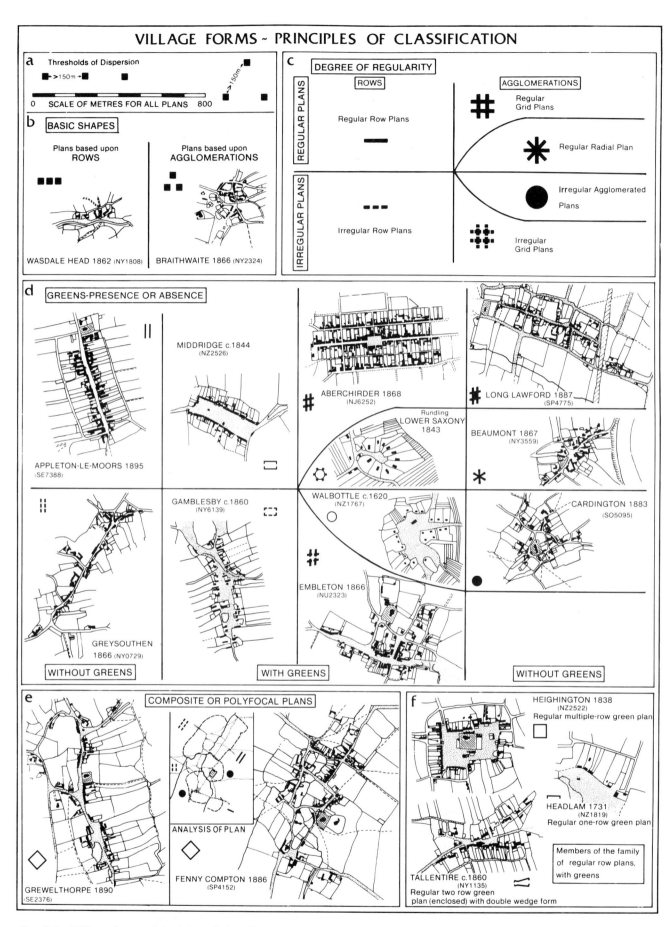

Fig. 2.5 Village forms: principles of classification

Linking Discussion I

The simple normative model discussed above does occur in reality and settlements with the characteristics described by the model are discoverable in both manuscript map sources and in the field. It can be legitimately argued that the model represents not a village but a hamlet, and although it is not intended to examine here the thresholds involved and the problems of definition, those settlement forms which lie below villages in the hierarchy and yet are demonstrably 'old' are worthy of close study, particularly those which represent township or parish foci, the latter containing, or associated with, the church. Indications of the presence of communal fields, or common grazing practices, showing, in fact, the presence of communality without close nucleation—for a mere scatter of farmsteads may be involved—may indicate the survival of a system of settlement of a type which could be antecedent to the development of true villages. Rodhuish, Somerset, consists to this day of no more than a scatter of four farmsteads with their associated cottages, with an isolated church set between two of the farms: all of the farmsteads are at least 150 m apart and the whole complex sprawls over about 750 m.[3] . In the light of recent discoveries of the dispersed patterns of Anglo-Saxon date (Taylor 1974, 5–11; Hall and Martin 1979), and of the composite character of many large villages (Taylor 1977), it is reasonable to ask if Rodhuish is indeed an antecedent type, still surviving. This interpretation, as yet unproven and thus merely hypothesis, is in accord with the absence of any visible village earthworks and Hoskins' arguments concerning the antiquity of single-farmstead settlement in the south-west of Britain (Hoskins 1963, 15–52). Such linked farm clusters are widely spread and must form the subject of further enquiry (Roberts 1982, 137–8).

Another antecedent type may be recognizable in what the author currently terms church-hallgarth, or church-manor complexes, where distinctive oval or polygonal enclosures containing an ancient church and the manor farm are found as survivals in areas as far apart as Somerset and Wales, Cumberland, Shropshire, Northamptonshire and Hertfordshire, an observation which must link this work with investigations of churchyards. In contrast to these rigidly bounded structures, three farmsteads around a small green can develop into a tight cluster which grows inwards on to the open space which becomes planted with cottages, so that public access ways blend with backyards, private spaces, in ill-defined ways. Such irregular clusters are common in the Heriott country of the Yorkshire dales.[4] In all of these types, settlement forms lying below the true village threshold, and indeed blurring the hamlet-single farmstead boundary, we see settlements which have still to be clearly defined and classified before they can be systematically studied as distinctive forms.

There are strong indications, however, that a careful study of both the living landscapes of today, supported by cartographic evidence from the last three or four centuries, will expand tremendously our understanding of forms which were both present in earlier centuries, and which may therefore be archaeologically detectable, and represent types antecedent to our present more complex villages.

All complex villages are made up of distinctive combinations of *plan-elements*, and Fig. 2.4 provides both a demonstration of the actual structures in question and the varied plans these can produce. Again this is not a subject for detailed discussion here, but in any study of villages one is faced with the problem of integrating studies of particular places, individual villages, into a border pattern of enquiry (Roberts, 1982c). Classification provides a vital link between these two scales of study, and the second model to be considered deals with this problem.

MODEL 2: Village Forms—Principles of Classification

One purpose of models is to help classification: Fig. 2.5 is a way of grouping the mass of unwieldy information achieved by the examination of large numbers of village plans into classes or 'sets', providing a logical foundation for further investigation. Such grouping leads inevitably towards the creation of a terminology to describe the varied types, but comparisons also emphasize the important of using a standardized scale, while the ideographic symbols attached to each category allow mapping and the exploration of the distribution of plan-types. It must be stressed that the classification presented here is not in any way time-constrained. It simply classifies forms, and is as applicable in the thirteenth century as in the nineteenth, and in Europe as in Britain (Uhlig 1972). Three fundamental morphological criteria are used to categorize plans; *basic shape*, there being two fundamental types, those based on rows and those based on agglomerations (2.5b); *degree of regularity*, the extent to which the plan-elements, buildings, boundaries and open spaces are arranged geometrically or without clear order (2.5c); finally, *the presence or absence of an integral green*, an interior open space used by the community (2.5d). These criteria serve to identify twelve basic plan-types, of which only eleven are exemplified in section d of Fig. 2.5.[5] The arrangement of the grid is, however, devised so that in practice the types grade into each other across both axes: thus plans can be discovered which fall between Appleton le Moors and Middridge. Moving across the grid from Appleton towards Middridge a range of plans can be discovered which reveal gradually widening streets: at what point a wide street becomes a true green is

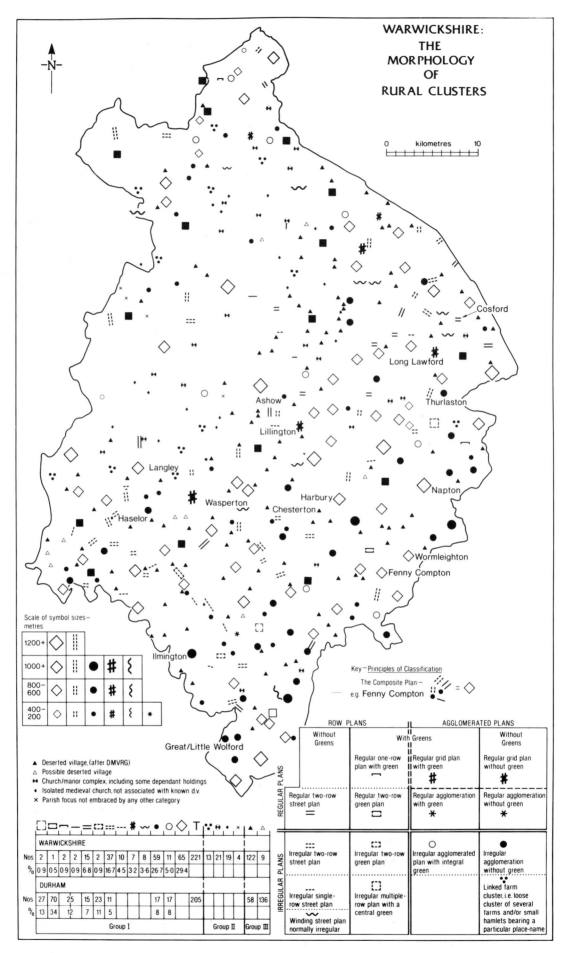

Fig. 2.6 Warwickshire: the morphology of rural clusters

debatable, but a threshold is indisputably crossed. Similarly, moving down the grid axes similar *catenae* of types could be identified, so that although based upon empirical evidence from visible plans the grid contains a theoretical core, the topological transfer of one distinctive arrangement of settlement space into another (Roberts 1982c). This means of course that a given settlement is classified by estimating its location on the grid: further evidence as, for example, the discovery of an earlier map, may demand that it be moved elsewhere. This does not in any way represent a failure of the classification; rather it is a sophistication of the use of the grid. Of course, while the symbols can be adapted to show variants, they inevitably present a rigidity within the system—but this is equally true of all cartographic symbols.

The grid, providing that it is used imaginatively, is not a procrustian bed and, while this is not the place to present them, a set of operating rules is gradually being created to allow the system to be applied by others. There are close parallels here between soil classification and soil mapping procedures. Indeed, the parallels are more exact then might at first appear because, like villages, modern British soils have evolved within a time matrix and must represent many phases of development. The grid provides a framework of reference within which to place particular studies, and for comparing and contrasting plans: as many of these are seen to be deliberate and careful creations this has a real value. In this way the subjective judgements involved can be refined. Figs. 2.5e and 2.5f are a reminder of some of the complexities: 2.5f shows that the regular two-row green village of Middridge is merely a representative of a family of regular row plans. Headlam is a single-row, Heighington possesses multiple-rows, while Tallentire is a variant of the regular two-row type; all of these possess, or have possessed greens. Fig. 2.5f follows a lead provided by Chris Taylor, who notes that many plans comprise not a single unitary plan type but are 'polyfocal' in character, made up of several nuclei (Taylor 1977). For the purposes of plan description the word 'composite' may be more appropriate as Taylor's coined word carries genetic implications, and, hair-splitting as the point may seem, growth from several original nuclei is a different process from growth from one nucleus by the addition of new plan-types, even though the end-products may be morphologically indistinguishable.

Linking Discussion II

One example of an English county is included (Fig. 2.6): this Warwickshire material has been discussed elsewhere, but the tabular comparison at the base of the map reveals a fact which is also becoming apparent from the six county maps and provisional national maps created by the author and his helpers:

that marked regional differences in plan-type assemblages occur (Roberts 1980, 1982b). Such a map is only a starting point for further analysis, for while it is possible to define the varied processes affecting plans, the forces generating them and causing the complex subsequent changes are easier to generalize than to demonstrate specifically. However, this map serves an important purpose, for while recording the morphology of all settlement clusters (excluding only a group of late hamlets bearing 'green' names, which require further study, and single farmsteads) it is a powerful reminder that patterns are made up of assemblages of forms, and that a pattern comprising several hundred individual foci contains forms which will have evolved at different temporal stages: the processes which affect individual forms are those which have moulded the pattern and while in some localities these forces can act divergently, each settlement going its own way, in others a single dominant process (perhaps itself the result of many different causes) can mould the overall pattern. A case in question in Fig. 2.6 would be the zones dominated by deserted settlements, but it is not difficult to find other areas where other forces were predominant. Beresford and Hurst (1971) demonstrate the variety of processes which can result in village depopulation, leading to shrinkage and desertion.

The next model of this series was created to do two things; first, to produce in a single diagram an integrated view of changing forms and patterns for teaching purposes, but second, to explore certain assumptions which were present in the author's mind concerning the value of plan comparisons. The latter can be demonstrated most clearly by a question: to what extent does a given landscape (and Warwickshire is a case in question) contain not only varied types of plan which have evolved at different times and in different ways, *but also the same plan-types seen at different stages of development?* If this is the case, and earlier work in the north of England would support both assumptions, then not only must the forces generating change be considered, but those engendering stability, a far more difficult proposition. To apply Berkhofer's questions, a checklist to apply when endeavouring to measure change, presents real challenges in this context (Baker 1972, 16–17).

MODEL 3: Rural Settlement: Patterns and Forms, Processes of Change

Figure 2.7 is a complex diagram: at the top is a settlement pattern divided into three regions. The inner region, the largest, corresponds to the champion lands of England, while the right and the left reflect wood pastures and upland open pasture zones (Thirsk 1967, 1–160). This is an attempt to recognize that the balance of forces generating settlement varies in response to

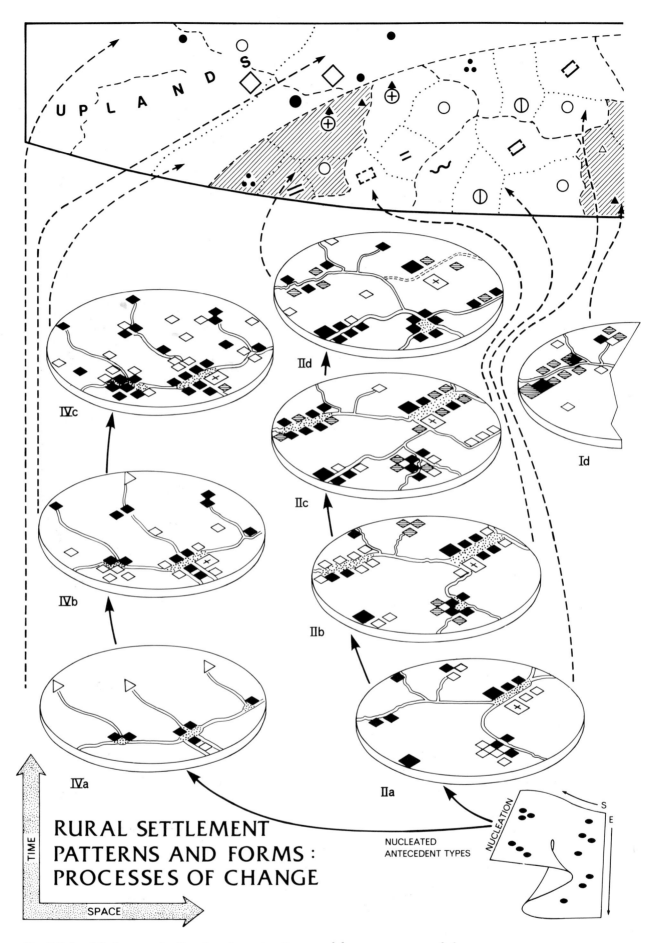

RURAL SETTLEMENT PATTERNS AND FORMS : PROCESSES OF CHANGE

TIME

SPACE

NUCLEATED ANTECEDENT TYPES

Fig. 2.7 (and facing page)   Rural settlement patterns and forms: processes of change

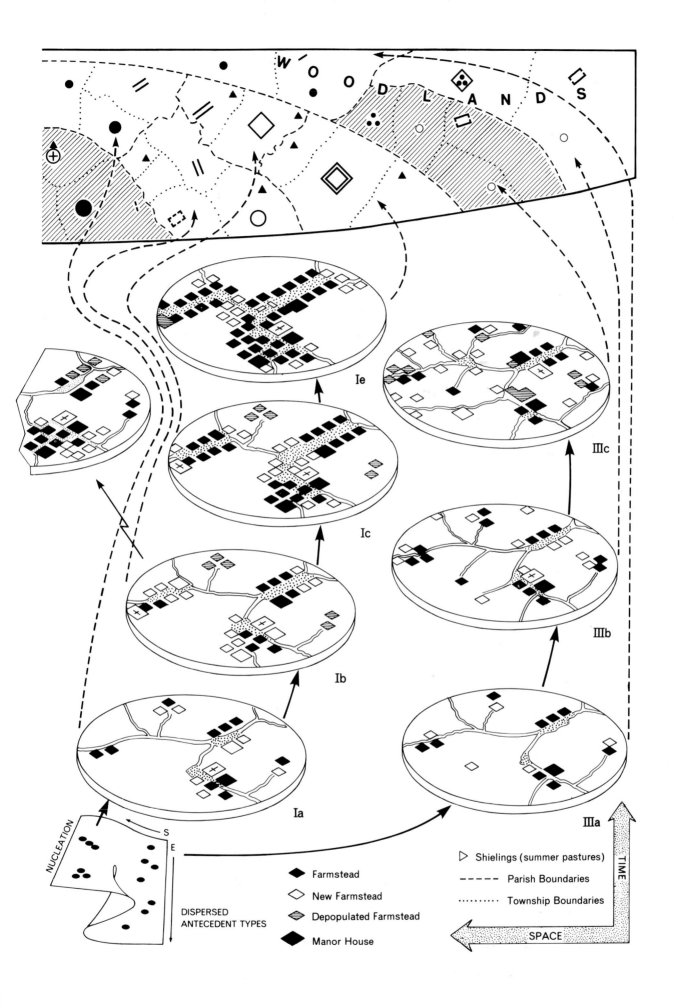

W O O D L A N D S

Ie

Ic

IIIc

Ib

IIIb

Ia

IIIa

NUCLEATION

S

E

DISPERSED
ANTECEDENT TYPES

◆ Farmstead

◇ New Farmstead

⬙ Depopulated Farmstead

◆ Manor House

▷ Shielings (summer pastures)

– – – Parish Boundaries

· · · · · · Township Boundaries

TIME

SPACE

broad environmental controls and hints that further work may well result in versions of this model which demonstrate developments within local regions. However, in this version the model creates a broad view of settlement forms evolving under the influence of six processes: (i) *expansion*, the appearance of new farmsteads and new clusters; (ii) *contraction*, the disappearance of farmsteads causing shrinkage and total depopulation; (iii) *aggregation*, the disappearance of some clusters linked with the expansion of others; (iv) *seigniorial factors*, the presence of lordship, manifest in manor houses and churches; (v) *colonization*, the taking in of new lands; and finally (vi) *commercial activity*, the establishment of markets in rural clusters. Quite obviously, no single model can reflect reality and the diagram portrays one possible end-product of the complex interactions possible. Analysis and descriptions can proceed via the numbers of letters allocated to each plate of the diagram, but it should be noted that the horizontal axis records spatial differentiation while the vertical axis is concerned with changes in time.

The phase characterized by plates Ia, IIa, IIIa and IVa (Fig. 2.7) contains certain assumptions: it will be noted that the black symbols, for farms present at the beginning of this phase, embrace the basic range of simple morphological types: (i) a single farmstead, (ii) a two-farmstead cluster, (iii) a three-farmstead row and (iv) a three-farmstead agglomeration. These, termed *antecedent types* are assumed to have been universally present, a fundamental weakness of the model, for such simplicity has no place in reality. Nevertheless, the two catastrophe surfaces (a duplication so that the diagram can be split for printing) are a reminder that there is a volume of evidence, noted earlier, which suggests that the middle and late Saxon period saw the presence of aggregative forces which drew elements of formerly more dispersed patterns into larger clusters. What balance of social and economic forces (S and E in Fig. 2.7) stimulated these is debatable (Fox 1981, 83–91), indeed, the evidence presently available from limited areas must be given wider substance, but there are some grounds for believing that a period of accelerated aggregation brought many protovillage nuclei into being and while the temporal duration of this phase has yet to be established with certainty it has a place in this general model. Within these antecedent clusters the placing of lordly farms and churches is not entirely random: thus in Ia two nuclei were selected for enhancement, whereas in IIb only one was chosen, a subjective decision designed to ensure that the plates of column I resembled developments found in the Midlands and to a lesser extent Eastern England while those of column II followed a course of events more typical of the North. Even at this level divergence had to be ensured.

The key to the symbols of this map is to be found in both Fig. 2.5 and Fig. 2.6 and the link between the stylized forms on the plates and the ideographic symbols on the map can be examined by focussing on the three shaded parishes. It can be seen that the map is divided into parishes and townships and it should be appreciated that areas where settlements are well spaced (as in the north of England) offer fewer opportunities for complex growth than where, in the Midlands and South, settlements are close packed within a densely settled landscape. In the former case composite plans will only result from the accretion of new plan-types to a pre-existing core. In the situation where antecedent types are more closely packed, often involving complex manorial linkages, then the potential exists for the emergence of a variety of composite plans, many developing from polyfocal antecedents. In this respect the model necessarily does some injury to local space relationships. Furthermore, a close comparison of the map and the plates emphasizes that essentially similar forms can appear at varied periods, the result of different processes: thus in Fig. 2.5 the grid at Long Lawford could be replaced by other examples drawn from other contexts, not least eighteenth-century Scotland, for Aberchirder is representative of a group of plans, a proportion of which are true grids (Lockhart 1980a, 1980b). The less regular grid of Long Lawford—a subjective but nonetheless valid judgement—is arguably medieval in origin (Roberts, 1982b).

The model can be examined in two ways, by describing the relationship it has to the four landscape types it demonstates, and by considering some particular case studies in relation to it. Column I is based on the Warwickshire-Northamptonshire experience, for both counties are dominated by former champion landscapes where a diversity of forms occur, but where large composite plans occur alongside areas of quite exceptional late medieval depopulations (plate Id). There is some evidence that villages increased in size in the medieval period by aggregation as well as population increases (Ia–Ib) (Ford 1976, 287), while both aggregation, expansion and the acquisition of market rights may account for the largest composite plans. Regular plans are less evident in these areas, suggesting the absence of cross-time discontinuities which stimulated replanning processes. Contraction is represented by both shrinkage and complete depopulation. The extent to which the emergence of big villages was associated with the reorganization of field systems must for the moment be speculative (Fox and Campbell, in Rowley 1981), but there are good grounds for seeing settlements evolving in parallel with more communally organized systems and this being one key factor leading to aggregation. When evaluating this section of the model it is important to grasp that a great midland composite plan can sprawl across a kilometre or more of countryside and occupy the space which could accommodate three or even more smaller villages or hamlets: this seems to have repercussions on settlement spacing generally. Preliminary work in Somerset suggests that column I is equally applicable in parts of that county, where rich farming land associated with handicraft industries engendered some of the largest continuously built-up composite plans yet encountered.

Turning from the general to the specific: plate Ic shows a situation where a parish contains a large composite village, a smaller regular plan and two small depopulated sites. The composite plan echoes Ravensdale's observations at Cottenham, Cambridgeshire, where he identified an ancient core, comprising a rectangular area of very irregular plots, with no consistent pattern, to which there were added two extensions whose regular strip boundaries suggest they were established over former arable strips. The extension, it is suggested, 'began in the Norman period' (Ravensdale 1974, 123). This situation is closely paralleled in Bower Hinton in Somerset, where the irregular grid of Bower Hinton has a northward extension which took place in two stages: at first there was a separate hamlet of Hurst, regularly laid out, and by the early fourteenth century the 40 regular tofts of Newton had been interjected between the two (Dunning, *V.C.H., Somerset,* 1978, 4, 82). Padbury in Buckinghamshire (Beresford 1979, 278–9) although smaller, seems to have a similar layout, with an irregular nucleus—Old End—being extended eastwards by a more regular row plan. The value of identifying, and where possible dating, such structural components hardly needs emphasis, and careful observations can reveal their presence even in long published and well-studied cases. Thus the 1680 plan of Leighton Bromswold, Huntingdonshire, shows that not only was the village composite at that stage, but that there is a complex relationship between the plan-types making up the composite plan and disposition of field strips in the furlongs. Indeed, in this case it is possible to postulate the presence of a depopulated antecedent hamlet beneath the arable furlongs to the west of the village, an indication that aggregation has taken place (Beresford 1979, 13–6; Page, Proby and Ladds, *V.C.H. Hunts.* 1936, 3, 86–92).

Column III shows the evolution of hamlets and single farmsteads in a woodland region such as the Arden of north-west Warwickshire, one context in which ancient linked farm clusters may in fact survive (Fig. 2.6), and a distinction may be noted between linked farm clusters (three dots) and linked clusters (three dots in a diamond). The implications of such distinctions have yet to be fully examined, but it is reasonable to suggest that there may well be a developmental sequence,

linked farmstead cluster, linked hamlet cluster, composite plan, irregular agglomeration, with the gradual fusion of originally separate components (Roberts 1982b). It is certainly possible to identify all of these in the landscape, but infinitely more difficult to demonstrate the process within a single village. A careful re-examination of Chibnall's study of Sherington, Buckinghamshire (1965), suggests that this composite plan could have originated in a scatter of farms, with manor houses providing growth cores. Column II presents a marked contrast, for it shows the development of northern villages. In this case there is probably a very well-marked catastrophe between the antecedent types and all subsequent developments, for the lower population of the region coupled with extensive devastations in the late eleventh century and a subsequent vigorous Anglo-Norman colonization of the region stimulated the growth of regular plans. In many areas, as for example in Northumberland, post-medieval engrossing has led to a decline in the number of farmsteads in well-established villages, causing both shrinkage and depopulation, while accretion and the establishment of new plans has sustained other clusters. Column I suggests the developments in an upland zone, where shielings are gradually brought into permanent occupation and the presence of looser ties of lordship, of partible inheritance and the presence of an extractive or craft industry within a dual economy, sustains a highly dispersed pattern interspersed with often very irregular market-town clusters.

The time-span of Fig. 2.7 falls between the late Saxon period and the mid-nineteenth century and in this brief analysis no attempt has been made to describe every facet. It should be emphasized that this model must be seen as an experiment, a framework for teaching, refining, discussing and perhaps rejecting, but it does touch upon another important theme in such anlayses based upon landscape evidence: the incorporation of the regional component serves as a reminder of the significance of transition zones. Thus, the formalized champion-woodland boundary of the model is seen in a real context in Fig. 2.6 and the question 'At what period did the observable settlement contrasts between the south and east and the north and west manifest themselves?' is integral to an understanding of the varied morphologies which are present.

Linking Discussion III
The third model of this series emphasizes the role of forces operating through time generating varied settlement morphologies: the gauge of any system of classification must always be the extent to which new data can be incorporated without destroying the framework which has been adopted. If flexibility is not apparent, then the criteria selected as the basis for classification must be questioned. At the time of writing

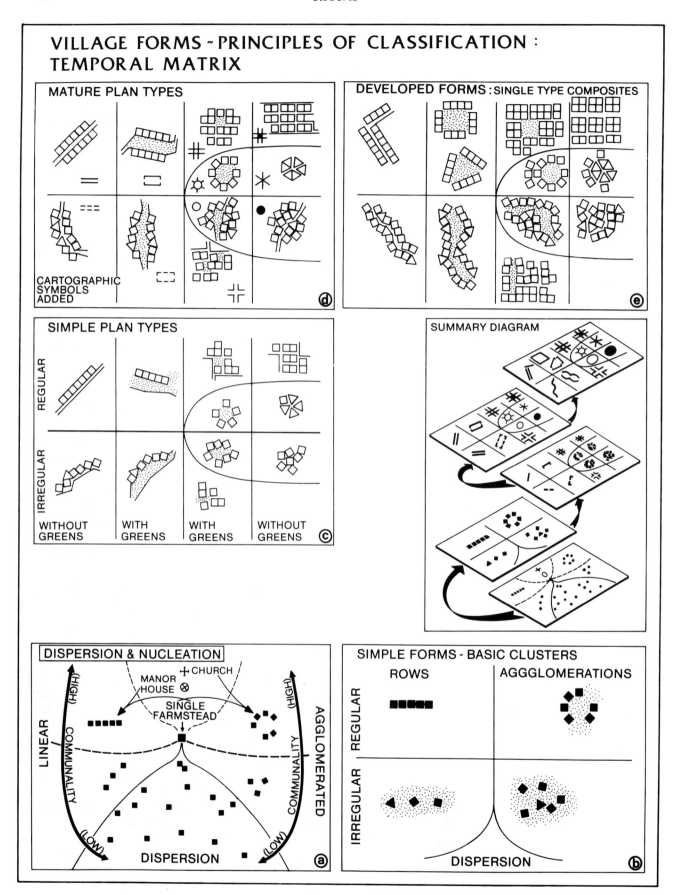

Fig. 2.8   Village forms: principles of classification, temporal matrix

the author faces three problems: first, a period of collection has vastly extended the data base available to him, and this has inevitably expanded the range of plan-types within his experience, bringing new questions and new problems of interpretation and explanation. Nevertheless, while with Maurice Beresford one can despair at this stage of gathering a 'representative collection' of plans, belief in the validity of the criteria selected as a basis for classification remains unimpaired. In the context of the grid examined as Model II, however, two aspects are seen to demand attention, the question of *scale*, the physical area embraced by the settlement land, and the intensity of occupation within that land. Fig. 2.6 incorporates an attempt to measure physical dimensions, albeit crude, while in another context the author has touched upon the threshold between true rural morphologies and simple urban morphologies, often only measurable in terms of intensity of plot use. Second, there is a fundamental problem of communicating perceptions within the necessary constraints of a paper: as was noted earlier, and in measure demonstrated in Fig. 2.2 there is no substitute for the physical shock of examining settlement contrasts via simple map sources, and while there is no doubt that an examination of processes and the creation of explanations must take place within the context of the study of a single village, or a small number of these, the broader perspective offers prospects of worthwhile stimulation. Thirdly, in the struggle to impose 'some sort of order upon' this 'vast flow of information from the real world' there is a temptation to take refuge in theoretical discussion, creating further deductive models, beds on which to stretch reality. That which follows derives from two roots; first, the grid of Model II, second, attempts by the author to refine the grid in order to create a computerized data storage system for the volume of empirical material he has generated. In particular, the question of locating an individual settlement upon the line of a *catena* of types was considered, a process which had repercussions on the concept of 'families' of plans (see above). It will be noted that in this case 'real' examples are not yet keyed in to the final model, individual tofts and their associated buildings being schematically depicted by geometric shapes. The deductive structure now requires testing against a multitude of particular cases.

MODEL 4: Village Forms—Principles of Classification: Temporal Matrix

The diagram (Fig. 2.8) converts the basic classificatory grid into a series of temporally discrete plates running in sequence (a) to (e): (a) and (b) examine the threshold between nucleation and dispersion. Plate (a) constitutes a reminder that all settlements were built of farmsteads

and their dispersion or nucleation is perhaps less a direct reflection of physical conditions (although these play a part) than an expression of the concentrating power of lordship, seen in the manor house and church, and the presence of communality—a necessity or desire to engage in group activity. Geographers have still to offer adequate explanations for this fundamental dichotomy. Plate (b) is a further step and defines four types of nucleations on the basis of two fundamental criteria, but the diagram is presented in a way which emphasizes the importance of the enclosed, private space of the house-plot and the surrounding through-passage space of the non-enclosed matrix—primevally the cave and the forest—and points towards more theoretical areas of the study of settlement spaces (Hillier *et al.* 1976). The step from this to the grid has already been examined, but plates (c), (d) and (e) demonstrate first, (c) the existence of very simple plan-types, combinations of a few farmsteads, which, nevertheless, are morphologically classifiable. The minimum number would be three, but a maximum size threshold is difficult to set, for a dozen and a half farmsteads strung along a single road retain an essential simplicity absent when the same number lie in boundary contact with each other in a formalized plan-structure. More mature types (b) are represented by the plans used to illustrate the grid (Model II) while the identification of developed forms, essentially single-type composite plans, provides a bridge between the grid and both composite plans made up of several plan-types, and urban plans, perhaps also placing Chris Taylor's term—polyfocal—for use in a genetic context. In theory, this revised grid recognizes not only morphological *catenae*, across the face of a plane grid, but also temporal *catenae*, successions of types resulting from the expansion, or, of course, contraction (for the process is reversible) of a single type. This is not to argue for the erection of an elaborate system of classification based upon these observations, but it is argued that, thus far, the frameworks presented do aid historical research by creating contexts for the appraisal of individual cases and by posing questions concerning likely lines of development. In the absence of excavation there can never be any certainty concerning the stages in the development of a village earlier than those known from documents, but the comparative method, when appropriately refined, undoubtedly has a place. Furthermore, a broader understanding of the likely lines of development of traditional forms is one basis upon which planners can create sensitive adaptations and ensure the retention of some of their qualities in the future.

One final word must be said on the content of this paper: the presentation of the four models is a question-posing exercise, involving the creation of generalizing structures within which particular cases can be evaluated. Of the two questions with which the paper commenced only the first has been answered: the evidence available does indeed suggest that there is much to be learned from the plans themselves of the processes which may have generated them. At the very least, their diverse character presents a challenge to all scholars who have eyes to see them and are prepared to admit such material as evidence. The demonstrable fact that a landscape may contain plans inherited from widely separated periods presents undoubted interpretational problems, involving balancing the forces which lead to stability as well as change, and evaluating the evidence available at several scales of enquiry. The pragmatic limitations on archaeological excavation and even on localized in-depth studies, while these must always form controls, makes the broader pictures provided by landscape evidence of vital importance.

Notes

1. The plan of Marnhall is redrawn from the Ordnance Survey (hereafter O.S.) 1:10,560 1st edn. sheets, VII NE, NW, SE, SW, (1886); Middridge is based on the O.S. 1st edn. 1:2,500 sheet 42.12 (1854–7), to which scale the Tithe map (Department of Palaeography and Diplomatic, Durham) has been transcribed.
2. 'What is it that stands upright in a bed and brings a tear to a maiden's eye' is a welcome demonstration of both Anglo-Saxon humour and horticulture; translated by Kevin Crossley-Holland, as part of 'The Battle of Maldon and other Old English Poems', Argo Records, 2PL 1058, Side 1, band 2. (An onion!)
3. O.S. 1:10,560 1st edn. sheet XLVII N.E. (1887).
4. Examples of such enclosures are as follows: Cumrenton, Cu. G. R. NY 4962, O.S. 1:10,560, XVII NE, in this case without a church; Bewcastle, Cu. NY 5675, VIII NW, set within the ramparts of a polygonal Roman fort; Brockley Court, Som. G. R. ST 4767, XI NW; Stanton Lacy, Salop, G. R. SO 4979, LXXI SE, where the churchyard clearly possesses a rampart; Bygrave, Herts. G. R. TL 2636, VIII NW; see also Litlington, Cambs. G. R. TL 3142 LVII NE and Pirton, Herts G. R. TL 1431, XXVI SE, both illustrated by Seebohm 1883, 426f. There are obvious parallels with Welsh sites, e.g. Llanynys, Denb. G. R. SJ 1063, XIV SW, see Jones in Finberg (1972), 344.

   Very small basic clusters can be seen as follows: Clatworthy, Som. G. R. ST 0530, LVIII SE, LIX SW; Exton, Som. G. R. SS 9233, LVII NE; Barrasford, Nb. G. R. NY 9274, LXXVII SW; Hawkshead, Lancs. G. R. SD 3598, V NW; Threapland, Cu. G. R. NY 1639, XXXVI SW; Muker, N. R. Yks. SD 9198, LI NW; Swinside, NR, Yks, G. R. SE 0682, LXXXIII NE; West Scrafton, NR. Yks. G. R. SE 0784, LXXXIII NE, LXXXIV NW.

   It is intended to publish a separate study of such small clusters.
5. The reader may easily test these points by spending a few hours with a copy of the 1680 plan of Leighton Bromswold (available in the *Victoria County History of Huntingdonshire*, 3, 86–92) and using coloured pens to shade both village and field strips. A fascinating pattern emerges, which seems to indicate the preservation of a pattern which would have evolved during the extension of the arable. An earlier settlement focus is postulated at approximately TL 096757 where farms 1–10 and the demesne all possess irregular pieces of land, anomalous to the general pattern of strips.

References

Ault, W. O. 1972: *Open Field Farming in Medieval England* (London and New York, Allen and Unwin).

Baker, A. R. H. 1968: A note on the retrogressive and retrospective approaches in historical geography. *Erdkunde* 22, 3, 243–4.

Baker, A. R. H. (editor) 1972: *Progress in Historical Geography* (Newton Abbott, David and Charles).

Beresford, M. W. and St. Joseph, J. K. S. 1958: *Medieval England: an Aerial Survey* 2nd edition (1979) (Cambridge, Cambridge University Press).

Beresford, M. W. and Hurst, J. G. (editors) 1971: *Deserted Medieval Villages: Studies* (London, Lutterworth Press).

Campbell, B. 1981: Commonfield origins—the regional dimension. In Rowley, T. (editor) 1981, 112–29.

Chibnall, A. C. 1965: *Sherington: Fiefs and Fields of a Buckinghamshire Village* (Cambridge, Cambridge University Press).

Clack, P. and Haselgrove, S. (editors) 1981: *Approaches to the Urban Past* (Department of Archaeology, University of Durham, Occasional Paper No. 2).

Clarke, G. R. 1971: *The Study of Soil in the Field* 5th edition (Oxford, Clarendon Press).

Conzen, M. G. R. 1949: Modern settlement. In *Scientific Survey of North-eastern England*. British Association for the Advancement of Science, 75–83.

Curtis, L. F., Courtney, F. M. and Trudgill, S. 1976: *Soils in the British Isles* (London and New York, Longman).

Dewdney, J. C. 1970: *Durham County and City with Teeside* (Durham, British Association for the Advancement of Science).

Dodgshon, R. A. 1980: Medieval settlement and colonisation. In Parry, M. L. and Slater, T. R. (editors) 1980, 45–68.

Dunning, R. W. (editor) 1978: *The Victoria History of the Counties of England. A History of the County of Somerset, Vol. 4* (The University of London Institute of Historical Research).

Emery, F. 1967: The farming regions of Wales. In Thirsk, J. (editor) 1967, 113–60.

Erixon, S. 1961: Swedish villages without systematic regulation. *Geografiska Annaler* 43, Nos. 1–2, 57–74.

Fenton, A. 1978: *The Northern Isles: Orkney and Shetland* (Edinburgh, Donald).

Finberg, H. P. R. 1972: Anglo-Saxon England to 1042. In Finberg, H. P. R. (editor) 1972, 385–525.

Finberg, H. P. R. (editor) 1972: *The Agrarian History of England and Wales, I, AD 43–1042* (Cambridge, Cambridge University Press).

Ford, W. J. 1976: Some settlement patterns in the central region of the Warwickshire Avon. In Sawyer, P. H (editor) 1976, 274–94.

Fowler, P. J. (editor) 1975: *Recent Work in Rural Archaeology* (Bradford-on-Avon, Moonraker Press).

Fox, H. S. A. 1981: Approaches to the adoption of the Midland system. In Rowley, T. (editor) 1981, 64–111.

Green, D., Haselgrove, C. and Spriggs, M. (editors) 1978: *Social Organisation and Settlement* (Oxford, British Archaeological Reports, International Series 47 (1978) Vol. 2).

Hall, D. N. and Martin, P. W. 1979: Brixworth, Northamptonshire—an intensive field survey. *Journal of the British Archaeological Association* 132, 1–6.

Harvey, D. 1969: *Explanation in Geography* (London, Edward Arnold).

Harvey, M. 1978: *The Morphological and Tenurial Structure of a Yorkshire Township* (Department of Geography, Queen Mary College, London, Occasional Paper 13).

Harvey, P. D. A. 1980: *The History of Topographical Maps: Symbols, Pictures and Surveys* (London, Thames and Hudson).

Helmfrid, S. 1972: Historical geography in Scandinavia. In Baker, A. R. H. (Editor) 1972, 63–89.

Hillier, B., Leaman, A., Stansall, P. and Bedford, M. 1976: Space syntax. In Green, D., Haselgrove, C. and Spriggs, M. (editors) 1978, 343–81.

Hoskins, W. G. 1963: *Provincial England. Essays in Social and Economic History* (London, Macmillan and Co.).

Lockhart, D. G. 1980a: The planned villages. In Parry, M. K. and Slater, T. R. (editors) 1980, 249–70.

Lockhart, D. G. 1980b: Scottish village plans: a prelimary analysis. *Scottish Geographical Magazine* 96, 141–57.

Miller, E. and Hatcher, J. 1978: *Medieval England: Rural Society and Economic Change 1086–1348* (London, Longman).

Myhre, B. 1973: The Iron Age farm in south-west Norway. *Norwegian Archaeological Review* 6, No. 1, 14–29: see also 7, No. 1 (1974) 44–83, for extensive discussion and models.

Northumberland County History Committee. Various dates. *A History of Northumberland* (Newcastle and London).

Page, U., Proby, G. and Ladds, S. Inskipp (editors) 1936: *The Victoria History of the Counties of England. A History of the County of Huntingdonshire*, Vol. 3. (London, The University of London Institute of Historical Research).

Parker, R. 1975: *The Common Stream* (London, Collins).

Parry, M. L. and Slater, T. R. (editors) 1980: *The Making of the Scottish Countryside* (London, Croom Helm).

Raftis, J. A. 1957: *The Estates of Ramsey Abbey. A Study in Economic Growth and Organization* (Toronto, Pontifical Institute of Medieval Studies. Studies and Texts No. 3).

Ravensdale, J. R. 1974: *Liable to Floods: Village Landscape on the Edge of the Fens AD 450–1850* (London, Cambridge University Press).

Roberts, B. K. 1972: Village plans in County Durham: a preliminary statement. *Medieval Archaeology* 16, 33–56.

Roberts, B. K. 1976–7: The historical geography of moated homesteads. *Transactions of the Birmingham and Warwickshire Archaeological Society* 88, 62–7.

Roberts, B. K. 1977: *The Green Villages of County Durham* (Durham County Library, Local History Publication No. 12).

Roberts, B. K. 1979: Village plans in Britain. In *Récherches de Gégraphie Rurale, Hommage au Professeur Frans Dussart*. (Numéro hors Série du Bulletin de la Société Geographique de Liège, Liège (1979) 34–49).

Roberts, B. K. 1981a: Townfield origins; the case of Cockfield, County Durham. In Rowley, T. (editor) 1981, 145–61.

Roberts, B. K. 1981b: Of towns and villages. In Clack, P. and Haselgrove, S. (editors) 1981, 7–16.

Roberts, B. K. 1982a: *Rural Settlement: an Historical Perspective*. Historical Geography Research Series, No. 9, Institute of British Geographers (Norwich, Geo Abstracts).

Roberts, B. K. 1982b: Village forms in Warwickshire: a preliminary discussion. In Slater, T. R. and Jarvis, P. J. (editors) 1982, 125–46.

Roberts, B. K. 1982c: The anatomy of the village: observation and extrapolation. *Landscape History* 4, 1982, 11–20.

Roberts, B. K. forthcoming: Rodwell, W. 1981: *The Archaeology of The English Church* (London, Batsford).

Rönneseth, O. 1975: 'Gard' und einfreidigung. *Geografiska Annaler special issue, No. 2*.

Rowley, T. (editor) 1974: *Anglo-Saxon Settlement and Landscape* (Oxford, British Archaeological Reports 6).

Rowley, T. (editor) 1981: *The Origins of Open Field Agriculture* (London, Croom Helm).

Sawyer, P. H. (editor) 1976: *Medieval Settlement: Continuity and Change* (London, Edward Arnold).

Seebohm, F. 1883: *The English Village Community Examined in its Relations to the Manorial and Tribal Systems ... An Essay in Economic History* (London, Longman).

Sheppard, J. A. 1966: Pre-enclosure field and settlement patterns in a Yorkshire township. *Geografiska Annaler* 48b, 59–77.

Sheppard, J. A. 1974: Metrological analysis of regular village plans in Yorkshire. *Agricultural History Review* 22, Part 2, 118–35.

Sheppard, J. A. 1976: Medieval village planning in northern England. *Journal of Historical Geography* 2, Part 1, 3–20.

Slater, T. R. and Jarvis, P. J. (editors) 1982: *Field and Forest: an Historical Geography of Warwickshire and Worcestershire*. (Norwich Geo Books).

Taylor, C. C. 1974: The Anglo-Saxon countryside. In Rowley, T. (editor) 1974, 5–15.

Taylor, C. C. 1977: Polyfocal settlement and the English village. *Medieval Archaeology* 21, 189–93.

Thirsk, J. 1967: The farming regions of England. In Thirsk, J. (editor) 1967, 1–112.

Thirsk, J. (editor) 1967: *The Agrarian History of England and Wales, 1500–1640* Vol. 4 (Cambridge, Cambridge University Press).

Thorpe, H. 1951: The green villages of County Durham. *Transactions of the Institute of British Geographers* 15, 155–80.

Uhlig, H. 1961: Old hamlets with infield and outfield systems in Western and Central Europe. *Geografiska Annaler* 43, Nos. 1–2, 285–312.

Uhlig, H. 1972: *Rural Settlements: Basic Material for the Terminology of the Agricultural Landscape* (Giessen, Levz-Verlag. Text in German, English and French).

Wade-Martins, P. 1975: The origins of rural settlement in East Anglia. In Fowler, P. J. (editor) 1975, 137–57.

3. Power and Conflict in the Medieval English Village

C. C. Dyer

This paper examines the recent revisionism among historians and geographers which has sought to diminish the importance of the English village community. It reaffirms the reality of the community organization, and seeks to define its functions. It emphasizes the complexity of relationships between the village, manor, and parish. Conflicts within the village are seen as expressions of feuds rather than class antagonisms. A review of the changing cohesion of the village leads to doubts being expressed on the fashionable orthodoxy that regular planned villages resulted from the intervention of landlords, as villagers themselves were capable of such planning.

The purpose of this paper is to define the village as it is seen and understood by documentary historians; this will lead to an emphasis on the village as a social entity. As the bulk of the written evidence comes from the later Middle Ages, the development of the village in that period will be the main theme, with a brief and more speculative venture into the early medieval history of the village at the end.

Anyone studying the village must clear from his mind a good deal of sentimental lumber that has surrounded the subject for more than a hundred years. The word 'village' inevitably conjures up pictorial images deriving from artistic and commercial representations of thatched cottages grouped round church towers, and from fictional accounts of village life from Thomas Hardy to the 'Archers'. The idealization of village life in recent times is a reflection of a real historical experience, the urbanization and industrialization that led people to look back to a way of life that seemed, in retrospect, to represent simple, innocent and communal values.

More recently historians have been concerned, with varying degrees of enthusiasm, with stripping away the layers of myth and sentiment that have formed around the pre-industrial village. This is an entirely proper exercise, but the revisionism has now reached the point where the very existence of the village as a community is being denied. Nineteenth-century scepticism on the subject (Maitland 1897, 184–8) has been revived by those who claim that the interests and actions of individuals were more important than those of any grouping of people (Macfarlane 1979); another line of attack has been to see the landlord rather than the village as the motive force behind the creation of field systems (Campbell 1981). Such arguments are an understandable reaction to the woolliness of some previous thinking, but in reviewing our state of knowledge here the reality of the village community will be reasserted.

There is a good deal of room for debate on this issue because the village has left us virtually no records. The institutions that did produce documents, the manor, the central government, and the church, give us information about villages, but when we read these documents we see the village through the eyes of the landlords, royal officials, or the higher clergy, people whose lives and experience lay outside the village. There are those who find this a minor problem, and believe that the records of the manor reflect closely the life of the village (Raftis 1965). This is wishful thinking, and if we are to overcome the problem of the bias of the records, and to glimpse the village from the point of view of the inhabitants, we need to work hard at our sources, and to treat them critically.

Firstly, the power of the landlord must be put into perspective. Lords lived a life of comparative leisure and comfort because they drew their income from the work of the rest of society. Their main interest in the peasants lay in gaining rents and services from them; this meant that they had some influence over many aspects of peasant life—farming, buying and selling, marriage and children. This influence stopped a long way short of a total dictatorial control of daily life. It is now even argued that the lives of serfs were not weighed down with particularly heavy burdens (Hatcher 1981); this is not very convincing in view of the obvious resentment of many serfs to their condition, which they clearly regarded as disadvantageous (Hilton 1973); but most historians would agree that lords exercised an intermittent and imperfect control over their subordinates. The main inhibition on their power lay in the inefficiency of medieval government at all levels. The existence of many tiers of overlapping and competing jurisdictions effectively prevented any single authority exercising absolute control.

The aristocratic mentality also prevented landlords from taking too much interest in their subordinate villagers. The nobility, both lay and clerical, saw their proper occupations as war, prayer, hunting, and courtly entertainment. Estate management was a tedious chore, delegated to inferiors wherever possible. The preferred method of running a landed estate was to lease out manors to farmers for fixed rents. The system broke down under the pressure of inflation round about 1200, and for two centuries the detailed administration of agricultural production became the concern of most landlords. Even then a cadre of professional managers took over the bulk of the necessary supervisory work. Many great lords, though they wandered from manor to manor, owned so much land that they never saw many of their properties. The lesser lords, the gentry, who often held land in only one or two places, were necessarily closer to the soil than the great magnates. Often the farmers of manors and the administrators of the large estates were recruited from their ranks. However, even these smaller landowners might be absentees from their own estates because they were pursuing military or administrative activities elsewhere. And the gentry who did live on their own lands were still limited in their powers over the peasantry because, in comparison with the magnates, they lacked servile and customary tenants (Kosminsky 1956). So at all levels the aristocracy lacked either the inclination or the opportunity to exercise a complete domination over the lives of the peasantry.

The main limitation on the power of the landlords lay in the underdevelopment of society that prevented the employment of full-time officials and police. Without these resources, the obvious method of governing a village was to enlist the help of the peasants themselves. The election of such officials as reeves and rent-collectors became an obligation on tenants; service for individuals elected was often a compulsory condition of customary tenure. The manorial courts, the principal tribunals of seigneurial justice, were each presided over by the lord's steward, a member of the gentry, but the other court officials, the jurors, chief pledges, ale-tasters and afferers, were all tenants. The advantage of involving the peasantry in such duties lay in the cheapness and ease of recruiting petty officials; the lord's rule was helped by the intimate local knowledge of the officials; above all, orders were more likely to meet with some compliance because they came from a locally respected neighbour. The lord was in effect enlisting the local hierarchy to carry out his administration. The disadvantage from the lord's point of view was that in gaining the co-operation of the local élite he had to share a little power and profit with them, and allow them to use their position to advance their own interests. Their involvement was bound to have a softening effect on the harshness of the lord's rule— indeed, that was part of their function, to make social exploitation more acceptable and therefore workable. It is out of this complicated relationship that we can

learn from the archives of the manor about the life of the village. Through the leading men acting as jurors, reeves, haywards and the like, manor and village became closely associated.

Let us turn to the village in its own right. The word was scarcely used in the Middle Ages. In Latin documents we read of the *villa* or *villata*, which is commonly translated as 'vill', though in Middle English the equivalent word was 'town'—still preserving its original meaning of a small settlement in modern North American speech. The use of this word tells us nothing about the form of settlement, as both compact, nucleated settlements and groupings of scattered hamlets and farms were called 'vills'. The terms 'hamlet', 'berewick', 'member' and so on were used to indicate the constituent elements of a single 'vill'. The term 'vill' then did not necessarily refer to a concrete grouping of homes and fields, but to a unit of government.

The vill oftens appears in the records of central government. It was the smallest unit of administration, and was expected in the later Middle Ages to provide representatives to attend various royal courts, to pay collective fines, to undertake public works, to be responsible for maintaining law and order (by setting a watch and electing a constable), to contribute foot soldiers to royal armies, and to pay taxes, even to the point after 1334 of assessing and collecting a quota of taxation.

Although the evidence for the obligations is abundant, we know very little about how they were carried out within the villages. Occasionally complaints about the non-payment of taxes by one villager to another came to the notice of the courts. Irregularities in the discharge of military obligations are also known, like the case at Halesowen, Worcestershire, in 1295, of Thomas Hill, who collected money from the men elected to serve by offering to go as a substitute and then absconded with the cash (Homans 1941, 330).

The normal routine of deliberation, assessment, and election of representatives was conducted verbally and is consequently not recorded. Yet the effectiveness of the internal governing machinery of the vill cannot be doubted. No doubt the tasks were carried out slowly and reluctantly, but in the long run taxes were paid, armies levied, and bridges repaired.

We are better informed about the self-governing role of the vill in organizing its own fields. Here the business of the vill sometimes overlapped with the jurisdiction of the lord's court, so that court rolls surviving from the mid-thirteenth century onwards record by-laws and the punishment of offenders against the by-laws (Ault 1972). The earlier by-laws tend to be preoccupied with the problems of the harvest, such as the prevention of sheaf-stealing and the regulation of gleaning. After 1400 the majority of by-laws deal with the control of animals and grazing. Here lay the heart of the matter for the village community, the protection and maintenance of the means of livelihood of the inhabitants.

Now we are more fully informed about those rules and regulations that were made and enforced through the lord's court, and it is possible to see the lord rather than the villagers as the guiding force behind the by-laws and the management of the fields. However, a good deal of this local legislation was of little interest to the lord, such as the by-laws dealing with the arrangements for the hiring of a common herdsman. Also there are occasional references to villagers acting on their own initiative, significantly from vills with many lords, like Wymeswold, Leicestershire, where a village meeting in *c.*1425 made decisions about the organization of the fields (Bland, Brown, and Tawney 1920, 76–9). Places like Wymeswold in which the villages did not coincide with a single manor were in a majority, so it is likely that such meetings were not uncommon. In the rare case of a manor containing more than one village, such as the huge manor at Wakefield, Yorkshire, the constituent vills held their own meetings, for which the lord's clerk used the term 'plebiscite' (Ault 1972, 66).

Although the regulation of the fields was the most important function of the villages' internal governing machinery, the vill was responsible for much else: for example, for the assessment and collection of lump sums paid to the lord, such as tallages, common fines, and recognitions. The villagers could act as collective tenants, as in agreeing to pay a rent for a pasture so as to preserve it as a common (Wilson 1933, 158–9), or by becoming group lessees of the lord's demesne. The ultimate development of this was at Kingsthorpe, Northamptonshire, where in the early thirteenth century the vill leased the whole manor, including the court, and it came nearer than any other English village to the privileged self-government of the continental rural communes (Ault 1960).

The villagers played a major part in the maintenance of law and order, and the reinforcement of prevailing norms and values. This was partly through co-operation with the view of frankpledge, the petty court of royal justice held by many lords, and the church courts. There were also more informal, ritualistic methods of dealing with those who failed to conform, such as the humiliation of 'rough music', which is well known from post-medieval incidents, and is also recorded in late medieval France (Thompson 1972; Gauvard and Gokalp 1974). The existence of rough music in the English medieval village is indicated by the semi-official institution of the 'hue and cry', raised against malefactors, which may well represent the origin of the custom.

The involvement of the vill with the church grew in the later Middle Ages, with the development of the responsibilities of the churchwardens as guardians of the cemetery, church building and furnishings (Mason 1976). They in turn reinforced the social ties that bound the villagers by organizing church ales, mass drinking sessions to raise funds. Normally money for the church was levied by the informal constraints of social pressure and neighbourly disapproval, but occasionally, as at Ingatestone, Essex, in 1359, the churchwardens used the lord's court to extract money for a new church tower from a reluctant parishioner.[1]

As is well known, the church extended its influence over the ceremonies of the village which were not necessarily Christian in origin or meaning. So the Rogation processions, or the celebration of Plough Monday, clearly had a secular, even magical purpose. We know very little about rural folklore practices in the Middle Ages, because they are often not documented until comparatively recent times, so we have to assume that the popular festivals and celebrations existed in the medieval village. (Phythian-Adams 1975). We are only rarely helped by specific references in our records; for example, at Polstead, Suffolk, in 1363 John atte Forth was fined 3s. 4d. because 'with others', 'he entered the close of the lord and ... played in the lord's hall a game called a summer game'.[2] This is likely to have been a traditional 'role reversal' ceremony in which social tensions were released through a temporary adoption of the lord's authority by a peasant, which in this case was greeted intolerantly by the lord, who, like many of his class in the generation after the Black Death, was not in the mood for jocular banter with his subordinates.

So the village had a real existence as an organization, a unit of government controlling its own fields and inhabitants, partly in the interests of the 'community', partly in the interests of external authorities, such as the state, the landlord, or the church. In addition to these formal, obligatory functions, it is also possible to glimpse activities, like 'rough music', church ales, or 'summer games', that in some cases originated out of the government of the village, which show the villagers joining in collective groups in pursuit of commonly agreed objectives. The problem for the social historian is understanding the nature of this collective action. in the past, as has already been mentioned, there was a tendency to idealize the sense of community, and to assume neighbourly co-operation and the identification of individuals with the village which has no real justification in the evidence. In investigating the processes of decision making which every vill carried out we must distrust the preambles to the by-laws which state that they were drawn up with the consent of all. By analogy with other examples of medieval government, it is likely that some opinions counted for more than others, and that the views of the 'wiser and better part', or the 'sad and discrete' men, prevailed at village meetings or court sessions. These were the men who filled the positions of reeves, jurors, churchwardens and constables. They were not a small clique, but there was an element of oligarchy in their selection. The same people often held more than one office, simultaneously or successively. Sons often followed their fathers as office-holders. There was a tendency for the wealthier peasants to occupy a high proportion of the offices. However, this should not be exaggerated; there were so many jobs that the oligarchy was necessarily broad. The better-off sections of village society were not divided from their poorer neighbours by an enormous gulf: in many villages in *c*. 1300 the best-endowed tenants had only a 15- or 20-acre holding. It therefore seems unlikely that the élite of the village ran things entirely for their own benefit, as they did not form an interest group separate from the other villagers.

This point can be examined by looking at the lines of conflicts in rural society. A classic form of dispute pitted the vill against the landlord; in the thirteenth and fourteenth centuries this involved the villagers bringing law suits in the royal courts to prove their freedom and their exemption from certain services and dues (Hilton 1949). They needed to organize financial resources and to brief lawyers to do this, and this was often done under the leadership of the élite. In other words, the government of the vill, so often employed in the service of outside authority, was turned against the lord.

Conflict between lords and peasants was not always as clear-cut as in the cases mentioned above. While some villagers might express their opposition to the lord by acts of insubordination, like failing to do labour services or pay dues, there would be others willing to take the easy course of co-operating with authority and therefore helping to punish their rebellious neighbours. Some peasants identified so strongly with their lords that we find them, in the civil wars of the mid-fifteenth century for example, joining the aristocratic armies in large numbers (Goodman 1981, 205–9).

Was there a serious tension between rich and poor villagers? We know that such hostilities exist now. Williams' well-known study of Gosforth in Cumberland in the 1950s revealed some embittered relationships between the different strata in a village that would have appeared socially harmonious to a casual observer (Williams 1956, 86–120). In the medieval village there was a potential division of interest between the employing tenants and the employed smallholder; almost every settlement contained holdings too small to provide for the needs of a family without supplementation of income by earnings in agriculture or industry, and a substantial minority of peasants needed to employ workers, at least in seasonal peaks of effort,

or in the old age of the tenant. By-laws sometimes sought to maintain a supply of wage labour in the harvest by forbidding the able-bodied to glean, or to leave the village in search of higher wages, indicating that the employing interest was influencing the deliberations of the vill. Also some by-laws imply a division of interest between the 'respectable' villagers and a potentially criminal group of gamblers, gossips, thieves and prostitutes. Yet it would be difficult to sustain the argument that there was a conflict between two entrenched groups within each village. Many employees were 'life-cycle servants', that is, young people beginning working life as servants in a neighbour's household, saving up money and gaining experience in preparation for life as a peasant or peasant's wife in later years. When a wealthier peasant died, his eldest son would inherit the holding, but the daughters or younger brothers were likely to have been provided with a smallholding. So wage-earning servants and smallholders might be the relatives of the substantial tenants, and therefore unlikely to be bitterly opposed to one another. Although we no longer believe that every village was organized into an elaborate system of co-aration, whereby every household contributed oxen to make up plough teams, there is no doubt that a good deal of borrowing went on, not just of draught animals, but also of a wide range of goods and services in what has been called a 'blurring of the distinction' between the economies of the different peasant households (Hilton 1975, 48–53).

'Social interactions', acts of co-operation and conflict between villagers, have been investigated by various researchers using the mass of information in series of court rolls. These studies indicate considerable differences in behaviour between social groups, so that in his work on late thirteenth-century Redgrave, Suffolk, Smith has shown that the poorest people had a very limited range of contacts with other villagers, in contrast with the number and variety of interactions of their wealthier neighbours (Smith 1979). Pimsler, in a study of Elton, Huntingdonshire, has again highlighted the frequency with which wealthier villagers appear as pledges, that is guarantors and sureties for those coming before the lords' courts, and argues that the pledging system was not a cosy manifestation of neighbourly co-operation (Pimsler 1977). In analysing violent conflict among villagers at Broughton, Huntingdonshire, Britton found that while a number of fights were between rich and relatively poor individuals, there was a great deal of quarrelling also among the élite families (Britton 1977, 115–23). Other researchers have also noted the lack of a clear social pattern in acts of violence (Dyer 1980, 370–2). All of these pieces of research suggest that indeed there were important social differences between villagers, but it is unlikely that these were sufficiently divisive to lead to a polarization of village society between rich and poor, employers and employees, substantial tenants and cottagers.

Such an interpretation is a long way from saying that villages were socially harmonious. Any glance at a set of court rolls reveals constant disagreements and conflicts. There was clearly a casual and easy resort to violence, not just the minor fist fights and assaults with sticks, pitch-forks, and knives recorded in manorial court rolls, but also murder, leading to a homicide rate well in excess of that of modern urban U.S.A. (Hanawalt 1979, 261–73). Can we make any sense of this quarrelsome behaviour? The best-documented fourteenth-century village in continental Europe, Montaillou in the Pyrenees, was split by a feud between a leading family, the Clergues, and others (Ladurie 1975). Many villagers belonged to the clientage of the Clergues and their opponents, and similar links of patronage have been detected in English villages (Smith 1979).

Certainly we are sometimes conscious of alignments of villagers, who involved themselves in struggles, but were also capable of settling them. For example, at Chaddesley Corbett, Worcestershire, in 1398 two inhabitants of the hamlet of Hill were at odds with one another. Richard Trowbrug was accused of trespass against John Eylof, and also beat him. John Eylof also had a reputation for violence, having made a very serious attack on Richard Ermyte. Evidently Trowbrug had friends in Hill, because the vill, which was supposed to report his wrong-doing, concealed the cases. But after this act of favouritism had been exposed, the machinery of law enforcement was invoked. Trowbrug was fined, and both he and Eylof were bound by four pledges each to be of good behaviour. If either broke the peace, their pledges would be liable to pay the enormous sum of ten pounds.[3] The point to notice in this case is that the two neighbours quarrelled over a real issue, trespass by animals in a crop of beans. Such incidents often originated in this way. The community of villagers became involved in two roles—initially as parties to the dispute, but then agreeing to settle the affair in the interests of good order. Later in the medieval period one is conscious of a growing number of conflicts between individuals and the community in which the differences of interest were so great that the problem could not be readily solved. A major source of such deep disputes was the use of grazing land in an increasingly pastoral age, when individuals sought to maximize their agricultural activities by over-stocking common pastures and enclosing land for their exclusive use. A striking example of such an individual was Thomas Baldwyn of Lower Shuckburgh, Warwickshire, who refused to accept the rulings of his vill from 1387 until his death in 1400 (Dyer 1981, 32). Such problems multiplied in the fifteenth and early sixteenth centuries, with the growth of yeoman farmers, the scale of whose agricultural operations made co-operation within an open-field system increasingly difficult to achieve.

To sum up, the late medieval village had a separate existence, influenced by, and overlapping with, the administration of the landlord, but retaining some independence from higher authorities. The internal life of the village was dominated by the élite, who occupied positions of authority and made important decisions. Village society was fractious, but the leaders sought to control violence, and the conflicts arose out of feuds and friction between neighbours rather than divisions rooted in differences in wealth and economic functions.

We are aware of important changes in the village in the relatively short period, less than three centuries, when we can observe it closely. The organization of the community was still developing in the thirteenth century. It was then that the institution of churchwardens developed, adding new administrative and social dimensions to the life of the vill, and the full growth of the village's hierarchy of officials did not come until the end of the thirteenth century (Beckerman 1972). Reports of the death of the village in the late fourteenth and fifteenth centuries have been shown to be much exaggerated (Razi 1981). Even in the early sixteenth century villages were alive and well, and the formal community organization still had a long history ahead of it. Stresses and strains are visible in the fifteenth century, in the anti-social behaviour of the yeoman graziers, and in the most extreme cases the collapse of a minority of villages in the adverse circumstances of population decline.

If so many developments are discernible in two or three centuries, we are justified in looking for other changes before 1200. We now believe that the village as a distinctive nucleated settlement originated in an evolutionary process, probably in the seventh to eleventh centuries, in association with the growth of regular field systems. The development of the vill as a unit of government and social organization is more problematical. As we have seen, its physical shape could take the form of dispersed settlements and hamlets, linked by invisible bonds of administration and common action. A plausible hypothesis, in view of the crucial importance of the regulation and defence of common pastures in the life of the village, would be to link the emergence of the vill as an organization with a growing scarcity of agricultural resources. We would expect this to appear very early in the fielden districts, and there is indeed evidence from tenth-century charters of the existence of distinct village territories that were available for alienation from larger land units to create new small estates. In woodlands and uplands we might expect the evolution of well-defined vills to be more protracted, and we find in the wooded north of Worcestershire, for example, that the precise boundaries between one vill and the next were still being defined in the thirteenth century.

Finally, in a paper addressed to those primarily concerned with the physical remains of the village, a note of caution is needed on the question of village planning. It is very tempting to see in the symmetry of some villages, in the use of units of measurements in their layout and in the regularity of field systems, the hand of the landlord as the single authority capable of such systematic organization. The bulk of planned villages probably dates back to before the period of full documentation, to the eleventh or twelfth centuries, so there can be no certainty in the matter. However, we do know that field systems were rearranged by a combination of lords and village communities in the later Middle Ages; cases involving lords were more likely to be recorded, and in view of the obvious capabilities of the village in self-government, we can assume that the lords need not have been involved directly in such tasks. Because of the remoteness of many lords from the concerns of the village, and the underdevelopment of administrative machinery in the period before 1200, we should surely open our minds to the possibility, indeed the likelihood, that villagers rather than lords were responsible for the planning of villages and field systems.

Notes

1. Essex Record Office, D/DP M19.
2. British Library, Add. Roll 27685.
3. The Shakespeare Birthplace Trust Record Office, Stratford-upon-Avon, DR5/2743.

References

Ault, W. O. 1960: Village assemblies in medieval England. In *Album Helen Maud Cam. Studies presented to the International Commission for the History of Representative and Parliamentary Institutions* (Louvain and Paris).

Ault, W. O. 1972: *Open-Field Farming in Medieval England* (London and New York, Allen and Unwin).

Beckerman, J. S. 1972: *Customary Law in English Manorial Courts in the Thirteenth and Fourteenth Centuries* (Unpublished PhD thesis, University of London).

Bland, A. E., Brown, P. A. and Tawney, R. H. 1914: *English Economic History. Select Documents* (London, G. Bell and Sons. Reissue 1930).

Britton, E. 1977: *The Community of the Vill, a Study in the History of the Family and Village Life in Fourteenth-century England* (Toronto, Macmillan of Canada).

Campbell, B. M. S. 1981: The regional uniqueness of English field systems? Some evidence from eastern Norfolk. *Agricultural History Review* 29, 16–28.

Dyer, C. C. 1980: *Lords and Peasants in a Changing Society. The Estates of the Bishopric of Worcester 680–1540* (Cambridge, Cambridge University Press).

Dyer, C. C. 1981: *Warwickshire Farming, 1349–c.1520. Preparations for Agricultural Revolution* (Dugdale Society Occasional Paper No. 27).

Gauvard, C. and Gokalp, A. 1974: Les conduites de bruit et leur signification à la fin du Moyen Age: le charivari. *Annales: Économies, Sociétés, Civilisations* 29, 693–704.

Goodman, A. E. 1981: *The Wars of the Roses, Military Activity and English Society, 1452–97* (London, Routledge and Kegan Paul).

Hanawalt, B. A. 1971: *Crime and Conflict in English Communities 1300–1348)* (London and Cambridge, Massachusetts, Harvard University Press).

Hatcher, M. J. (1981): English serfdom and villeinage: towards a reassessment. *Past and Present* 90, 3–39.

Hilton, R. H. 1949: Peasant movements in England before 1381. *Economic History Review* 2nd series 2, 119–36.

Hilton, R. H. 1973: *Bond Men Made Free: Medieval Peasant Movements and the English Rising of 1381* (London, Temple Smith).

Hilton, R. H. 1975: *The English Peasantry in the Later Middle Ages: the Ford Lectures for 1973, and Related Studies* (Oxford, Clarendon Press).

Homans, G. C. 1941: *English Villagers of the Thirteenth Century* (Cambridge, Massachusetts, Harvard University Press).

Kosminsky, E. A. 1956: *Studies in the Agrarian History of England in the Thirteenth Century* (Oxford, Blackwell).

Le Roy Ladurie, E. 1975: *Montaillou, Village Occitan de 1294 à 1324* (Paris, Gallimard).

Macfarlane, A. 1979: *The Origins of English Individualism: the Family, Property and Social Transition* (Oxford, Blackwell).

Maitland, F. W. 1897: *Domesday Book and Beyond: Three Essays in the Early History of England* (Cambridge, Cambridge University Press).

Mason, E. 1976: The role of the English parishioner, 1100–1500. *Journal of Ecclesiastical History* 27, 17–29.

Phythian-Adams, C. 1975: *Local History and Folk Lore* (London, Standing Conference for Local History).

Pimsler, M. 1977: Solidarity in the medieval village? The evidence of personal pledging at Elton, Huntingdonshire. *Journal of British Studies* 17, 1–11.

Raftis, J. A. 1965: Social structures in five east Midland villages. *Economic History Review* 2nd series 18, 83–100.

Razi, Z. 1981: Family, land and the village community in later medieval England. *Past and Present* 93, 3–36.

Smith, R. M. 1979: Kin and neighbours in a thirteenth-century Suffolk community. *Journal of Family History* 4, 285–312.

Thompson, E. P. 1972: 'Rough Music': le charivari anglais. *Annales: Économies, Sociétés, Civilisations* 27, 285–312.

Williams, W. M. 1956: *The Sociology of an English Village: Gosforth.* International Library of Sociology and Social Reconstruction (London, Routledge and Kegan Paul).

Wilson, R. A. 1933: *Court Rolls of the Manor of Hales, Part 3* (Worcestershire Historical Society).

4. Mapping the Village: the Historical Evidence

P. D. A. Harvey

This paper looks at the problems that arise in using historical evidence to draw a map of the medieval village and its fields. Two places in the Oxford region are examined by way of illustration. Both have unusually good surviving records from before 1500, but these records are of different sorts: from Cuxham we have manorial accounts, court rolls and surveys, while from Boarstall we have a large collection of deeds as well as maps of both the fifteenth and the sixteenth centuries. We see how these records tell us a great deal, but can also fail us, or positively mislead, when we use them to reconstruct the detailed layout of village and fields on a map.

Introduction

It is a salutary experience for the local historian to draw a detailed historical map of his area. The map is a remarkably uncompromising medium for conveying information. When he writes, the historian will obviously write a lot about the things he knows and much less about the things he does not know. Whether deliberately or not, he will usually avoid drawing attention to the gaps in his knowledge, leaving his readers, and often himself, with the impression that he knows more than he really does, and that the gaps are unimportant or even nonexistent. The map will have none of this. It gives equal emphasis to every part of the whole and there can be no sliding over doubtful points. Either the house was there in 1600 or it was not. The boundary ran either this way or some other way. The sheep market was either here or it was there. Faced with the questions posed by any reconstruction on a map one realizes just how imprecise one's knowledge is, how many gaps there are that on the map will have to be represented by blank spaces or the most hesitant of outlines.

Few local historians in the past submitted themselves to this discipline. E. F. Jacob used to tell his Oxford postgraduate class on historical bibliography that 'topographical history is one of the glories of English historical scholarship'. So indeed it is, a tradition of research and exposition extending from William Lambarde in the sixteenth century to the present day. But detailed topography—where precisely buildings, estates, boundaries lay on the ground—forms no part of this tradition. The county historians, even in their early days the Victoria County Histories, have all been concerned with the detailed succession to landed property over the centuries but not at all concerned to discover exactly where this property lay. This reflects the legal interest at the root of the tradition, though given the interest in maps shown by William Dugdale and some other notable practitioners, it is surprising

that none of them tried to draw maps of the estates and fields whose ownership they traced in such loving detail. The possibility of linking manorial descents with the realities of fields and meadows and woods on the ground has recently been demonstrated by A. C. Chibnall in his studies of Sherington and its surrounding villages in north Buckinghamshire (1965, 1979). His careful maps never let us forget that the lands defined in the legal and feudal terminology of the records had a real location that can often still be precisely pinpointed.

How do we set about finding just where lands and buildings lay? How can we reconstruct maps of the medieval village? The urban historian faced with the same task sometimes has the help of demonstrable regularities: a grid-iron street pattern or even, as at Salisbury, individual tenements of a known uniform size. This type of regularity seems much rarer in the village, though it is not unknown and may be more common than we realize: pointers in this direction are June Sheppard's work on the street-frontage lengths of village holdings in Yorkshire (1974) and Sölve Göransson's demonstration that at least in certain villages some sort of *solskifte* system operated in the distribution of arable strips among the villagers. Far more obvious is the help we get from the physical evidence on the ground. When we are dealing with a deserted site archaeology can lay bare the outline and many details of the medieval village plan. And where the settlement has continued in occupation, existing building sites and boundaries are inevitably our starting point, though we must always be careful not to take their antiquity for granted, whether consciously or unconsciously. Anything may have happened over the centuries, and we must keep our minds open to any possibility. There are very few villages indeed with a substantial number of medieval buildings, though Harwell, Oxfordshire, with its thirteenth- to fifteenth-century farmhouses is an example (Fletcher 1965–6).

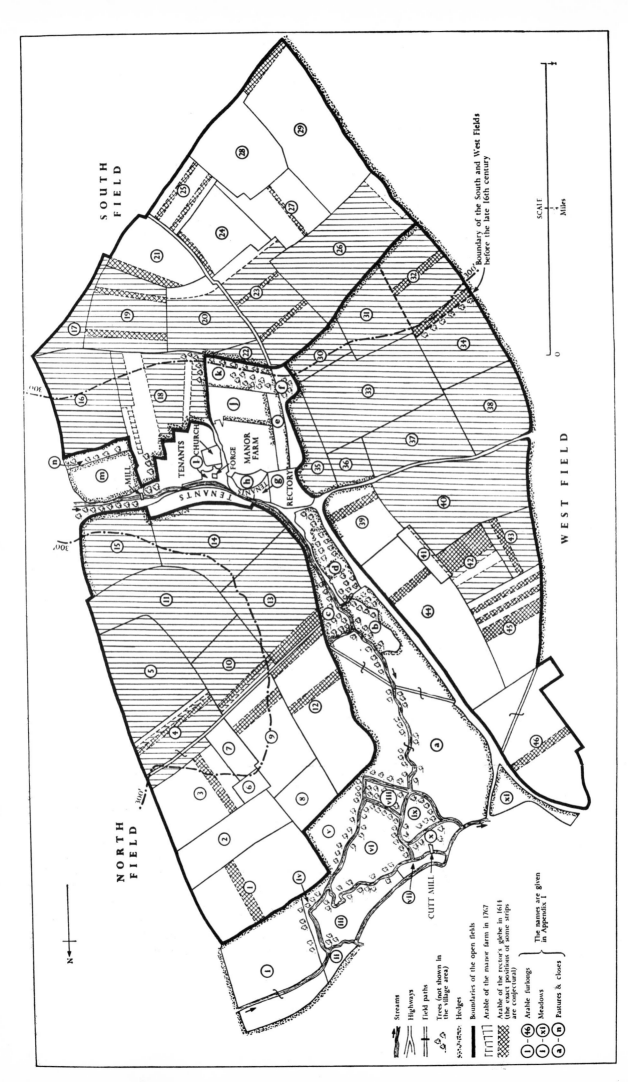

Fig. 4.1 The fields of Cuxham in 1767 from the map by William Chapman

Usually there will be no houses earlier than the Great Rebuilding of the sixteenth and seventeenth centuries, and the church will be the only medieval building. Very often, of course, there will have been continuity of site though not of structure; mills in particular may be shown to have occupied a single site through several successive rebuildings. But often too there will have been significant changes; Richard Morris reminds us that even the village church may have wandered and we cannot assume that its site is older than the earliest datable feature of the existing building. For the medieval layout of a surviving village, for the detailed map of its buildings and fields, we are bound to rely largely on written records that mostly give no more than hints or mere snippets of information, calling for a great deal of reading between the lines.

Taking two villages as examples will show what sort of problem arises, what sort of information can be gleaned from the documents and how it can be interpreted—as well as what traps lie in wait for the unwary. Both villages are near Oxford: one, Cuxham, Oxfordshire, is ten miles to the south-east, the other, Boarstall, Buckinghamshire, is eight miles to the north-east. Both are very well documented; anyone setting out to map a medieval village will be extraordinarily lucky to have anything like the quantity of records that survive from both these places. In each case we have a splendid starting point in early maps of the village—from the eighteenth century for Cuxham, and, amazingly, from the fifteenth century onwards for Boarstall. Beyond this, each has a fine range of written records from the thirteenth century onwards, but of contrasting types: from Cuxham we have manorial surveys, accounts and court rolls, and from Boarstall a cartulary containing over 400 relevant deeds. Because we have so much evidence from these two places they illustrate very well both how we can extract relevant information and what risks we run of misinterpretation where sparser records give us less chance for cross-checking and controls.

Cuxham

Our eighteenth-century map of Cuxham was drawn by William Chapman in 1767; Fig. 4.1 is based on what it shows us of the layout of the village fields. It is particularly valuable, as it predates the enclosure of 1846–7 and is the only map we have of Cuxham's open-field arable. This lay in three fields—the North Field, the South Field, the West Field—subdivided into some 50 furlongs, and the lands of the manor farm mostly formed a single block in each field. This picture of Cuxham's fields can be carried back some 300 years by a terrier of 1447–8; this takes each field in turn and lists the lands that the manor farm (the demesne in medieval terminology) held in every furlong, measuring them in

both customary and measured acres. It shows that there had been remarkably little change since 1767. Pre-enclosure maps are rare; medieval written surveys are much more common. Often a terrier will cover not just the manorial demesne (as at Cuxham) or the lands of a particular tenant, but all the lands of a manor, or, indeed, all the lands of a vill that was divided between two or more manorial lords. In this case the terrier becomes a veritable talking map (*carte parlante*) as F. de Dainville put it. Of one such mid-fourteenth-century terrier, covering all the thousand-odd parcels of land in the West Fields of Cambridge, F. W. Maitland wrote 'In each field it describes the various furlongs or shots in such a manner that an ingenious man, who had time to spare and taste for the Chinese puzzle, might depict them on a map'. So he might indeed, and D. G. Kendall has demonstrated, with increasing precision and subtlety, how a computer can be used to make a map from the information in a detailed field terrier.

For this our Cuxham terrier, covering only the demesne, would be inadequate, but, given our map of 1767 as a basis, it carries us a long way towards being able to draw a map of Cuxham's fields in the Middle Ages, the more so as we are able to supplement it with other early evidence. Three seventeenth-century terriers take our picture of the rector's glebe lands back to 1614; fourteenth-century account rolls show us that the arable was then, as in 1767, divided into the North, South and West Fields, that these were the basis of a three-course rotation of crops, and that the area of demesne in each field was 87 acres, 88 acres and 93 acres respectively; here and there in the medieval records we find quite a number of occasional references to individual furlongs. All this helps us to fill in our map of the medieval arable and its divisions.

But with caution. The three fields may have had the same names in the fourteenth century as in the eighteenth, but this need not mean that they had the same bounds. The 1614 glebe terrier notes that two arable strips 'are nowe tilled, as the wholl furlong is also togither with the west fielde: though lately within memory of man they have bin tilled as parte of the South fielde'. Here the area in question was only some seven acres (furlong no. 32 on Fig. 4.1), but it is mere chance that has given us this note, and other, larger, transfers of land from one field to another may well have taken place without leaving any trace at all in our records. Our knowledge of the area of demesne in each field in the fourteenth century will not serve as a check, for the demesne then was not the same as the demesne of 1447–8: it was reduced by 100 acres in 1441. And if it is risky to carry the names and bounds of the three fields back from the eighteenth century into the Middle Ages, it is even riskier to do this with their subdivisions, the furlongs. Sometimes we find that that a single furlong bears the same name over many centuries: the Stir

Furlong (no. 3 on Fig. 4.1) and Fifty Acre Furlong (no. 29) of 1767 both seem to have been so-called in the thirteenth century. But some furlongs had several successive names over the same period: Mackney Furlong in 1767 (no. 24) was Short Gravel Furlong in 1614 and Whiteland in 1447–8, while Gibbons Piece in 1767 (no. 23) was New Close Furlong in 1685, Grove End Furlong in 1614 and the Furlong above the Court Garden in 1447–8. At Cuxham we can make these identifications because we have such full written sources; more often we would have no way of linking one name with another across the centuries. Moreover, furlong names can be positively misleading. In 1767 the furlong numbered 12 on Fig. 4.1 was called Moor Furlong; but what was called Moor Furlong in various sources from the fifteenth century to the seventeenth was not this furlong at all but the furlong numbered 44 (in 1767 the Oxford Road Furlong). And just as the names of the fields may have changed less than their bounds, so too with the furlongs; the area numbered 29 had been known as Fifty Acre Furlong for at least 500 years in 1767, but before the seventeenth century the furlong also included no. 32 and half of no. 26 as well—and indeed the name itself would lead us to suppose that it had originated with a larger area than no. 29, though the 50 acres will have been customary ones, not measured statute acres. In all these cases it is simply because we have so many records from Cuxham that we know what happened. It is all too easy to see how badly our reconstruction of the medieval fields could go astray if our evidence were scantier. And of course even at Cuxham there may well be gaps in the evidence that have led to mistakes, to misidentifications. It is significant that we have in the thirteenth- and fourteenth-century Cuxham records references to arable furlongs (and even more to meadows and closes) which we cannot identify from later sources and thus cannot locate on the ground.

Parish and estate boundaries may help in our reconstruction for periods where written records fail us, though their evidence too must be used with the greatest caution. By 1086 probably all of Cuxham's arable was under cultivation: Domesday Book makes no reference to woodland there. But it is likely that cultivation had started in the areas beside the floor of the valley, spreading up the low hills on either side until it finally replaced woods that covered the hilltops. This is suggested by the shape of the manor (and parish) bounds: long, sweeping curves, except in the north-west corner of the parish, near the stream, where we have straight lines and right angles that clearly follow the lines of existing fields. Moreover a charter of AD 995[1] refers to a *wudu wic*, or 'dairy farmstead by the wood', which seems to have stood on the south-east boundary. It seems as if we can tentatively draw a rough map of land use in Anglo-Saxon Cuxham, showing the likely areas of woodland, arable and meadow or pasture.

At the same time it can only be very tentative. The bounds of *Cucces hamm* set out in the charter of AD 995 have been identified with the modern parish boundaries, though at best they only confirm the general outline. Where the evidence of place-names and of boundary patterns seems to point in the same direction they may serve as a useful guide to probabilities. But either can be misleading. At Cuxham we distinguished between the straight lines and angles of bounds drawn among cultivated fields and the gently curving bounds drawn across uncultivated wood or pasture. If we look at a group of parishes around Haverhill, Suffolk, the area where Essex, Suffolk and Cambridgeshire all meet, we see the same contrast on a different scale (Fig. 4.2). West Wratting, crossed by the Icknield Way at its western end, has bounds that were mostly drawn across uncultivated land, while just as clearly the bounds of several parishes to the east—Haverhill, Withersfield, Great Wratting, Little Wratting—were drawn to follow the lines of existing fields. We know that the Fleam Dyke was drawn across the Icknield Way in the sixth or seventh century; on the west it ended in the waters of the fenland, and it is reasonable to suppose that on the east it ended in woodland thick enough to serve as a defensive barrier. We might then suppose that West Wratting's bounds were drawn through woodland, and that this part of the area was reduced to cultivation later than the lands around the River Stour, where we have the bounds of straight lines and right angles. But this is a dangerous assumption without other evidence pointing the same way: the parish bounds (or the bounds that were to become parish bounds) may not have been drawn at the same period. Boundaries can be valuable clues to the landscape of the past, but they are clues that need great care in interpretation.

Returning to Cuxham, we have seen the problems that arise in mapping the medieval fields, but what of the village itself? We have a little help from standing structures: the oldest building in the village today is the church, which has a Norman tower. We have some help too from the traces, visible in air photographs, of five abandoned house sites along the stream at the village's north-west end; one of these plots formed an enclosure called Wallridges in 1767, a name we can link with the Waldrugge family which died out in the Black Death of 1349, and it is likely that the desertion of all five followed the reduction in the number of tenants that we know occurred after the mid-fourteenth century. The earliest map of the village to show all its houses and other buildings in detailed outline plan is a Tithe Apportionment map of 1848; the village area does not appear very clearly on the map of 1767, though we can see that the manor farm, the rectory, the mill and individual house sites were all in the same positions. Let us assume that this continuity extended back into the Middle Ages, to the thirteenth century, and that the village plan then was essentially the same as it was 500

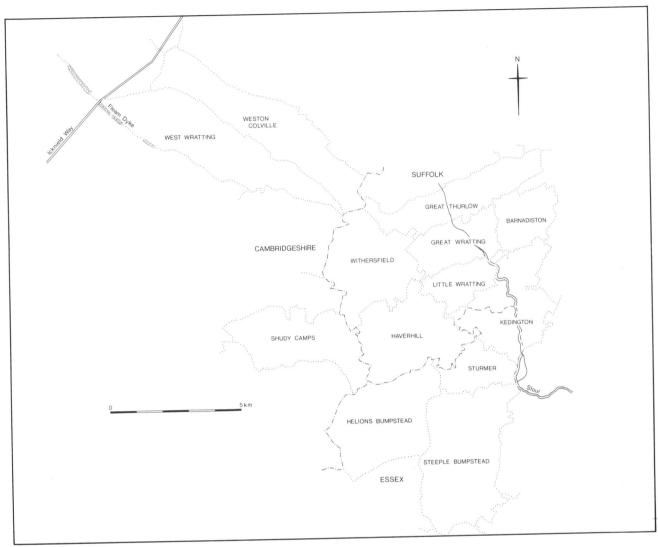

Fig. 4.2   Parish boundaries around Haverhill (Suffolk)

years later with just the addition of the five houses on the deserted sites. It is a risky assumption, as we shall see when we look at Boarstall, but at Cuxham it is a reasonable one: all the hints and stray references to the village layout that we find in the medieval records fit this pattern.

The question then arises whether we can go further than this and identify the house plots with the individual families mentioned in the medieval surveys and court rolls. In fact we can, mostly with fair certainty. We have seen that one of the five abandoned sites took its name from the Waldrugge family; fifteenth-century deeds show that another was then still remembered as the Waleys holding (another family that disappeared in 1349), while, a third, Greneheys, preserved the name of the Grenes, a family of freeholders. Elsewhere in the village we have no direct evidence of this sort, but chance references to particular villagers' houses occasionally give us a clue to where

they stood. We know, for instance, that the Hethe family holding adjoined the manor farm, as in 1297–8 the reeve accounted for the cost of repairing the walls 'between the *curia* and the house of Adam atte Hethe'. Some reading between the lines may be called for: in 1315 members of the Bovecheriche and Sawyere families were amerced in the manorial court for making a path across the demesne corn to go to Watlington, the next village, and we can deduce from this that they lived to the south of the church as this is the only part of the village from which it would be a short cut to go across the fields. We can get further help from looking closely at the order of the villagers' names in contemporary lists—manorial surveys and royal tax assessments are the most obvious. The most likely order for the clerk to choose (to make sure everyone was included) was topographical; it need not be the same topographical order every time—it might or might not take each side of the street in turn, for instance, while there would be

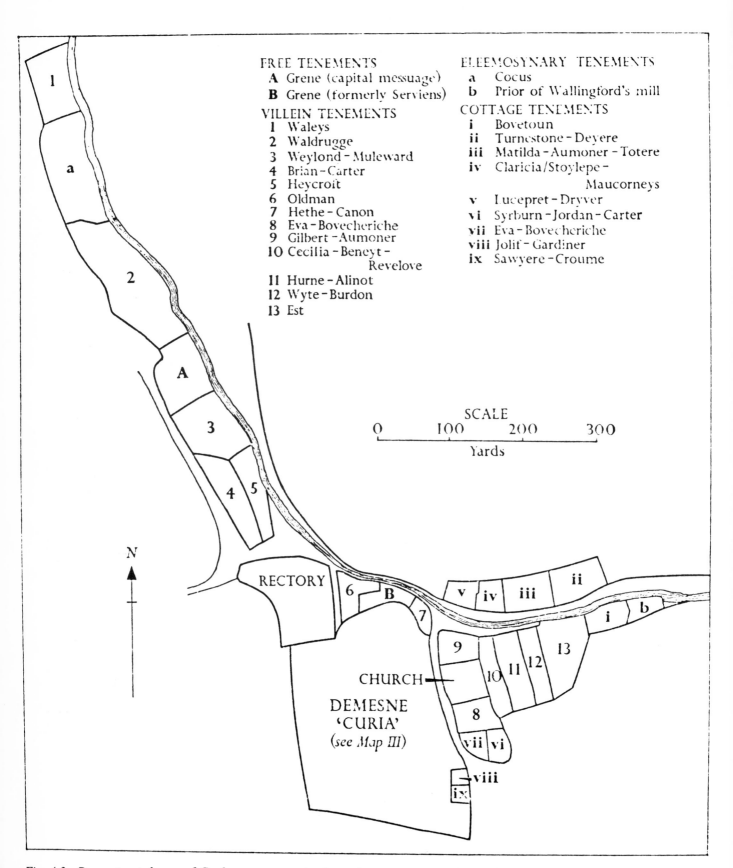

FREE TENEMENTS
A Grene (capital messuage)
B Grene (formerly Serviens)
VILLEIN TENEMENTS
1 Waleys
2 Waldrugge
3 Weylond – Muleward
4 Brian – Carter
5 Heycroft
6 Oldman
7 Hethe – Canon
8 Eva – Bovecheriche
9 Gilbert – Aumoner
10 Cecilia – Beneyt –
                    Revelove
11 Hurne – Alinot
12 Wyte – Burdon
13 Est

ELEEMOSYNARY TENEMENTS
a Cocus
b Prior of Wallingford's mill
COTTAGE TENEMENTS
i Bovetoun
ii Turnestone – Deyere
iii Matilda – Aumoner – Totere
iv Claricia/Stoylepe –
                    Maucorneys
v Lucepret – Dryver
vi Syrburn – Jordan – Carter
vii Eva – Bovecheriche
viii Jolif – Gardiner
ix Sawyere – Croume

SCALE
0   100   200   300
Yards

RECTORY

N

CHURCH

DEMESNE
'CURIA'
(see Map III)

Fig. 4.3 Reconstructed map of Cuxham tenements in the early 14th century

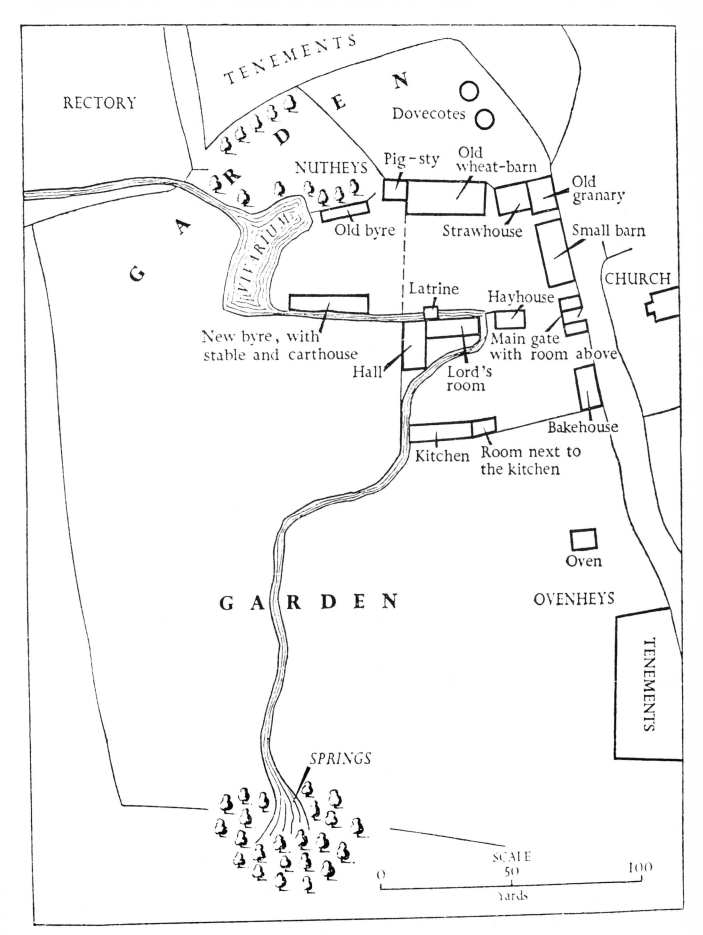

RECTORY

TENEMENTS

GARDEN

Dovecotes

NUTHEYS

Pig-sty

Old wheat-barn

Old granary

VIVARIUM

Old byre

Strawhouse

Small barn

CHURCH

New byre, with stable and carthouse

Latrine

Hayhouse

Main gate with room above

Hall

Lord's room

Bakehouse

Kitchen

Room next to the kitchen

Oven

GARDEN

OVENHEYS

TENEMENTS

SPRINGS

SCALE
0   50   100
Yards

Fig. 4.4 Conjectural plan of the manorial buildings at Cuxham c. 1315

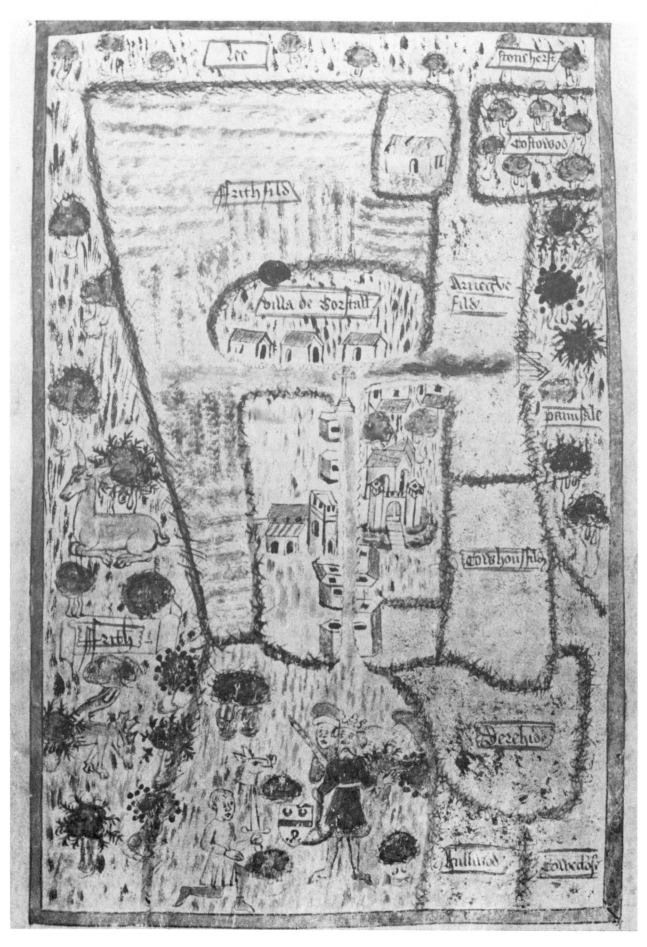

Fig. 4.5 Map of Boarstall and its fields from the Boarstall Cartlary, 1444–6

various ways of covering side roads—but there would be enough points of similarity between the lists to show that this was how they were compiled and to give some clues to the positions of particular houses. From Cuxham we have nine lists of village households dating from 1279 to 1329, and all but one seem to have been drawn up topographically. Thus when we find that seven of them name the Aumoner and the Beneyt households one after the other it seems reasonable to assume that they were next-door neighbours on the village street. When we put the evidence of these lists alongside our various scraps of evidence from other sources, we find that they give us a fully consistent pattern of the households in the village (Fig. 4.3). In three instances the villagers' surnames confirm our conclusions: the family living in the easternmost of the villeins' houses was named Est (i.e. East) while beyond them, in a cottage probably put up in 1304, was a family named Bovetoun (i.e. Above-town), and as we have seen, the Bovecheriche (i.e. Above-church) family lived beyond the village church. In all this we are using various sources to corroborate each other's evidence and to build up, between them, a picture which is credible just because different sources all seem to point in the same direction. To base our reconstruction on less varied evidence, to draw conclusions from one source alone, would be much more risky.

Often, indeed, our sources give us a great deal of topographical information but just not quite enough for us to plot our map of the medieval village. We see this in what the Cuxham records tell us of the buildings of the manor farm, the *curia* . Almost all the manorial accounts from 1276 to 1359 refer to costs of repairing these buildings or of putting up new ones; often these entries are very detailed, listing the amounts and costs of materials used. Often too they tell us something of the locations of these buildings. The hay-house, for instance, was rebuilt in 1320–3; it had stone walls, a wooden stairway and a door fitted with a lock, and the reconstruction included replacing a thatched roof with 12,000 tiles or slates. A new wheat barn, built in the 1320s, ran from north to south, for corn would be stacked at its north and south ends, and it must have adjoined the manorial garden, for one of its doors was 'at the end of the barn towards the garden'. But when we put all the evidence together we cannot reconstruct a plan of the manor-farm buildings without a substantial amount of guesswork (Fig. 4.4)—guesswork that has indeed proved wrong in one respect since this plan was drawn, for recent work on air photographs and on the site itself has shown that what is called the *vivarium* or fishpond was in fact a moat and that the real fishponds (two of them) lay some 20 yards to the west. It is a useful reminder that even our well-documented medieval village is likely to have blanks on its reconstructed map.

Boarstall

From Boarstall, as from Cuxham, we have many medieval records but, as we have seen, records of a different sort. From Cuxham we have primarily manorial records, from Boarstall the deeds that were copied into the mid-fifteenth-century cartulary of Edmund Rede, whose family were lords of the manor throughout the Middle Ages. There are contrasts too in the history of the two places, contrasts that are crucial in reconstructing their medieval plans. At Cuxham we find continuity and stability, with little change in either village or fields from the the thirteenth century to the eighteenth. At Boarstall the layout of both village and fields underwent substantial changes in the 250 years after the date of the cartulary.

Some of this appears from the map of Boarstall that was probably meant as the cartulary's frontispiece (Fig. 4.5). It is a colourful production, if rather crudely drawn. At the bottom is a drawing of Edmund Rede's ancestor, Nigel the Forester, presenting to King Edward the Confessor the head of a ferocious boar he had just killed, receiving in return the hereditary wardenship of Bernwood Forest (the incident is apocryphal). Above is a plan of the fields and woods around Boarstall, each with its name, and, at the centre, the village drawn disproportionately large. One building in the village is clearly recognizable as still standing today: the gatehouse of the Redes' manor house with its hexagonal towers (Fig. 4.6), drawn distinctively, if not very accurately, on the map. But the rest of the village is not so easily recognized, and H. E. Salter, who edited the cartulary in 1930, wrote that 'It is impossible to make the plan harmonize with the geography of the village'. He will have had in mind the way the map places the gatehouse and the village church on opposite sides of the street, whereas in fact they both lie on its west side; and also the T-junction it shows at the end of the village street with houses at the crossing, for the road comes at one end to a T-junction certainly, at the other simply to a sharp bend, but in both cases well beyond the village's built-up area.

In fact it is the village that has changed. The street now makes a broad sweep round the east end of the church; it does the same on a map of 1697 (Fig. 4.7) and on a bird's-eye view of the manor house by Michael Burghers in 1695 (Fig. 4.8), but on both these we see an enclosed walk just inside the boundary wall of the manor grounds, its line forming a chord to the arc made by the street. Probably this was once the line of the street itself, passing between church and manor house as on the fifteenth-century map: an extension of the manor grounds will have brought it within their enclosure, with the street realigned on the farther side of the church. This would have been made easier by the reduction of Boarstall's population. In the Civil War

Fig. 4.6   The gatehouse at Boarstall

the manor house, a centre of royalist resistance, was besieged and attacked; houses in the village were destroyed, and the parish registers point to severe depopulation in the 1650s, presumably because many who left the village during the war did not return. In 1524 33 villagers, most or all of them householders, contributed to the Lay Subsidy besides the Redes themselves; the map of 1697 shows only eight houses at Boarstall besides the manor house. The fifteenth-century map marks some 11 or 12 villagers' houses, all it has room for; there must have been more at that time, but we can reasonably suppose that the map at least shows the general layout of the village. It follows that houses extended up to and beyond the present sharp bend in the road south of the village, a bend that could then be seen as a T-junction with another road now lost.

The moral of this is not that early maps are reliable and accurate. They are not, and it is worth noting that a 1590 map of Boarstall (Fig. 4.9) puts not only the church but also the manor house on the east side of the village street, a quirk that really cannot be explained by any change in layout or alignment. But the changes illustrated from the fifteenth-century map serve as a corrective to the unchanging continuity we found at Cuxham; they remind us that we must be flexible in our approach to the written evidence, neither accepting nor rejecting it lightly, and that in reconstructing the village plan and landscape we should draw our evidence from as many different sources as we can.

We find more changes when we turn from the village to the fields of Boarstall. Beside the village the fifteenth-century map names Arngrove Field, Cowhouse Field and Frith Field, each with arable strips and furlongs roughly painted on. Deeds of the 1430s and 1440s in the cartulary show that these were the three open fields where the arable of the lord and his tenants lay: particular furlongs are said to be in one or other field. However, the cartulary's fourteenth-century deeds

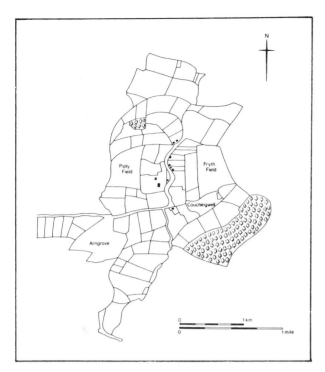

Fig. 4.7   The fields of Boarstall in 1697 from the map by J. Burges

mention not three fields but four: Arngrove Field, Frith Field, Northcroft Field and Quechenwelle Field. Northcroft Field was probably the same as Cowhouse Field, for Chalcroft Furlong is said to lie first in one then in the other. Quechenwelle Field, last mentioned in 1350, seems to have been turned into a southern extension of Frith Field: Lee Furlong lay in Quechenwelle Field in 1322 and in Frith Field in 1447. But changes in the Boarstall fields did not stop there. If we look at the 1697 map (Fig. 4.7) we find no open fields and furlongs at all, but a system of closes. Among them, however, we find relics of the old fields. Two of the three largest closes are named Arngrove (52 acres) and Fryth Field (67 acres); presumably each was the nucleus of one of the old open fields from which whole series of closes had been hived off. The third large close was called Piply Field (67 acres), and it is tempting to see this as the surviving core of the old Northcroft or Cowhouse Field, having undergone another change of name. Another, smaller, close, Couchingwell (24 acres) preserves the memory of the long vanished Quechenwelle Field. At Cuxham we could map the medieval fields on the basis of the map of 1767; at Boarstall the 1697 map gives us no more than a few barely recognizable vestiges of the medieval field system.

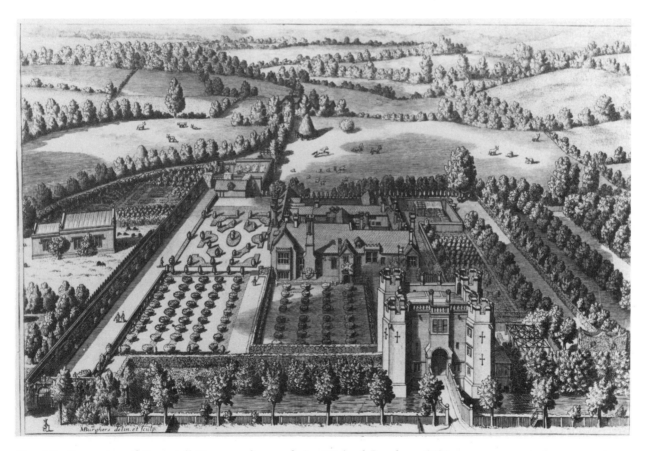

Fig. 4.8   Engraving of Boarstall House and grounds by Michael Burghers, 1695

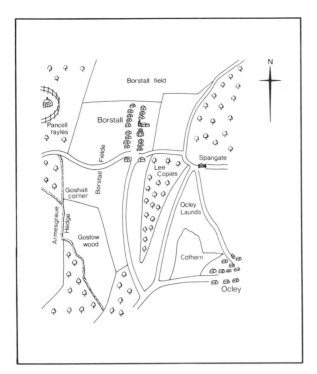

Fig. 4.9   Plan of Boarstall from the map of Boarstall, Oakley and Brill, c. 1590

The deeds in the Boarstall cartulary confirm the outline picture that the fifteenth-century map gives us of the fields as well as enabling us to fill in many details. However, even where we have as many deeds as we have from Boarstall, they are no substitute for a detailed survey in reconstructing the layout of a village's fields—they are far from serving as a talking map. Like the references to the manorial buildings in the Cuxham records, one is apt to find that they give a great deal of detail—names of furlongs and their abuttals, the allocation of furlongs to fields, and so on—but never quite enough to enable us to fit the whole patchwork together, to see how more than a few furlongs here and there lay in relation to others. But worse than this, the topographical descriptions in deeds can be positively misleading. When a piece of arable had already changed hands before, with a written deed to attest the conveyance, the clerk might copy the description of the property verbatim from the earlier deed, unconcerned (or, indeed, not knowing) that this description was now out of date. Thus we find arable strips defined as bounded by the lands of men actually long dead, or—more confusingly to our reconstruction of the fields—references to agrarian arrangements superseded long

before. It is not beyond the bounds of possibility, for instance, that Quechenwelle Field at Boarstall had already disappeared by 1350, the date of the latest surviving deed to mention it. Moreover, few deeds name more than one or two furlongs or other features, unlike the survey which offers a conspectus of an entire field system; thus we have no guard against the risks that we found in looking at the Cuxham fields, the risks of failing to recognize a furlong when it appears under more then one name, and of wrongly identifying two furlongs that (like the two Moor Furlongs at Cuxham) bore the same name at different dates. We have no guarantee that the Lee Furlong in Quechenwelle Field in 1322 was the same as the Lee Furlong in Frith Field in 1447. All we can say is that this identification—and the identification of the two fields that we based on it—fits in with what the other deeds and the maps suggest was happening in the Boarstall fields and fits in too with what evidence we have of the position of the two fields on the ground. It is the same sort of probability falling short of clear proof that we had to assume in carrying Cuxham's village plan back to the Middle Ages. Mapping the medieval village will almost always involve a good deal of balancing of probabilities.

Conclusion

Cuxham and Boarstall are both exceptional in the number of their medieval records, Cuxham in its manorial documents, and Boarstall in its deeds and early maps. The historian who tries to map the medieval village will normally have far scantier sources of information at his disposal. To this extent our two villages are hardly a fair sample: they give no hint of the basic problems of layout of houses and fields that will often confront us. But there is a particular value in looking at these two unusually well-documented places. For one thing they show that even where a great deal of evidence survives there are still likely to be gaps or, at best, very hesitant reconstructions on our map, as well as a great deal more for which our evidence gives us less than absolute certainty. But beyond this it is easy to see, in the abundance of records from Cuxham and Boarstall, just what traps there are, traps that we can all too easily fall into if we base our deductions on more limited evidence. Mapping the medieval village may be a valuable exercise for the local historian, calling on all his experience and expertise. But he would be unwise to place great confidence in the result.

Notes

1. The Cuxham charter of AD 995 is no. 1379 in Sawyer, P. H. 1968: *Anglo-Saxon Charters, an Annotated List and Bibliography*, printed in Kemble, J. M. 1839–48: *Codex Diplomaticus Aevi Saxonici*, no. 691.

References

Chibnall, A. C. 1965: *Sherington: Fiefs and Fields of a Buckinghamshire Village* (Cambridge, Cambridge University Press).

Chibnall, A. C. 1979: *Beyond Sherington: the Early History of the Region of Buckinghamshire Lying to the North-east of Newport Pagnell* (London and Chichester, Phillimore).

Fletcher, J. M. 1965–6: Three medieval farmhouses in Harwell. *Berkshire Archaeological Journal* 62, 45–69.

Göransson, S. 1961: Regular open-field pattern in England and Scandinavian *solskifte*. *Geografiska Annaler* 43, 80–104.

Sheppard, J. A. 1974: Metrological analysis of regular village plans in Yorkshire. *Agricultural History Review* 22, 118–35.

The accounts of Boarstall and Cuxham are based on:

Harvey, P. D. A. (editor) 1965: *A Medieval Oxfordshire Village: Cuxham 1240–1400* (London, Oxford University Press).

Harvey, P. D. A. (editor) 1976: *Manorial Records of Cuxham, Oxfordshire, circa 1200–1359* (London, Her Majesty's Stationery Office, Historical Manuscripts Commission, Joint Publications 23; Oxfordshire Record Society, Vol. 50).

Salter, H. E. (editor) 1930: *The Boarstall Cartulary* (Oxford, Oxford Historical Society, Old series Vol. 88).

Skelton, R. A. and Harvey, P. D. A. (editors) 1984: *Local Maps and Plans from Medieval England* (Oxford, Clarendon Press), 211–19.

Fig. 5.1

All Saints, Wighill, North Yorkshire. The church occupies the summit of a small but prominent knoll, as do churches at the neighbouring villages of Walton and Healaugh. A hall stands amid trees to the north of the churchyard. In plan the modern village takes the form of an inverted letter L. Housing along the 'upstroke' is new, and in the nineteenth century the village and church were separated by open ground. The single-street village shows a clear relation with the zone of ridge-and-furrow visible at the centre of the photograph. The strips depart from, or drain towards, a green lane which is connected to the east end of the village street, and they have acquired a cyclonic aspect from being bent around the small fields that abut the village tofts. It is possible that the linear village replaced an earlier settlement at the foot of the church hill. Pre-Conquest sculpture re-used in the south wall of the church suggests that the site was in ecclesiastical use before 1000. The church thus acquires importance as a steady component in a changing pattern of settlement and land use.

5. The Church in the Countryside: two Lines of Inquiry

R. K. Morris

Inconsistencies have arisen between hypotheses about the origins of villages and of village churches. Consideration is given to the numbers of churches which stood at different times. A figure of 4,500 is suggested as a minimum total by the late eleventh century. While the sites of most medieval churches have remained unchanged, attention is drawn to instances of closure and shifts of position. The existence of an ephemeral and hitherto unrecognized class of pre-parochial local church is postulated.

The question which is probably asked most often by the new visitor to a parish church is 'How old is it?'. This matter of site, the church as a component of rural settlement, bears upon the wider theme of the medieval village, not least in those parts of England where we are being taught to recognize the almost kaleidoscopic appearance of some village developments, and where the church, at least, might be expected to hold out some promise of stability.

Once a church is known to be in existence it can be used as a point of reference when we come to examine the topographical evolution of the village (Fig. 5.1). However, our two original questions—of time, and of place—cannot really be separated, and the ultimate application of this use of the church as a sort of benchmark turns upon the availability of information about when it was that the site of the church was designated and became fixed. Here we meet a difficulty. In the words of Mrs Dorothy Owen: 'It is very rare indeed to discover a precise, or even an approximate, date, for the foundation of any parish church or chapel known to have been in existence before 1100' (1976a, 22). For reasons which will be explained below, the minimum figure for churches in this category cannot be less than 3,000, and the actual total could be nearer twice that number. Put differently, the origins of *at least* 35 per cent and perhaps as many as 70 per cent of all medieval parish churches are unreported in written records. Archaeology can furnish dates, but the sample of churches which have been explored in enough detail for the origin of the ecclesiastical use of the site to be known is woefuly small and disproportionately urban in emphasis.

It may be wondered how it was that our predecessors in this field, lacking even the surety of a small corpus of dated sites, arrived at the consensus which enabled the late G. W. O. Addleshaw to say that 'the large majority of old parish churches in England were founded in the tenth and eleventh centuries' (1970, 13) (Fig. 5.2). Over 90 per cent of all medieval parochial provision stood in the countryside, so Addleshaw's statement, if it is correct, clearly carries implications for the student of the medieval village. Are we, to borrow Norman Scarfe's apt remark about the pattern of churches in Suffolk in 1086 (1972, 140), looking at the true 'bone-structure' of pre-Conquest settlement when we contemplate a map of our older parochial sites?

In order to discuss this question it is first necessary to look at something of the historiographical tradition which lies behind its asking. It is fair to say that until quite recently the study of churches and the study of settlement marched more or less hand in hand. Ideas about the significance and dates of village church sites were comfortably accommodated within a wider system of opinions about English settlement history in general. To give an example, the analysis offered by William Page in his pioneering essay about churches in Domesday Book was in full accord with, and fed upon, the doctrines of his day about the course of colonization and the making of the landscape. Page was prepared to believe in the possibility that extensive areas of southern England lacked churches in 1086 because they were still largely unsettled (1915, 92). In his discussion of the ecclesiastical organization of Sussex at this time Page also drew a distinction between what he regarded as the 'older settled districts in the south... and the later settlements on the verge of the forest in the north'. The former, Page opined, were served by an 'older system of minsters', whereas in the latter 'manorial churches only are to be found' (1915, 79–81). Mrs Owen has described the relationship between parish churches and chapelries in the Kesteven portion of Lincolnshire, where 'the oldest and most populous centres formed parishes, while chapels or field churches occur only where the settlement is recent, or very sparse' (1976b, 66).

Thus far, the broad lines of the picture are clear. The oldest settlements are to be expected on the best land, and it is in a proportion of these preferred centres that the first secular churches are likely to be encountered. When agricultural activity and settlement were subsequently extended into less attractive terrain, this

Fig. 5.2

St John the Baptist (formerly St Quintin), Kirk Hammerton, North Yorkshire. Addleshaw described this as a 'typical stone village church of the second half of the eleventh century. A priest and church are recorded here in Domesday Book. Possibly the church was built through the initiative of Turchil, Gamel and Heltor, who had six and a half carucates for geld in the time of Edward the Confessor' (1970, Pl. IV). A different caption might read: 'The building dates of the primary fabric of this church have not yet been established with certainty; nor is it known if this was the first church on the site, or the first ecclesiastical site in the neighbourhood.' The fabric of the church should be considered in relation to the settlement history of the area: some, if not all, of the large blocks of stone which occur in the walls are of Roman origin. The great size of these stones renders a local source unlikely, unless they were taken from the piers of a bridge where the main Roman road from York to Aldborough crossed the River Nidd *c.* 1 mile to the north-east, and rather suggests a building date for the church at a time when massive structures were being demolished in York. (Photo: Derek Phillips)

expansion could be either accompanied or followed by the founding of secondary churches or chapels.

According to Stenton, the primary unit in the early medieval pattern of settlement was the village. Stenton took good care to say that 'no single type of settlement can ever have prevailed throughout the whole, even of southern England'. But he continued: '...as late as the eighth century life for perhaps a quarter of the English people was a struggle for existence against the unprofitable soil and scrubland vegetation which would spread again over cultivated fields on any slackening of effort. It was by individual enterprise that these poor lands had been brought into cultivation, and innumerable isolated farmsteads bearing Anglo-Saxon names remain as memorials of the process. Nevertheless, throughout Old English history it was not the farm but the village which formed the basis of social organization' (1971, 286).

Recent years have seen the appearance of studies which, if they do not deny a measure of validity to Stenton's thesis, at least tend to accord as much, if not more, importance to the first part of the foregoing quotation as to the second. Professor Sawyer, for example, has argued that the 'rural resources of England were almost as fully exploited in the seventh century as they were in the eleventh and that although some settlements were established, or moved, in the late Anglo-Saxon period, the settlement pattern is, in general, much older than most scholars have been prepared to recognize. Our sources are certainly consistent with the view that, in general, the Anglo-Saxon period was a time of shifting but not expanding settlement' (Sawyer 1976, 2, with further references). Fluidity, rather than fixedness, has also emerged as a leading theme in the work of C. C. Taylor (e.g. Taylor 1974; 1977; 1978). Other scholars have engaged in detailed local studies, with results which point in the same direction (e.g. Foard 1978; Wade-Martins 1980).

What concerns us here is that whereas ideas about early medieval English settlement have been substantially reshaped and given new directions, opinion about the origins of village churches—and hence, by implication, about the selection and chronology of their sites—remains much where it stood 50 years ago, when the multiplication of churches was seen as a concomitant of slow growth. So, on the one hand we have freshly minted theories about the extensiveness of pre-Conquest settlement, which embrace dispersal and mobility, and on the other the hand-me-down perceptions of an older generation of scholars who were wedded to precisely those tenets about village origins which are now being modified or challenged. If this assessment is anywhere near the truth, it could explain why churches, despite their prominence and ubiquity, have received such exiguous treatment at the hands of landscape archaeologists. Apart from an appreciation of the value of lonely churches as possible advertisements for vanished villages, there has been no systematic attempt to consider, from an archaeological standpoint, the *loci* of village religion within the broader context of village studies.

By now it should be clear that the subject of the church as a component of settlement demands a more extensive treatment than can be provided in the space of one essay. For this reason, it is best to single out just a few lines of inquiry, and to follow these for a short distance. There will be two such lines, as follows:

i) The matter of quantities: how many churches can be reasonably expected to have been in existence at different times?

ii) The doctrine of stability: should we continue to suppose that the church has remained rooted to its site, or that, if we investigate it and assign a date to its beginning, we have found the first and only church to have existed in that locality?

Alongside these principal topics some attention must also be given to the relative importance of churches at different times, together with the significance of ecclesiastical hierarchy and rank in theories about the progression and chronology of settlement. Are we entitled to assume that certain types of church—whether assessed according to their status, staffing, or plan—are 'early', and others 'late', and to relate conclusions about the development of villages to these assumptions?

(i) The matter of quantities (Table 5.1)

We cannot begin to discuss questions of church location without thinking first about numbers: roughly speaking, how many churches, and by when?

The conventional answer has already been given. It may be summarized as a 'big bang' theory for the origins of most village churches. Briefly stated, this visualizes the local or—to use slightly later terminology—the parish church, as being a relatively late arrival within the pattern of settlement. We are told that the foundation of such churches was mainly a phenomenon of the period *c.* AD 900–1100.

Now, almost everyone can agree that the parochial system was in the process of emergence during these years. Certain features of parochial organization had been introduced at earlier dates, and refinements were to follow later, but it was in the eleventh and twelfth centuries that the system as we know it crystallized. Moreover, it is during these years that we first begin to meet appreciable numbers of contemporary references to the building of local churches, and it has sometimes been claimed that these statements betoken a more comprehensive movement of churchbuilding which was then in progress. The evidence of architecture and sculpture could be cited in support of this. In Yorkshire, for example, more than 70 per cent of all surviving medieval parochial churches either contain fabric which can be assigned to the period *c.* 1050–1200 on stylisic grounds, or have yielded carved stones of the tenth to eleventh centuries, or both. Of course, it is likely that an Anglo-Norman building boom would have involved the modernization of existing churches as well as the creation of new ones. In most cases, however, we lack the criteria which would help us to differentiate between works of renovation and fresh foundation. The total of Yorkshire sites which have produced Anglian sculpture is low by comparison with the Viking period, and it is tempting to interpret this difference as meaning that the region was more lavishly provided with local churches in the tenth and eleventh centuries than it had been formerly. This is possible, but since most of the places which have yielded Anglian carving were, in some sense, monastic (Bailey 1980, 80–3), the restricted distribution of such sculpture in northern England can have little bearing upon what was going on in the secular sphere. As for written references to 'new' churches, the example of Weaverthorpe, Humberside, is instructive. The church of St Andrew contains an inscription which tells that *Herebertus Wintonie hoc monasterium fecit.* Herbert the Chamberlain probably commissioned the church between 1108 and 1121, and the greater part of the present building is considered to be the product of his patronage. As to whether Herbert's church was the first to occupy the site, we have no information, one way or the other.

For comparison, let us now turn to look at Wiltshire, where the tally of village churches

'...seems to have been more or less complete by the middle of the 13th century, for a list of pentecostal obligations paid to the cathedral in 1251 records practically the same number of parish churches in

Table 5.1 Church numbers

Source	Date	England	Wales	England & Wales	Subject
Census	1801			11,379	Parish churches
A Direction for the English Traveller (1)	1635	8,861	873	9,734	Parishes
Valor Ecclesiasticus (2)	1534			8,838	Benefices
Taxatio Nicholai (3)	1291			8,085 457	Parishes Parochial chapels
Domesday Book (4)	1086	*c.* 2,700			Churches Chapels Priests interpreted as representing churches

(1) Not consulted directly; cited by Dr J. H. Harvey in his edition of *William Worcestre Itineraries* 1969, p. 63, note 1.

(2) This figure was kindly supplied by Mrs Dorothy Owen.

(3) The extraction of accurate figures from the *Taxatio* would be an arduous task. On this occasion I have had to rely upon the results which have been published by others. Unfortunately, they do not agree. According to Moorman, J. R. H. 1945: *Church Life in England in the Thirteenth Century*, 4–5, the range is from 12,280, which does not seem reasonable, to 8,085 plus 457 chapelries, which does.

(4) The figure given is based upon a general count which was made in 1980 for *The Church in British Archaeology* 1983. Council for British Archaeology Research Report 47, Table VII. Since undertaking this work, which was based partly upon an examination of editions of the text and partly upon figures derived from secondary sources, it has become clear that the original results are in need of revision. This has not yet been completed, but it seems unlikely that any change will disturb the general conclusions that are offered here.

the county as that given in the *Valor* [270] nearly 300 years later. Domesday Book told a very different story. It recorded only about 30 churches in Wiltshire, but it was only concerned to enumerate those with glebe charged with geld. By supplementing Domesday Book with other scraps of evidence, mainly from early charters and from architectural remains, it is possible to make a list of about 80 places with a church existing within 50 years of the Norman Conquest. Even if this total is reckoned as a considerable underestimate of the churches actually there at the time, it still looks as though the main work of organizing the parish system in the county was done by the men of the 12th century' (Templeman 1956, 3).

The contribution of Domesday will be considered in due course, but before proceeding further it is worth pausing to ask whether the origins of an ecclesiastical parish are necessarily, or even normally, equatable with the origins of its church building. The question may seem to be pedantic, but just as the first written reference to a village is still occasionally accepted as an indication of the date of the settlement, so the earliest mention of a church is sometimes equated with the appearance of its parish, and *vice versa*. That this need not be so is illustrated not only by such a case as that of Allerton Mauleverer, North Yorkshire, where the promotion of a chapel to full parish status is recorded in a chapter of 1109 x 14 (Farrer 1914, 729), but also by

archaeology, which can testify that even apparently insignificant churches, like Raunds, Northamptonshire, and Burnham, Humberside, were already in existence by the middle of the tenth century (Boddington and Cadman 1981; Coppack 1978). Churches and churchyards were quite often chosen as hiding places for coins and valuables. Deposits were made throughout the Middle Ages, as for example at Wedmore, Somerset (*c.* 1050), Crosthwaite, Cumbria (twelfth century), Hickleton, South Yorkshire (*c.* 1230), and St George's, Stamford, Lincolnshire (*c.* 1465). The list of places which have produced caches that are earlier than the eleventh century included some important churches, like Bath, Somerset, St John's, Chester, and Hexham, Northumberland. However, there is a larger catalogue to be compiled of otherwise seemingly unexceptional village churchyards which have yielded hoards, such as Satley, County Durham (*c.* AD 871–5), Dunsforth, North Yorkshire (*c.* AD 875), Goldsborough, North Yorkshire (AD 925–30), Hundon, Suffolk (*c.* AD 953), and Kintbury, Berkshire (*c.* AD 957–60). Doubtless there were occasions when a deposit was made before the site was designated for ecclesiastical use, or at a spot sufficiently close to a church for it to have been taken within the bounds following an expansion of the churchyard. The group of ninth-century disc brooches from the churchyard at Pentney, Norfolk, may belong to this class of 'absorbed' hoards. Nevertheless, in other instances it is evident that the site was already being used as a graveyard when the material was secreted, or the hoard was deposited with reference to a feature of the churchyard which still survives, such as a boundary. Nor should we forget those village churchyards like Farndon, Nottinghamshire, and Wensley, North Yorkshire, which have produced furnished burials of Scandinavian type. Presumably these funerals of the ninth and tenth centuries took place in graveyards, if not churchyards, which already existed (cf. Wilson 1967; 1976). Around the year 1060 no fewer than 11 East Anglian churches were specified in just one Old English will, including an *elde kirke* at Wreningham, Norfolk, (Whitelock 1930, 86–9). Did all these churches spring up simultaneously, or could it be that the growth of ecclesiastical provision at neighbourhood level was more gradual, and that what has commonly been regarded as an explosion of churchbuilding in the eleventh century was actually the climax of a process that had been begun several centuries earlier? Outside the towns, there must be doubt as to whether written records can enable us to choose between these two possibilites, since whatever the process may have involved, it is not described in any detail until it is virtually over. But archaeology is capable of providing an answer to the question. Meanwhile, it would be unwise to suppose that the founding of local churches and the formalization of the parochial system were movements which invariably went in parallel. In itself this is not a very controversial thing to say, but it does require that the terminologies which we use to discuss the church as a building, and the parish as an institutional concept, should be kept separate, at least until the twelfth century. If Malvolio had taken any interest in these things he might have said that some churches were born parochial, some achieved parochial status, and that others had had the parochial system thrust upon them. Among the latter were some churches which could be very old indeed (Plummer 1896, Bede 5, 4–5).

Having set the scene, let us now turn to see that definite figures are available. Between the reigns of William I and George III there were several occasions when national surveys were made. Details extracted from some of these are presented in the accompanying table. The various totals must be used with care, because they were compiled for different reasons and in accordance with separate sets of criteria. Hence, we are unable to compare like with like. Nonetheless, for the needs of a general discussion the figures are serviceable.

Before we consider the question of how many churches there were, or could have been, in the eleventh century, there is an important point to be derived from an examination of the more secure data that are available later on. The 1801 total of 11,379 is especially instructive because it refers to parish *churches,* and

gives a snapshot of the ecclesiastical pattern as it existed on the eve of the nineteenth-century expansion. The totals in *Valor* and the seventeenth-century *Direction* involved benefices and parishes, respectively, and so must be regarded as understating the numbers of effectively parochial buildings which then existed. Numerically, the omissions become particularly significant in areas of northern England such as Cheshire, Cumbria, and the Pennine portion of Yorkshire, where parishes tended to be large and few, and chapelries many. A large part of the difference between the figures of *Valor* and 1801 (2,541) can be explained as the result of the upgrading to parish status of chapels-of-ease which had been excluded from previous surveys. In his study of the architecture of Stuart and Georgian churches, Marcus Whiffen observed: 'Very few new parishes were formed during the period... The machinery for the formation of a new parish was complicated and cumbersome, involving as it did (at least until the Church Building Act of 1818) a special Act of Parliament. And so the vast majority of Stuart and Georgian churches... either are the outcome of the rebuilding of earlier fabrics or came into existence as proprietary chapels or chapels of ease ' (1948, 4).

From all this we may guess at the presence of between 9,000 and 11,000 parish churches and parochial chapels in the sixteenth century. The Taxation of Pope Nicholas IV (1291) indicates that the great majority of these churches were already in existence before the end of the thirteenth century. The Taxation, like *Valor*, excluded many parochial chapels, and the churches in some areas, such as Merionethshire, were overlooked almost entirely. Between the dates of the Taxation and *Valor*, therefore, the line of our graph must be very close to the horizontal. Entirely new churches, like those of St Mary and St Cuthbert built at Barton, North Yorkshire, in the 1450s, were rare. In the period 1300–1600 there is more evidence in written records for the abandonment of village churches than there is for fresh creations, although there are special classes of settlement, such as new towns and some types of chapelry, which reverse this trend. This broad picture of early, sometimes excessive provision, followed by stability or contraction is clearly visible in the older towns, a few of which had amassed totals of such size before the end of the twelfth century that deletions, rather than additions, were to be the order of the day thereafter.

When were all these churches built? Our next checkpoint is Domesday Book, which either records or indicates the presence of about 2,700 churches. By comparison with the later figures this total is very low; however, when the circumstances in which the survey was carried out are taken into account, the figure begins to look astonishingly high. In the first place, virtually all of Wales and considerable portions of England were

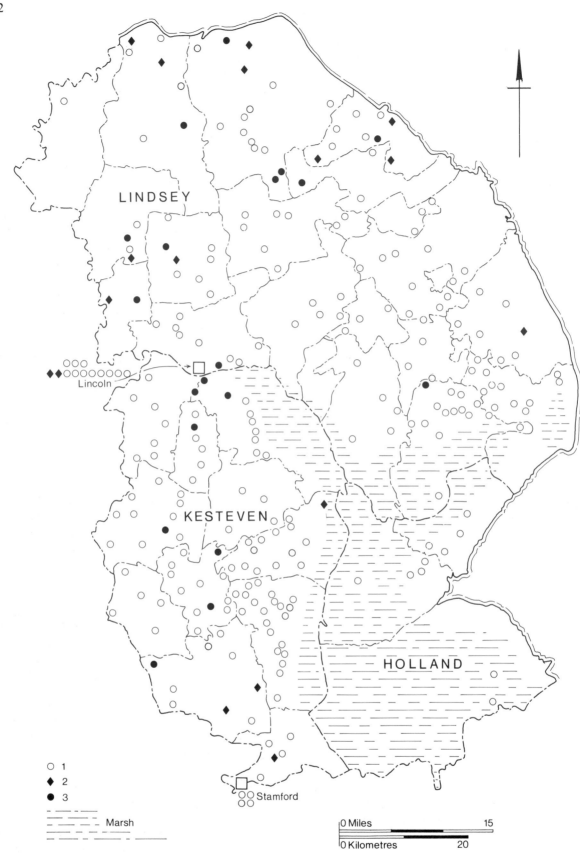

Fig. 5.3

Lincolnshire: map depicting churches (1) mentioned in Domesday Book; (2) claimed as pre-Conquest in part or whole by Taylor (1978), or on other archaeological grounds; (3) mentioned in Domesday Book and claimed as Anglo-Saxon on architectural and/or archaeological grounds. About half of the churches that are mapped as containing pre-Conquest fabric or providing evidence for an existence before 1100 do not appear in Domesday Book. The lesser boundaries are those of wapentakes. (Source for boundaries: Foster and Longley 1924)

excluded. Secondly, the compilers were not concerned with the enumeration of churches or the systematic listing of places. The aims of the project were set forth at the time in the Anglo-Saxon Chronicle. King William

'... sent his men all over England to ascertain how many hundreds of hides of land there were in each shire, and how much land and live-stock the king himself owned in the country, and what annual dues were lawfully his from each shire. He also had it recorded how much land his archbishops had, and his diocesan bishops, his abbots and his earls... and how much each man who was a landholder here in England had in land or live-stock, and how much money it was worth' (*ASC (E) s.a.* 1085, trans. Garmonsway 1955, 216).

The Conqueror wanted an economic profile of his new kingdom; his officials were interested mainly in places through which payments of rent and tax were made (Sawyer 1976, 2). As an illustration of how this could affect our conception of the priority of churches in an area, let us return to the contrast noted by Page between the 'older settled districts' in the south of Sussex, and the forest edge settlements, which he regarded as recent, where 'manorial churches only are to be found'. According to arguments which have been advanced by Sawyer and developed on several occasions (e.g. 1976, 3–4; 1978, 136–8), the Weald was not uncolonized forest at this time, 'and the explanation for this group of Sussex estates is simply that they had been detached from their parent estates, and therefore needed separate treatment. The reason they had not been assessed for taxation was not that they were recent clearings but that they had formerly been treated as parts of larger estates' (1976, 4). An important aspect of Sawyer's discussion about the character of settlement in the Weald is that it is based upon the position in Kent, 'where some eleventh-century lists of places with churches reveal the existence of no fewer than 400 eleventh-century churches, 159 of them in places that are not even mentioned in Domesday Book' (1978, 136, see too Fig. 5.3).

Thirdly, the survey was undertaken by several groups of compilers, and their interpretations of the articles of inquiry differed from circuit to circuit. The variations stand out clearly in a tabulation of ecclesiastical data. Thus, in the county of Huntingdon over 50 churches are mentioned, whereas the totals in the neighbouring counties of Cambridge and Bedford scarcely reach double figures when they are added together. Suffolk may be the most instructive county, for it was here and probably here alone that a complete count was attempted. By my reckoning Domesday Book for Suffolk mentions at least 416 churches. Nearly all of them stood in the countryside.

The interest of the Suffolk figure lies not so much in its immensity as in the opportunity it provides for a comparison with the grand total of churches which existed in that county in the later Middle Ages. It has been said that this total was not less than 558. If this is true, it follows that about 75 per cent of the medieval churches in Suffolk were present by 1086 (Scarfe 1972, 139).

If this degree of establishment were to be applied uniformly across the country we should be thinking of a figure in the region of 5,850 churches before the end of the eleventh century. Despite the crudity of this calculation, it gives a figure that may be no wild exaggeration. It accords, for example, with the extent of twelfth-century architecture that has been noted in northern England. More importantly, it is based upon proportions of eventual totals in different counties, not upon a direct extrapolation from the absolute total that Suffolk provides. Hence, it is a figure with some claim to economic realism, and one which automatically adjusts itself at least to later regional differences in the density of ecclesiastical provision.

When all is said and done, a late eleventh-century total for England between 4,500 and 5,000 would not seem to be too high, and could be too low. This estimate can be refined and checked. In many counties there are areas which contain blocks of parishes wherein archaeological, onomastic, literary and sculptural evidence all combine to testify to the presence of pre-Conquest churches. There is one such area in Ryedale, North Yorkshire (Fig. 5.4), and Dr. Rodwell has drawn attention to another, in Essex (1977, 92–3). These blocks are unlikely to be exceptional, other than in the fortuitous survivals of evidence that they contain. There is ample scope here for local endeavour by part-time archaeologists, amateur historians, and schools.

If the foregoing figures can be agreed upon as provisional working totals, it becomes necessary to reflect upon their implications. It is a paradox that the higher the total we have *c.* 1100, the less likely it is that there was a sudden escalation of church founding. Five—or four, or even three—thousand churches can hardly have been begun within the space of a few decades. If we are to believe in the detonation of a big bang around 1000, then we must also believe in the existence of a craft organization which could provide sufficient manpower to erect, say, 200 churches in a decade. In proposing this figure allowance has been made for the pre-existence of ministers, and for the likelihood that an appreciable number of the new foundations began as wooden buildings which might be constructable without calling upon more than local resources. It may well be that the appearance of the local stone church as an architectural type owes as much, if not more, to the emergence of a class of skilled technician and a quarry industry, as to the downward diffusion of church-building habits from kings and aristocrats to local lords. The technical capability to

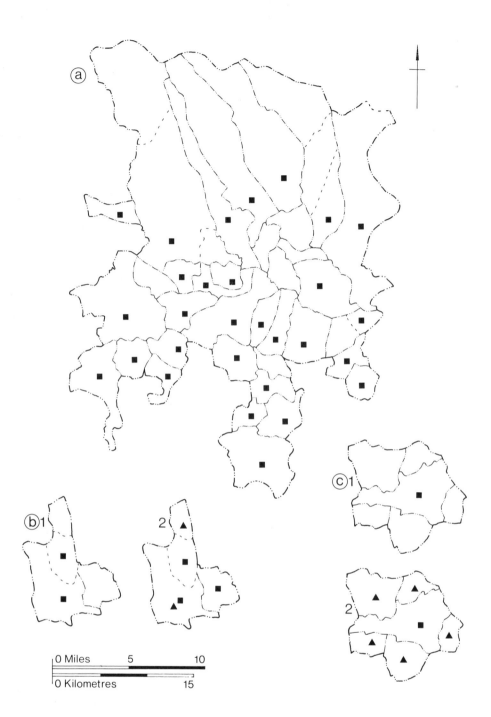

Fig. 5.4

A: Ryedale, North Yorkshire. A block of 35 parishes wherein no fewer than 29 churches can be claimed to have been in existence before the end of the eleventh century (evidence: architecture, sculpture, Domesday Book). B: Allertonshire, North Yorkshire. No churches are mentioned here in Domesday Book. However, (1) the presence of at least two churches well before this time is indicated by pre-Conquest sculpture at Brompton and Northallerton, and (2) a more elaborate pattern is revealed in a document purporting to date from 1091–92 which granted the churches of Brompton, Northallerton and Kirby Sigston *cum omnibus capellis* to the prior and monks of St Cuthbert at Durham. The grant is judged to be a fabrication of the later twelfth century, but it may be considered in conjunction with a series of confirmations of the Allertonshire churches to Durham from the 1140s onward. For discussion of the charter consult Offler, H. S. 1968: *Durham Episcopal Charters 1071–1152*. Surtees Society 179, 48–53. C: Hunmanby, Humberside. Ecclesiastical pattern as revealed by (1) Domesday Book (church at Hunmanby), and (2) a document of 1125 recording the gift by William de Gant of the mother church of Hunmanby with its chapels to Bardney, the greater parish at that time including (from north, clockwise): Muston, Reighton, Burton Fleming, Wold Newton and Folkton. (Sources for B and C: Farrer, W. (editor) 1915: *Early Yorkshire Charters II*, 266, 428.)

erect large numbers of stone churches did not exist in England during the seventh and eighth centuries. Royalty, bishops, and the wealthier religious communities would have had the first call upon the few craftsmen who were available. The distribution of pre-Danish sculpture in northern England could be held to tell the same tale. But this is not to say that local, secular churches did not exist in the eighth and ninth centuries. It is clear from statements in the writings of Bede, episcopal correspondence, and certain official documents that some of them did. Rather, we should at least entertain the possibility that there may have been different sorts of church building: almost exclusively of wood, perhaps 'secular' in aspect (cf. Yeavering, Northumberland: Hope-Taylor 1977), potentially ephemeral, and occupying sites which may not always have coincided with those of their more durable and conspicuous stone-built successors.

(ii) The doctrine of stability

Here are some quotations culled from several recent, and wholly imaginary, books on landscape archaeology:

(a) 'The church is in the middle of the village, and represents the nucleus around which the settlement grew.'

(b) 'The church is on the edge of the village, and it is likely that the settlement has migrated some distance from its original centre beside the church.'

(c) 'An isolated church is all that now survives of the deserted medieval village of...'

(d) 'The church stands by itself, but despite intensive fieldwork in its vicinity, no sign of any former settlement has yet been recognized.'

An idea, or, rather, an unspoken assumption that underlies all these sayings is that while we may allow settlement to be dynamic, mobile, or mutable, we expect the church to be stable. A second assumption is that, for any given village, the site of the church is likely to be unique. When we speak of Wharram Percy we say 'the church', rather than 'a church'.

It is worth recalling that since the fourteenth century, at least, many hundreds of village churches have been abandoned, their functions united with others, or have been transferred to new sites (Fig. 5.5). Such changes have occurred for a variety of reasons. In our own time it is the imbalance between the distribution of the population and the distribution of the Church's resources—chiefly, buildings and manpower—that has brought about an upheaval which in 13 years has seen the closure of about 1,000 churches.

It is less easy to give quantitative dimensions to losses sustained in earlier centuries. There is no reliable national figure even for those churches which stand in ruins today. Forster's handlist of English church dedications, published in 1899, mentions over 280 rural

parish churches and parochial chapels which were then either in ruins or had disappeared within recent memory. This total is likely to be far below the actual figure. Forster indentified about 74 ruined or vanished churches in Norfolk, for example, whereas a recent detailed survey made under the auspices of the Norfolk Achaeological Unit disclosed 197 known abandonments before 1900. The ecclesiastical fatality rate in Norfolk is of course exceptional. However, while it is true that no other English county has seen anything like the number of losses that have occurred in Norfolk, there are particular areas where losses have been high. About nine per cent of the eventual medieval total of churches in Suffolk are gone (Scarfe 1972, 139). In Kent, some 13 per cent of the churches and chapels mentioned in the *Textus Roffensis* (before 1115) had gone before the present century. Appreciable numbers of churches have disappeared from the marshland areas of Thanet and Romney, Kent. The parish of Hartland, Devon, contained ten medieval churches, but only one survives (Swanton 1980, 86). Modern redundancies and former chapels aside, there are at least 18 ruined parish churches in Herefordshire, and more than 16 in the old North Riding of Yorkshire.

Although it is difficult to arrive at a national total for all these disappearances, the minimum figure is evidently well in excess of 400: the equivalent of all the churches in a fair-sized diocese. A total twice as large could emerge from a national survey. This means that, down to 1900, between six and ten per cent of medieval parish churches can be regarded as casualties. Inevitably, this assessment will usually exclude churches that fell redundant before the era of continuous written records, although there are exceptions, as in the instance of the 'old church' mentioned in the bounds of a grant of land at Ducklington, Oxfordshire, in AD 958 (Sawyer 1968, no. 678; Gelling 1979, 132), or the shadowy *cadan mynster* to which reference was made in several West Midland charters (Sawyer 1968, nos. 80, 786, 1599; cf. Hooke 1981, 298). By *c.* AD 730 the stone church of 'wonderful workmanship' which Bede thought had been built in Lincoln a century previously was derelict (Plummer 1896, Bede, 2, 16). A ruinous church was recorded at Netheravon, Wiltshire, in 1086. The rededicatory inscription at Kirkdale, North Yorkshire, dating to 1055 x 1065, states that the church was bought as a ruin and rebuilt (Fig. 5.6). It is reasonable to inquire if there were other cases in which the church was not rehabilitated, fell down and passed out of memory. Archaeology suggests that there were. The case of Raunds, Northamptonshire, has already been mentioned. Excavations at Barrow, Humberside, disclosed the remains of a church which was probably out of use before the thirteenth century (Whitwell and Boden 1979). Traces of two middle Saxon timber churches

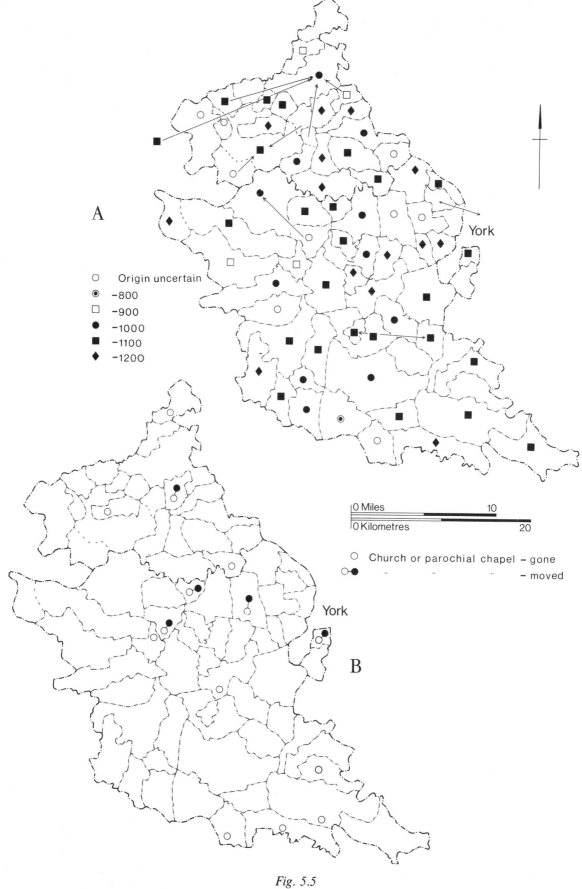

A

○ Origin uncertain
⊙ −800
□ −900
● −1000
■ −1100
◆ −1200

York

0 Miles   10
0 Kilometres   20

○ Church or parochial chapel – gone
○─● ˮ ˮ ˮ – moved

York

B

Fig. 5.5

Deaneries of New Ainsty and Boroughbridge, medieval Diocese of York (now Ripon). A: conventions signify dates by which churches can reasonably be suggested to have been in existence (evidence: architecture, sculpture, Domesday Book, charters), *not* supposed periods of origin. The majority of churches appear to have been in existence before 1100. B: the same deaneries after the Reformation, showing main losses, late- and post-medieval movements. (Source for boundaries: Harvey, J. H. and Payne, D. 1973: *Yorkshire: Ancient Parishes and Chapelries* (map published by Yorkshire Archaeological Society).)

Fig. 5.6

St Gregory, Kirkdale, North Yorkshire. Inscription above south door of nave: 'Orm, son of Gamal, bought St Gregory's minster when it was all broken and fallen, and he enabled it to be made anew from the ground, to Christ and St Gregory, in the days of Edward the king, and the days of Tosti the earl'. Central panel: 'This is the day's sunmarker at every tide'. 'Haward wrought me, and Brand, priest(s)'.

have been found at Nazeingbury, Essex (Huggins 1978), and a previously unsuspected church has been found at Winwick, Cheshire. At Cowage Farm, near Malmesbury, Wiltshire, the outline of a rectangular church-like building with an eastern apse has been identified from the air (Hampton 1981).

Definite reasons for the loss or dormancy of a church before 1200 are seldom forthcoming, but in later centuries there are three main groups of factors which can be identified. These may be summarized as natural processes, depopulation, and shifts of population. Let us now look at these in turn.

(i) Natural processes

Medieval builders generally took care to locate their churches out of reach of flood and tide. Problems did arise occasionally, however, and over the years there were quite numerous losses of churches which can be attributed to the movement of sand dunes, river and coastal erosion. At St Piran, Cornwall, Penmaen, Pennard and Rhossili, Glamorgan, for example, churches were engulfed by wind-blown sand. In 1703 the church of St Kentigern, Grinsdale, Cumbria, was in

ruins and falling into the River Eden. The parishioners were obliged to revet the churchyard in order to prevent the remains of their ancestors from being washed away. At Alnmouth, Northumberland, the church of St Waleric was cut off from the settlement by a change in the course of the river. A new church was built and the site of the old one lies amid sand dunes. Coastal erosion has claimed a large number of villages and several towns on the eastern littoral, such as Dunwich, Suffolk, and its nine churches, and Eccles, Norfolk. About 30 settlements have been washed away all along the coast of the old East Riding of Yorkshire since the fourteenth century. The church at Withernsea was rebuilt on a new site in 1445, and other churches were erected away from their doomed predecessors at Skeffling (1469) and Hollym (1488). At Little Colden the chapel of St John the Evangelist was drowned *c.* 1690. In 1335 human remains were being washed out of the cemetery at Ravenser. The church at Kilnsea was in ruins and on the verge of destruction by the sea in the 1820s; in 1899 a party of antiquaries inspected the remains at low tide. If given in full, this melancholy roll call would be quite long (Sheppard 1912).

(ii) Failed settlements

This is not a category that requires much discussion, since the fact that the disappearance of a hamlet or village has often led to the loss of its church is well known. Examples are legion. They include relatively early failures, such as Argam, Humberside, where the site of a twelfth-century parochial chapel which was demolished before 1632 awaits identification within the earthworks of the deserted village, as well as the more familiar cases like Goltho, Lincolnshire, and Wharram Percy, North Yorkshire, where the churches managed to outlive the demise of their settlements by several centuries and are only now redundant. Wharram Percy reminds us that between the extremes of complete disappearance and full survival there are numerous churches which still commemorate deserted settlements but stand in ruins. Examples, taken at random, include Aldeby and Knaptoft, Leicestershire, Pudding Norton, Norfolk, Sockburn, County Durham, and Whorlton, North Yorkshire. A systematic count is needed.

(iii) Shifts of population

Many churches have been moved in order to adjust to changes in the pattern of settlement. In circumstances of this sort the old church may not count as a loss in the tally of disappearances, but there will be a ruin, or a flat site, in some cases forgotten, which lies apart from the present building.

Transfers were often made in the nineteenth century, sometimes over short distances, as at Yazor, Herefordshire, or Marton, North Yorkshire, but on other occasions to a different part of the parish, as at Baddesley Ensor, Warwickshire, Lower Sapey, Worcestershire, Merston, Kent, or Treyford, Sussex. Comparable processes may be noted in the seventeenth and especially the eighteenth centuries, when sometimes for aesthetic or social reasons it was not unknown for entire villages to be moved from one place to another if they interfered with the sight-lines or privacy of newly-created parks. On such occasions the church might be retained as a prominent feature in the grounds of the hall, as at Harewood, West Yorkshire, or Fawsley, and Holdenby, Northamptonshire, where the churches mark the sites of former villages. Parkland churches could be rebuilt in keeping with changing tastes, as at Stapleford, Leicestershire, reconstructed in 1783, or Shobden, Herefordshire, where bits of the old church were re-erected north of the house as an eye-catcher at the time of the rebuilding of 1752–56. Alternatively, there could be a change of site, as at Croome D'Abitot, Worcestershire, where the church was repositioned in 1763. In other cases the removal of a settlement from the immediate environment of the hall eventually led to the decay of the church. This happened at Annesley, Colston Bassett and Colwick, Nottinghamshire, where ruined churches stand next to halls and the relocated villages were provided with new churches in the nineteenth century. Similar sequences are observable elsewhere, as at Madresfield, Worcestershire, where the old church stood close to the hall and a new church was erected in 1866. Birdsall, North Yorkshire, provides another example, and there are many more to be collected.

With the foregoing cases in mind, it is interesting to ponder the possibility that some of the 'Newchurch' place-names which occur in the eleventh and twelfth centuries could have arisen as the result of comparable processes towards the end of the Old English period. Certainly, there is a good number of adjustments to be found before the Reformation. In 1455 the church of St Michael, Cowthorpe, North Yorkshire, was transplanted from its pre-Conquest site to a new position half a mile away, for the convenience of the villagers and the patron. Earlier still there are such examples as Lamplugh, Cumbria, were a transfer seems to have occurred in the twelfth century, and the well-documented case of Sutton-in-Holland, Lincolnshire, where before 1180 an earlier wooden church was replaced by a new building on a different site. On this occasion the process of change extended even to the translation of the burials which had been inside the old church (Owen 1971, 5).

For reasons given above, transfers which took place before 1200 will seldom feature in written records, although Domesday provides an interesting quota of churches which cannot now be placed. However, there may be clues. There are a number of anomalous cemeteries comprised of findless, oriented graves which could be reconsidered from this point of view. Local traditions and folk-tales, if used with discrimination, may also be able to assist. There is for example a widespread class of legend which relates how a particular church was moved from one place to another, usually by a supernatural agency. Many of these stories concern churches which occupy odd sites, such as the tops of steep hills, but there are quite a number of tales which specify churches where no topographical peculiarities are involved. Each of these must be judged individually, but in a proportion of cases it could be that the story originated with the closure of one church and the construction of a successor on a different site.

Discussion

The parochial system abhors a vacuum, and where shrinkage of settlement took place leading to the closure of a church it was inevitable that the territory of the abandoned church should be united with that of a neighbouring parish. Thus the depopulation of the village of Hutton Wandesley, North Yorkshire, in the fourteenth century led to the closure of its church *c.* 1400 and the concentration of remaining resources in the church of the adjacent village of Long Marston.

Naturally enough, these amalgamations were particularly common in areas which had previously been provided with many churches in close proximity. This led to a thin share of tithes and bequests: limitations which were bearable in times of growth, but could prove fatal if economic conditions deteriorated and the population fell. The problem could affect an agriculturally wealthy county, like Norfolk, were there were dense concentrations of churches by 1086, as well as less profitable areas into which there had been expansions of settlement that proved to be abortive. Many cases in the latter category turn out upon inspection to concern extinct chapelries, but the casualty list also includes some parish churches, such as West Wykeham, Lincolnshire, where the parish of St Lawrence was absorbed by Ludford Magna in 1396. In 1437 the rector and patrons of the church of Hameringham and the patron of the church at Dunsthorpe presented a lugubrious petition to the Bishop of Lincoln, claiming that:

'...the church of Dunsthorpe, which was wont to be ruled by a secular rector, is so decreased on account of the lack of parishioners, the fewness of peasants, their low wages, the bareness of lands, the lack of cultivation, pestilences, and epidemics with which the Lord afflicts his people for their sins, that it is hardly sufficient for the eighth part of the salary of a stipendiary chaplain, much less of a rector who has to bear necessary charges; and that there is no likelihood of its sufficing in the future since the world is going from bad to worse, and that the church of Dunsthorpe has no parishioners; and praying that the two churches may be united.' (Forster and Longley 1924, liv–lv)

Where two churches were united it was sometimes the custom to add the dedication of the redundant church to that of the survivor, as in the case of St Peter, Stainton by Wadingham, Lincolnshire, which was pulled down sometime after 1602 and united with St Mary, Wadingham, the surviving church thereafter being known by the double dedication of St Mary and St Peter (1924, lxvi). Parishes containing churches bearing double dedications in 'high risk' areas would be worth careful scrutiny with the possibility of a lost church in mind.

To conclude, it is useful to recall the tentative suggestion which was made at the end of the first portion of this essay: '...we should at least entertain the possibility that there may have been different sorts of church building: almost exclusively of wood, perhaps 'secular' in aspect... potentially ephemeral, and occupying sites which may not always have coincided with those of their more durable and conspicuous stone-built successors.'

If the settlement pattern really is, in general, 'much older than most scholars have been prepared to recognize', and if, in general, the Anglo-Saxon period 'was a time of shifting but not expanding settlement', then many of the processes which have just been discussed, mainly on the basis of later medieval and post-Reformation evidence, may hold lessons which could affect our conceptions of what was happening to ecclesiastical geography before the Conquest as well.

It is fair to ask if the primitive one- and two-cell church must always represent the first stage in local provision. We are accustomed to these structures because where excavations have taken place they have often been identified as the ancestors of later medieval parish churches. In a sense, however, this feeds on itself, because the sites were selected for excavation in the first place precisely because they *were* those of later medieval churches. This has reinforced the conviction that the underlying simple buildings, which in general seem to date from the tenth and eleventh centuries, are to be regarded as the first village churches, and hence as occupying the first village church sites. This belief, in its turn, has exerted quite considerable influence upon thinking about the origins and development of the medieval village.

A different view would accommodate the possibility that some of these tenth- and eleventh-century churches represent the *second* stage in the emergence of local ecclesiastical provision. The first stage, alongside the minsters at royal *tūn*-centres, might involve growing numbers of vernacular *ecclesiae propriae*, perhaps affiliated with the residences of local lords, of the sort which have been postulated above. This idea is not new (cf. Godfrey 1974), although some of the arguments which have been presented in its favour may be additional to those which have been heard before. An important feature of the hypothesis is that it envisages no significant break between the local settlement patterns or building traditions of 'pagan' and 'early Christian' England. Indeed, with Yeavering in mind as an exemplar, the model would permit a closer relationship between heathen cult sites, meeting-places, and early churches than has normally seemed to be admissible. Change, where there was change, comes rather within the Christian period, and the time it could take to occur becomes progressively longer the lower down the social scale we go.

Sources and Acknowledgements

The examples from hoards in churches and church-yards were taken fom *Coin Hoards* (Royal Numismatic Society) 4 (1978), 343, 347, 349; 5 (1979), 274; Thompson, J. D. A. 1956: *Inventory of British Coin Hoards AD 600–1500 and Metcalf, D. M. 1960–1: Some finds of medieval coins from Scotland and the north of England, British Numismatic Journal* 30, 88–123. Several colleagues have kindly supplied information. The statement about the context of the Pentney brooches is based upon a note written by A. Rogerson and S. Ashley, provided by the Norfolk Archaeological Unit. The figure for abandoned churches in Norfolk is derived from an interim note on the survey of ruined churches in that county which has been undertaken by N. Batcock under the auspices of the Norfolk Archaeological Unit. The case of Winwick is included on the basis of information given by D. J. Freke about

excavations by the Liverpool University Rescue Archaeology Unit in 1980. I owe special debts of gratitude to Professor P. H. Sawyer, who not only delivered the original paper on my behalf but also suggested ways in which it could be improved; to Dr L. A. S. Butler, who gave much help and encouragement while the paper was being rewritten; and to Dick Raines, who produced the drawings.

References

Addleshaw, G. W. O. 1970: *The Development of the Parochial System from Charlemagne (768–814) to Urban II (1088–1099)* 2nd edition (St. Anthony's Hall Publications No. 6).

Addyman, P. V. and Morris, R. (editors) 1976: *The Archaeological Study of Churches* (London, Council for British Archaeology Research Report 13) 21–7.

Bailey, R. N. 1980: *Viking Age Sculpture in Northern England* (London, Collins).

Bede: *Historia Ecclesiastica Gentis Anglorum.* In Plummer, C. (editor) 1896.

Boddington, A. and Cadman, G. 1981: Raunds: an interim report on excavations 1977–1980. In Brown, D., Campbell, J. and Hawkes, S. C. (editors) 1981, 103–22.

Brown, D., Campbell, J. and Hawkes, S. C. (editors) 1981: *Anglo-Saxon Studies in Archaeology and History* (Oxford, British Archaeological Reports 92).

Colgrave, B. and Mynors, R. A. B. (editors) 1970: *Bede's Ecclesiastical History of the English People.* (Oxford, Oxford Medieval Texts).

Coppack, G. 1978: St Lawrence, Burnham, South Humberside. *Bulletin of the Council for British Archaeology Churches Committee* (London) 8, 5–6.

Farrer, W. (editor) 1914: *Early Yorkshire Charters* Vol. 1 (Edinburgh).

Foard, G. 1978: Systematic fieldwalking and the investigation of Saxon settlement in Northamptonshire. *World Archaeology* 9, 357–74.

Foster, C. W. and Longley, T. (editors) 1924: *The Lincolnshire Domesday Book and the Lindsey Survey* (The Lincoln Record Society 19).

Garmonsway, G. N. (translator) 1954: *The Anglo-Saxon Chronicle* 2nd edition (London, J. M. Dent).

Gelling, M. (editor) 1979: *The Early Charters of the Thames Valley* (Leicester, Leicester University Press).

Godfrey, J. 1974: The emergence of the village church in Anglo-Saxon England. In Rowley, T. (editor) 1974, 131–8.

Hampton, J. 1981: The evidence of air photography: elementary comparative studies applied to sites at Mount Down, Hampshire, and near Malmesbury, Wiltshire. *Antiquaries Journal* 61, 316–21.

Hooke, D. 1981: *Anglo-Saxon Landscapes of the West Midlands: the Charter evidence* (Oxford, British Archaeological Reports 95).

Hope-Taylor, B. 1977: *Yeavering: an Anglo-British Centre of Early Northumbria* (London, Her Majesty's Stationery Office).

Huggins, P. J. 1978: Excavation of Belgic and Romano-British Farm with Middle Saxon Cemetery and Churches at Nazeingbury, Essex, 1975–76. *Essex Archaeology and History* 10, 29–117.

Limbrey, S. an Evans, J. G. (editors) 1978: *The Effect of Man on the Landscape: the Lowland Zone* (London, Council for British Archaeology Research Report 21).

Owen, D. M. 1971: *Church and Society in Medieval Lincolnshire* (Lincoln, Lincolnshire Local History Society).

Owen, D. M. 1976b: Chapelries and rural settlement: an examination of some of the Kesteven evidence. In Sawyer, P. H. (editor) 1979, 66–71.

Page, W. 1915: Some remarks on the churches of the Domesday Survey. *Archaeologia* 66, 61–102.

Plummer, C. 1896 (editor): *Venerabilis Bedae Opera Historica*, 2 vols. (Oxford).

Pugh, R. B. and Crittal, E. (editors) 1956: *The Victoria History of the Counties of England. A History of the County of Wiltshire*, Vol. 3 (The University of London Institute of Historical Research).

Rodwell, W. J. with Rodwell, K. 1977: *Historic Churches—a Wasting Asset* (London, Council for British Archaeology Research Report 19).

Rowley, T. (editor) 1974: *Anglo-Saxon Settlement and Landscape* (Oxford, British Archaeological Reports 6).

Sawyer, P. H. 1968: *Anglo-Saxon Charters: An Annotated List and Bibliography* (London, Royal Historical Society).

Sawyer, P. H. 1976: Introduction: Early medieval English settlement. In Sawyer, P. H. (editor) 1976, 1–7.

Sawyer, P. H. (editor) 1976: *Medieval Settlement: Continuity and Change* (London, Edward Arnold).

Sawyer, P. H. 1978: *From Roman Britain to Norman England* (London, Methuen).

Scarfe, N. 1972: *The Suffolk Landscape* (London, Hodder and Stoughton).

Sheppard, T. 1912: *The Lost Towns of the Yorkshire Coast* (London, A. Brown and Sons).

Stenton, F. M. 1971: *Anglo-Saxon England* 3rd edition (London, Oxford University Press).

Swanton, M. 1980: Church archaeology in Devon. *Archaeology of the Devon Landscape* (Exeter, Devon County Council) 81–95.

Taylor, C. C. 1974: The Anglo-Saxon countryside. In Rowley, T. (editor) 1974, 5–15.

Taylor, C. C. 1977: Polyfocal settlement and the English village. *Medieval Archaeology* 21, 189–93.

Taylor, C. C. 1978: Aspects of village mobility in medieval and later times. In Limbrey, S. and Evans, J. G. (editors) 1978, 126–34.

Templeman, G. 1956: Ecclesiastical History 1087–1547. In Pugh, R. B. and Crittal, E. (editors) 1956, 1–27.

Wade-Martins, P. 1980: *Village Sites in the Launditch Hundred*. East Anglian Archaeological Report 10.

Whiffen, M 1948: *Stuart and Georgian Churches* (London, Batsford).

Whitelock, D. (editor and translator) 1930: *Anglo-Saxon Wills* (Cambridge, Cambridge University Press).

Wilson, D. M. 1967: The Vikings' relationship with Christianity in northern England. *Journal of the British Archaeological Association* 3rd series, 30, 37–46.

Wilson, D. M. 1976: The Scandinavians in England. In Wilson, D. M. (editor) 1976, 393–403.

Wilson, D. M. (editor) 1976: *The Archaeology of Anglo-Saxon England* (Cambridge, Cambridge University Press).

6. Late Saxon Topography and Early Medieval Estates

D. N. Hall

Fieldwork techniques for the reconstruction of medieval field-system layouts are outlined. The resultant plans are used to plot details of tenurial structure and land use for townships that have pre-enclosure surveys of their open fields. Retrospective analysis reveals much evidence about the late Saxon and early medieval landscape. The following themes are discussed: late Saxon topography, structure and origins of subdivided fields, demesne, tenurial rearrangements, taxation assessments and peasant holdings, and early estates.

Introduction

This paper will discuss the results obtained from studies of field systems rather than villages. The detailed and extensive surveys now being undertaken throw light on the variable nature of village plans, but those results will be discussed on another occasion.

Medieval field systems have received attention from historians since the days of Maitland and Seebohm, the understanding and approaches being subsequently refined and defined (for a convenient recent summary see Dodgshon 1980).

Beresford (1957) and Hoskins (1957) pointed out the importance of evidence surviving on the ground and since 1961 field-system plans in the East Midlands have been reconstructed from the linear earthworks that still survive, even in modern arable fields (Hall 1972, 1982). Various multi-disciplinary approaches were discussed at Oxford in 1978, and surprising results were put forward regarding the probable origins and dating of medieval fields (Rowley 1981). Since then considerable research has taken place, particularly on the field systems of the East Midlands and Yorkshire. Although some of the details have been presented at various international meetings, (Biddick forthcoming; Roberts and Glasscock 1983), it is convenient to review developments here and comment on further supporting evidence.

Techniques

The techniques have been fully discussed by Hall (1982a), and they consist of a combined historical and landscape-archaeological approach. For detailed studies of field systems it is essential to have three types of information; a plan of the open fields, a *field book*, or survey, which describes every parcel of land, and supporting medieval documentation.

Some townships have plans of open fields made during the sixteenth to nineteenth centuries. For those that do not, the field pattern can be reconstructed using archaeological fieldwork survey. The action of the plough transferred soil from each strip to the ends, causing accumulation over the centuries. The edges of furlongs, where there had been a series of turning points, were demarcated by a considerable bank of soil. The effects of modern ploughing rapidly render a field of earthwork ridge and furrow planar, but leave the furlong boundaries as long linear banks which are fairly easy to identify and survey. Examination of every modern field in a parish, and the plotting of the linear banks, allows a reconstruction of the furlong pattern of subdivided fields. Orientations of the strips within the boundaries can usually be observed on the ground or on older aerial photographs.

Many townships have surveys, often called *field books,* town books or terriers. They are descriptions of all the individual strips, and usually group information by field and furlong, and they give the size of the holding, most commonly in an estimated form such as 'one rood' or 'half an acre', or 'one land'. In exceptional cases strip widths, the length, and the area are recorded. Owners and tenants are named, and often the nature of the holding identified, i.e. whether it is glebe, freehold, demesne, former monastic land etc.

Most field books state or imply the cardinal orientations of lands by adding after the furlong names such comments as 'begin west' i.e. implying that the lands run north and south. Abuttals relating a furlong to its neighbours or to topographical features are sometimes given. Such abuttals are also available from charters and terriers etc, all of which should be carefully studied.

For furlong identification the field book is a major source of data. It is necessary to add up the numbers of strips in each furlong and compile a table of names and statistics. The next type of information needed is a compilation, in map form, of all the modern field-names recorded on Tithe maps, estate maps, and sale catalogues. Many of these will be furlong names, which can thus be accurately located on a modern 1:10,000 (or 1:10,560) map.

We are now in a position to attempt to identify furlongs using the three types of data compiled by the

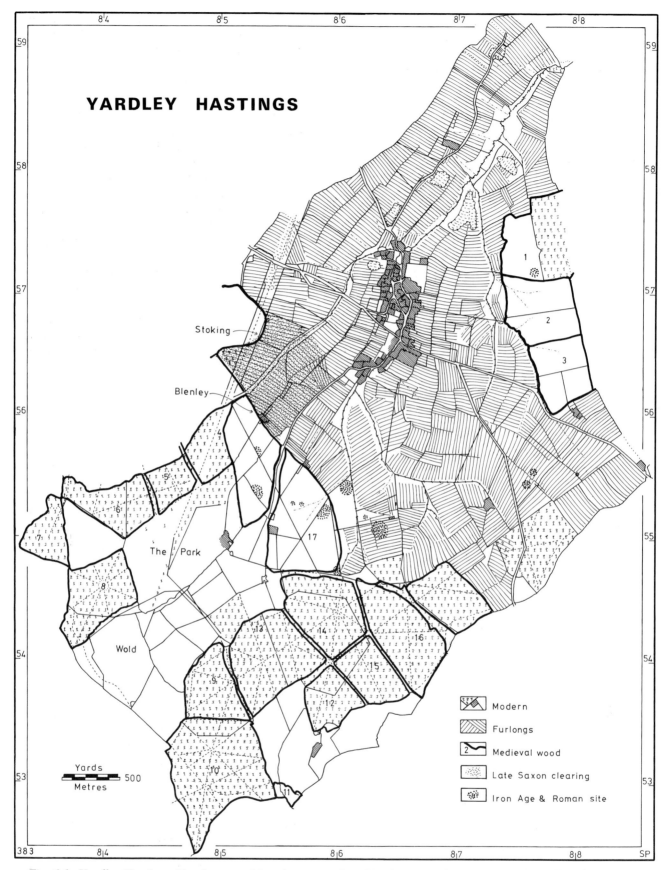

Fig. 6.1 Yardley Hastings, Northamptonshire, showing medieval land use. The furlongs west of the village have names suggesting clearance of woodland.

methods indicated above. The furlong map provides the physical landscape, the collected enclosed field-names give locational data, and the furlong list gives the medieval field-names, their sizes and abuttals. A simultaneous usage of all three should lead to an accurate and precise plotting of furlongs on the reconstructed plan.

In clear-cut cases where there is a field book, a good set of post-enclosure field-names, and plenty of furlong abuttals, it is an easy matter to start from a known point, say on the parish boundary, and plot the furlongs directly on to a 1:10,560 plan. On this scale lands of average 7 m width are 0.7 mm wide, i.e. there are 14 lands to the centimetre.

In an area where the data is not so good, a slightly different procedure has to be adopted. A strip of thin cardboard, no more than 2.5 cm wide, is marked off in 'furlongs' measured to scale. These are then cut up and the name of the furlong written on, with any abuttal information and the land orientation. It is then possible to arrange and rearrange these 'furlongs' on the reconstructed plan until they form a reasonable interpretation of all the evidence.

The sizes (widths) of the furlongs are known by either adding up the stated widths of the lands or by using an appropriate average value. Further details of how to identify furlongs have recently been given (Hall 1982a).

Analysis of results

As a result of a series of detailed case studies of field systems, analysing the topography as well as the tenurial information, the following interrelated major themes have emerged.

i) Late Saxon topography.
ii) Structure and origins of subdivided fields.
iii) Demesne.
iv) Tenurial arrangements.
v) Taxation assessments and peasant holdings.
vi) Early estates: township, field system, and parish.

All the examples discussed are in Northamptonshire unless stated otherwise.

(i) Late Saxon topography

Field books, of whatever date, give an accurate glimpse of the landscape then operating, i.e. how much pasture and meadow there was, how much was enclosed, or left as woodland, etc. By the late thirteenth century very little of Northamptonshire was left as woodland, except for three royal forests (and much open field existed within the official legal area of the woodland). However, the furlong names themselves reflect ancient topography, such as the presence of heaths, moors, or woodland. It can be shown in many cases (see below) that the landscape was already completely opened up to

agriculture by the early twelfth century, or even by the eleventh, in the form that prevailed until enclosure. It is likely therefore that most references to woods and heaths etc. reflect a landscape still extant before that, i.e. in the middle or late Saxon period, when fields were being laid out.

Examples have already been given showing the former existence of woodland at Little Oakley, and in part of the Huxlow Hundred (Hall forthcoming b, Figs. 4 and 5). At Great Addington an attempt has been made to quantify the area of woodland (Hall 1983).

Another similar example is evident at Yardley Hastings. The name itself indicates a settlement in or adjacent to cleared land within or near woodland (*lēah*). The area of open field in the medieval period is shown on Fig. 6.1. To the west, adjacent to surviving medieval woodland, are furlongs bearing the names of *stoking* and *blenley,* which are indicative of land cleared from woodland.[1]

Adjacent to the surviving medieval forest areas clearance was probably later than in the champagne regions and resisted by forest laws. References do occur to newly assarted land, e.g. at Monk's Barn in Paulersbury where 80 acres are described as assart in *c.* 1220 (Elvey 1968, 162–76), and at Weedon Bec where 48 acres were new assart in 1203.[2] Generally such references are to small pieces of assarting, as at a view of Rockingham Forest in 1251, when it was noted that there had been assarts of eight and a half acres at Dene, and seven acres at Liveden.[3]

At Cold Ashby the last piece of intake on the edge of the parish is recorded in *c.* 1230 when the Abbot of Pipewell complained that the lord, Eustace de Watford, had ploughed a furlong next to the road which used to be part of *syfletemore* common pasture.[4]

Thus the documented land clearance, just 'caught' by early monastic records, represents the very end of a process which has a much earlier origin. The early stages have to be studied by an analysis of furlong names, and with more work would allow a fairly precise reconstruction of a county's landscape in the later Saxon period.

(ii) Structure and origins of subdivided fields

Archaeological and physical evidence was put forward in 1978 to show that there had been major changes in the furlong patterns of Midland England, notably that the patchwork of small furlongs with strips about 200 m long had been created by lateral division of furlongs with strips very much longer, up to 1,000 m long (Hall 1981).

The physical evidence may be summarized as follows. Aerial photographs show that some small furlongs have been created by changing parts of the strips of a larger furlong through 90 degrees. In many other cases the strips of one furlong can be seen to go through (under) one or more boundaries of adjacent furlongs (Hall 1982a). Most striking are those cases which show that a massive furlong, forming a reverse-S aratral curve, is divided into several furlongs (e.g. at Raunds where six furlongs are so formed from a single one (Hall 1982a, Fig. 29).

Historical evidence has also been forthcoming showing the subdivision of such large units. At Hardingstone, near Northampton, there were repetitive cycles of tenurial holdings intimately related to the furlong pattern and suggesting an older and simpler arrangement (see below, and Hall 1980). Generally the furlong names themselves point to an earlier larger scale unity in that they frequently occur with adjacent 'upper' and 'lower' elements, often with 'middle' furlongs between them.

Away from the Midland region there are many parishes which had simple 'long land' fields unchanged until enclosure, e.g. in Yorkshire (Harvey 1980, Hall 1978a) and in the Cambridgeshire silt fens (Hall 1981b). Lands of 1,000 m length are very common. This is also the case in much of Germany and Austria (H. J. Nitz 1983 and F. Eigler 1983). It is, after all, the so-called classic English Midlands which are different. The dating of the Midland subdivision is before the twelfth century, according to terrier and charter evidence.

Archaeological fieldwork results show that there was a drastic change of settlement pattern in the middle Saxon period (*c.* AD 650–850). A landscape consisting of numerous small settlements was rearranged to form fewer large villages (the ancestors of the present-day ones). On pottery evidence this process occurred before the middle of the ninth century. The furrows of the open-field strips cut across these Saxon sites and are therefore later. Saxon charters demonstrate that subdivided fields were in existence at least by the tenth century. There were thus two major landscape rearrangements occurring at a similar date: it is likely that the two events happened together, as part of a large-scale replanning of the countryside. An eighth- to ninth-century date is therefore probable for the original field systems.

Such an early date is compatible with the German evidence, where planned villages and long strips can be dated to the period AD 775–850 (Nitz 1983).

Since the above papers were written, evidence continues to accumulate that Midland-type fields were laid out in a planned and simple manner. Countless aerial photographs show blocks of furlongs with lands lying at exactly the same angle.

A most remarkable case of furlong alignment is evident on an open-field map of Wollaston[5] where 14 furlongs have strips in exactly the same orientation, suggesting they originally consisted of one set of strips 12,500 m long (reproduced in Hall 1983, Fig. 1). Two roads, in existence before the fourteenth century, cut across this alignment.

Hardingstone has produced historical evidence that its furlongs were once simpler with long strips, but that later small furlongs were made by lateral division and realignment. It was possible to reconstruct a plan showing the half-way stage between a simple arrangement and the final complex one (Hall 1980).

Current work for the Wharram Project (by D. N. Hall and P. W. Martin) also shows the extreme variety of the physical nature of field systems. The Yorkshire Wolds have simple field structures with long lands frequently running from dale to dale, yet on the Plain of York there are typical 'Midland-type' field systems with a chequerboard pattern of small furlongs. Settrington lies on the edge of the Wolds and the Vale of Pickering. Here the furlong pattern around the village itself is exactly that postulated for Hardingstone in *c.* 1300 (see above), i.e. it represents a half-way stage between an unchanged elemental layout and a complex array of furlongs about 190 m (40 poles) long.

The models discussed above do not, of course, preclude examples of forest villages with field systems built up by assarting. Such processes may have occurred in the examples discussed before there was a large-scale remodelling.

(iii) Demesne estates

This theme has been covered by Hall (1982a and forthcoming). In essence it was shown that there is evidence for an early (*c.* twelfth century) demesne estate lying close to a settlement, followed by its subsequent dispersal fairly uniformly throughout the township field systems. The dispersal is complete by the sixteenth and seventeenth centuries, although even then the demesne is usually distinguished by being in small groups of two to six lands rather than individual ones.

Rushden has proved to be another extremely interesting case study of demesne estates. At the time of the Domesday survey the main manor belonged to William Peverel, and subsequently descended to the Duchy of Lancaster (Kerr 1925, chapters 1–5). Domesday Book also states that in the Higham Ferrars Hundred (of which Rushden forms a part) there were ten and a half hides belonging to the Soke of Thingdon (Finedon, adjacent) which formed part of the ancient demesne of the crown. An enquiry of 1318 specifies that these lands in Rushden consisted of ten and a half virgates, each consisting of 40 acres which amount to five and a quarter hides of land (Kerr 1925, 7–8). The total acreage is therefore 420.

It so happens that this estate can be identified. The tithes of the Peverel estate were given with one virgate of land to Lenton Priory in Nottinghamshire in the twelfth century (Bridges 1791 2, 192), but the ancient demesne of the crown was not, and so the vicar of Rushden retained the tithes. The ancient demesne was later called boonhold (bondhold) land, and a glebe terrier of 1749 states that it consisted of 144 acres in

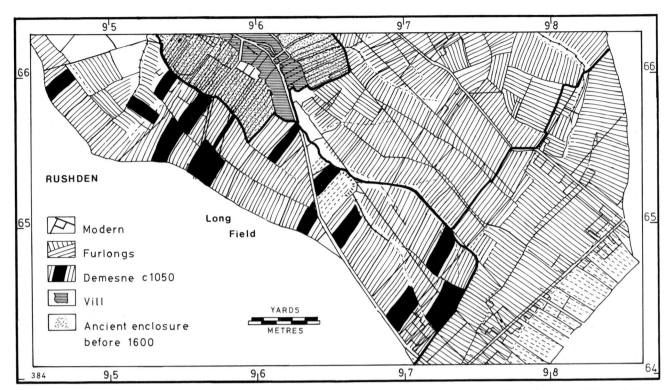

RUSHDEN

Long
Field

◻ Modern

▨ Furlongs

◼ Demesne c1050

▤ Vill

▨ Ancient enclosure
before 1600

YARDS
METRES

Fig. 6.2   Rushden, Northamptonshire, showing the location of an 11th-century estate. The precise position of the parcels in each furlong is not known, but the evidence is clear that most furlongs contained a parcel.

each of the three fields (i.e. a total of 432 acres, close to the estimate of 1318). A glebe terrier of 1755 described all the lands in each furlong,[6] and part of this is plotted on Fig. 6.2. So far it has only been possible to work out the whereabouts of Rushden furlongs in one of the three great fields. It is remarkable that an estate of the early eleventh century can be plotted in such detail. The demesne is dispersed, but lies in parcels of seven to twenty-one lands. Such a dispersion does not disagree with the suggestion above that early demesne estates lie near the settlement, because this 'demesne of the crown' is merely an ancient estate and not demesne in the sense of the lord of the manor's personal holding.

(iv) Tenurial arrangements

Individual peasant holdings (small virgates or yardlands) are dispersed throughout a township. In most cases the precise arrangement appears to be irregular, and it is assumed that such a distribution was achieved by lottery. However around Northampton

there are a number of townships with a fixed and regular cycle of tenurial units. Tenurial cycles of 32 and 19 lands are 'hidden' in field books of *c.* 1660 and 1433 respectively, for Hardingstone and Muscott. These have been discussed in some detail (Hall 1980 and Hall forthcoming), and further developments will be given below.

Great Billing has a sketch plan of its regular tenurial cycles made in *c.* 1690, and Ecton has an estate map of 1703 showing repetitive cycles of groups each containing 10 lands (Hall 1983). Göransson (1961) and Harvey (1980) have published other Yorkshire examples. All these field systems are therefore organized in the manner of a Scandinavian *solskifte*.

In these cases the yardland appears on the ground as a rood, or ridge, recurring once in each tenurial cycle at a rigidly fixed interval thoughout the parish furlongs. Great Billing, Hardingstone and Ecton have additional structure, for within each tenurial cycle are subdivisions called *hides*, as shown in Table 6.1.

Table 6.1   Tenurial cycle subdivisions

Place	No. hides	No. strips (roods) in each hide	No. strips in cycle	Date
Great Billing	3	20, 10, 13	43	1684[7]
Hardingstone	8	4	32	1660
Ecton	11	10	110	1464

The hides of Hardingstone and Ecton have Middle English names attached to each, and must date from at least this period; in other words they are a fundamental component of the field-system spatial structure.

Again the only parallels are Scandinavian—this time the Danish *Bolskifte* system. Since this system is unknown in Germany, Holland or Belgium (E. Ulsig, pers. comm. 1981), it seems reasonable to look to the tenth century for an explanation of its occurrence only in Denmark and England, when the political ties between the two countries were close. Further evidence to support this early date comes from the large number of Scandinavian elements in the furlong names, particularly the use of the Danish *dale* instead of the English *slade* for a 'valley' (Hall 1978b for Billing). At Ecton there is the use of the word *wandale* for a division of a meadow which is a striking characteristic of northern 'Danish' counties (Gover *et al.* 1933, 274). More details and a plan on the Ecton *bolskifte* are given in Hall 1983.

(v) Taxation assessments and peasant holdings

At a 1981 Durham meeting evidence was presented to show that there is a relationship between the number of peasant holdings (yardlands or small virgates) in a township and the Domesday assessment (Hall 1983).

Most frequently there seems to be a reckoning of 10 or 12 small virgates to a Domesday hide (not to be confused with the *bolskifte* hides discussed above). Since fractional units of one-tenth and one-twelfth (and their multiples) are abundant in the Norhamptonshire Domesday returns, it is implied that the small virgates were already in existence. It is therefore possible that the hides were assessed by ascertaining the number of small virgates and dividing by 10 or 12. Such a procedure would account for the variability of the size of the hide, since the small virgate varies in acreage from 15 to 80, although 20–25 acres is a common value.

The townships of Ravensthorpe and Teeton well illustrate that Domesday assessments were concerned with yardlands and not acreages. The townships form one parish (see below) but have separate field systems: the statistics are presented below in Table 6.2.

Here there is no doubt that the Domesday assessors were considering either 10 or 12 yardlands as a hide and not taking any account of the actual size. The difference was noted in 1643 when the inhabitants of Teeton complained that it was unfair for them to be taxed more than Ravensthorpe because their yardlands were only one-third as big.[9]

The impossibility of turning Domesday hides into acreages without more information is further made clear by an enquiry of 1318 into Finedon Soke lands already mentioned (Kerr 1925, 8). The following figures are given (Table 6.3).

These are interesting figures. Although the number of virgates to a hide is either two or four, the constant value that underlies the calculation is that a hide is 80 acres; this in contrast to what has been said above. Another differing factor is that *small virgates* are being used at two or four to the hide, so that these hides are small compared to the usual ones that have 10 or 12 small virgates (see above). Yet in the Domesday survey the Finedon Soke is stated as a total of 27 hides, giving the impression that a very large estate is involved, but it is not.

It is clear, therefore, that little idea of the acreage involved at the time of Domesday can be calculated until something is known about yardlands, which, fortunately, because of great stability in field-system structure, can be ascertained from the more copious records left by later centuries.

Another example of the continuing stability of field-system structure and estates is given by the demesne of Rothersthorpe. There were three Domesday estates consisting of two and a half, a half, and a half, hides, i.e. a total three and a half (Thorn and Thorn 1979). Only

Table 6.2   Township sizes

Township	Acreage (modern)	Domesday hides	No. yardlands in fieldsystem[8]	Acreage of yardland
Ravensthorpe	1437	2	20.5	c80
Teeton	666	2	25	c25

Table 6.3   Statistics of Finedon Soke lands in Higham Hundred

Township	No. of virgates	Acreage of virgate	Assessment in hides	No. virgates to hide
Irchester	19	20	4.75	4
Knuston	0.5	–	0.125	4
Raunds	1	40	0.5	2
Rushden	10.5	40	5.25	2

the largest had any demesne, which was rated at two out of seven ploughlands, i.e. $2/7 \times 2.5/3.5$ of the total, or 0.204. The enclosure award of 1810 gives the total number of yardlands as 64, so the demesne, if unchanged, would be $0.204 \times 64 = 13$ yardlands. Amazingly, a 1694 mortgage of the manor states that there were 13 yardlands belonging to it (Hall 1982b).

(vi) Field systems and estates

So far the examples discussed have mainly been concerned with the smaller subdivision of estates and holdings within a given township or field system, but field systems are extremely useful tools to unravel the problems of larger temporal and ecclesiastical holdings. Often in the Midlands, manor, parish, field system and settlement are a single entity, so that the potential complexities are not evident. It is not until a multi-settlement parish is studied that problems arise. A study of the field systems will often resolve the matter, because an agricultural entity must represent one of the earliest features of organized settlement, no matter how many actual settlement sites are involved within it. Field systems are therefore the smallest and most ancient entity that can be called an 'estate'.

The present day parishes of Ravensthorpe, Hollowell and Guilsborough are good examples of complexity and confusion. At present the hamlet of Coton, near to Guilsborough, is part of Ravensthorpe parish and the hamlet of Teeton is included in Hollowell parish. The latter, however, was only created in 1840 with the erection of St James Church. Previously Hollowell was

part of Guilsborough parish and Teeton was part of Ravensthorpe, still leaving the oddity of Coton as part of Ravensthorpe parish even though it is in a different hundred (Bridges *c.* 1720) and physically close to Guilsborough (Fig. 6.3).

Medieval records demonstrate that this latter arrangement was of long standing. Field-system studies show that Teeton, Ravensthorpe and Hollowell are independent agricultural units. Their physical bounds are evident on various eighteenth- and nineteenth-century estate maps.

Guilsborough is much more complicated. It contains a hamlet called Nortoft contiguous with it to the north. This turns out to be a separate settlement with its own field system enclosed in 1588. Guilsborough and Coton form a single field system, as is evident, for instance, from a glebe terrier of 1634.[10] The individual strips were plotted on a reconstructed furlong plan, and shown to envelop both settlements (unpublished work by the author). The terriers of Guilsborough state that the holdings lie in the 'fields of Guilsborough and Coton'. That this was the medieval arrangement is clear because the glebe consists of land granted to the church in *c.* 1480 (Bridges 1791; 1, 537, 571). It is therefore established that in agricultural terms there are five separate field systems.

We have to turn to the political holdings of the eleventh century to get an explanation of the parishes. Table 6.4 shows the Domesday landholders of the various manors within the villages, and the Saxon holders in 1086 (Thorn and Thorn 1979).

Table 6.4 Holders of manors in parishes of Guilsborough and Ravensthorpe in 1086 and 1066

Reference (in Morris)	Owner in 1086	Township	Number of hides	Owner in 1066
35–19	William Peverel	Coton manor		
		Hollowell	$^1/_4$	
		Coton	$^7/_8$	
		Thornby	1	Saxon estate
		Winwick	$^3/_4$	held by Drogo
		Wesh Haddon	$^3/_8$	in 1086
		Cold Ashby	$^3/_8$	
		Nortoft	$^1/_2$	
35–18	William Peverel	Teeton	2	Drogo
35–17	William Peverel	Ravensthorpe	$1^1/_4$	Drogo
35–23	William Peverel	Guilsborough	$^7/_8$	Gytha
18–80	Count of Mortain	Guilsborough	$^1/_4$ +church	
		Nortoft	2	Leofwin
		Hollowell	$^1/_{12}$ mill	
18–96	Count of Mortain	Hollowell	$^1/_{12}$	Alric
18–6	Count of Mortain	Ravensthorpe	$^1/_2$	Edmer
5–1	Bishop of Lincoln	Hollowell	$1^2/_6$	Bardi
57–3	Gilbert the Cook	Hollowell	$^2/_{12}$	
57–4	Gilbert the Cook	Ravensthorpe	$^1/_4$	Norman

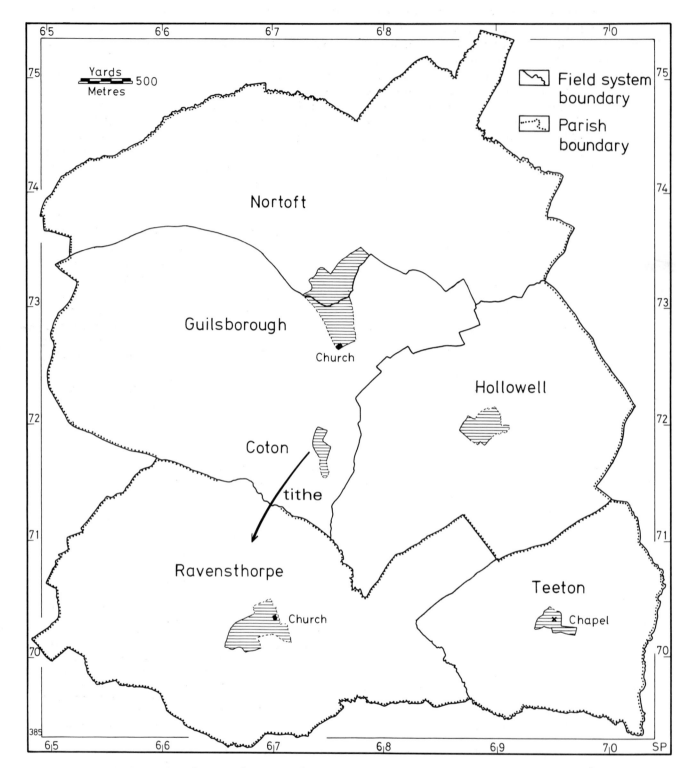

Fig. 6.3 Guilesborough and Ravensthorpe parishes, Northamptonshire, showing how the field systems relate to the settlements and parishes.

Drogo, under William Peverel, was the chief landowner in 1086; he held all of Teeton and most of Ravensthorpe, and a manor at Coton that consisted of a hotchpotch of smallish estates from nearby villages and 7/8 hide at Coton (i.e. in the fields of Coton and Guilsborough). It seems clear that when Ravensthorpe parish was created there was one church for this main holding at Ravensthorpe and Teeton but, because of the proximity of Coton to them, that part of the Coton manor was also added. This meant that in the open fields the lands owing tithe to Ravensthorpe church were physically mixed with those of Guilsborough throughout the field system.

Such an arrangement cannot be later than 1086, because William Peverel held all this Saxon estate and another 7/8 hide in Guilsborough that belonged to Gytha in 1066. Had he created the medieval parish system then this last might also have been added to Ravensthorpe.

The siting of Guilsborough church is also of considerable interest. The Domesday entry for the Saxon estate of Leofwin (then belonging to Robert, a tenant of the Count of Mortain) shows that the main estate was at Nortoft with a very small detached holding and part of the mill at Hollowell. The entry also states 'to this land belong a church with a virgate of

land in Guilsborough' (Thorn and Thorn 1979, 18–20). It seems extraordinary that a manor should possess a church in another settlement until we look at the physical layout. The double village of Nortoft and Guilsborough and the smaller hamlets of Coton and Hollowell form a triangle. A church at the southern extremity of Guilsborough places it almost exactly in the centre of all the three settlements. In all likelihood such an arrangement appreciably pre-dates the eleventh-century holdings, going back to a stage when the four settlements had a simpler ownership. The medieval systems of settlement, field and parish, are shown in Fig. 6.3.

All of these rather complex details of the eleventh century illustrate fragmented holdings, with a simple underlying unity of parish and field system that must be much older, supporting Maitland's remark that at Domesday England was a 'very old country'.

In conclusion, it can be seen that field systems provide a valuable tool for the study of medieval estates, and their spatial and tenurial characteristics. They yield evidence of many archaic features and a long term stability that betrays their extreme antiquity. Further studies should enable a comprehensive approach to be made towards understanding land use and division in late Saxon England.

Notes

1. Map and survey of Yardley Hastings 1760, Northamptonshire Record Office (NRO), Maps 4155–7.
2. Weedon Bec, Northamptonshire, Eton College Records: Catalogue of Archives, Volume 27, compiled by N. Blakiston.
3. Bru. O. vii. 6, NRO.
4. Cartulary of Pipewell Abbey, Northamptonshire; British Library, Cotton Mss. Calig. A 12, f. 135.
5. Wollaston open field map, 1774, NRO.
6. Rushden glebe terriers, NRO.
7. Great Billing glebe terriers, NRO.
8. LT 85c, about 1603, NRO.
9. LT 416, NRO.
10. Guilsborough glebe terrier, 1634, NRO.

References

Beresford, M. W. 1957: *History on the Ground* 2nd edition, 1971 (London, Methuen).

Biddick, K. (editor) forthcoming: *Proceedings of Session on Medieval Archaeology and Ecology* at Sixteenth International Congress on Medieval Studies at Kalamazoo, Michigan, U.S.A., 1981.

Bridges, J. 1971: *The History and Antiquities of Northamptonshire* (Material compiled in *c.* 1720 and edited by Whalley, London).

Dodgshon, R. A. 1980: *The Origin of British Field Systems: an interpretation* (London, Academic Press).

Eigler, F. 1983: Regular settlements in Franconia founded by the Franks in the early Middle Ages. In Roberts, B. K. and Glasscock, R. E. (editors) 1983, 83–91.

Elvey, G. E. (editor) 1969: Luffield Priory charters. *Northamptonshire Record Society* 26.

Göransson, S. 1961: Regular open-field pattern in England and Scandinavian *solskifte*. *Geografiska Annaler* 43, 80–104.

Gover, J. E. B., Mawer, A. and Stenton, F. M. 1933: *The Place-Names of Northamptonshire*. English Place-Name Society 10 (Cambridge, Cambridge University Press).

Hall, D. N. 1972: Modern surveys of medieval field systems. *Bedfordshire Archaeological Journal* 7, 53–66.

Hall, D. N. 1978a: In *Annual Report of the Medieval Village Research Group*, reproduced in Hall, 1982a, Fig. 32.

Hall, D. N. 1978b: Great Billing parish survey. *Northamptonshire Archaeology* 13, 161–7.

Hall, D. N. 1981a: The origins of open-field agriculture—the archaeological fieldwork evidence. In Rowley, T. (editor) 1981, 22–38.

Hall, D. N. 1981b: The changing landscape of the Cambridgeshire silt fens. *Landscape History* 3, 37–49.

Hall, D. N. 1982a: *Medieval Fields* (Princes Risborough, Shire Publications).

Hall, D. N. 1982b: Rothersthorpe field survey. *Council for British Archaeology Group 9 Newsletter* 12, 55.

Hall, D. N. 1983: Fieldwork and field books: studies in early layout. In Roberts, B. K. and Glasscock, R. E. (editors) 1983, 115–31.

Hall, D. N. forthcoming: Fieldwork and documentary evidence for the layout and organization of early medieval estates in the English Midlands. In Biddick, K. (editor) forthcoming.

Harvey, M. 1980: Regular field and tenurial arrangements in Holderness, Yorkshire. *Journal of Historical Geography* 6, 3–16.

Hoskins, W. G. 1957: *The Making of the English Landscape* (London, Hodder and Stoughton).

Kerr, W. J. B. 1925: *Higham Ferrer and its Ducal and Royal Castle and Park* (Northampton private publication).

Nitz, H. J. 1983: Feudal woodland colonization as a strategy of the Carolingian empire in the conquest of Saxony; reconstruction of the spatial patterns of expansion and colonist settlement morphology in the Leine-Weser region. In Roberts, B. K. and Glasscock, R. E. (editors) 1983, 171–84.

Roberts, B. K. and Glasscock, R. E. (editors) 1983: *Villages, Fields and Frontiers.* (Oxford, British Archaeological Reports International Series -S185).

Rowley, T. (editor) 1981: *The Origins of Open Field Agriculture* (London, Croom Helm).

Thorn, F. and Thorn, C. (editors) 1979: *Domesday Book 21, Northamptonshire* (Chichester, Phillimore).

7. Dartmoor and the Upland Village of the South-West of England

D. Austin

The publication of the Houndtor report now allows a detailed appraisal of the nature of deserted villages in the uplands of the south-west. Particular problems about the Houndtor material centre on the interpretation of a sequence of turf predecessors to the stone longhouses and the dating of this sequence to the later Anglo-Saxon period. The argument should be regarded as 'not proved' by the Houndtor evidence and a narrow dating of twelfth to fourteenth centuries should accompany these upland settlements. There are also dangers in simple descriptions of function and tenurial role, since documentation is slender and evaluation of size and morphology should be the result of formal analysis. The function of buildings and the arrangements within the settlement space would suggest that the village is inappropriate in the upland context and that the morphological forms are reflective of the fundamentally dispersed pattern of the south-western lowlands.

In the upland regions of Britain the term 'village' has often had a rather indeterminate usage particularly by archaeologists describing deserted clusters of farmsteads and enclosures. Nowhere is this more true than the south-west of England where a small number of classic sites has dominated the literature. In this part of the country the granite massifs have provided the source for a great deal of good fieldwork and excavation which is still continuing, but their sites have also distorted our vision of both the settlement forms and their chronologies. The very well-preserved remains of stone buildings and fossilized field systems contrast sharply with the surrounding lowlands and intersected plateaux of Devon and Cornwall. Here the forms and chronologies of settlement have received only scant attention from archaeologists, although these ought to be the regions of maximum and continuous utilization throughout the medieval period. By contrast, the abandoned sites of the present moorland fringes are the wreckage left between the low and high tide lines of medieval settlement, and represent relatively temporary exploitation.

Recently three sites excavated by Mrs Minter on Dartmoor have finally received publication by Guy Beresford (1979). Completing a report on somebody else's excavation solely from site records is an onerous and often frustrating task and Mr Beresford must receive both our congrautlations and our sympathies. Publication, however, now gives us the opportunity to review some of the conclusions which have become entrenched for some years in medieval settlement studies (e.g. Beresford and Hurst 1971 and recently Cantor 1982). Particularly, it is worth reconsidering conclusions about the vernacular architecture, the chronology, the economy, the morphology and the status of such settlements on the present margins of Dartmoor.

In relation to the vernacular architecture, the stone structures excavated at Houndtor, Dinna Clerks and Hutholes belong to a well-known class and sequence of buildings: the south-western longhouse. The excavated features can be readily related to the well-documented characteristics of standing examples in Devon and Cornwall. There are, however, considerable problems of origin for the type. Beresford's report supports the view of Minter that the later forms develop from a tradition of turf-walled longhouses which can be attributed to a date as early as the middle Saxon period. The suggested development passes from turf-walling revetted by stakes and wattle, through turf revetted by stone, to the entirely dry-stone constructions. It is the first part of this sequence which causes most problems.

There can now be no doubt that stakes driven into the subsoil were used in the south-west both on and off Dartmoor as part of the structural repertoire of the medieval peasant farmer. They have an average diameter of about 10 cm and are probably the product of pollarding hedges or local woodland trees. At times they were clearly used for minor internal subdivision, providing no load-bearing support but forming the framework for wattle and sometimes daub as room dividers, fire hoods and screens. At Okehampton Park 59 (Austin 1978) they could be clearly seen in the wall angles of the stone buildings and there were lines of stake-holes within the byres which were interpreted as tethering posts or hay-racks. Here, within single period stone buildings, a proliferation of stake-holes suggested constant renewal perhaps on an annual basis over a relatively short period, perhaps 100 years at maximum. In contrast, at Houndtor and other south-western sites included in the recent and other reports, lines of such stake-holes have been offered as evidence of revetment for turf-walled buildings, each one having a putative life of approximately 30 years (Beresford 1979, 113).

Floors for these buildings were defined by hard 'edges' which were coupled with the stake-hole lines and 'hearths'.

Beresford has assembled an impressive array of parallels for the turf-walled house ranging from the neolithic in Ireland to the nineteenth century. Although the links between them chronologically and typologically are far from clear, the general evidence for turf walling is unequivocal. What must be in question, however, is the relationship of the Devon evidence to the other sites. Many of those quoted by Beresford occupy a far more northerly distribution in the British Isles where timber for an alternative building tradition was, and remains, scarce. This is not true generally for the edges of Dartmoor where quite substantial stands of timber seem to have been available in valley locations and where a post-Roman regeneration of woodland seems to have occupied the more exposed flanks of the moor (Ausin, Daggett and Walker 1980). Thus framed buildings would have been a distinct possibility, as demonstrated at Okehampton Park 59. The first buildings quoted as parallels also provide evidence for the turf *in situ* either still retained by stone or as dumps which appear as earthwork features prior to excavation. From all the evidence produced for Houndtor, there are no sections or photographs showing turf, let alone any which can be directly related to a single line of stakes or a floor edge. Moreover at none of the excavated sites and nowhere in the south-west do there exist earthworks of proven turf-walled buildings other than those which are stone-revetted. Considering the suggested length of time they were in use at Houndtor, for example, this is surprising. In addition one might assume that a series of turf-walled houses on a single location should have produced a 'tell' effect with a great depth of humic laminated soil. Nothing of this nature seems to have been produced at any of these sites.

At a more general level, there has been no questioning of the logic behind turf construction in these upland landscapes, especially if it is asked how they ought to be related to nearby field systems. This question in itself has important implications for the economic life of the community, but is is worth observing here that the massive stone clearances needed to create the fields would have generated enough building material for a complete settlement even if it were not already available on the clitter-strewn slopes. It is difficult to understand how the Dark Age peasant, unlike his counterpart at Mawgan Porth (Bruce-Mitford 1956) should fail to use such abundant stone supplies. In fact, the farmer of every other age who has worked the same landscapes has turned to this building material first. The impression of illogicality is increased when it is realized that a single turf building such as the

one under House 1 at Houndtor (Beresford 1979, 120) would require about a quarter of an acre of two-inch thick turfs cut from good grassland. To strip cleared pasture in this way, especially when it was won with great difficulty, seems absurd, but the alternative would be either the wholly unsuitable material in the regenerated scrub and light woodland or dried peat for which there was also no evidence.

Another problem relates to the criterion for selecting from a great mass of stake-holes in the growan sub-soil the lines which form the building indicators. Their selection depends largely on their coincidence with the 'floor edges', which, however, seem always to have only one major side and usually part of a second, but rarely a third and never a fourth. In other words 'floors' simply fade away without complete definition, leaving nothing which is a whole structure. As a subsoil, growan is highly susceptible to the creation of zones of softness and hardness, producing natural lines of difference in soil texture caused by such effects as iron-panning, solifluxion and superficial drainage. The 'floor' interpretation is also dificult in itself, since they seem to have no traces of occupation surface in asociation with them other than the 'hearths'. These seem to be burnt patches of subsoil without attendant structures such as stone-settings, and it should be noted that the same effect can be created by the most casual of bonfires. Finally, the floors of the overlying stone houses which were trampled and worn into the growan and which were terraced 'into the sides of the hill' (Beresford 1979, 129) seem to have had no impact on the distribution of stake-holes, hearths or floor edges. One could have suspected that earlier stake-holes would have been removed. This might suggest that such features are either contemporary with, or later than, the stone structures. Yet no stake-holes are attributed by Beresford to the stone buildings other than door posts (except curiously in the caption to Fig. 10, p. 121).

This introduces the matter of chronology, and here there are two principal points in the argument which takes the turf structures back into the Anglo-Saxon period. The first is the suggested multiplicity of superimposed turf-building phases and the second is the assignment of a notional 30 years (a generation) to each phase. The argument for multiplicity rests on the quantity of perceived lines and floor edges, the perception of which has already been questioned here. It should be further noted, however, that the case for superimposition in itself is not securely made, since no one line of stake-holes has been proved to overlie another by the accepted convention of one negative feature in a series cutting another. Indeed it was not proved during excavation that the stake-holes lay under the stone buildings, since the walls were not removed. This imprecise study of relationships leaves a question mark over conclusions about numbers of buildings involved and even more importantly about how many stake-holes could be linked ultimately with stone buildings, both those extant as foundations and others which may have been robbed clean during the life of the settlement. Constant renewal of stakes inside stone buildings as at Okehampton Park 59, and outside in yards as pens for beasts would produce the swarm of holes so characteristic of these sites.

Even if, for a moment, we accept the basic interpretation of turf buildings, we must examine the second, temporal assumption, and we are forced to ask what foundation such structures had, before we can assume that their average life-span was 30 years. The lack of proper floors and internal arrangements, especially the diagnostic byre drains which should have been so apparent even under severe erosion, means that the turf buildings cannot be unquestionably related to the stone longhouse tradition. Only their general length and some occasional evidence of opposed entrances in the long sides supports the theory. As longhouses they would imply all-year-round settlement and some degree of permanent supervision of the fabric. Under these circumstances they may survive for long periods, although the constant need to replace stakes under the damp and acid soil conditions of the moor would still be a factor, as is witnessed at Okehampton Park. Turf buildings might, however, fit better into the transhumance tradition in which a continuous cycle would require abandonment in the autumn and rebuilding and refurbishing in the spring. Under such conditions a rapid turnover in the temporary building stock can be inferred and phases would lie closer to the one year span than that of 30 years.

Early medieval documentation for the structures and practice of transhumance in the south-west, as in all the British uplands, is however pitifully scarce and the degree in interchange with the lowlands can only be a matter of conjecture. The movement of stock on to the moors in the summer is well-attested, for example, in the Venville arrangements for the parishes of the Dartmoor perimeter, and it has always been assumed that the late medieval sources reflect ancient customs. It seems to have been part of this practice to establish temporary huts in the 'predas' or good grazing areas of the medieval Forest of Dartmoor (Fogwill 1954, 107). These contrast, however, with the more substantial remains on the moorland fringes of medieval farms and their related enclosures which are assumed to be attempts at permanent settlements by farmers operating at the very limits of crop production. Certainly the bulk of evidence from the stone buildings, which belong predominantly to the high medieval optimum of the twelfth to fourteenth centuries, would tend to confirm this assumption. Moreover the same evidence would suggest that although the farming

economy was fundamentally mixed, proximity to extensive tracts of moor ensured that pastoralism predominated. The proportions in the mixture of farming activity may have been different from site to site and from year to year. Recent evidence, for example from Bodmin Moor (N. Johnson pers. comm.) might suggest that the extent of arable exploitation (or at least ridge and furrow) may have been underestimated. Although re-evaluation of the high medieval upland economy may be required in the future, it is already certain that it is impossible to extend even the current evaluation into any period earlier than the twelfth century. This is not to deny that permanent mixed agricultural settlements existed at such sites as Houndtor in the late Anglo-Saxon or Norman periods, but simply to stress that the evidence is not yet available. It is not enough to antedate conclusions on the vaguest hints of similarity.

At Houndtor some support for such a conclusion seems to have been derived from the analysis of documentary evidence. In this the manorial history of Houndtor from Domesday Book onwards has been unequivocally attached to the site excavated by Mrs Minter. This is too simplistic, since all the documents refer to the 'vill' and 'manor' of Houndtor which are essentially territories or areas of land and not individual places. Beresford in his conclusions, however, has taken the identification of documents and sites even further by suggesting that an otherwise unrecorded manor-house, the embodiment of a *manerium,* is to be found within the excavated cluster of buildings. This is Houndtor 1 Building 3, which is singled out simply because it is the largest and sits obviously within the enclosure. A quick look at the topography of this area (Fig. 7.1) would suggest that the most favourable location for farming is in the valley to the east of the excavated site since it lies in a less exposed position below the 800 foot (244 m) contour. With this broader perspective the probable arable core of the manor, held T.R.E. by Abbot Sihtric of Tavistock and subsequently by the Dennys family, is the current farm of Great Hound Tor, with its fields on the south-facing slopes of the small valley. If a manor-house existed, the ruined longhouse in the farmyard here would seem to indicate a much more likely contender (Alcock 1969, 95).

The question of *villa, manerium* and manor-house raises the broader and more intricate problems of the settlement morphology and tenurial status of these earthwork sites in the south-west. It has been a tacit assumption that the medieval exploitation of the moorland edge was undertaken by freehold farmers assarting on the waste much in the manner of their contemporaries in Arden or the northern Pennine dales. In reality very little is known of the inhabitants of these farms and by what forms of tenure they held their lands since reference to their existence is only

Table 7.1   Buildings excavated in the South-West: Internal characteristics

Building Number (Fig. 3)	Site	Site No.	Length in ft	A Dwelling Length (ft)	B Byre/Shippon Length (ft)	C Opposed Doors	D Stone Hearths	E Cooking Pit	F Annexe Rooms	Type
1	HTI	1	47	21	20	x	x	—	—	1A.
2		2	24	—	—	—	—	—	—	4.
3		3	57	31	22	x	x	x	x	1A.
4		4	25	—	—	—	x	x	—	3.
5		5	22	—	—	—	—	—	—	4.
6		6	32	—	—	—	—	—	—	4.
7		7	52	27	22	x	x	x	x	1A.
8		8	40	—	—	—	—	—	—	4.
		Barn 1	29	Corn drier						5.
		Barn 2	28	Corn drier						5.
		Barn 3	26	Corn drier						5.
9	HTII	1	38	20	14	x	x	—	x	2.
10		2	30	—	—	—	—	—	—	4.
		3	22	Corn drier						5.
11	D.C.		55	29	22	x	x	—	x	1A.
12	H.H.	1	34	19	13	—	x	x	x	2.
13		2	21	—	—	—	—	—	—	4.
14		3	46	25	18	—	x	—	x	1A.
15		4	34	—	—	—	—	—	—	4.
16		5	25	—	—	—	—	—	—	4.
17		6	30	—	—	—	—	—	—	4.
18	O.P.59	A1	54	28	22	x	x	—	x	1A.
19		A2	—	—	—	x	—	—	—	4.
20		A3	32	11	19	x	x	x	—	2.
21		A4	21	—	—	—	—	—	—	4.
22		B1	38	—	—	—	—	—	—	4.
23		B2	62–73	42	16–28	x	x	—	x	1B(?)
24		B3	34	—	—	—	—	—	—	4.
25	G.T.	1	46	28	13	x	x	—	—	1A.
26		'Barn'	26	—	—	—	—	—	—	4.
27	L.M		28–48	17–37	9	x	x	—	x	1A.
28	B.	1	36	23	10	x	x	—	x	2.
29		'Barn'	24	—	—	—	—	—	—	4.
		'Kiln'	—	'Corn drier' (?)						5(?)
30	D.M.	'House'	27	12	10	—	—	—	—	3.
31		'Byre'	49	15	29	x	—	—	—	1A.
32	Td.	1	67 (?)	40 (?)	18 (?)	x	x	x	x	1B.
		2	30 (?)	14 (?)	12 (?)	x	—	—	—	3.
34	Tn.	1	23	14 (?)	7 (?)		—	—	—	3.
35		2	22	—	—	—	—	—	—	4.
36		3	20 (?)	—	—	—	—	—	—	4.
37	Ta.		71	36	29	x	x	—	x	1B.

H.T.I & H.T.II. Houndtor 1 and 2 (Beresford 1979).   D.C. Dinna Clerks (Beresford 1979).   H.H. Hutholes (Beresford 1979).   O.P. 59 Okehampton Park Site 59. (Austin 1978).   G.T. Garrow Tor (Dudley and Minter 1962–3).   L.M. Lanyon-in-Madron (Minter 1964).   B. Beere, North Taunton (Jope and Threlfall 1958).   D.M. Dean Moor (Fox 1958).   Td. Treworld, Lesnewth (Dudley and Minter 1966).   N.B. Measurements in the text do not accord with measurements taken from published plans. The latter are used in the table.   Th. Tresmorn, St. Gennys (Beresford 1971).   Ta. Trewortha (Baring-Gould 1892–3).

x indicates presence of a characteristic feature.

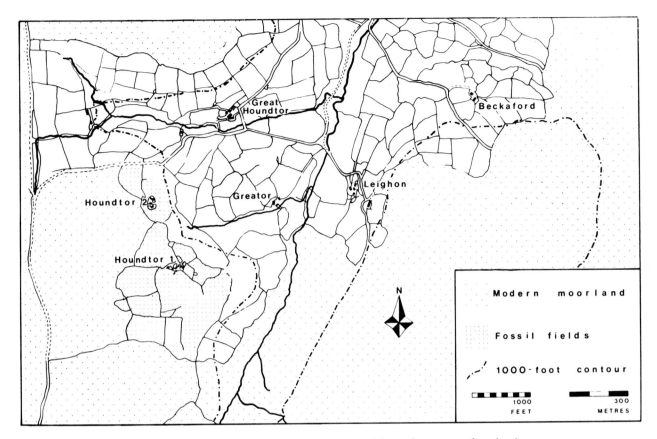

Fig. 7.1   Houndtor, Devon: the relationship of settlement and fields to the surrounding landscape

infrequently made in the surviving documents. Again the relationship of the deserted tenements to those that have survived must be examined. How often, for example, can it be suggested that the farms at high altitudes are in some kind of dependent relationship to the more low-lying manors? The Houndtor earthwork site may be just such a case and the excavated longhouses may belong to bond tenants of a demesne experimenting by expansion on to the waste, exploiting favourable conditions of demographic growth, improved climate and a buoyant economy. The failure of the experiment in the fourteenth century would coincide well with the general retreat from the demesne in the harsher conditions of the later Middle Ages. A simplistic model such as this is, of course, susceptible of criticism, not least because of a lack of evidence, but it might help to explain, for example, the phenomenon of deserted sites interspersed with still functioning units in adjacent holdings otherwise similar in topography and aspect. This has already been noted on the northern side of Dartmoor where the demise of the farms in the demesne of Okehampton Park is sharply contrasted with the survival of Halstock which lies on the same contour. The phenomenon may be explicable in a contrast between the demesne of the Park and the freehold of Halstock. On the western side of Dartmoor it can be suggested that at least some of the deserted

sites are dependent off-shoots of still surviving manorial neighbours e.g. Butterbury in Peter Tavy (Linehan 1966, 137).

More work clearly needs to be done, but there are interesting questions to be asked also about the morphology of these settlements, since shape and disposition of individual units is an aspect of tenure as well as of economic and social function. Here we return to the use of the term 'village'. Definitions in rural settlement are never easy, especially when the words employed are part of the common fabric of language with its hazy and regionally varying usage as well as being required to have very specific and technical meanings (Roberts 1977, 81–5). The commonest terms are, therefore, least susceptible of precision, particularly 'farm', 'hamlet', 'village' and 'town' which represent the fundamental expression of hierarchy in the classification of rural settlement (Uhlig 1972, 102–7). In the uplands of the south-west the problem of classification is acute, and is not assisted by the vague application of 'village' to the settlement forms.

In morphological terms the problem is easily stated. The essential unit, the building block of plans, is the individual, discrete grouping of farm buildings within their home close or 'toft', which is the physical indicator of tenurial allocation within the settlement space. The interrelationships and location of the enclosed farms within the plan form the basis of classification. In the south-west however it has been difficult to isolate the essential units of space and structure and this has led to some confusion. Surviving enclosure walls do not in general surround clearly discrete clusters of buildings, suggesting that subdivision of settlement space into units of tenure either was not important, even irrelevant, or was expressed in some other way.

Morphological understanding of these sites, therefore, must be achieved by an examination of the whole functional interrelationship of the structures within the settlement, of which tenure is only one aspect. Any discussion of function, however, rests on the interpretation of building use and in this the selection of a systematic terminology is important. Beresford, for example, makes a general application of the word 'house' to the majority of the excavated structures at Houndtor, Hutholes and Dinna Clerks, but is prepared to qualify certain of them as longhouses although with little consistency. Imprecision of this nature is understandable because of the equivocal quality of some of the evidence, especially since the prevailing tradition of the longhouse in itself demonstrates mixed function beneath a single roof line. Yet the difficulties of interpretation do not arise from this type of structure but from the range of usually smaller buildings which contain few, and perhaps fugitive traces of their former use. To call these 'houses' which refers to human dwelling areas, is perhaps presumptive.

Table 7.1 lists a number of excavated and published stone structures from the uplands of the south-west, and indicates their length and the presence of certain internal characteristics. The internal length of these stone buildings of the twelfth to fifteenth centuries is used as a single, general indicator of size and measurement is limited to the space which may reasonably be considered to lie beneath one ridge-line and roof. Six further characteristics are chosen in an attempt to provide positive criteria for distinguishing the function of classic longhouses from those of other structures. For this reason selection was restricted to features which may be diagnostically attributed to the longhouse type, that is: (A) presence of byre or shippon indicated by central or lateral drains, (B) presence of domestic arrangements separated from the byre, (C) presence of cross passage separating the two areas, indicated by opposed doorways in the long-sides, (D) presence of hearths indicated by laid burnt stones rather than simply burnt patches which may be related to destruction, or any form of temporary heating for stock and stockmen alike, (E) presence of cooking pits, usually found close to the main hearth, (F) presence of subdivided dwelling space or annexes and outshots which demonstrate complex arrangements of habitation. Other features could have been selected, but most are ephemeral, difficult to interpret or limited by other

factors, such as stone benches, which are largely restricted to Cornish sites and seem to be a regional sub-type.

In Fig. 7.2, the characteristics are plotted against length for all structures other than the very obvious buildings containing corn-drying facilities (type 5). Four other groups seem to emerge. The principal longhouses (type 1) can be subdivided into the majority, 46–56 feet (14–17 m) in length (1A) and a few larger buildings 66–76 feet (20.1–23.1 m) in length (1B), and all (except 31) display at least four of the diagnostic features. The small or subsidiary longhouses (type 2) have similar features but are substantially shorter, 31–39 feet (9.5–11.9 m) in length. The barns and outhouses (type 4) are generally 20–40 feet (6.9–12.2 m) long and contain none of the selected elements (except 8 and 19). This leaves a small group (type 3) which are shorter than all the longhouses, but which seem to display some of their characteristics. In some respects, therefore, the best description may be 'subsidiary dwellings', and be functionally similar to the small longhouses (group 2). Within this classification it is possible to define the essential operating units in the settlement forms. If the principal longhouses are the core of the unit, the other buildings will have direct relationship with these, including all other dwellings. The unit may be expressed as an extended family, although it may be more accurate to describe them as belonging to 'stem families', where additional rooms and dwellings are added to accommodate ageing parents and married children. In particular, one feature, the room attached to the house end of the principal longhouse, is of interest in this context, especially at Okehampton Park 59, B2, where it is heated by its own hearth and has no access from the rest of the building, just its own door to the yard. The sociology of the relationships is difficult to recover without direct documentation, but the speculation is important in helping to investigate the morphological elements of the settlements. If there is a pattern of one principal longhouse with satellites constituting one functioning unit, it will be possible to demonstrate whether the settlements represent single components or nucleations within the terms 'hamlet' or 'village'. At Okehampton Park 59, (Fig. 7.3) for example, it would seem clear that there are two units (A and B) which are spatially well separated, but at Houndtor 1 and 2 and Hutholes the elements are not so apparent. On the model of one principal longhouse to a unit, however, both Houndtor 2 and Hutholes would appear to be each single units. Houndtor 1, in contrast, has three principal longhouses, each with well-defined associated enclosures, and it is perhaps no coincidence that there are three corn-drying kilns. Houndtor 1, therefore, must be a 'hamlet', but all of these sites exist essentially as part of a dispersed settlement pattern.

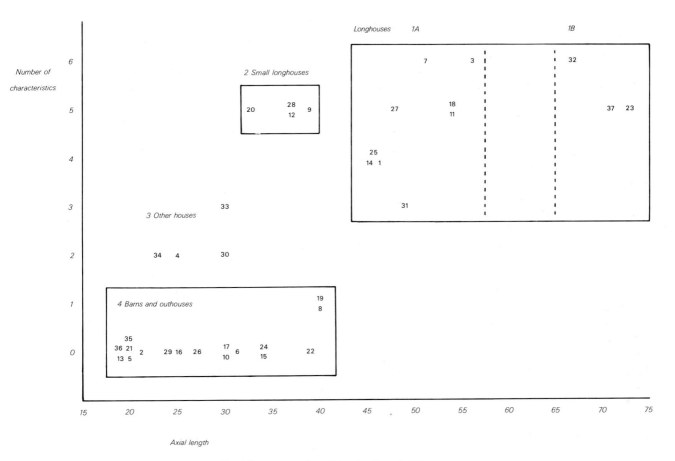

Fig. 7.2 Architectural analysis of building types found in the South-West

Elsewhere in the south-west, analysis of settlement form is made rather more difficult because of partial excavation, incomplete survey and a lack of integration with surrounding settlements. At Garrow Tor, for example, it is not possible from published sources to assess the place of the excavated longhouse (type 1A) and barn (type 4) within the whole community. This will be made easier when the survey by the N.M.R. and C.C.R.A. of Bodmin Moor and West Penwith is published. Similar comments could be made on other sites in Cornwall with the exception of Tresmorn, St Gennys, which in many respects is very unusual. Beresford has described for this site 13 specific crofts defined by surviving walls or earthwork enclosures. Each croft, however, is very small and contains only one stone building, none of which can be described as a longhouse, although one (Table 7.1 34) belongs to the anomalous type 3. The rest are barns or outhouses (type 4). It is doubtful, therefore, that we are dealing here with full farm units as defined above, but it is difficult to know how else they could be described except perhaps as cottage tenements. If 13 is the number of units at Tresmorn, it must, therefore, rank as the only candidate for a village excavated in the south-west and its coastal location may be important in this assessment. In Devon, by contrast, the two sites of Beere and Dean

Moor can be easily identified as single, dispersed farms. The internal arrangement of buildings at Dean Moor suggests that the large 'barn' of Lady Fox's report was probably built as a longhouse while the 'house' across the yard started as an outhouse, but, somewhere quite late in the sequence, the roles were reversed.

Complexity, however, is added to the discussion when we ask two further questions: did the units represent separate tenure by different families and were the units contemporary? At Okehampton Park 59 for example there was a suggestion that the settlement developed out of one or perhaps two ill-defined timber structures on the 'A' complex site. The two thirteenth-century units may, therefore, have resulted from a subdivision of ownership within a single family's tenure, an impression which is heightened by the lack of internal partition walls and enclosures. There it was felt that all the stone structures were contemporary during the last phases of occupation, and this general assumption would seem to apply also to all the other sites under consideration. The dates at which stone buildings were added to the communities and stages of growth are unclear, both because there is little stratigraphy and because the pottery types may look similar for over a hundred years on the poorer peasant sites of the south-west. With the chronology so

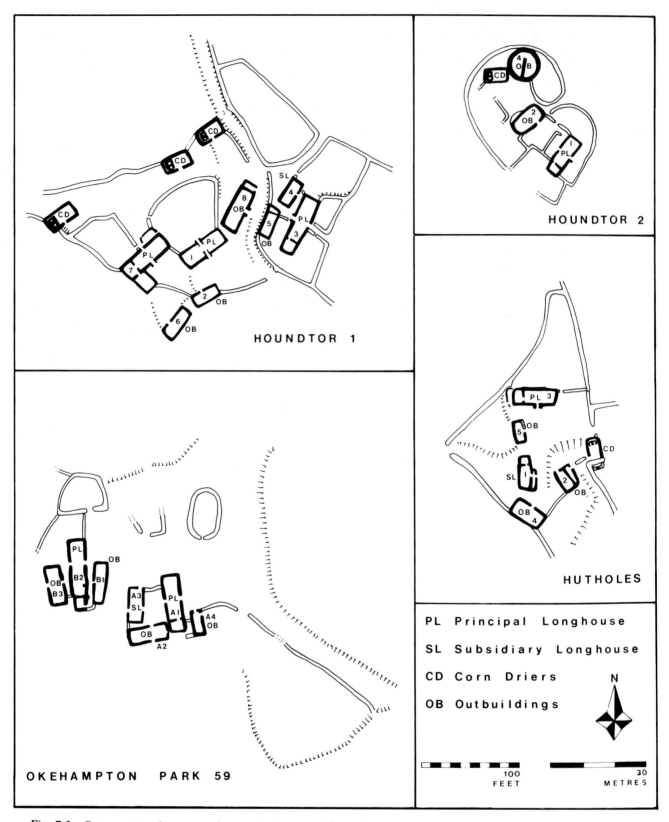

Fig. 7.3 Comparative diagrams of some Dartmoor settlements

imprecise, the processes of settlement evolution and creation can only remain a source of speculation and hypothesis. Despite, therefore, the amount of work already undertaken in the south-west uplands, too little is certainly known and a rather more systematic approach to excavation and field-work is needed in the next generation. It will also become increasingly important to link the examination of the sites to detailed studies of the environmental sequences.

References

Alcock, N. W. 1969: Devonshire farmhouses, Part 2. Some Dartmoor Houses. *Transactions of the Devonshire Association* 101, 83–106.

Austin, D. 1978: Excavations in Okehampton Deer Park, Devon, 1976-78. *Devonshire Archaeological Society Proceedings* 36, 191–239.

Austin, D., Daggett, R. H. and Walker, M. J. C. 1980: Farms and fields in Okehampton Park, Devon; the problems of studying medieval landscapes. *Landscape History* 2, 39–58.

Baring-Gould, S. 1892–3: An ancient settlement on Trewortha Marsh. *Journal of the Royal Institute of Cornwall* 11, 57–70.

Beresford, G. 1971: Tresmorn, St Gennys. *Cornish Archaeology* 10, 53–73.

Beresford, G. 1979: Three deserted medieval settlements on Dartmoor: a report on the late E. Marie Minter's excavations. *Medieval Archaeology* 23, 98–158.

Beresford, M. W. and Hurst, J. G. (editors) 1971: *Deserted Medieval Villages: Studies* (London, Lutterworth Press).

Bruce-Mitford, R. L. S. 1956: A Dark-age settlement at Mawgan Porth, Cornwall. In Bruce-Mitford, R. L. S. (editor) 1956.

Bruce-Mitford, R. L. S. (editor) 1956: *Recent Archaeological Excavation in Britain* (London, Routledge and Kegan Paul).

Cantor, L. M. 1982: *English Medieval Landscapes* (London, Croom Helm).

Dudley, D. and Minter, E. M. 1962–3: The medieval village at Garrow Tor, Bodmin Moor, Cornwall. *Medieval Archaeology* 6–7, 272–94.

Dudley, D. and Minter E. M. 1966: The excavation of a medieval settlement at Treworld, Lesnewth, 1963. *Cornish Archaeology* 5, 34–57.

Fogwill, E. G. 1954: Pastoralism on Dartmoor. *Transactions of the Devonshire Association* 86, 89–114.

Fox, A. 1958: A monastic homestead on Dean Moor, S. Devon. *Medieval Archaeology* 2, 141–57.

Jope, E. M. and Threlfall, R. I. 1958: Excavation of a medieval settlement at Beere, North Tawton, Devon. *Medieval Archaeology* 2, 112–40.

Linehan, C. D. 1966: Deserted sites and rabbit-warrens on Dartmoor, Devon. *Medieval Archaeology* 10, 113–44.

Minter, E. M. 1964: Lanyon in Madron. *Cornwall Archaeological Society Field Guide* No. 10, 3–7.

Roberts, B. K. 1977: *Rural Settlement in Britain* (Folkestone, Dawson).

Uhlig, H. 1972: *Die Siedlungen des Landlichen Raumes: Materialen zur Terminologie der Agrarlandschaft* (Geissen, Levz-Vering).

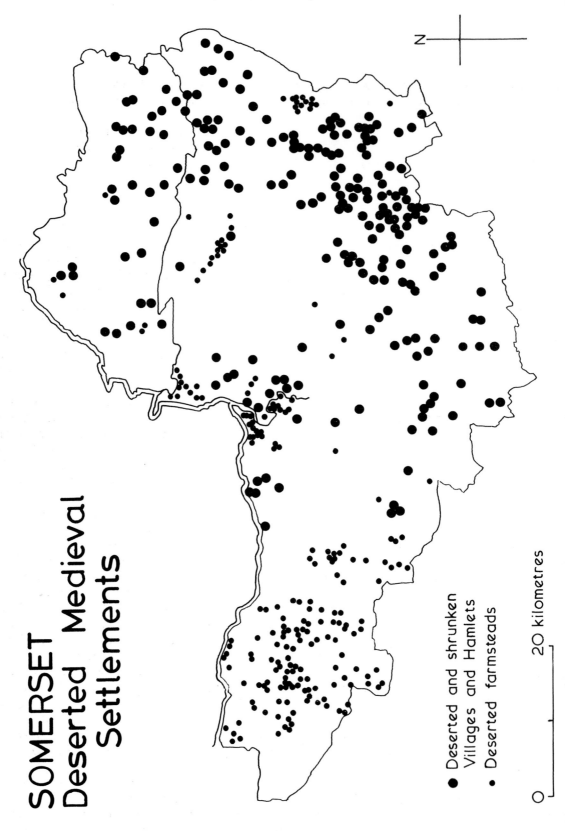

SOMERSET
Deserted Medieval
Settlements

N

M. Aston 1982

● Deserted and shrunken
   Villages and Hamlets
• Deserted farmsteads

0   20 kilometres

Fig. 8.1 Somerset: deserted medieval settlements

8. Rural Settlement in Somerset: some Preliminary Thoughts

M. A. Aston

This paper looks at the origins of nucleated settlements in Somerset in the early Middle Ages. Somerset is not a county with predominantly village settlement; hamlets are most common with, in the west, scattered individual farmsteads.

Various methods of analysis are used, based on research elsewhere in the country, in an attempt to understand when and why nucleated settlements developed. No firm conclusions are reached (further research is necessary) but, on balance, villages seem to be of possibly late Saxon or, more probably, early medieval date, in Somerset.

Introduction

A glance at the 1:50,000 or 1:25,000 maps of Somerset will show very quickly that the county has a wide variety of settlement types, from isolated farms and hamlets to fully developed villages, but such maps also show that there are some areas with more nucleation of settlement than others. Overall, however, Somerset is not a county of villages. This is especially true if, in a definition of villages, we insist on large nucleated settlements existing singly in their own parish with parish church and manor house. It is a county of large and small hamlets and almost all the early parish and administrative units had a variety of settlement types and forms.

Previous Research

Remarkably little attention has been paid in the past to the origin and development of the present settlements in the county. Beatrice Swainson's studies in 1932 and 1935 on rural settlement were typical of the sterile, geographically deterministic methods of the time and they were not followed up by other students (Swainson 1932 and 1935). The work of another geographer, Harry Thorpe, while attempting to classify rural settlements in Britain, resulted in a tortuous classification for Somerset, from predominantly villages with many scattered homesteads, occasional hamlets and market towns, in the east of the county, to predominantly hamlets with many scattered home-steads, occasional villages and market towns, in the area west of the River Parrett. While his classification had the merit, at least, of drawing attention to the obvious differences between the scattered settlements of the west of the county and the more nucleated pattern of the east, Thorpe still had to include anomalous areas elsewhere in the county (Thorpe 1964, Fig. 47).

Somerset did not share initially in the upsurge of interest created by the work on deserted villages by Maurice Beresford, John Hurst and other members of the Deserted Medieval Villages Research Group. In 1954, Beresford could only refer to 15 deserted and possibly deserted settlements in the county, located largely from documentary sources (Beresford 1954, 385), and even in 1971 Beresford and Hurst listed only 27 sites (Beresford and Hurst 1971, 202–3). (Both figures refer to the larger pre-1974 county of Somerset).

This lack of work on deserted villages in Somerset reflected the greater antiquarian attention in the county to prehistoric and Roman sites, to the virtual exclusion of the study of Saxon and medieval settlements (Fowler 1982). Although a few excavations had taken place on rural medieval sites, generally in the north of the county, little basic fieldwork or scanning of aerial photographs had taken place before the mid-1970s. Then, as part of the compilation of the County Council's Sites and Monuments Record, large numbers of settlements were located, principally from fieldwork and air survey, considerably supplementing the sites located by Beresford and others. By 1980, over 500 deserted, shrunken and migrated settlements had been located in the new, post-1974, county of Somerset, ranging from completely deserted village sites which formerly had churches (such as Whitcombe, Fairoak and Sock Dennis) to hamlets, with or without chapel sites, and to abandoned farmsteads of medieval and later date. The vast majority of the deserted sites in the county, however, consist of deserted and shrunken hamlets, without church or chapel in the medieval period (Aston 1982) (Fig. 8.1).

Although of considerable interest, and greatly supplementing the amount of medieval settlement archaeology undertaken in the county, the location of this large number of abandoned and partially deserted settlement sites has not helped greatly in answering questions about rural settlement origins and developments in the county. Only a couple of further excavations have been carried out recently (Long

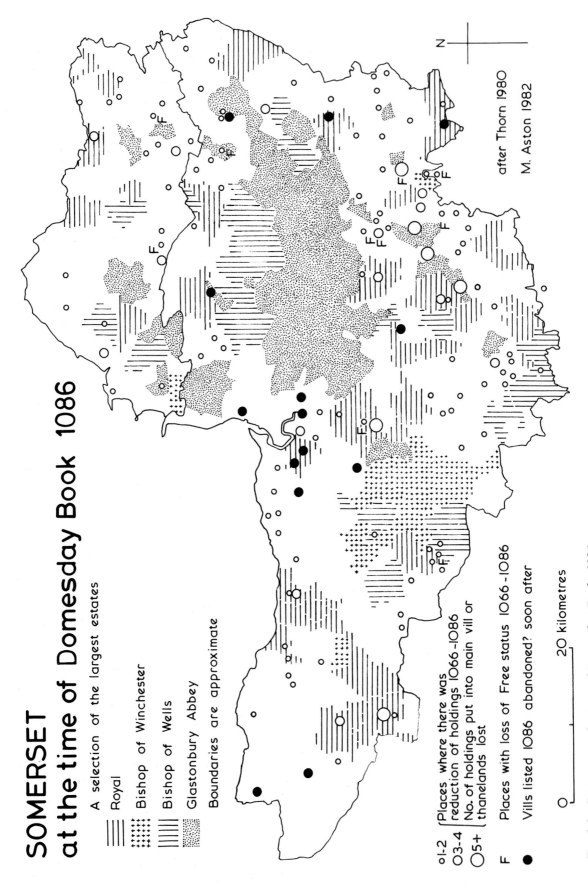

SOMERSET
at the time of Domesday Book 1086

A selection of the largest estates

|||| Royal

∷∷∷ Bishop of Winchester

⦀⦀⦀ Bishop of Wells

⣿ Glastonbury Abbey

Boundaries are approximate

o1-2   ⎱ Places where there was
O3-4   ⎰ reduction of holdings 1066-1086
○5+   ⎱ No. of holdings put into main vill or
       ⎰ thanelands lost

F   Places with loss of Free status 1066-1086

●   Vills listed 1086 abandoned? soon after

after Thorn 1980

M. Aston 1982

0 ————————— 20 kilometres

Fig. 8.2 Somerset at the time of Domesday Book, 1086

Ashton, Hurscombe in Brompton Regis and several sites on the Wincanton by-pass) but since 1974 the publication of further volumes of the Victoria County History of Somerset has begun to fill in, for some areas, the detailed history from documents which has hitherto been relatively inaccessible (Dunning, *V.C.H. Somerset* 1974, 1978).

Finally, Ann Ellison has carried out a topographical survey of villages in a large part of south Somerset. Although this was in the nature of an implications survey for use by planners, the work did draw together much field and documentary evidence. Both the approach and the information contained within it will be useful for researchers elsewhere in the county (Ellison 1976 and 1984).

Faced with this situation, what can be said of the origins and development of rural settlement in the county of Somerset? What was the 'typical' settlement type and pattern in pre-Norman times? Does the county exhibit any of the characteristics of village origin and development to be seen elsewhere: are there, for example, instances of planted planned villages as in Yorkshire and Durham? Has there been agglomeration of hamlets into villages and can we find examples of polyfocal settlement in the county? These questions have occupied the writer's attention for some time and it is proposed to discuss some of them in the rest of this article. Since so little work has been done, however, much of what is said below must be regarded as speculative. It is based on models, hypotheses, speculations and ideas from elsewhere but it is hoped at least that the framework and some of the ideas will prove useful in further research.

The Origins of the Settlement Pattern

Roger Leech, in a masterful survey of Romano-British settlement in Somerset and north Dorset, has drawn attention to the similarity in distribution and density between Roman sites and medieval settlements (Leech 1977). He suggests that many Romano-British sites continued in existence into the post-Roman period to emerge as medieval and modern villages and that where a Roman site has been located, it is principally because it is an abandoned site not overlain by later settlements. Elsewhere, he implies that Roman sites remain to be discovered under medieval settlements. Such 'continuity' should be expected in Somerset (and perhaps Dorset as well) since there was a long (almost 300 years) 'post-Roman' period through to the late seventh century, followed by a smooth Saxon take-over (whatever this might imply in Somerset at that date). Philip Rahtz and Peter Fowler drew attention to this some years ago and marshalled a convincing dossier of evidence; if anything this has now been reinforced (Rahtz and Fowler 1972). Ian Burrow, in re-examining

the hill-forts of the region, has demonstrated that in the west, and particularly in Somerset, there is good evidence for reoccupation after (or continuous occupation through) the Roman period in a number of cases (Burrow 1981). This at least did not continue as a legacy into the Middle Ages since there seem to be no examples of medieval settlements in hill-forts in Somerset (but see the discussion below on 'ring-works').

Despite the vitally important evidence of late Saxon activity at the royal palace of Cheddar (Rahtz 1979), no contemporary middle or late Saxon settlements have so far been located in the county. Work on the early medieval pottery assemblages from such sites as Ilchester and elsewhere is, however, enabling tentative identification of rural sites occupied in the tenth and eleventh centuries from field scatters (Leach 1984). Terry Pearson suggests, for example, that surface finds of sherds from Barrow (Odcombe), Holbrook (Bratton Seymour) and around the church at Milton Clevedon may be of this date. Further north, the large-scale excavations at Long Ashton by Roger Leech produced much pottery of pre-Conquest date.

Evidence from Domesday Book?

As in most counties, our clearest picture of settlement distribution begins to emerge with the compilation of Domesday Book in 1086. All of the caveats to which attention has been drawn by Peter Sawyer and others apply in Somerset but the detailed nature of the entries and the existence of the Exeter Domesday, which includes Somerset, enable some cautious remarks to be made about settlements in the late eleventh century (Thorn and Thorn 1980).

In the west of the county, the situation in 1086 was probably similar to that in Devon, with numbers of farms being indicated, but unrecorded, under the name of a single manor in the way elucidated by Professor William Hoskins (1965). Susanna Everett shows this for the Minehead area but little work has been done in detail elsewhere (Everett 1968). However, this writer believes that in the rest of the county Domesday Book is indicating changes in the status and arrangement of holdings which may well indicate developments on the ground. It is possible that some of the general developments of the Middle Ages (Duby 1968) and specific changes particular to Britain are taking place in Somerset at this time (Allerston 1970, Taylor 1977 and 1978). In particular, four main themes seem to be relevant, and we seem to be seeing a continuing process of 'feudalization', agglomeration and nucleation of settlement, and the abandonment of part of the earlier pattern (Fig. 8.2).

On the larger and more important estates, particularly those of the king, Glastonbury Abbey and the Bishop of Wells, no great changes other than ownership seem to have taken place between 1066 and 1086; earlier privileges have been maintained. The implications of this situation (especially with reference to the discussion below) are that any major changes in settlement organization and pattern have either taken place by 1066, or have yet to take place, and, if the former, that the contemporary organization was acceptable to the new Norman lords. It is thus possible that any changes which the Normans might be expected to want to make, such as the imposition of a rigid feudal structure, may already have been in operation and that the existing arrangements were regarded as satisfactory. This might imply that the pattern of large villages we see on these former estates today was then already in existence; but even if this were not the case these estates stand in marked contrast in 1086 to others at that date.

In a number of cases, what are clearly regarded as 'irregular arrangements' in 1066 had been 'regularized' by 1086. One of these was the extinction of a number of instances of 'free' status. This is particularly the case with the smaller and perhaps less significant (often unnamed) landholders. The Domesday account implies resentment of these changes, and perhaps the ways they were carried out, in such phrases as 'he could go to whichever lord he would' (Lydeard St Lawrence and Leigh), 'this land has been added to Brictric's lands, but the holders before 1066 could go where they would' (Lytes Cary). Other entries seem to imply the extinction of the free status of lands. Examples include Stringston, where half a virgate had been added which had been held freely in 1066, and Stratton in South Petherton, where two hides held by Merleswain in 1066 as thaneland were *now* (the Domesday word) paying 60 shillings into the king's revenue.

Related to the above, there are many instances in the county where there had been consolidation of holdings between 1066 and 1086, usually with numbers of small holdings, often thanelands, being incorporated into single, presumably larger, manors. Extreme examples include Dulverton, where two hides of land less half a furlong, which 13 thanes held before 1066, had been added to the manor, as well as a virgate which Doda held *freely* before 1066, and Stoke sub Hamdon, where the three estates of 1086 had been fashioned from the lands of nine thanes in 1066. At Sock Dennis near Ilchester the single manor had been held by seven thanes before the Conquest. Examples such as these exist widely in the county but are particularly in evidence in the south-east, where there are most villages. They are, in the main, absent from the larger royal, episcopal and ecclesiastical holdings (as with the removal of free status) and the situation might therefore represent changes already having occurred (or which had not yet taken place) on these estates (see Fig. 8.2).

Thirdly, there are references in Domesday Book to places which either disappeared later or are not later given the prominence they had in 1086. Are these places deprived of some earlier status in the Norman period in the same way as the manors discussed above, or are they abandoned in some process of agglomeration? Some survive as farms but none develops as a centre of any importance in the Middle Ages.

What might Domesday Book be telling us of settlement in Somerset in 1086? One possible explanation for all the developments discussed above might be the application of a 'feudalization' process, part of which could be the initiation of more nucleated settlements. The complex historical arguments for the rise of feudalization have been widely discussed by historians but the feature of interest to the settlement researcher is probably the organization of resources on manors to produce surpluses for the support of highly trained knights, their expensive armaments, and their well-bred, well-equipped, well-trained and well-fed warhorses (White 1962). The changes in settlement pattern which these developments might have necessitated have been little discussed but the *nucleation* of settlement into an efficient communal system of villages might be one manifestation. In the case of Somerset, this seems to have involved the consolidation of holdings into manors, the extinction of the anomalous free status of some estates and the possible abandonment of some sites.

Clearly this 'feudalization' hypothesis needs to be discussed further but if it resulted in a more nucleated settlement pattern there would have been both widespread abandonment of the late Saxon settlements (for which there is good evidence in other counties, e.g. Northamptonshire) and the necessity for newly-planned villages or extensions to existing settlements (for which again there is good evidence elsewhere). Where the applications of feudalism had occurred before 1066, there might be little indication of any changes in Domesday Book and such seems to be indicated on the royal and ecclesiastical manors in Somerset. Elsewhere, where the older(?) or less well-developed(?) settlement pattern existed in 1066, it would either persist without alteration or it would be altered to conform more to the idealized feudal model. The former pattern, with its lack of development, would result in the settlement arrangements seen over much of west Somerset and Devon and for which there is other evidence of an early origin, while the latter may well be reflected in the sort of references cited from Domesday Book.

The detailed picture given by Domesday Book in 1086 could well be giving a 'single-shot' static view of a long dynamic process of reorganization and perhaps settlement change. It is likely that any changes filtered down from the highest levels of society and the richest estates to the rest. Thus the royal and ecclesiastical estates seem stable—the villages there may already have been in existence. In the middle ranks, great changes were taking place and had been over the 20 years before Domesday Book was compiled. The status of settlements and lands was being altered. Some sites were being abandoned and a rigid feudal system may have been applied. Villages may well have been created at this time (this will be discussed further below) and doubtless older settlements were abandoned; we last hear of some of them in Domesday Book. In other parts of the county such changes had not taken place. They may never have been applied over much of the west, but even if they were, the settlement pattern was not greatly affected.

Earlier work in Somerset suggested that the dispersed pattern of settlement in west Somerset was the result of 'Celtic' survival and that the more nucleated villages and hamlets of the east were 'Saxon' introductions. With current research suggesting the relatively late origin of some village plans in other parts of the country (Roberts 1979, Taylor 1981, Sheppard 1976) such a simplistic hypothesis is no longer tenable. In any case, arguments for continuity of estates and territories, if not settlement sites themselves (Jones 1961, 1979), mean that there is little room for massive expansion in settlement *numbers* (and hence the general pattern) over much of the country in late Saxon and medieval times. It becomes difficult to point to areas were *new* medieval colonization into *empty* areas occurred on any scale, and even more difficult to prove them either from documents, which rarely if ever give the date of *origin* of a settlement, or from place-name study, which has lost the faith in a reliable chronological development of names which was essential for its use in a study of settlement development.

That colonization did exist is certain, in parts of Yorkshire and north Warwickshire for example (Roberts 1976), but it is difficult in Somerset to point to areas which were filled up with new settlements in the pre-Conquest or early medieval periods. A case could be made however, for the establishment of seasonally-used sheilings along the coastal clay belt, developed on land drained and improved in the late Saxon to thirteenth-century period and there was probably some colonization around the Forests of Neroche and Selwood.

If, therefore, we reject the 'racial' and the 'colonization' models for an explanation of the different settlement types in Somerset, the 'feudalization' hypothesis has some attraction as a further idea for discussion. More thought is clearly needed but it may well be that Domesday Book has even more material for the settlement historian than has been realized.

The Origins of Settlement Plans

If we ask the questions why a particular village is in the form it is or why the plan is like it is and why the buildings and properties are arranged as they are, we run into great difficulties, but such questions have always been central to historical geography and recently, with the work of Brian Roberts, Christopher Taylor and others, considerable progress has been made. Beatrice Swainson hardly considered the matter in 1932 and there has been little research in Somerset until recently.

Some of the difficulties lie in the availability of data. There are only two cases in Somerset where an approximate foundation date can be guessed at for village plans. In Mells, Abbot Selwood of Glastonbury (1456–92) intended to lay out several streets in a replanning exercise south of the church. Leland describes the plan thus: 'Selwood Abbate of Glessen-byri seeing the welthines there of the people had thought to have reedified the townelet with mere houses of square stones to the figure of an Antonie Crosse; whereof yu deade be made but one streatelet' (Toulmin-Smith 1910). In the one street which was built, several fifteenth-century houses still remain (Fig. 8.3). The second case is Newton in Martock parish, where it seems likely that a planned extension was built on to the existing settlements over open-field strips; the settlement still has a regular plan created before 1327 (Bush 1978) (Fig. 8.3). But the general lack of documentation is in stark contrast to the available material for town developments. In Somerset, which has a strong Saxon urban background (Aston 1984), almost 40 places have some claim to urban status in the Middle Ages (Leech 1975, Aston and Leech 1977). In some cases the mechanisms of town foundation and the ways in which the sites were laid out are reasonably well documented and topographical study can aid understanding of plan development (Conzen 1960, 1968). Examples include Chard and Montacute in south Somerset and Stoford in the south-east. Many of these new medieval towns in Somerset, as elsewhere, were no different in size of plan layout to adjacent villages—the distinction being of course in their status as market or fair centres, sometimes with burgage tenure.

Similarly, the compilation of maps comes too late to record villages being laid out. In Somerset, the earliest map is of 1573, and although it shows the plan of Hazelgrove, a village now abandoned, as well as the site of Padel deserted village, it and its successors show villages already well established and developed. As elsewhere, there are no contemporary documents indicating village plantation in the county and there has not been enough archaeological excavation to give dates for all or part of any village plan. The researcher is

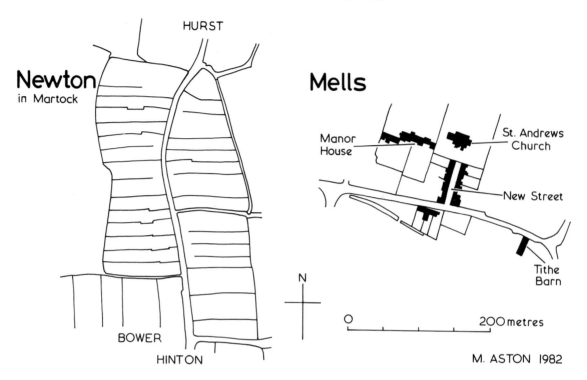

Fig. 8.3   Somerset: new medieval settlements

therefore driven to reconsider documentary and topographical evidence for village plan development.

One of the basic problems lies in terminology, both in the words used by medieval clerks and in our translation, and the implications put on the interpretation. For example, although most entries in the Somerset Domesday refer to manors, in the recent edition the use of the word 'villa' is translated as 'village' for Rode and 'town' for Glastonbury (Thorn and Thorn 1980). Similarly, the Victoria County History entry for Huish Episcopi speaks of the 'villages' of Littleney, Huish, Combe and Pibsbury confirmed by Edward the Confessor to Bishop Giso of Wells in 1065 but the term used in the document is not given.

Were all or any of these places *villages* in the eleventh century and if so, were they typical or exceptional in the local settlement pattern? It is only in 1284, with the compilation of Kirby's Quest, that we get clear distinctions made between towns (*burgus*) villages (*villata*) and hamlets (*hamel*) (Dickinson 1889).

Let us look therefore at the approaches of other researchers and see if any of their methods are helpful in Somerset. Again the earliest, most useful documentary

source is Domesday Book and, following on from the discussion above, we might expect it to be referring to established settlement plans and circumstances in which village planning may have taken place in the late eleventh century.

Evidence from Domesday Book?

There are three possible ways of dealing with the data of Domesday Book in looking for settlement plans at that date. Firstly, there is the possibility that places described as 'waste' in 1066 or 1086, but which are known to have existed at a later date, may have been refounded and replanned in the Norman perod. Such an approach has been used by June Sheppard for Yorkshire, where many places were laid waste by William's 'harrying of the north'. Very many settlements were replanned and redeveloped after this event and although June Sheppard is very cautious in her interpretation of the evidence, some replanning on formerly waste manors seems certain to have taken place; 'a chi-square statistical text of probability shows that, at the level of the individual vill, there is no significant degree of association between the two

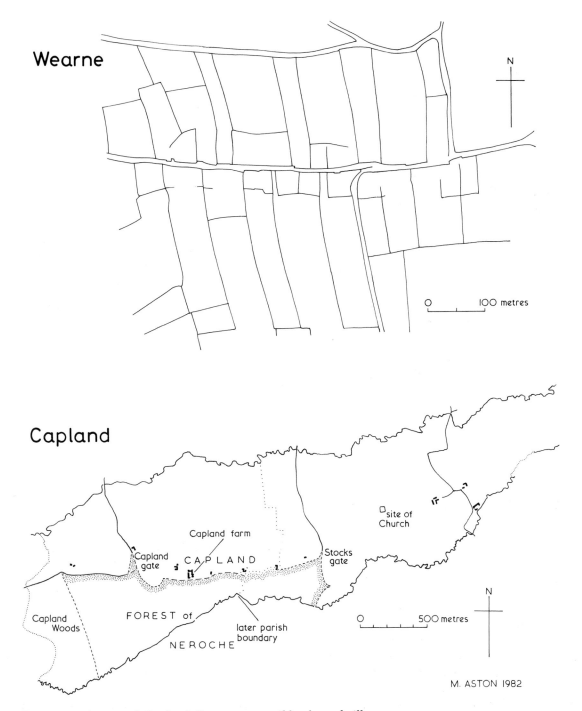

Fig. 8.4 *Wearne and Capland, Somerset: possible planned villages*

characteristics (harrying and planning). In view of the possible considerable differences between 1070 and 1086 distributions, this does not mean that regular plans were unrelated to 1070 waste; it does indicate, however, that no relationship can be demonstrated using the limited evidence available' (Sheppard 1976).

Bearing this caution in mind, we can look at the evidence for waste vills in Somerset in 1086. Seven places are recorded, most of them forming a group around Exmoor. It has been suggested that these represent a local catastrophe of poor climate, harvest or the like (Darby and Finn 1967, 189) and where they have survived only farmsteads remain today. However, two other places are described as waste and as they now exist as small hamlets, they might be expected to have been replanned after 1086. One such place is Wearne in Huish Episcopi (Fig. 8.4), which in 1086 had only one bordar and one serf. It was a small estate of two and a

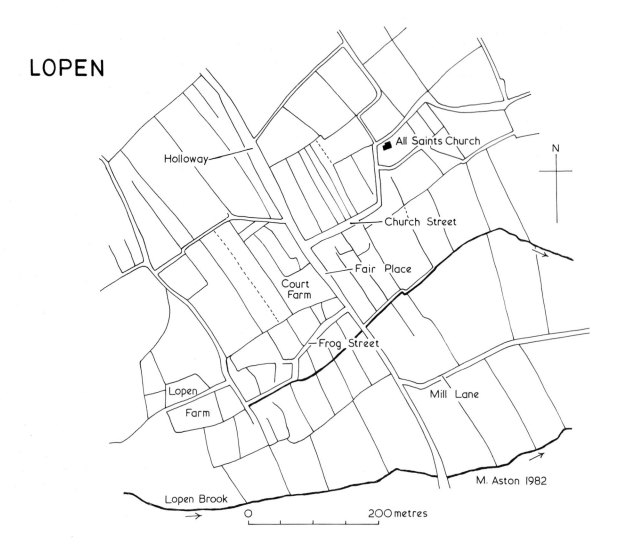

Fig. 8.5 Lopen township, Somerset

half virgates with half a plough, which had never paid tax. It was said to be worth 15 shillings but it was waste when its tenant, Robert of Auberville, received it. The present settlement is of prehistoric and Roman origin and has the characteristic earthworks of medieval settlement shrinkage (Leech 1976). However, the overall plan of the surviving plots and the outline of the settlement on the earliest surviving plans is very regular, being based on an east-west road with regular crofts running to the north and south. There is thus every indication that Wearne was planned at some time and the almost empty and waste condition of the place in the late eleventh century may have provided the opportunity for a new settlement to be laid out shortly afterwards. Capland in Beercrocombe provides the second example (Fig. 8.4). In 1086 half a hide of land

which had belonged to the king's manor of Curry Rivel had been added to Capland, but it was said that it had been laid waste. The main manor was only of one hide, with one plough and one bordar and one serf, although its value had increased from five to 20 shillings. Today, Capland consists of a few farms strung out along an east-west road which led to the former church. There is a persistent tradition of a village here (Hunt 1967) and the few remaining farms were certainly part of a more extensive settlement shown on nineteenth-century maps. On present evidence little more can be said but the general arrangement of the settlement and the former separate parochial status suggest that there may have been a planned village here as well. It is interesting to note that there are no references to waste places in the south of the county around Montacute, since in

1069 there had been a local Saxon insurrection against the Normans for despoiling the holy place of St Michael's Hill at Bishopston with the building of Montacute castle. Perhaps little damage had occurred or there had been time to rebuild; possibly the regular plan of Bishopston, the first urban development of Montacute, may be significant in this context.

The second use of Domesday Book data concerns those places with more than one manor or estate assessed for them. Such assessments could indicate different settlement elements within an overall plan, forming 'polyfocal' villages in the ways suggested by Christopher Taylor (1977). Very many places are recorded in 1086 in Somerset with more than one manor but a number can be dismissed from the discussion for various reasons. The three Adbers recorded near Mudford, for example, almost certainly relate to Over Adber, Nether Adber and possibly Hummer (Aston 1977); the two Bagboroughs are East and West Bagborough and the three Bradons are North, South and Goose Bradon in Curry Rivel parish. Stephen Morland has sorted out many of these examples for the county (Morland 1955, 1963). Other references, however, clearly indicate separate parts of the same estate and probably the same settlement. In some cases, as we have seen, even these entries are amalgamations and rationalizations of pre-Conquest holdings, but an example will serve to show that some, at least, might indicate separate parts of the same settlement and hence imply the existence of nucleated village settlements in 1086. At Lopen near South Petherton (Fig. 8.5) three estates are recorded in Domesday Book but it is not clear if one of these refers to Little Lopen, a deserted site nearby. Robert Dunning does suggest, however, that the other two manors reflect the separate parts of the present village: 'Church Street, formerly Higher Street... leads past the parsonage barn and the site of (the) manor house complex to the church... Frog Street, further south leads westwards to Lopen Farm and the nucleus of a secondary Domesday settlement' (Dunning, *V.C.H. Somerset* 1974, 164). Both these streets lead off from the medieval cross and fair site, the latter of which may have been ancient even when it was first recorded in 1201. The Domesday manors are traceable later because the estate at Lopen Farm was Templar property. The present village plan, therefore, clearly reflects the tenurial arrangements in 1086 but it is not possible to be sure that the relatively regular pattern of properties was in existence at that date.

Thirdly, if we are correct in suggesting the possibility that the consolidation of holdings indicated in Domesday Book might reflect changes in settlement form, then places with less manors recorded in 1086 than holdings in 1066 should be examined for evidence of agglomeration and/or nucleation of a larger number

of settlements into one or more villages. As has been indicated, consolidation of holdings into manors can be seen on a number of estates in Somerset which had been held by thanes in 1066 but which had been grouped under single tenants by 1086, and also by the holding of groups of earlier manors as single manorial units. Could this indeed indicate nucleation of formerly dispersed holdings or were they places in separate ownership within one settlement? Maitland says that thanes were landed proprietors whose main duties were military (1897, 201–6). We might expect the thanes, therefore, to be based in and supported by a feudal society; but conversely, if they were landholders with with special privileges, (especially 'to go to which lord they pleased') then references to thanes might, in fact, be an indication of free status and perhaps of separate (isolated farmstead?) settlements. If reference to thanes were to indicate the latter, then the administrative picture of Somerset in 1086 was very different to that of 1066, because in many instances a Norman tenant has replaced a number of earlier thanes. Could this development be indicated in processes of settlement agglomeration into nucleated villages with attendant abandonment of earlier farmsteads? Such a process would result in nucleated villages, presumably newly planned, where there had formerly been, perhaps, a scattered settlement. Pamela Allerston was able to show in the Vale of Pickering that numbers of Domesday vills were amalgamated into medieval villages. In some cases, such as Thornton Dale and Hutton Buscel, several centres were connected up with later infilled holdings, while elsewhere, as at Appleton le Moors and Spaunton, one or more earlier centres were abandoned at the foundation of a planted planned new village. The place-name 'oldfield' was noted in some cases to have referred to the infield around the earlier settlement (Allerston 1970).

Examples of the consolidation of holdings in Somerset include:

Dowlish—'To this manor have been added 7 hides which three thanes held before 1066 as three manors'. There is now one large village, the deserted site of West Dowlish, with the hamlet of Moolham.

Chaffcombe—'To this manor have been added 1 hide and 3 virgates of land. Two thanes held them before 1066 as two manors'.

Donyatt—'Adolf, Saewin and Dunstan held it as three manors before 1066'.

Curry Mallet—two estates; Roger of Courseulles held all these lands as one manor.

Knowle St Giles—'Godric and Aelfric held it before 1066... Eleigh has been added to this manor. Browning held it as a manor before 1066'.

In most of these examples and others, there is only a single village on the estate in question in the Middle

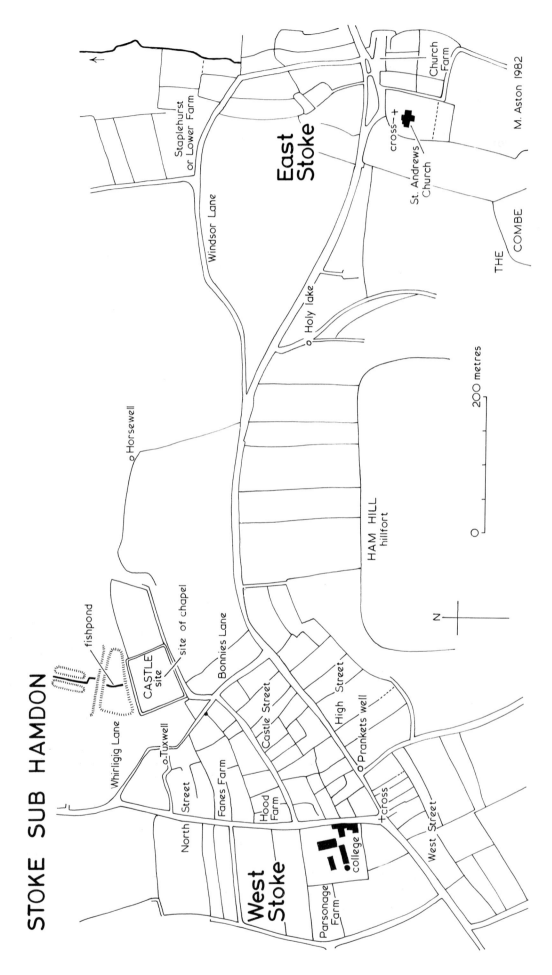

Fig. 8.6 *Stoke sub Hamdon, Somerset: West and East Stoke*

The SEAVINGTONS

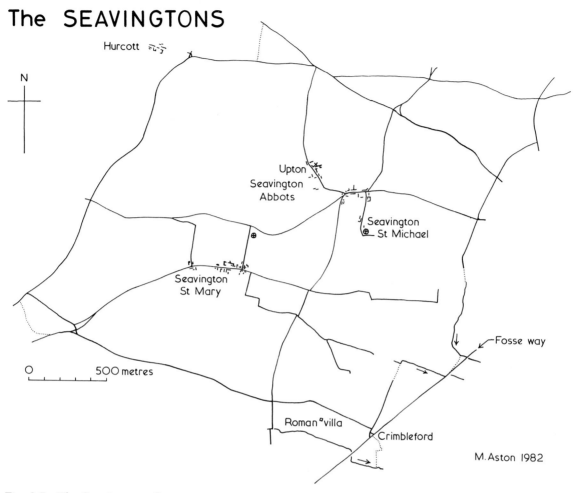

Fig. 8.7 *The Seavingtons, Somerset*

Ages. Also in this part of Somerset, the area east of the Forest of Neroche, such consolidation might reflect recent colonization and we may be seeing reorganization of relatively recently created settlements. All this land belonged to much more important and wealthier estates, especially royal estates, away to the east, at South Petherton, Martock and Crewkerne. There is other slight evidence for 'new' developments here which will be discussed below (Sun division).

Perhaps the clearest case of consolidation, however, is at Stoke sub Hamdon (Fig. 8.6). Here there are now two main villages of East and West Stoke (the latter now the main village). There was another settlement on Ham Hill, called South Ameldon or Suth Meldon, possibly a quarrying hamlet, but this is now deserted. In 1066, however, there were eight separate holdings held by thanes; these had been reduced to three manors by 1086. Not only do the present two villages have relatively regular plans, but because of the disposition of known medieval structures in them, we can be more

certain of their medieval topography than for many settlements. At West Stoke there was formerly a castle, a collegiate chapel and a fishpond of the Beauchamp family and at the other end of the the village a College of priests, while the parish church was at East Stoke.

Another example, not so much indicated by Domesday data but by place-name evidence, is the Seavington villages (Fig. 8.7). There are now three villages called Seavington on the estate, Seavington St Michael (or Denys), Seavington St Mary (or Vaus) and Seavington Abbots (or Upton). There are also two other hamlets, Hurcott, which has been added from Ilton parish, and the lost Crimbleford.

The place-name, however, indicates seven settlements (Seven hampton), so that even if the Roman villa site is taken as one, and each of the existing settlements represents another, there are still two lost late Saxon settlements on the estate. The villages of Seavington St Michael, Seavington St Mary and Hurcott are still very regularly aligned on east-west streets, while at

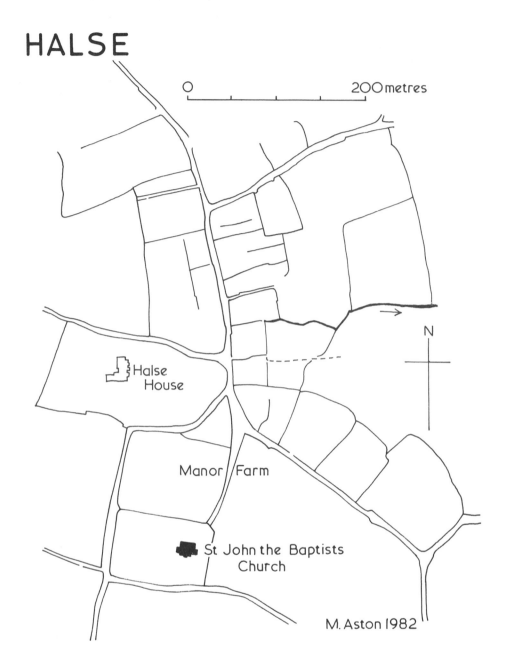

HALSE

0   200 metres

Halse
House

Manor Farm

St John the Baptists
Church

M. Aston 1982

N

Fig. 8.8   Halse, Somerset

Seavington St Michael and Seavington St Mary, there are noticeably detached churches which are of early medieval foundation, at least.

The name 'oldfield' (and oldland), to which very little attention has been paid in the past, occurs a number of times in the county at, for example, East Pennard (1265), Halse (1327), Beercrocombe or Capland (1327) and Mells (1840). Each of these needs to be more fully investigated but at Halse there is a very regular village with a large detached church; the estate belonged to the Knights Hospitallers, well known for settlement plantation in France and elsewhere (Fig. 8.8). Beercrocombe lies within the area east of Neroche Forest referred to above; Capland has already been discussed. No doubt further 'oldfield' names exist but as yet Somerset lacks a Place-Name Society volume, thus making any such work on field- and place-names extremely difficult.

Periods of Village Planning and Plantation

The late eleventh century is not the only time when villages might be expected to have been planted and new settlement plans laid down. The possibility of the reorganization of such estates as those of the Crown, Glastonbury Abbey and the Bishop of Wells in the pre-Conquest period has already been hinted at. This might explain why Domesday Book has relatively simple accounts for these estates. With the major landowners in close touch with developments in northern and western Europe, and having the power and wealth to effect such changes as they felt necessary on their estates, it is perhaps not such an unlikely possibility that village planning and plantation did occur earlier. There are several occasions in the pre-Conquest period, in Wessex at least, when such developments could have taken place.

Under Alfred and the other Wessex kings many changes were engineered. The creation of *burhs,* and the means to support them from estates, had far-reaching implications, not least on the development of trade and urban activities, but the possibility that there were changes in the countryside as well, particularly on the more important royal and ecclesiastical estates, seems not to have been considered, since documentary evidence seems to be lacking. Many of the developments alluded to above could have taken place in the ninth and tenth centuries, especially as Somerset had a high proportion of important Wessex royal estates, centred on places like Somerton, Cheddar, Taunton, Cannington, Carhampton, South Petherton, North Petherton, Martock and Crewkerne. Similarly, the refounding and reorganization of many monasteries in the tenth century would also have provided for, or even necessitated, the reorganization of ecclesiastical estates and perhaps settlements. Dunstan, architect of the tenth-century monastic reform, was, after all, Abbot of Glastonbury. The abbey possessed estates which were later among the best organized in the county, with very regularly planned villages. Dunstan would have been in touch with developments in Europe and could be expected to have applied good estate management ideas to the Glastonbury estates. The Viking raids themselves, with their destruction of land and property, might also have provided opportunities for change.

In the post-Conquest period there were numerous occasions when warfare might have necessitated new settlements. One such period was the aftermath of the anarchy and civil war between King Stephen and the empress Matilda. The West Country was deeply involved in this, as is indicated by the *Gesta Stephani* and William of Malmesbury's *Chronicle*. There was much local destruction and damage in Somerset and although there are no lists of destroyed or damaged settlements, the Pipe Rolls for 1155–6 suggest degrees of damage between counties. Somerset figures low in these assessments but Professor Davis (pers. comm.) thinks that this does not reflect accurately the large-scale damage that must have been inflicted on the country in the 1140s. Places within a few miles of the sites of battles and castle sieges might be expected to have suffered particularly. A number of motte and bailey castles, especially in the east of the county, were probably in use at this time (Fig. 8.9). The *Gesta Stephani* describes some of the conditions around Bristol at the time of this civil war, with the men of the city rampaging over the local countryside: 'yokes of oxen, flocks of sheep, whatever tempting object either their eye saw, or their proud heart desired, they seized and took away, sold or consumed. When whatever was within their reach and compass has been bought into the pit of destruction and *utterly laid waste'* (my italics) (Potter 1976). M. W. C. Davis (1903) shows that in the period 1138–48 Somerset (with Gloucestershire and Monmouthshire) was the centre of the power of the Earl of Gloucester, chief supporter of the empress Matilda against Stephen. Somerset marched with lands held by men loyal to Stephen, or taken over by him, in Wiltshire, Dorset and the Cotswolds, and we can thus expect disturbances to be in the east of the county. It is here, in a part of the county with many villages, that destruction of early settlements would have occurred, destruction which could have provided a necessity for change. We have perhaps underestimated such destruction in the mid-twelfth century; Davis describes the type of warfare at that time: 'during the siege, the attacking army lived by plunder, and usually before it withdrew, destroyed all the means of subsistence which were still to be found in the neighbourhood. The garrisons, both the castle and the counter forts, maintained themselves by forays in which they ranged further and further afield. *Consequently every castle which had been the object of attack stood at the centre of desolate country'* (my italics) (Davis 1903, 634).

It is difficult to show such effects for Somerset but some indication of the amount of destruction is given in the first extant Pipe Roll of Henry II in 1155–6, where the figures for the Danegeld in each shire give some indication of relative damage. Somerset comes some way down the list but the *Gesta Stephani* for 1143 for the Thames Valley and the south-west counties states 'You might behold villages of famous names standing empty because the country people... had left them' (Davis 1903, 635). It is reckoned that nearly one-fifth of Somerset was waste in the 1150s.

We have to reckon, therefore, with widespread disruption in Somerset in the 1140s and 1150s, perhaps mainly in the north and east. This had been put right by the eighth year of Henry II, when little waste is referred to. Even if 'six years of ordered government had sufficed to restore prosperity' (Davis 1903, 641), there had been

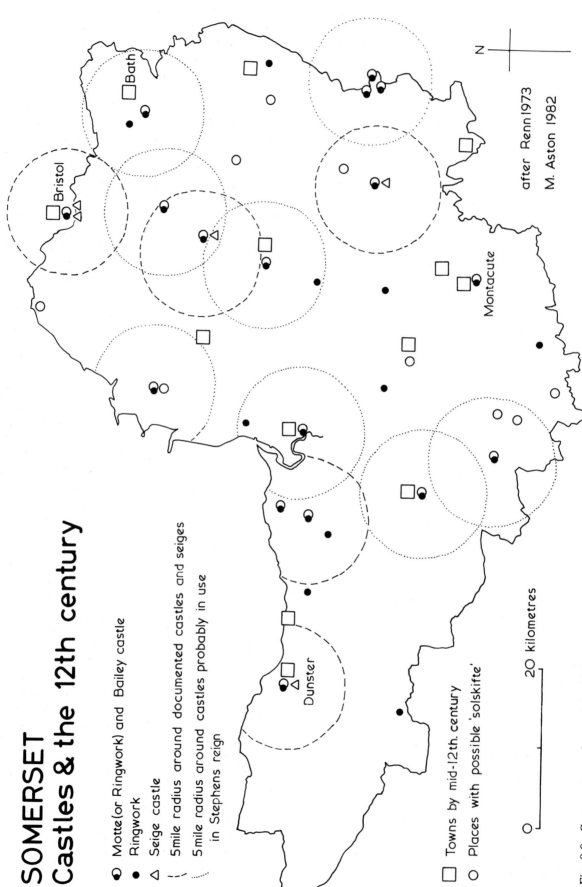

SOMERSET
Castles & the 12th century

◑ Motte(or Ringwork) and Bailey castle
● Ringwork
△ Seige castle
–– 5mile radius around documented castles and seiges
⋯ 5mile radius around castles probably in use
in Stephens reign

□ Towns by mid-12th. century
○ Places with possible 'solskifte'

Bath

Bristol

Montacute

Dunster

N

after Renn1973
M. Aston 1982

20 kilometres

Fig. 8.9 Somerset: castles and the 12th century

ample opportunity and necessity over the previous 15 years and more for considerable changes in the settlement forms of the county. How many of the settlements near castles in the east and north of the county could have been damaged, perhaps abandoned and possibly resited and replanned in the mid-twelfth century?

Such redevelopment of settlements is frequently related in the north of England in the twelfth century to the existence of planned and regulated field systems. Many of these can be traced from the existence of land division according to the passage of the sun over individual holdings and strips in the common fields and hence called 'sun division', (or *solskifte* after its recognition and study in Scandinavia (Homans 1941)). A great deal of further work needs to be done on this but in 1961 Sölve Göransson published a map of its possible incidence in Britain with 13 places indicated in Somerset (Fig. 8.9). If these places *could* be shown to have used 'sun division' in their field systems, and the link between planned villages and such regulated field systems could be shown to clearly exist, then solskifte might prove to be very useful evidence in predicting the existence of planned regulated villages. Of the 12 possible settlements (one, Badlesmere, is probably not in Somerset), two cannot be identified from a number of places with the same name (Wyke, Knoll) and one is unintelligible (Yuest). The others are Lidmarsh (+) (*) (Chaffcombe), Wick Perham (*) (Curry Rivel), Dunpole (+) (Ilminster), Lamyatt (*), Portishead, Stratton on the Fosse (*), Horton (+), Locking (*) and Nunney (*). Each of these places needs much further research but several have regular plans (*) and three (+) are in the zone of possible early medieval colonization east of the Forest of Neroche which has already been referred to. Clearly, the relevance of these settlements to any discussion of village plan origins and any relationship to village planning (and the relevance of 'sun division') must await more detailed general research by historians on *solskifte* in England.

The 1327 Lay Subsidy

Finally, there is the evidence of the 1327 lay subsidy and its implications for settlement study (Dickinson 1889). The use of subsidies for demographic studies has been widespread but only in a few cases have the surnames contained in them been used in settlement study (Allerston 1970, 100; Yates 1961).

The 1327 lay subsidy for Somerset contains the earliest detailed list of places in the county and this writer has found it very useful in the implications for settlement distribution and form. Under each place or manor there is a list of persons paying the subsidy. Most have surnames indicating either occupation or a place-name (while others seem unintelligible). Since in the early fourteenth century surnames are still evolving and

probably represent actual employment and places of current or recent domicile, they can be used with confidence in an analysis of the subsidy. In many cases the place-names indicated by such surnames tally neatly with farmsteads and hamlets near to the main place or manor entry. Such surnames can thus be used to give some general idea of which settlements are in existence over the whole county in the early fourteenth century.

In the west of the county there is a close relationship between surnames indicating places and farmsteads on the ground (Fig. 8.10). In Withypoole parish, for example, although the entries are included under nearby Exton, almost all the existing farms seem to have existed as separate holdings in 1327. Elsewhere the list of surnames indicates some places no longer in existence. Field-names from the Tithe maps have been used to locate some of these places and fieldwork has revealed earthworks of such abandoned sites. The implication from the 1327 lay subsidy for the west and centre of the county, then, is of a persistent settlement pattern with a high correlation between farmsteads on the ground today and surnames in the early fourteenth century.

Thus the present settlement pattern as indicated in place-names is early medieval in origin at least. Two pieces of evidence suggest it may be older. Firstly, before Wimblehall Reservoir was built, a farmstead called Hurscombe (in Brompton Regis) was excavated by Peter Leach for CRAAGS (now The Western Archaeological Trust). This farm seems to be indicated by the reference to Adam de Hurclescombe in 1327 and it has been abandoned since the early 1900s. The excavations indicated a farm site back to at least the twelfth century, around 200 years earlier than 1327.

Secondly, in west Somerset, as elsewhere in Devon and Cornwall, at least part of the Roman and post-Roman settlement pattern was in the form of 'ring-works' ('rounds' in Corwall)—small farmsteads with encircling banks and ditches. A number of these are recorded in west Somerset and many more have been found as a result of Richard McDonnell's survey of air photographs of Exmoor (McDonnell 1980). None has so far been excavated in Somerset but in a few cases they seem to be associated with medieval farmsteads. At Bagley and Sweetworthy (Luccombe), for example, two medieval farms are associated with two ring-works. Bagley is recorded on 1086, but it was not until an excellent air picture was taken by John White that the adjacent ring-work was recognized, while at Sweetworthy the fine ring-work has been known for years. During recent clearance of bracken and gorse, a previously unidentified deserted farmstead was found next to Sweetworthy. Thus, in this upland area north of Dunkery Beacon, the highest part of Exmoor, we seem to be seeing, perhaps, continuity of land use (infield/outfield?) from prehistoric to medieval times,

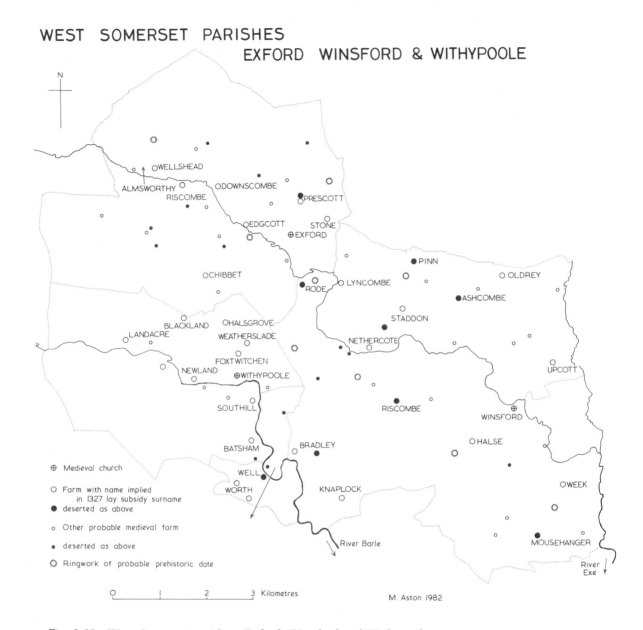

WEST SOMERSET PARISHES
EXFORD WINSFORD & WITHYPOOLE

N

OWELLSHEAD

ALMSWORTHY   ODOWNSCOMBE
RISCOMBE   PRESCOTT

OEDGCOTT   STONE
            ⊕EXFORD

OCHIBBET   ● PINN

        RODE O LYNCOMBE   O OLDREY
                                ●ASHCOMBE

                        STADDON
        OHALSGROVE
BLACKLAND
LANDACRE   WEATHERSLADE   NETHERCOTE
        FOXTWITCHEN
NEWLAND ⊕WITHYPOOLE   UPCOTT

SOUTHILL   ● RISCOMBE
                                ⊕ WINSFORD

        BATSHAM   O HALSE
        WELL
        WORTH   BRADLEY   OWEEK

            KNAPLOCK

                River Barle   ● MOUSEHANGER

                                River
                                Exe

⊕ Medieval church

O Farm with name implied
   in 1327 lay subsidy surname
● deserted as above

o Other probable medieval farm

• deserted as above

✧ Ringwork of probable prehistoric date

0   1   2   3 Kilometres   M. Aston 1982

Fig. 8.10   West Somerset parishes: Exford, Winsford and Withypoole

with only slight shifts of settlement site. The settlement form seems to have been the same—isolated farmstead—although in earlier periods slight defences of banks and ditches were felt advisable. Other examples in west Somerset suggest medieval farm sites continuing on the same site as earlier farmsteads. At Twitchen (Oare) and Spangate (Wootton Courtney), deserted farm sites exist apparently inside ring-works.

If the present settlement pattern and forms in west Somerset can be seen to have some connection with pre-Conquest sites and distribution, and if this is to some

extent indicated by the surnames in 1327, can the lay subsidy be used to say something of the origin of settlements in the east of the county? As has been indicated, settlement in the east of the county is more nucleated and Roger Leech has suggested that since it was a more Romanized area, the pattern may relate to Romano-British settlements. Surnames in 1327 for this area clearly indicate something of nucleated settlement. There are references to 'townsend' and to localities which would have been recognizable to people at the time, for example

West Chinnock   Nicholas atte Boghe
                         Johanne and Petro in le Lane
                         Johanne atte Ford

Chiselborough   Nicholas Biweye
                        Roberto atte Welle
                        Matilda atte Halle
                        Christina atte Halewey

Norton sub Hamdon   Johanne atte Water
                                Willelmo in the Lane
                                Matilda atte Mulle

Sandford Arundel   Waltero atte Tounesende

There are also, however, numbers of settlements implied in the surnames. In many cases these can be correlated with hamlets and farmsteads in existence today or well known from the research into deserted settlements. An example is Kingsbury Episcopi (Fig. 8.11), a large manor belonging to the Bishop of Bath and Wells in the middle of the county. Surnames in 1327 indicate the hamlets of

Rodwell   Roberto de Radewelle

Southay   Johanne de Southeye
              Willelmo Bysoutheye

Lake   Thoma atte Lake
        Phyllippo atte Lake

Wick (deserted)   Ade atte Wyche

However, in a number of cases surnames indicate places which cannot now be related (at least locally) to the main entry. It is clear from the surnames that there was both emigration and immigration, since a place is implied by a surname listed under an adjacent manor, and in the towns many surnames suggest long-distance movement of a few people. But in general there is a high correlation between surnames and places existing, or formerly existing, in the vicinities of the main entry. In one case, Kingsdon, near Ilchester, two Wick names—Roberto atte Wyche and Willelmo atte Wyche—do not refer to an existing settlement but the Tithe map shows that many fields in the empty southern half of the parish have Witch names and it is in this area that the implied settlement of Wyche must have existed. An example of many topographical surnames referring to unlocated settlements is Lovington (Fig. 8.11), where there is today a very nucleated village with farms in use and areas of abandoned settlement earthworks. In 1327 all the 11 surnames refer to places and none of them can be located in the parish. Even allowing for the probability of names referring to out-parish places (Stone in West Bradley, the adjacent parish) and others indicating locations in the main settlement (atte Yatte, atte Pole or atte Stone), there are still eight names which could be expected to refer to six places. Where are Arderne,

Wellesleghe, Raleye (two names), Cotteleghe (two names), Wyke and Welde?

In the east of the county, it can be seen then that many more places may be referred to in 1327 and here the settlement pattern may appear more nucleated now than it was formerly. Several difficulties arise if this is the case and these can only be solved by further research. Firstly, since the early fourteenth century was a period when surnames were still evolving and may still have had relevance to people's occupations and origins, can they be relied upon to indicate settlements? Secondly, since elsewhere in the county the surnames *do* seem to indicate settlement, were there many more hamlets and villages in 1327 in east Somerset than are indicated on the ground today? Is it possible, indeed, that the surnames refer to places which had already gone by that date, in a process of agglomeration or nucleation associated with village development and perhaps planning? This process occurred earlier elsewhere. June Sheppard suggests that the largest group of planned villages in the north relates to the late eleventh and early twelfth centuries, while smaller groups may relate to the pre-Conquest period and post-1150. Brian Roberts has found examples of the remodelling of villages taking place up to the sixteenth century (Sheppard 1976). Is it possible to envisage surnames in 1327 retaining the names of places that may have been abandoned a century or more before in Somerset or is the late thirteenth to early fourteenth century a period in which some sites were being abandoned in the county and some villages were emerging?

Future Research

In this paper the writer has speculated on the periods and mechanisms by which the medieval settlement pattern and the types of settlement then in use might have originated and developed. Considerably more research needs to be undertaken in Somerset before the hypotheses suggested can be rejected or developed further. In particular, there is a need for much more historical analysis of the mass of available documentation. The large collections of records relating to the Glastonbury Abbey estates and the properties of the bishops of Bath and Wells must contain useful material. The detailed examination of the county's place-names and Saxon charter material, being so ably undertaken by Michael Costen, will inevitably be of considerable assistance in settlement studies. Further fieldwork, paying great attention to every small detail, must continue but, sooner rather than later, several settlements will need to be systematically excavated. It is perhaps not yet possible to indicate which ones should be selected but one of the deserted farm sites in a possible prehistoric ring-work in the west of the county

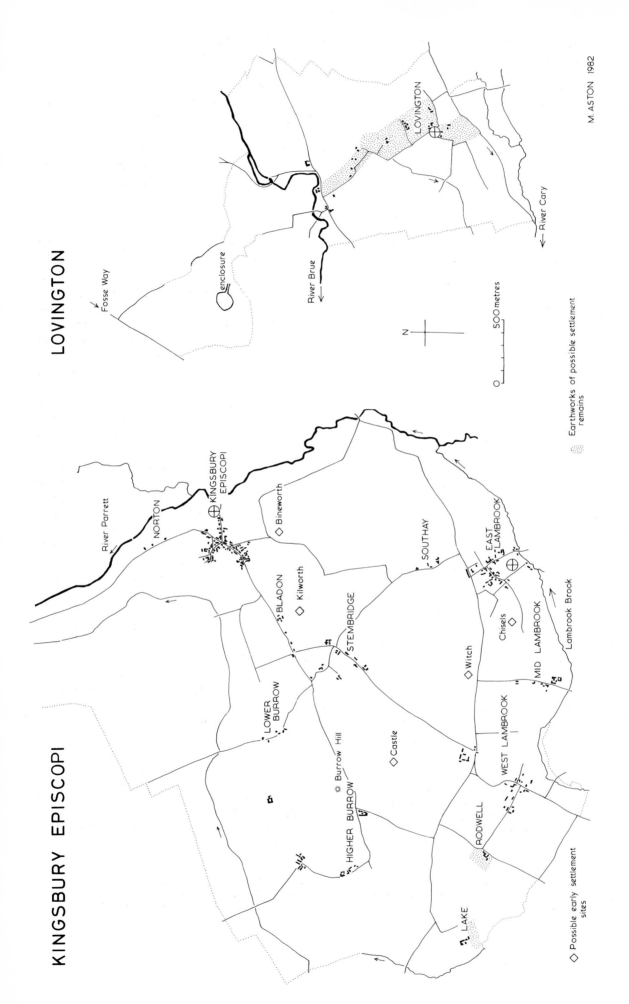

KINGSBURY EPISCOPI

LOVINGTON

M. ASTON 1982

Fosse Way

enclosure

River Brue

River Cary

N

500 metres

◇ Possible early settlement sites

Earthworks of possible settlement remains

River Parrett

NORTON

KINGSBURY EPISCOPI

◇ Bineworth

BLADON

◇ Kilworth

LOWER BURROW

STEMBRIDGE

Burrow Hill

SOUTHAY

HIGHER BURROW

◇ Castle

◇ Witch

EAST LAMBROOK

Chisels ◇

MID LAMBROOK

Lambrook Brook

WEST LAMBROOK

RODWELL

LAKE

LOVINGTON

Fig. 8.11 Kingsbury Episcopi and Lovington, Somerset

would be a possibility; in the east a well-documented, surviving village should perhaps be selected.

Some settlement research strategy has already begun to emerge in the county. The need to define more closely the types of settlements in late Roman and post-Roman times is important. Was the pattern mainly one of hamlets or were there villages and how were they organized? Was Catsgore (Somerton) for example, a village in Roman times and was it typical? (Leech 1982). Harold Uhlig (1961) has argued that the primeval settlement pattern of western Europe was in the form of hamlets with infield/outfield field systems. Is it possible to see this in the archaeological record? It seems to be so at such sites as Houndtor on Dartmoor (Devon) where three or four farmsteads worked an extensive infield with limitless outfield beyond (Beresford 1979). Are Bagley and Sweetworthy such examples in Somerset?

In view of Uhlig's work, we need to know for Somerset how extensive were such early (and perhaps primitive or underdeveloped?) settlement forms as the *clachan* (or Uhlig's *drubbel*), along with their fields. There is at least the possibility, one which this writer finds attractive, that over much of the county the hamlet with its infield was the 'normal' settlement and that this was 'developed' into the more conventional village with its open fields later on, in some areas and on certain estates. Much of the evidence assembled above could be viewed in this way; it could indicate greater settlement development in the east with earlier and/or less developed forms in the west.

This suggestion needs to be viewed in the light of the research of Glanville Jones and others into earlier estate structure. Somerset is third only to Kent and Worcestershire in the number of Anglo-Saxon charters available, and these should enable the relationship between multiple and composite estates and their constituent settlements to be clarified. Related to this is the recognition of a *hierarchy* within settlement structure, something appreciated more by the prehistoric archaeologist than the researcher in the post-Roman period. Some places have always had a higher *status* than others and may turn out to be the earliest villages in the landscape, founded perhaps because of the more varied functions which needed to be undertaken at estate centres, particularly those of estate administration, religious provision and perhaps exchange (i.e. the marketing of goods).

In the post-Conquest period, this analysis is easier but we still lack the detailed analysis of estates (or 'baronies') which might indicate whether the policies of particular landlords were affecting the way settlements developed. Again, June Sheppard's work in Yorkshire suggests very strongly that this was the case.

Finally, there is much local topographical research to be undertaken. Place-names indicating 'newness' or 'oldness' need more attention—they are at least indicating something of a chronology. Where this can be related to settlements like Sevenhampton, containing reference to the *number* of places in existence at some date, real progress should be possible. But equally important must be the metrological analysis of village plans. They need to be quantified, not only in the categories being developed by Brian Roberts (which enable order to emerge from apparent chaos and provide thought stimulation), but also objectively as in June Sheppard's measurement of plot sizes in Yorkshire and the relationship of these data to early fiscal arrangements (Sheppard 1974).

It is a truism that the study of the English landscape must progress on a multi-disciplinary basis and increasingly this is happening—we are all becoming at least apprentices in a number of trades. What is also needed, however, is a greater rigour in the use of the material in each of these disciplines. If the origin and development of settlements was an easy problem to sort out it would have been solved a long time ago. Although the amount of data has increased over the years, it will not be larger quantities of information which will solve the problems discussed here. Our approach, the breadth of latitudinal thought, and the degrees to which we can develop new concepts (see for example, Randsborg 1980; Hodges 1982) will in the end lead to a greater understanding of settlement evolution.

Acknowledgements

I am grateful to my colleagues at Bristol University, Dr. Joseph Bettey, Michael Costen and Robert Machin for much helpful discussion, and to Mrs. Suzie Sampson for typing an impossible script.

References

Allerston, P. 1970: English village development: findings from the Pickering district of North Yorkshire. *Transactions of the Institute of British Geographers* 51, 95–109.

Aston, M. A. 1977: Deserted settlements in Mudford parish, Yeovil. *Somerset Archaeology and Natural History* 121, 41–53.

Aston, M. A. and Leech, R. H. 1977: *Historic Towns in Somerset—Archaeology and Planning* (Committee for Rescue Archaeology in Avon, Gloucestershire and Somerset).

Aston, M. A. 1982: The medieval pattern 1000–1500 AD. In Aston M. A. and Burrow, I. (editors) 1982, 123–33.

Aston, M. A. and Burrow, I. (editors) 1982: *The Archaeology of Somerset* (Taunton, Somerset County Council).

Aston, M. A. 1984: Anglo-Saxon towns in Somerset. In Haslam, J. (editor) 1984, 167–201.

Beresford, G. 1979: Three deserted medieval settlements on Dartmoor: a report on the late E. Marie Minter's excavations. *Medieval Archeology* 23, 98–158.

Beresford, M. W. 1954: *The Lost Villages of England* (London, Lutterworth Press).

Beresford, M. W. and Hurst, J. G. (editors) 1971: *Deserted Medieval Villages: Studies* (London, Lutterworth Press).

Burrow, I. 1981: *Hillfort and Hilltop Settlement in Somerset in the First to Eight Centuries AD* (Oxford, British Archaeological Reports 91).

Bush, R. J. E. 1978: Martock. In Dunning, R. W. (editor) 1978, 78–109.

Conzen, M. R. G. 1960: Alnwick, Northumberland. A study in town plan analysis. *Institute of British Geographers* 27.

Conzen, M. R. G. 1968: The use of town plans in the study of urban history. In Dyos, H. J. (editor) 1968, 113–30.

Darby, H. C. and Finn, R. Welldon 1967: *The Domesday Geography of South West England* (Cambridge, Cambridge University Press).

Davis, H. W. C. 1903: The anarchy of Stephen's reign. *English Historical Review* 18, 630–41.

Dickinson, F. H. 1889: Kirby's quest for Somerset. *Somerset Record Society* 3.

Duby, G. 1968: *Rural Economy and Country Life in the Medieval West* (London, Edward Arnold).

Dunning, R. W. (editor) 1974, 1978: *The Victoria History of the Counties of England. A History of the County of Somerset*, Vols. 3 and 4 (The University of London Institute of Historical Research).

Dyos, H. J. (editor) 1968: *The Study of Urban History* (London, Edward Arnold).

Ellison, A. 1976: *Villages Survey : an interim report* (Committee for Rescue Archaeology in Avon, Gloucestershire and Somerset. Occasional Paper No. 1).

Ellison, A. B. 1984: *Medieval Villages Survey. A Survey of the Archaeological Implications of Development within 93 Surviving Medieval Villages in South-east Somerset* (Bristol, Western Archaeological Trust).

Everett, S. 1968: The Domesday geography of three Exmoor parishes. *Somerset Archaeology and Natural History* 112, 54–60.

Fowler, P. J. (editor) 1972: *Archaeology and the Landscape, Essays for L. V. Grinsell* (London, John Baker).

Fowler, P. J. 1982: Introduction. In Aston, M. A. and Burrow, I. (editors) 1982, 1–3.

Göransson, S. 1961: Regular open-field pattern in England and Scandinavian *Solskifte. Geografiska Annaler* 43, 80–104.

Haslam, J. (editor) 1984: *Anglo-Saxon Towns in Southern England* (London and Chichester, Phillimore).

Hodges, R. 1982: *Dark Age Economics—the Origins of Towns and Trade AD 600–1000* (London, Duckworth).

Homans, G. C. 1941: *English Villagers of the Thirteenth Century* (Cambridge, Massachusetts, Harvard University Press).

Hoskins, W. G. 1965: *Provincial England—Essays in Social and Economic History* (London, Macmillan and Co.).

Hunt, T. J. 1967: Capland—deserted medieval village. *Notes and Queries for Somerset and Dorset* 28, part 286, 325, September 1967.

Jones, G. R. J. 1961: Early territorial organisation in England and Wales. *Geografiska Annaler* 43, 174–81.

Jones, G. R. J. 1979: Multiple estates and early settlement. In Sawyer, P. H. (editor) 1979.

Leach, P. J. 1984: *Ilchester Excavations Volume 1, 1974–75* (Bristol, Western Archaeolological Trust).

Leech, R. H. 1975: *Small Medieval Towns in Avon—Archaeology and Planning* (Committee for Rescue Archaeology in Avon, Gloucestershire and Somerset).

Leech, R. H. 1976: Romano-British and medieval settlement at Wearne, Huish Episcopi. *Somerset Archaeology and Natural History* 120, 45–50.

Leech, R. H. 1977: *Romano-British Rural Settlement in South Somerset and North Dorset* (Unpublished PhD thesis, University of Bristol).

Leech, R. H, 1982: *Excavations at Catsgore 1970–73—a Romano-British Village* (Bristol, Western Archaeological Trust).

Limbrey, S. and Evans, J. G. (editors) 1978: *The effect of Man on the Landscape: the Lowland zone* (Council for British Archaeology Research Report 21).

Maitland, F. W. 1897: *Domesday Book and Beyond, Three Essays in the Early History of England* (Cambridge, Cambridge University Press).

McDonnell, R. 1980: Report on the survey of aerial photography in the CRAAGS region (Unpublished typescript, Committee for Rescue Archaeology in Avon, Gloucestershire and Somerset).

Morland, S. C. 1955: Some Domesday manors. *Proceedings of Somersetshire Archaeological and Natural History Society* 100, 34–48.

Morland, S. C. 1963: Further notes on Somerset Domesday *Proceedings of the Somersetshire Archaeological and Natural History Society* 108, 94–8.

Potter, K. R. (editor) 1976: *Gesta Stephani* (Oxford, Oxford University Press).

Randsborg, K. R. 1980: *The Viking Age in Denmark—the Formation of a State* (London, Duckworth).

Rahtz, P. A. 1979: *The Saxon and Medieval Palaces at Cheddar* (Oxford, British Archaeological Reports 65).

Rahtz, P. A. and Fowler, P. J. 1972 Somerset AD 400–700. In Fowler, P. J. (editor): 1972.

Roberts, B. K. 1976: The historical geography of moated homesteads: the Forest of Arden, Warwickshire. *Transactions of the Birmingham and Warwickshire Archaeological Society* 88 (1966–77), 61–70.

Roberts, B. K. 1979: Village plans in Britain. In *Récherches de Géographie Rurale, Hommage au Professeur Frans Dussart* (Numéro hors série du Bulletin de la Société géographique de Liège, Liège) 34–49.

Sawyer, P. H. (editor) 1979: *Medieval Settlement, Continuity and Change* (London, Edward Arnold).

Sheppard, J. A. 1974: Metrological analysis of regular village plans in Yorkshire. *Agricultural History Review* 22, 118–35.

Sheppard, J. A. 1976: Medieval village planning in northern England: some evidence from Yorkshire. *Journal of Historical Geography* 2, 3–20.

Swainson, B. M. 1932: *A Study of Rural Settlement in Somerset* (Unpublished MA thesis, University of London (External Degree).

Swainson, B. M. 1935: Rural settlement in Somerset. *Geography* 31 112–24.

Taylor, C. C. 1977: Polyfocal settlement and the English village. *Medieval Archaeology* 21, 189–93.

Taylor, C. C. 1978: Aspects of village mobility in medieval and later times. In Limbrey, S. and Evans, J. G. (editors) 1978.

Taylor, C. C. 1981: Saxon Remains, Medieval and later settlement. In Royal Commission on Historical Monuments (England) *An Inventory of the Historical Monuments in the County of Northampton*, Vol. 3 (London, Her Majesty's Stationery Office).

Thorpe, H. 1964: Rural settlement. In Watson, J. Wreford, with Sissons, J. B. (editors) 1964, 358–78.

Thorn, F. and Thorn, C. (editors) 1980: *Domesday Book 8, Somerset* (London, and Chichester, Phillimore).

Toulmin-Smith, L. (editor) 1910: *The Itinerary of John Leland in or about the Years 1535–1543* (London, George Bell and Son).

Uhlig, H. 1961: Old hamlets with infield and outfield systems in Western and Central Europe. *Geografiska Annaler* 44, 285–312.

Watson, J. Wreford with Sissons, J. B. (editors) 1964: *The British Isles, a Systematic Geography* (London, Nelson).

White, L. 1962: *Medieval Technology and Social Change* (Oxford, Oxford University Press).

Yates, E. M. 1961: A study of settlement patterns. *Field Studies* 1, part 3, 65–84.

9. Medieval Oxfordshire Villages and their Topography: a Preliminary Discussion

C. J. Bond

This paper reviews the progress of research on medieval rural settlement in Oxfordshire over the past quarter-century and attempts to assess the present state of knowledge. The question of village origins and the relationship between Romano-British, Anglo-Saxon and medieval settlement patterns is briefly considered. Medieval village plans are then discussed. A considerable variety of forms is represented, from complex polyfocal arrangements to simple linear plans whose regularity seems to imply seigneurial intervention. Central 'core' areas with a well-marked perimeter are a recurrent feature. There is widespread evidence for major changes of plan, including churches detached from the present village and crofts apparently laid out over earlier open fields. The diverse forms of village greens reflect a variety of origins and functions, but many green-centred villages are felt to be a product of comparatively late reorganization or extension of settlement. Many Oxfordshire greens have been lost through encroachment or enclosure. Many aspects of medieval rural settlement are not yet fully understood, and much more work remains to be done.

Introduction

It is perhaps surprising that almost the only general account of rural settlement in Oxfordshire available in print is that contained in two of the chapters of the local handbook published for the British Association's meeting at Oxford as long ago as 1954 (Hoskins and Jope 1954; Paget 1954). These papers represent a significant landmark in local settlement studies and are a valuable statement of ideas at the time; but inevitably in the ensuing quarter-century they have become outdated and ripe for revision. Several aspects now require complete reassessment:-

(i) The deterministic view of settlement location, which emphasized the attraction of spring-lines and the preferences for dry sites in the clay vales, can no longer be upheld. While not suggesting that environmental factors were totally irrelevant, they must now be considered in proper perspective and not in simplistic terms of cause-and-effect. Much greater prominence needs to be accorded to the elements of human perception, choice and decision, influenced as they were by a range of needs, pressures and aspirations which were themselves subject to temporal change.

(ii) The 1954 survey accepted the then prevalent view of a discontinuity of settlement at the end of the Romano-British period and the introduction of a completely new pattern by the incoming Anglo-Saxon settlers. Evidence whch has subsequently accumulated allows us to admit much more widespread possibilities for some strands of continuity, which will be discussed further below.

(iii) In 1954 Paget undertook what was probably the first attempt to identify common village plan-forms in Oxfordshire. He admitted to encountering considerable difficulties in this project, but distinguished six basic categories, namely (a) loose, irregular groupings, including clusters around greens, (b) street-line groupings, (c) composite villages with street-line tentacles, (d) twin villages, (e) estate villages and (f) dispersed settlements. While at its date this was a valiant attempt to impose order upon apparent chaos, with the advantage of hindsight it can be seen that there are weaknesses both within the classification and in its implications. The criteria used to define the six categories are an uneasy mixture of morphology, siting, context, historical origin and function, and there is an assumption that internal village plans were basically stable. More recently important work has taken place elsewhere, both on the classification of settlement forms according to more strictly morphological principles (e.g. Roberts 1971, 1972, 1975, 1977, 1978; Sheppard 1974) and on the potential for fundamental changes in village plans (e.g. Ravensdale 1974; Taylor 1978; Wade-Martins 1975). Surveys carried out in neighbouring counties (e.g. R.C.H.M. 1975, 1979, 1982; Roberts 1982) clearly have particularly important implications for Oxfordshire.

(iv) It was assumed in 1954 that, from the Anglo-Saxon period onwards, the overall distribution of settlements remained essentially static. The mobility of early Saxon settlement was unrecognized. The possibility that medieval colonization in areas such as Wychwood and the Chilterns was accompanied by the foundation of new villages was realized, and some inklings of the existence of deserted medieval village sites were also beginning to appear; but these still tended to be viewed as unusual aberrations rather than as an intrinsic part of a larger dynamic process of settlement change.

Since 1954 there have been some very important contributions on more limited local or special aspects of medieval rural settlement in Oxfordshire. The Victoria County History volumes published since 1957 have displayed a steadily increasing awareness of village morphology, in addition to their more traditional concerns (*V.C.H. Oxon* 1957 *et seq.*). A considerable volume of work on deserted villages has grown up since the publication of Beresford's classic study (Beresford 1954), particularly the Deserted Medieval Village Research Group's monograph on the county (Allison, Beresford and Hurst 1965). There have been some notable detailed local studies, outstanding amongst which is that of Cuxham, where a superb series of documents in the Merton College muniments has allowed this village to be studied in exceptional detail from the topographical as well as the historical point of view (Harvey 1965). There has been some archaeological investigation of medieval village sites, a little of which will be discussed further below. Finally, studies of 'open' and 'closed' villages (e.g. Emery 1974, 170–6; 1975) and of certain estate villages (e.g. Havinden 1966) have emphasized the importance of post-medieval changes and the dominant influence of landownership upon present village morphology.

The ensuing discussion, while acknowledging a considerable debt to these published accounts, is based primarily upon work currently being carried out on behalf of Oxfordshire County Council's Department of Museum Services. The peculiar functions of a local government department inevitably exert a profound effect upon its approach to the investigation of any topic. Techniques, objectives and priorities are determined by demands which are not primarily of an academic nature. It has not been possible to pursue a systematic, structured programme of survey and research, and this inevitably imposes certain limitations which cannot be ignored. Nonetheless, although progress has been less methodical than one would have wished in an ideal world, it has become apparent that the mere accumulation of raw information in the County Sites and Monuments Record, and the need to interpret this information for a variety of local authority services, has inexorably contributed towards a fuller understanding of rural settlement in Oxfordshire, even if we are still a long way from making any definitive general statements.

The remainder of this paper will concentrate upon a review of recent progress in two of the areas where the 1954 survey is now most clearly seen to be defective, namely (i) the origins of villages and the question of continuity and (ii) village plans. Other aspects covered at the Oxford conference in January 1982, the

contraction and desertion of villages and the impact of post-medieval reorganization, require fuller treatment than they can be accorded here, and they will therefore feature only incidentally in the ensuing discussion. The boundaries of the study area are those of the present administrative county of Oxfordshire, i.e. including the Vale of White Horse which was transferred from Berkshire in 1974.

Village Origins

The most radical readjustment of our ideas has probably taken place in our theories of village origins. The traditional view of the end of Roman Britain in an orgy of conflagration and slaughter, followed by the movement of immigrant Anglo-Saxon settlers into a desolate wasteland, avoiding or ruthlessly obliterating all traces of the culture of their predecessors and imposing their own Germanic patterns of nucleated villages and open fields, has long been untenable. Withington, scene of one of the classic propositions for continuity (Finberg 1959), lies less than 20 km from the Oxfordshire border. However, while arguments for a degree of continuity between Romano-British and Anglo-Saxon estates and settlements become increasingly persuasive, there is still considerable debate about how this can be defined, and how the processes of Anglo-Saxon settlement relate to the patterns of both earlier and later periods.

There are two basic problems. One is that it is much easier to produce evidence of change than it is to demonstrate continuity. Deliberate destruction, abandonment or wholesale reorganization are far more susceptible to positive identification in the archaeological record than continuous, unbroken use. The best evidence for supposed continuity which the field archaeologist can hope to observe may in reality represent no more than the survival of relict features in the landscape which happen to be respected by subsequent phases of land use: features which serve as a passive constraint but play no active part in a system of life to which they are no longer directly relevant. Even where coincidence of occupation of different periods can be demonstrated on the same site, it may still be difficult to determine whether what is happening is continuous unbroken occupation, the deliberate reoccupation of a site where signs of former habitation were still evident (e.g. squatters moving into an abandoned ruin), or a completely fortuitous reoccupation of a site which had passed out of human memory.

The second problem is one of definition, and there can be little doubt that considerable confusion has arisen from indiscriminate use of the word 'continuity' without defining exactly what is supposed to be continuous. A variety of circumstances where the term might be appropriate can be envisaged: continuous, unbroken habitation on the same site; continuity of community, with succeeding generations remaining in the same area; continuity of agrarian regime; unbroken descent of estate ownership or tenurial arrangements; or continuity of estate boundaries. The occurrence of any one of these forms of continuity does not exclude the possibility of fundamental changes in any of the other parameters.

Bearing these problems in mind, what can now be said about the evidence for village origins in Oxfordshire? If we begin by looking to the fifth century, when the great disruption of Roman settlement is traditionally supposed to have occurred, we find a number of sites where there appears to be a significant relationship between the location of Roman and early Saxon settlements, notably at Shakenoak (Brodribb, Hands and Walker 1968–78) and in the vicinity of Abingdon (Miles 1974) and Sutton Courtenay (Benson and Miles 1974a). There is little here to suggest a violent incursion of unwelcome invaders; on the contrary, the evidence points to a degree of contact and co-operation between the two racial communities. While minor relocations of settlement occurred, there seems every possibility that these took place within a framework of estate boundaries which remained constant; and whatever changes took place in the agrarian regime appear to have followed a course of slow devolution and adaptation rather than sudden supersession by an introduced system of open fields. Although none of these sites continued as a settlement nucleus into the Middle Ages, the critical break in the sequence of habitation occurred not in the fifth century, but in the middle or late Saxon period.

If we attempt to tackle the problem retrogressively from the standpoint of the present village, we can point to a number of settlements in Oxfordshire which lie within areas which have undergone intensive occupation at various periods since prehistory. Over twenty years ago Hoskins, discussing the possibility that some villages had had a continuous existence from Romano-British times to the present day, put forward Cassington as an example for consideration (Hoskins 1959, 42). All the way along the Thames valley villages such as Kelmscott, Clanfield, Aston Bampton, Cote, Stanton Harcourt, Appleford, Long Wittenham and Warborough lie adjacent to or are surrounded by crop marks indicating earlier settlements (Benson and Miles 1974b). It is, however, very difficult to prove any direct relationship between these ancient settlement areas and the present villages other than the self-evident one of propinquity. The chronological link is missing, and we do not know what has been obliterated or rendered inaccessible beneath the buildings of our extant villages. Over a long period of time the systematic collection of pottery from gardens, observation of

service trenches and other disturbances and selective excavation of available vacant plots within the village envelope has some potential, but these tactics can only ever produce an incomplete picture. Only in the case of deserted medieval villages is all the evidence theoretically available, though its recovery by total excavation is a daunting prospect; and there must remain doubts about the validity of assumptions that evidence from a failed settlement can be used as a model for the origins and development of successful villages.

Occasionally the sheer precision of the juxtaposition of sites of different periods makes the inference of some direct relationship between them very tempting. At the deserted medieval village of Widford the parish church, in its present form a predominantly thirteenth-century building, stands directly on top of a Roman villa; part of a tessellated pavement is exposed in the chancel floor. However, it should not be forgotten that a gap of nine centuries separates the two visible structures. The dedication of the church to the seventh-century St Oswald does not necessarily provide a stepping-stone across this chronological gulf, since Widford was a possession of St Oswald's Priory in Gloucester. Nor does the Domesday record of four villeins, three bordars and four serfs on the priory estate at Widford necessarily imply that they were living in a single nucleated community on the estate or that their dwellings lie buried beneath the earthworks of the later medieval village clustered round the church. Other deserted villages, such as Lea and Woodperry, also lie on top of Roman settlements, and at Kidlington the medieval church stands immediately adjacent to the site of a Roman building.[1] Two Oxfordshire hamlets, one in Wychwood Forest, one in the Vale of White Horse, bear the name Fawler, which is derived from the Old English words *fāg*, meaning variegated, and *flōr*, meaning floor; clearly this indicates knowledge of a tessellated Roman pavement in the vicinity surviving at the time these places received their present name. Excavations at Middleton Stoney have revealed a second-century farmstead directly beneath the Norman castle.

However evocative some of these individual juxtapositions may be, however, we cannot assume that they are necessarily meaningful in terms of any form of continuity. The sheer density of Roman and medieval settlement sites on the ground is such that an occasional fortuitous coincidence between them is inevitable. What needs to be determined is whether the actual frequency of such juxtapositions greatly exceeds the theoretical number of accidental coincidences which might be anticipated if the distributions of Roman and medieval settlements were entirely unrelated. To this end some preliminary and rather primitive statistical tests have been carried out. On present evidence it would not be unreasonable to assume that Roman

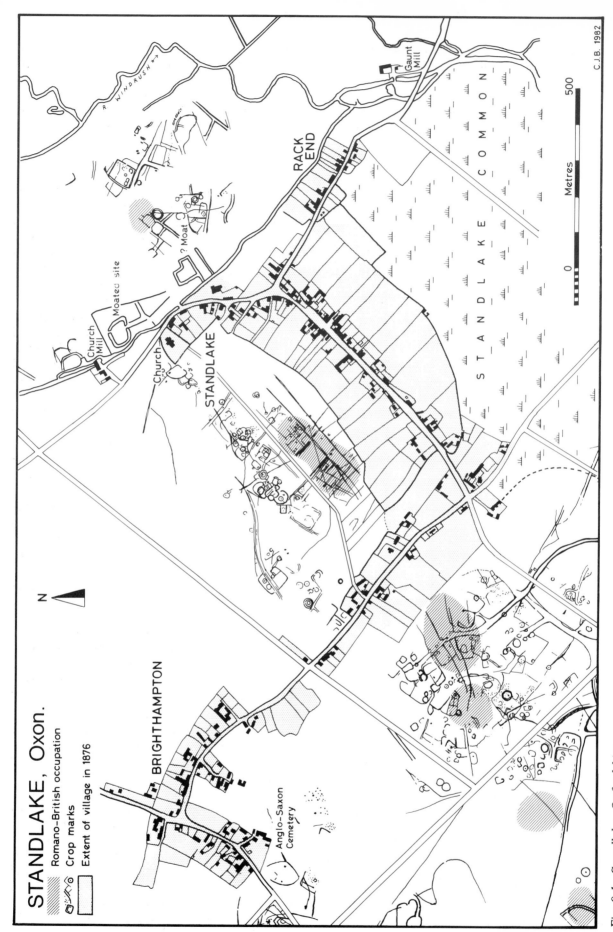

STANDLAKE, Oxon.

Romano–British occupation
Crop marks
Extent of village in 1876

N

BRIGHTHAMPTON

Anglo-Saxon
Cemetery

STANDLAKE

Church
Church
Mill

? Moat

Moated site

R WINDRUSH

Gaunt
Mill

RACK
END

S T A N D L A K E   C O M M O N

Metres

0   500

C.J.B. 1982

Fig. 9.1 Standlake, Oxfordshire

settlements of various kinds were quite densely distributed, the average interval between them being about 1 km. Medieval nucleated villages in Oxfordshire tend to lie between about 2 km and 2.5 km apart. The extent of Oxfordshire villages varies considerably, but an average area based upon the measurement of 50 examples works out at about 170,000 sq. m. If one assumes a Romano-British settlement distribution based upon the intersections of a 1 km square grid, then the chances of a medieval village overlapping a Romano-British settlement are of the order of 17 per cent.

This percentage presupposes no relationship between the two distributions whatsoever; shared environmental preferences of even the most rudimentary kind, e.g. avoidance of the bleakest hilltops, are likely to increase the proportion of coincidences quite considerably, without in any way increasing the probability that the two distributions are historically linked. Comparison of the theoretical predicted rate of coincidence with the actual observed rate in Oxfordshire is not entirely straightforward, because of the uneven standards of the recording of the Roman material. Nonetheless, from the evidence at present available, it can be estimated that somewhere between 1.5 and eight per cent of all medieval villages in Oxfordshire lie partly or wholly over known Roman settlements of some sort. The wide spread of these figures reflects the range of ambiguities resulting from the somewhat unsatisfactory nature of the basic data. The real point of interest, however, is that even the highest percentage of actual coincidences, derived from the most generous possible interpretation of the data, is still below the rate predicted. Whether this picture will be much altered by improvements in the data base or by the application of more sophisticated statistical techniques remains to be seen. It remains difficult on present evidence to read too much significance into the occasional cases of Roman and medieval settlement overlap which are known. Statistically they occur no more frequently than would be expected if they were entirely fortuitous. The view that even a significant minority of villages stand on sites which have been continuously occupied since the Roman period receives little support.

Even in an exceptional individual case such as Dorchester-on-Thames, where the general evidence for people living on more or less the same site from the Roman period to the present is unusually complete, it remains difficult to see much evidence for the continuity of Roman instituitions, commerce, industry, settlement plan or local community into the Saxon period (Rowley 1974). Elsewhere, despite the overlap of ancient and medieval occupation, the evidence points to a very positive break in the continuity of occupation. The village of Standlake (Fig. 9.1) is almost surrounded by complex concentrations of crop marks, and the evidence of surface finds and discoveries in the neighbouring gravel pits confirms the intensive prehistoric and Romano-British settlement of the area (Benson and Miles 1974b, 44–8; Armstrong 1979). Although Saxon occupation is attested on several sites no more than a couple of kilometres away, however, there is no indication of continuing occupation on the site of the present village. Brighthampton, now little more than an appendage at the west end of Standlake, is first recorded by name in AD 984 and appears in the Domesday survey as an independent seven and a half-hide vill divided between two landowners. By contrast, Standlake itself fails to appear in any documentary reference before the mid-twelfth century, which is also the date of the oldest recognizable fabric in its parish church. The present village is a long, straggling place, with the church almost isolated at the north-eastern end, and with some vestiges of a planned development along the High Street which is conceivably connected with the acquisition of a market and fair charter in 1230. The social structure revealed by the Hundred Rolls assessment is unusual, with no less than 38 free tenants. Emery has drawn a comparison with the Dutch polderland villages, and sees Standlake as a new settlement on the cultivation frontier, growing up in association with twelfth-century marshland reclamation in the Thames valley, a process which may also have brought neighbouring villages such as Northmoor and Hardwick into existence (Emery 1974, 81). If this view is correct, we have an interval of six or seven centuries elapsing between the abandonment of the Roman settlements and the re-establishment of permanent settlement on the site during the great expansion of the Middle Ages. At Seacourt, the only deserted village in Oxfordshire to have been subjected to extensive archaeological investigation (Biddle 1961–2), there were slight traces of Roman occupation underlying the northern end of the settlement, but none of the structures along the main street was of earlier date than the mid-twelfth century. There were some indications that this, too, was a consciously planned development. Early Saxon material was conspicuously absent, and there was only a thin scatter of late Saxon pottery which suggests that the focus of the estate documented in a charter of *c.* AD 957 and the homes of the Domesday population of 12 villeins and 15 bordars must be sought elsewhere.

Uninterrupted continuity of occupation on the same site is not, however, the only possible meaningful link between Roman, Saxon and medieval settlements. The widespread evidence that the exact form and siting of settlements may fluctuate in no sense rules out the possibility that other forms of continuity occurred. In many instances a somewhat dispersed pattern of settlement in the Roman or early Saxon period seems to have been superseded by a single nucleated village by

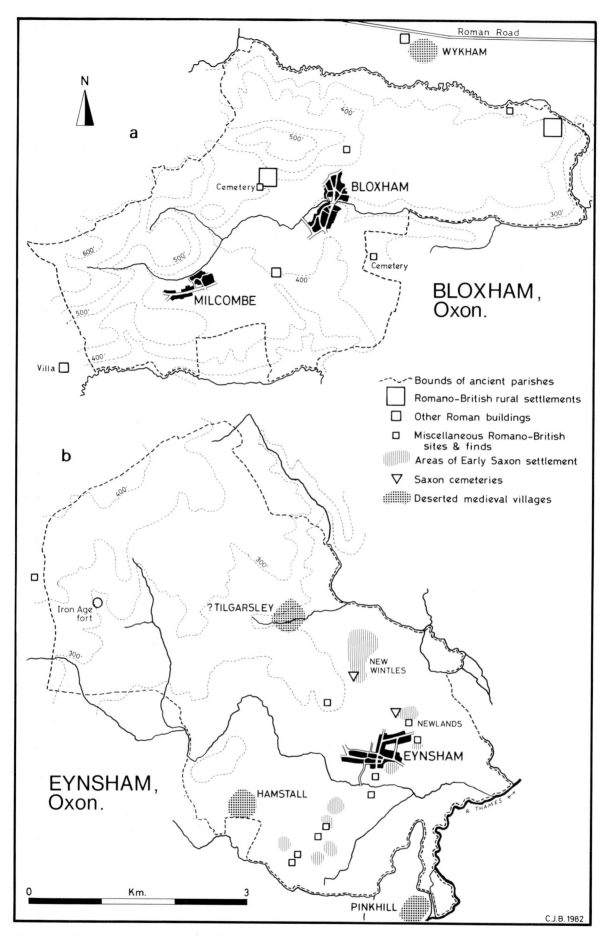

Fig. 9.2 Bloxham and Eynsham, Oxfordshire

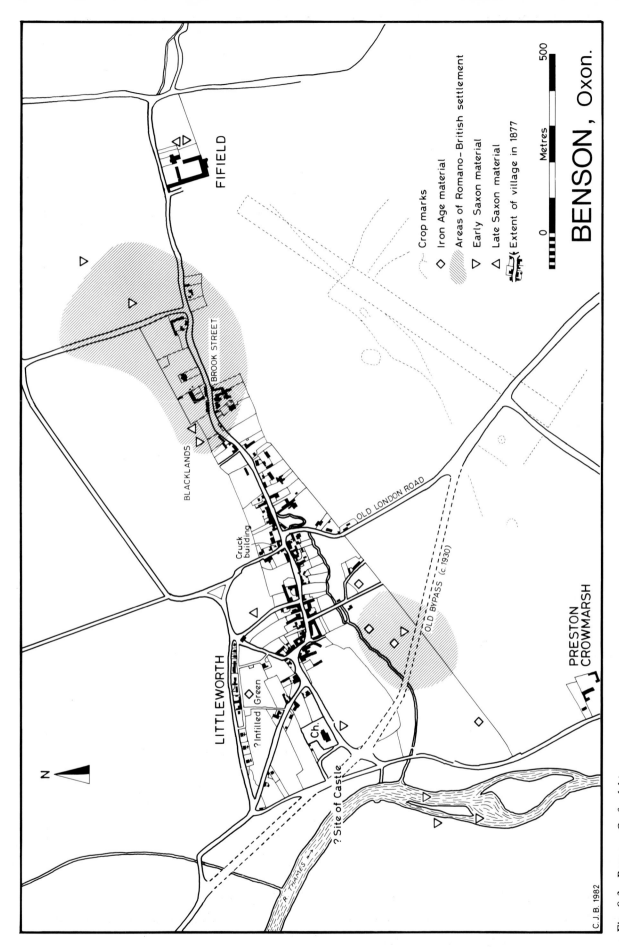

BENSON, Oxon.

Crop marks

◇ Iron Age material

▨ Areas of Romano–British settlement

▽ Early Saxon material

△ Late Saxon material

⌂ Extent of village in 1877

0   Metres   500

N

FIFIELD

BLACKLANDS

BROOK STREET

Cruck building

OLD LONDON ROAD

OLD BYPASS (c.1930)

LITTLEWORTH

? Infilled Green

Ch.

? Site of Castle

R. THAMES

PRESTON CROWMARSH

C.J.B. 1982

Fig. 9.3   Benson, Oxfordshire

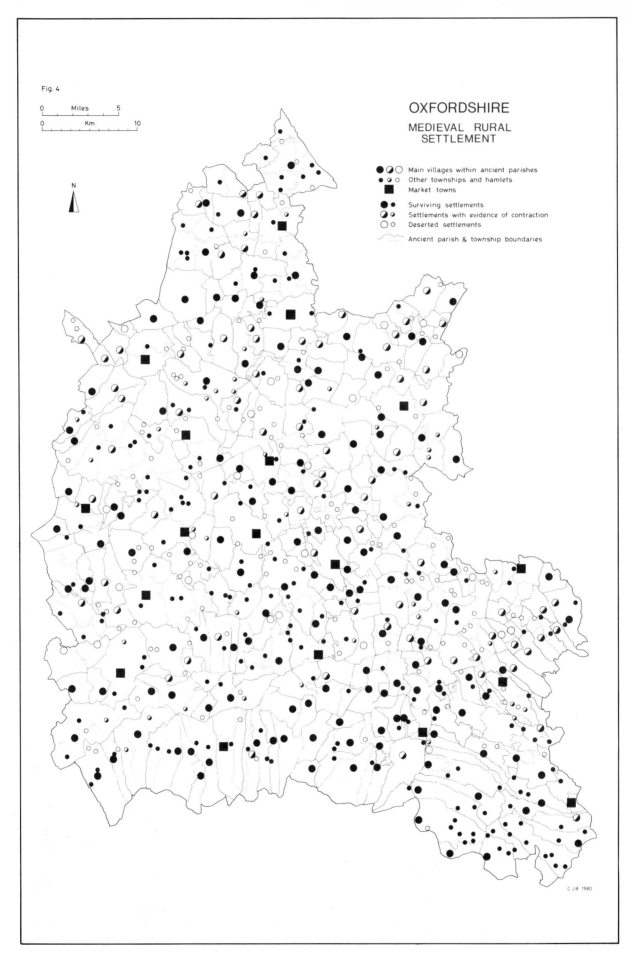

Fig. 9.4 Oxfordshire: medieval rural settlement

the eleventh century or thereabouts. At Bloxham the Romano-British settlement which underlies the northern margins of the present village cannot be regarded as its sole antecedent, since there are at least four other Romano-British settlements scattered around the remainder of the parish (Fig. 9.2a). Similarly in the early Saxon period, although Eynsham is one of the first places to be documented by name—according to the Anglo-Saxon Chronicle it was one of four places captured during Cuthwulf's campaign of AD 571—it remains an open question whether any part of the present village was settled at that date. Instead, in addition to the early Saxon occupation discovered during gravel-working immediately to the north-east at Newlands, and the loose-knit scatter of early Saxon buildings excavated about 1 km to the north at New Wintles (Hawkes and Gray 1969; Gray 1974), further groups of sunken-featured buildings can tentatively be identified from aerial photography on several sites in the southern part of the parish (Fig. 9.2b). Scattered groups of early Saxon buildings sited away from the present village nucleus, sometimes including over 30 individual structures, can now be demonstrated in about 20 other Oxfordshire parishes (e.g. Arthur and Jope 1962–3, 1–4). What seems to be happening is a process of internal movement or adjustment of the settlement pattern within the confines of an established and constant framework of boundaries. Although the details are imperfectly understood, there may be a degree of continuity in the exploitation and administration of some estates, despite the fact that the settlements within them display a marked capacity for mobility.

Detailed local studies are needed to throw further light upon the relationship between these comparatively impermanent dispersed settlements and the more stable nucleations which succeeded them. One Oxfordshire village which would repay further investigation is Benson (Fig. 9.3). In the late Saxon period this was the centre of a vast royal estate extending in a strip some 18 km long across the Chiltern escarpment to Henley. In addition to extensive prehistoric features around the present village, at least two Romano-British settlements are known near its margins. Both of these have also produced early Saxon material, and it is of interest that Benson was another of the four 'towns' captured from the Britons by Cuthwulf in AD 571. For long after this date, however, settlement on the estate seems to have taken the form of small clachans or farmsteads which were physically dispersed—late Saxon pottery has come from three separate localities around the fringe of the present village—but were presumably administratively or tenurially linked. The foundation of the church provided the first positive focus: although the present building contains nothing recognizably pre-Norman,

there is a traditon that it was built in the seventh century by Birinus, first Bishop of Dorchester, and it has a locally unusual dedication to the Romano-British St Helen (only three other examples are found in the Oxford diocese). The medieval castle, of which little is known and no trace survives, was apparently built immediately to the west of the church, and the two together seem to have become the centre of a more strongly nucleated settlement in the early Middle Ages. Subsequently the centre of gravity seems to have shifted again, eastwards towards what was then the main Oxford-Henley-London road. The presence of a cruck house in Crown Square (Blair 1979) shows that building had already spread over 500 m east of the church by the late thirteenth or fourteenth century. By the seventeenth century the village had extended still further eastwards along Brook Street, reoccupying one of the areas which has produced evidence of both Romano-British and Saxon settlement, so that what now looks superficially like a late addition to the village is in fact a recolonization of one of its several earlier centres of habitation.

The large nucleated village, which has remained the most characteristic feature of rural settlement over most of Oxfordshire from the Middle Ages into the present century, can no longer be viewed as the medium by which the first English settlers colonized a sparsely-populated wilderness. It now appears to be the result of a reorganization carried out in the late Saxon, or perhaps even post-Conquest, period, which took place within a pre-existing framework of much older estates. The reasons why dispersal gave way to nucleation as the local settlement norm are still far from certain, but the influences at work must surely include the rising pressure of population upon land resources, the development of the agricultural system into the classical communal open-field operation, the reorganization of the church into the parochial system, and the final imposition of feudal authority.

Village Plans

Although the tendency towards nucleation and towards greater stability of site had become pronounced well before 1300, when the high-water mark of medieval expansion was reached, settlement forms were still far from static. Expansion, contraction and internal reorganization continued to alter the plan of individual villages, and the overall settlement pattern was itself still to experience far-reaching changes through the widespread village desertions of the later Middle Ages.

Before we turn to the question of village plans, it is worth reminding ourselves of the scale of the problem which confronts the investigator in this field. Fig. 9.4 is an attempt to plot all nucleated rural settlements in

Oxfordshire, subdivided in two ways:

(i) The larger symbols indicate the village which formed the focal point of ecclesiastical organization, and often also of manorial administration, in each medieval parish. The smaller symbols represent hamlets and townships of nucleated form which were originally subordinate to them, though in a number of cases they acquired independent parochial status at a later date. It should be emphasized that the smaller symbols do not necessarily imply that these places were invariably smaller in extent or population than the parish centre, or that they were necessarily 'secondary' in the sense of being a product of later colonization. Single manorial complexes or medieval farmsteads which stood in isolation or formed part of a generally dispersed settlement pattern have been omitted from this map. The relationship between parishes, villages and hamlets is very variable. Some parishes contain a single centrally-placed nucleated settlement, which may be an extant village like Cuxham or Upper Heyford or a site like Widford or Little Rollright which is now deserted. There are some parishes of wholly dispersed settlement wihout any recognizable early nucleus, such as Swyncombe in the Chilterns. There are several large, multi-township parishes such as Enstone or Pyrton which include a number of nucleated hamlets in addition to the village containing the parish church; one or more members of such parishes have often suffered partial or total depopulation. In some cases, such as Ascott, Little Milton and Chilworth in Great Milton or Fencott and Murcott in Charlton-on-Otmoor, the 'minor' settlements had their own compact land units within the parish and field systems operating independently of those belonging to the main village. By contrast the four Baldons shared an integrated field system which was worked in common between all the members.

(ii) The form of shading on Fig. 9.4 distinguishes fairly crudely between places which survive to the present day apparently intact within their medieval perimeter, places which have undergone a degree of contraction or shift, and places which are virtually deserted. There are many obvious difficulties in applying a classification of such rigidity to a subject as fluid and dynamic as rural settlement, and the totals of 356 'intact', 113 'shrunken' and 148 'deserted' settlements shown here represent a somewhat subjective view which will be liable to revision and can do no more than indicate the approximate proportions. Particular difficulties surround the definition of 'settlements with evidence of contraction': at one end of the scale many large, thriving villages have the odd gap where one or two medieval crofts are no longer occupied, while at the other extreme few so-called 'deserted' villages are entirely devoid of occupied buildings. Any division within the range of options is of necessity an arbitrary

and subjective one. The proportion of sites distinguished here as 'intact' and 'shrunken' is likely to be overbalanced in favour of the former, since the phenomenon of contraction has attracted comparatively little detailed research and examples are often disguised by recent infilling and expansion. Finally, even where earthworks or pottery scatters adjoin an occupied settlement, it may not always be clear whether these represent a genuine contraction or simply a local shift of site which did not necessarily involve any loss of population.

Even the most superficial scanning of these 617 nucleated settlements can hardly fail to recognize the enormous diversity of shapes, sizes and degrees of complexity represented. One can feel considerable sympathy for Paget's dilemma in 1954 when, outlining his sixfold scheme of village types, he nonetheless found himself forced to conclude that 'The present-day forms are as remarkable for their individual characteristics as for their broad similarities. For this reason no clear-cut classification of settlement forms is possible'.

While the techniques of morphological analysis have undergone considerable refinement since 1954, the approach itself has attracted some criticism, and it may be well to consider how far it can be regarded as a valid exercise before attempting to apply it to Oxfordshire examples. The shape of any village can be regarded as the product of the interaction of several different influences and processes working within a framework of physical and historical constraints. Some of the factors involved are summarized in Fig. 9.5. The effectiveness of the various influences and the extent of their impact upon the village plan is likely to be subject to temporal fluctuation. While the study of the present arrangement of village streets and open spaces, property boundaries and public and private buildings is entirely justified in its own right, it is also apparent that these aspects of village topography cannot be understood without reference to their past development. The greatest problem in projecting morphological studies back into the historical dimension is to gauge how far back in time one can safely project the various individual surviving elements; and the greatest pitfall lies in the over-ready assumption that settlement forms or the disposition of any elements within them were necessarily static over any period longer than that for which stability can be proven.

What we cannot assume is that the form of the village today, or that shown on the earliest available cartographic source, necessarily reflects the broad outlines of the village in the high Middle Ages; even less can we assume that it represents the essential shape of the Domesday vill or of the first Anglo-Saxon settlement. The antecedents of the rural settlement pattern in Oxfordshire have already been discussed above and the view expressed that the large nucleated

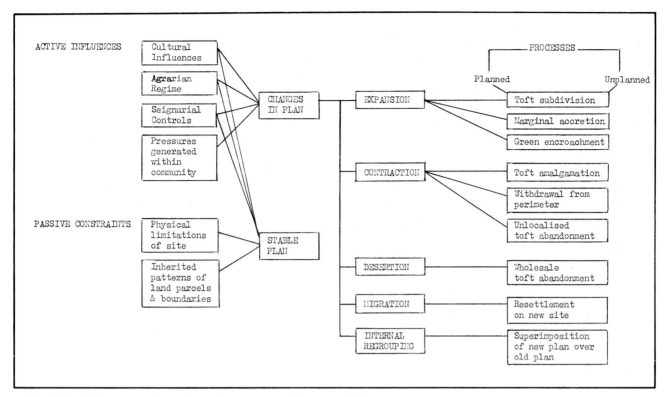

Fig. 9.5 Influences and processes determining village morphology

village is itself a comparatively late arrival on the scene. Even in the high Middle Ages, it is clear from excavated evidence elsewhere that there were considerable variations in the stability of village plans as a whole, and in the length of time over which their individual components were likely to persist. While block plans of medieval peasant buildings reveal a marked predilection for frequent realignment within their tofts, at least some property boundaries seem to have been remarkably enduring (cf. Beresford and Hurst 1979).

It is essential that the study of present village forms is properly integrated with the examination of the documentary evidence and the recording of all related earthworks and pottery scatters. Given that certain elements are likely to survive from the Middle Ages, it is then possible to detect at least some of the instances where significant medieval or post-medieval changes in layout have occurred. A pattern of ditches resembling medieval croft boundaries has long been known extending out beyond the perimeter of the twelfth-century castle at Ascott d'Oilly (Jope and Threlfall 1959, 239–9). The orientation of these enclosures does not conform with the alignment of the present village High Street, where considerable quantities of twelfth- and thirteenth-century pottery have been turned up in gardens. This could be interpreted as evidence for some fundamental reorganization in the plan of the settlement outside the castle gate at an early date. On a smaller scale, a recent survey of the earthworks of the

deserted hamlet of Coat (M.V.R.G. 1981, 9) has shown that one farmyard complex had encroached over and caused the diversion of a hollow-way entering the south-east corner of the settlement, an event which must have occurred before the final abandonment of the site, which apparently occurred in the middle of the fourteenth century. Other possible examples will be discussed below.

The justification of the morphological approach is the belief that village plans themselves contain evidence of their own historical development. A study of the present village morphology provides the launching-pad for an examination by retrogressive analysis. We need to maintain a keen awareness of the inherent limitations of this approach and to exercise extreme caution in the interpretation of evidence which, by its very nature, is imperfect and incomplete. Certainly the conclusions which can be drawn become increasingly tentative the further back we attempt to project them. Nonetheless, for all its limitations, this approach yields evidence and suggests ideas which can be obtained in no other way. Short of the ultimate resort of total village excavation, which can only ever be feasible in a tiny minority of cases, it is difficult to envisage any more productive, realistic alternative.

Village plans may be linear or agglomerated, tightly cohesive or loose-knit, regular or irregular, and with or without certain special features such as a green. As in other Midland counties (cf. Roberts 1982), many

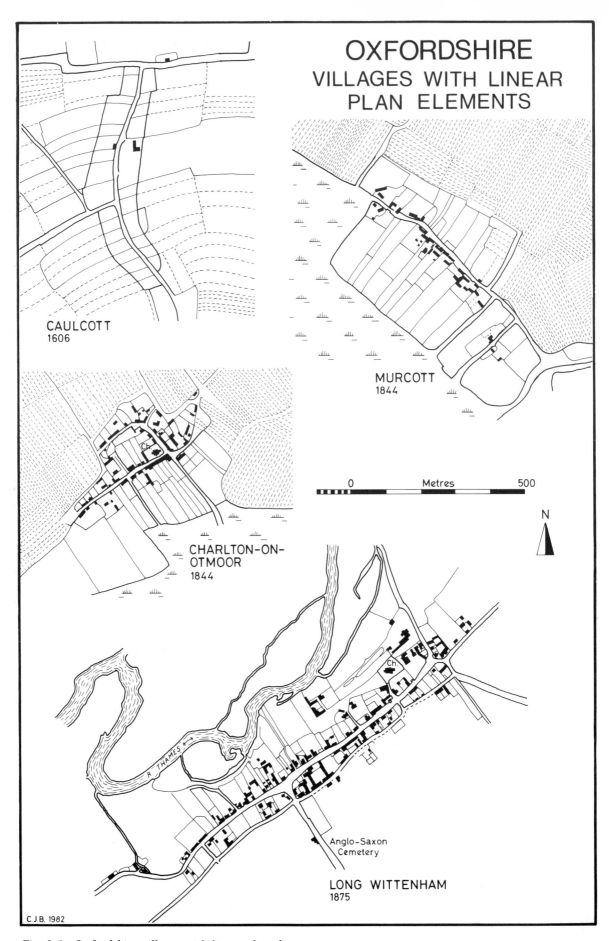

OXFORDSHIRE
VILLAGES WITH LINEAR
PLAN ELEMENTS

CAULCOTT
1606

MURCOTT
1844

CHARLTON-ON-
OTMOOR
1844

Metres
0   500

N

Anglo-Saxon
Cemetery

LONG WITTENHAM
1875

C.J.B. 1982

Fig. 9.6 Oxfordshire villages with linear plan elements

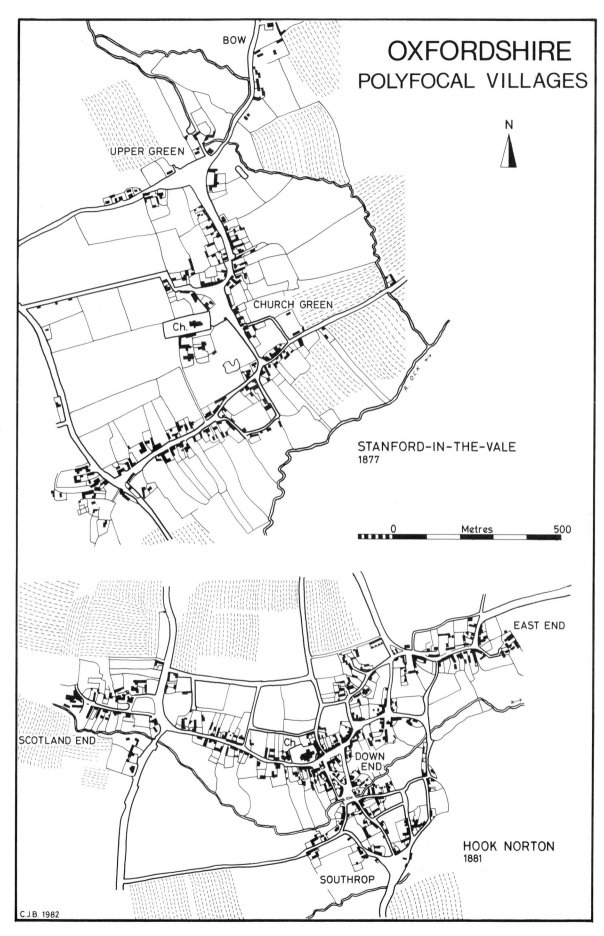

Fig. 9.7 *Oxfordshire polyfocal villages*

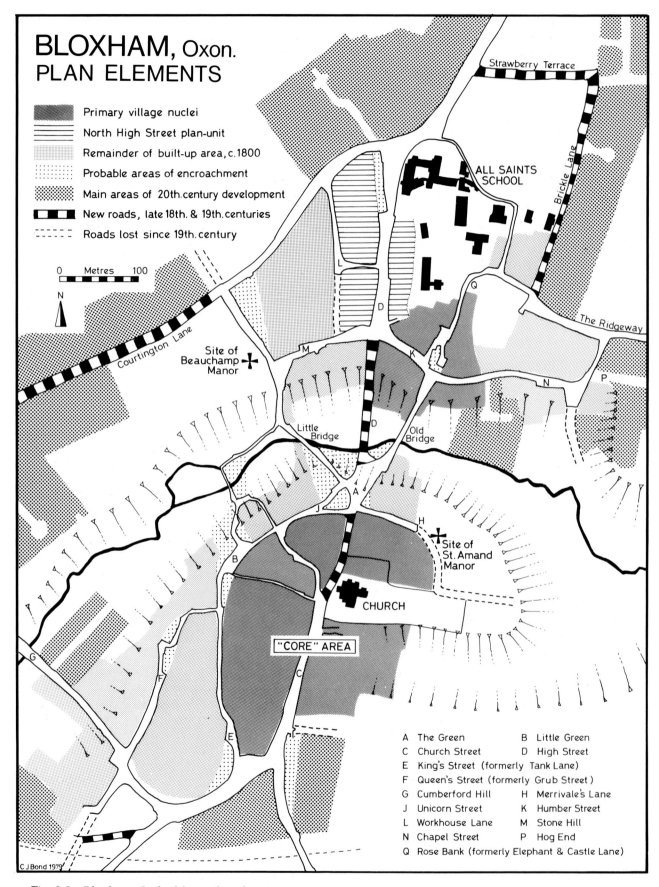

**BLOXHAM, Oxon.
PLAN ELEMENTS**

Primary village nuclei

North High Street plan-unit

Remainder of built-up area, c.1800

Probable areas of encroachment

Main areas of 20th.century development

New roads, late 18th. & 19th.centuries

Roads lost since 19th. century

0   Metres   100

N

Courtington Lane

Site of
Beauchamp
Manor

Strawberry Terrace

Brickle Lane

ALL SAINTS
SCHOOL

The Ridgeway

L

D

Q

M

K

N

P

Little
Bridge

D

Old
Bridge

A

J

H

Site of
St.Amand
Manor

B

CHURCH

"CORE" AREA

G

F

E

C

A The Green   B Little Green
C Church Street   D High Street
E King's Street (formerly Tank Lane)
F Queen's Street (formerly Grub Street)
G Cumberford Hill   H Merrivale's Lane
J Unicorn Street   K Humber Street
L Workhouse Lane   M Stone Hill
N Chapel Street   P Hog End
Q Rose Bank (formerly Elephant & Castle Lane)

C J Bond 1979

Fig. 9.8   Bloxham, Oxfordshire: plan elements

Oxfordshire villages display hybrid or composite forms composed of more than one individual plan-unit and including various combinations of these characteristics. The detailed analysis of village plans in Oxfordshire is still in its preliminary stages, and it would obviously be premature to suggest any firm conclusions from work still in progress. Nonetheless, it is worth considering some of the recurring features which seem to be emerging:-

(1) Regular plans

While Oxfordshire has few villages of such well-ordered simplicity as some of those which have been described in the north of England (Roberts 1972, 1978; Sheppard 1974, 1976), there are nonetheless a number of examples which have a strikingly compact and regular arrangement. The simplest form is represented by Long Wittenham (Fig. 9.6), a large village which, despite its size, consists essentially of a single main street with a parallel back lane. The church stands at one end, enclosed within the envelope of the village boundary. Long Wittenham lies in a part of the Thames valley with a long and complex settlement history, but it is difficult to escape the feeling that the village in its present form is a product of deliberate planning or replanning. If this is due to seigneurial intervention, then it seems most likely to have occurred before the early thirteenth century, when the manor was leased out subdivided into three separate portions. Similar apparently planned elements can be detected in other villages, such as Standlake and Charlton-on-Otmoor, and further examples will be described later.

(2) Polyfocal plans

At the other extreme, Oxfordshire contains a number of large, sprawling, open villages, the plans of which, at first sight, border on chaos (Fig. 9.7). Closer examination reveals most of these to be made up from a loose-knit linkage of several different hamlets. There are several examples in the north-west of the county, notably Hook Norton and Chadlington, with up to four or five separate nuclei, each of which has its own local name, usually incorporating the word '... End'. Elsewhere large settlements with multiple greens occur, such as Stanford-in-the-Vale or Kirtlington. These villages clearly provide a parallel for the polyfocal settlements which have been distinguished elsewhere in the East Midlands and East Anglia (Taylor 1977). Their origins are as yet unclear, but at least three possible explanations can be suggested:

(i) The individual nuclei are to be seen as successive accretions caused by expansion from a single early centre, either by organic growth or by planned additions.

(ii) The constituent parts of each village correspond with divisions of seigneurial jurisdiction or social organization.

(iii) They may even represent an inheritance from a more dispersed pattern of Anglo-Saxon or Romano-British settlement, arrested and fossilized before the process of coalescence or reorganization into a single large nucleation was complete.

(3) Core areas

Within the bounds of some villages it is possible to identify what may be either an early core or some sort of special precinct, defined by a distinct perimeter alignment. This plan feature was first recognized at Bloxham (Fig. 9.8), where the parish church stands in the larger of the two village nuclei, in the centre of an ovoid area partly ringed by lanes which look very much as if they follow the circuit of an early boundary bank. Outside this perimeter are the remains of several small marginal greens, much broken up by later encroachments (Bond 1980). Apparently similar features can be detected at Milton near Bloxham, at Kidlington, and elsewhere.

In this context, villages bearing names incorporating the Old English element *burh*, often translated as 'fortified place', may be of some significance. Some examples appear to derive their names from the presence of prehistoric hill-forts nearby, but at East Adderbury, Charlbury, Spelsbury, Burdrop in Sibford Gower and Bourton near Faringdon, possible hints of a Bloxham-type 'core' can be detected from the alignment of lanes and property boundaries within the village. It may also be significant that modern field-names incorporating the word 'bury' occur close to the church and village centre at Hook Norton, Garford, Culham and Tetsworth. A site immediately adjoining the field in Tetsworth called Old Bury was excavated in advance of construction of the M. 40, and produced evidence for an embanked enclosure with a deep ditch surrounding a fairly substantial farmhouse and croft of Norman date (Robinson 1973).

Within a number of village centres in Oxfordshire, then, there appears to be some evidence of areas or precincts which were separately enclosed. The deliberately noncommittal term 'core area' has been adopted to describe these as a morphological feature, without any implication that they necessarily have a common date, internal function or defensive strength. Some may be relict features dating from before the establishment of the village, which have subsequently influenced the pattern of its development; some may represent an early village perimeter which, on occasions, may have been reinforced with some sort of defences; others may be no more than an enclosed manorial demesne. Further work is clearly needed.

(4) Detached churches

It is a fairly common occurrence in Oxfordshire that the parish church stands somewhat apart from the village centre itself (Fig. 9.9). There are several possible

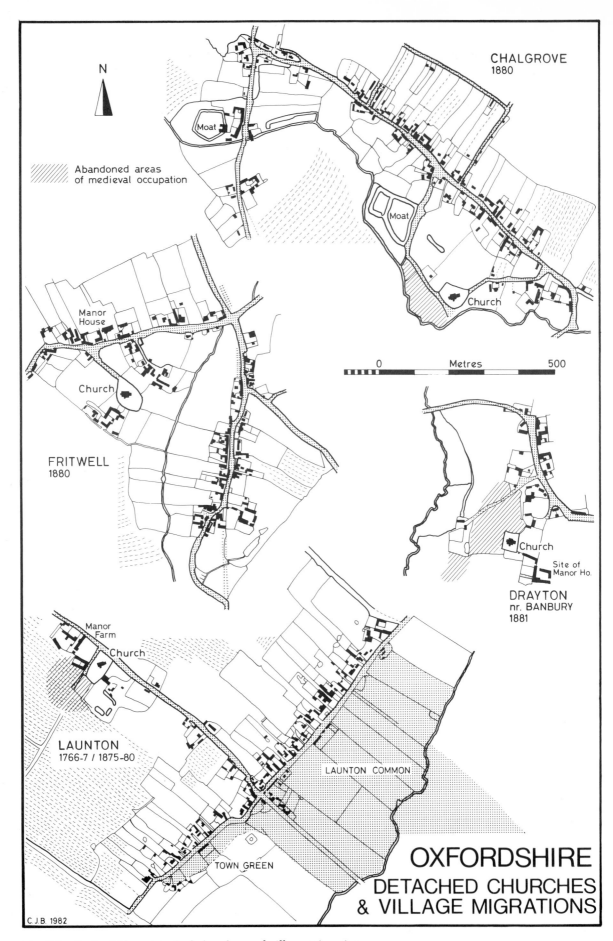

Fig. 9.9 Oxfordshire: detached churches and village migrations

interpretations of this phenomenon:

(i) The church may be a comparative late-comer, forced to take up a position on the margins of a nucleated settlement, the centre of which was already completely occupied. There is a well-documented post-medieval example at Nuneham Courtenay, where the new church built in 1872–4 was sited at a short distance outside the eighteenth-century estate village. Definite medieval examples are more difficult to find. Sometimes it might be supposed that churches which originated as subsidiary chapels within the bounds of ancient parishes were established after the villages which they served had taken shape. While the chapels at Shutford, Epwell, Mollington and Wardington Lower End are indeed sited in marginal positions, however, examples rarely seem to occur at any significant distance away from the village perimeter.

(ii) The church may have been built in a central position in a parish of generally dispersed settlement, within which a secondary nucleation has subsequently developed in a different location. A slightly more complicated example of this process may have occurred at Bix in the Chilterns, where the present village on the main Henley road is at a distance from both the vanished church of Bix Gibwen and the ruined church of Bix Brand. The surroundings of neither of the earlier churches have yet produced any clear evidence to suggest that they themselves ever formed the centre of substantial earlier nucleations.

(iii) The church may have been built to serve two or more separate nuclei, being sited equidistantly between them. The best example is probably at Ascott-under-Wychwood, where the late twelfth-century chapel-of-ease was located midway between the two earlier nuclei of Ascott Earl and Ascott d'Oilly. It has itself acted as the focus of a third nucleation, but its surroundings have so far produced little early medieval pottery. The now-isolated hilltop church of Baldon St Lawrence, which includes Norman features, lay midway between the two principal nuclei of Toot Baldon and Marsh Baldon. Originally it probably served them both, but it became more closely linked with Toot Baldon when Marsh Baldon gained its own church. A further complication here, however, is that slight earthworks in the adjoining field suggest that there may have been another small settlement nucleus by St Lawrence's church itself.

(iv) The village centre may have shifted to a new location, leaving the church isolated in its original position. The case of Benson has already been discussed, and other examples include Tetsworth (Hinton 1973; Robinson 1973), Souldern, North Leigh and Alvescot. It is rare that we can identify any clear motive for such movements, but sometimes commercial ambitions may have played a part. At Drayton near Banbury there are signs of an early nucleus around the now-isolated church, including a small area of earthworks. The present village is concentrated round what was once a long, rectangular green, bisected by the main Banbury-Stratford road, which appears to have acted as a magnet. Although there is no record of Drayton ever having a market, its lord, Robert Arden, did acquire a fair charter in 1329.

(v) All the above interpretations need to take into account the further possibility of multiple church provision before the twelfth century. Before the emergence of the parochial system and the establishment of the principle of one church per village supported by tithes, there appear to have been a large number of private chapels which were the personal property of local estate-owners. Polyfocal villages in multiple ownership may have had more than one such chapel, and normally only one of these will have been elevated subsequently to serve as a parish church.

A note of caution should also be sounded against the assumption that, once the parish church was established, its position was immutably fixed. While excavations have confirmed many examples of churches continuing to occupy the sites of earlier medieval or Saxon predecessors (e.g. Chambers 1979), exceptional instances do occur where the church was rebuilt on a new site. At Combe the Norman church in the valley bottom was abandoned after the de-population of the old village, and in 1395 a new church in perpendicular style was built on the margins of the green of the new village on top of the hill some 800 m away (Emden 1951).

(5) Settlement over open fields

In a number of cases where there is a reason to suppose that the centre of a settlement has shifted away from its original location, or that a new settlement has been established within the bounds of an older township, we might expect to find some indications that the new village was laid down over land previously under open-field cultivation. The curved or reversed-S courses of croft boundaries in parts of Fringford, Launton, Blackthorn, Fencott, Murcott, Caulcott in Heyford, Steeple Aston, Nethercott in Tackley and Chalgrove, may well betray such an origin. The situation at Launton is particularly interesting, for here part of the medieval nucleus near the church was subsequently overridden by ridge and furrow (Chambers 1981), while at some unknown date a new settlement had grown up 600 m away, along the edge of the former Launton Common (Fig. 9.9). Today there is still a distinct contrast here between the tightly-packed crofts on the north-west side of the Poundon road, with a distinct trace of reversed-S curvature in their boundaries, and the much more loose-knit building pattern on the opposite side of the road, where the boundaries are all straight. The former must have been carved out of the

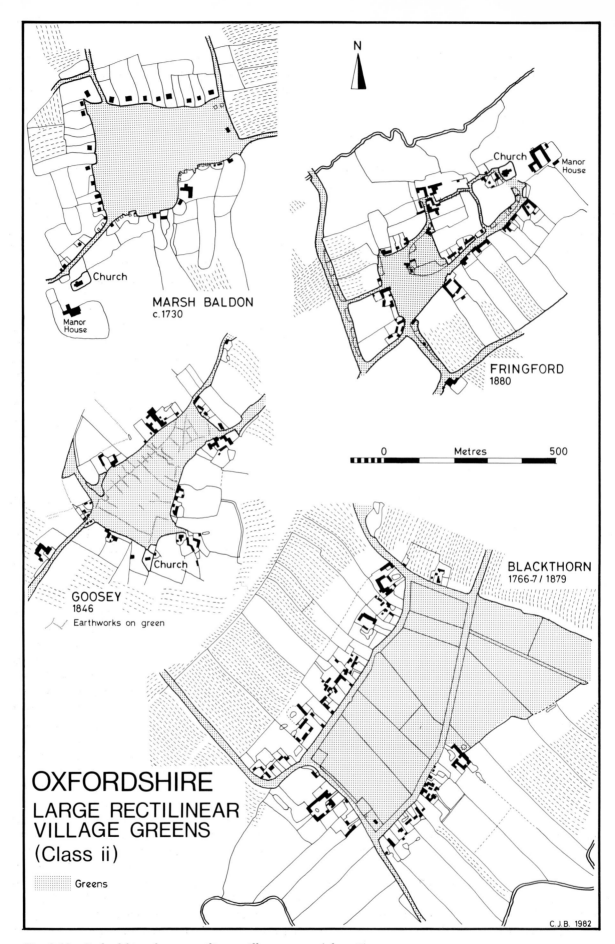

N

MARSH BALDON
c.1730

Church

Manor
House

FRINGFORD
1880

Church

Manor
House

0   Metres   500

GOOSEY
1846

Church

Earthworks on green

BLACKTHORN
1766-7 / 1879

OXFORDSHIRE
LARGE RECTILINEAR
VILLAGE GREENS
(Class ii)

Greens

C.J.B. 1982

Fig. 9.10   Oxfordshire: large rectilinear village greens (class ii)

open fields some time during the Middle Ages, the latter are a product of the enclosure of the common after 1814.

(6) Village greens

Oxfordshire village greens come in a wide range of shapes and sizes, which may reflect an equally diverse variety of origins and functions. It seems probable that their exact shape is of less significance than their extent, their degree of regularity and their relationship to the village tofts. At least four broad categories can be distinguished, though the divisions between them are sometimes imprecise:

(i) Small greens, generally less than 0.5 ha in extent, which appear to be essentially organic features of the village plan, usually occurring at road intersections and consequently often of triangular shape. Examples include Great Milton, Finstock and the Upper Green at Stanford-in-the-Vale.

(ii) Larger rectilinear greens, up to 10 ha in extent, which are more or less entirely surrounded by tofts (Fig. 9.10). The more striking examples, such as Marsh Baldon or Blackthorn, appear to be a product of conscious planning.

(iii) Large marginal greens, again sometimes up to 10 ha in extent. The essence of these is that they lie at the edge of the settlement and never appear to have been fronted by buildings on more than one side (Fig. 9.11). Examples include North Aston, Merton, Binsey, Stadhampton and Warborough.

(iv) Still more extensive commons with hamlets clinging to their margins. The commons themselves have now generally been enclosed, but Jefferys' county map of 1768 clearly shows a number of settlements, including Grafton, Lew, East End in North Leigh and Woodcote, which then occupied such positions. Some of these hamlets may have begun as temporary settlements, perhaps occupied seasonally by herdsmen using the common grazing. In other instances an element of illegal encroachment by squatters may be involved.

The exact total of village greens in Oxfordshire is difficult to determine. Some examples, including Garsington, Islip and Hook Norton, have been lost, or much reduced, through the encroachment of island blocks of buildings. Many more have been lost by enclosure. The Victoria County History account of Weston-on-the-Green remarks upon the fact that all its houses lie exclusively on the western side of the main Oxford-Brackley road, but postulates a lost green between the two lanes leading westwards from this road to account for the place-name (Lobel *V.C.H. Oxon* 1959, 6, 346–7). In fact, Jefferys' map of 1768 shows a long, wedge-shaped marginal green running the entire length of the village on the east side of the main road. This had already been divided into closes prior to

Davis' survey for his county map, published in 1797, but the east margin of the former green still survives as a hedgerow (Fig. 9.11). At Blackthorn the large rectangular green was enclosed and converted to arable fields in 1776 (Fig. 9.10). At Chesterton the triangular green was lost in 1799 when the Akeman Street was diverted in order to enlarge the grounds of the manor-house. At Kidlington both green and common were enclosed in 1810 (Fig. 9.11). The loss of other examples is undocumented, and their former existence can be deduced only from topographical evidence. Immediately north of Benson a row of cottages at Littleworth is built with the rear side fronting the road, and the frontages facing over a curious open area, now split up into gardens and allotments, which looks suspiciously like a former green.

The only general survey available (Stamp and Hoskins 1963, 249, 307–8) listed 42 extant greens in Oxfordshire, to which must be added another dozen examples then in Berkshire. This survey also lists nine examples described as small commons, which could equally be regarded as large village greens. Jefferys' map, the earliest available which is on a sufficiently large scale to provide some details of village topography over the whole of the old county, provides evidence for at least another 40 greens lost since the middle of the eighteenth century, in addition to a score of villages then lying marginal to larger commons. A more comprehensive study of early estate maps will certainly add many more examples, and it can confidently be anticipated that the final total will approach, and probably exceed, 200.

It becomes increasingly difficult to escape the feeling that many, if not most, of the 'green' villages in Oxfordshire are a product of a relatively late extension or reorganization of settlement, taking place some time during the Middle Ages. A few greens contain earthworks which suggest that they have been opened up by the clearance of earlier buildings and crofts; conspicuous examples include Baulking and Goosey (Fig. 9.10), both in the Vale of White Horse. Baulking now has a long marginal green some 8 ha in extent, with a thin scatter of farms and cottages on its western side only; the Tithe map shows that about a dozen buildings have disappeared since 1840, leaving wide gaps in this western fringe of occupation. The small thirteenth-century church, built as a chapel-of-ease to Uffington, stands in an island position on the green, and at first sight this looks like the sort of encroachment which was sometimes permitted for buildings of communal benefit—cases of churches built on greens are evident at Woodeaton, Culham and perhaps also Warborough (Fig. 9.11). However, the earthworks on Baulking green suggest an alternative interpretation. There are some indications that the village street originally ran along what is now the western edge of the green,

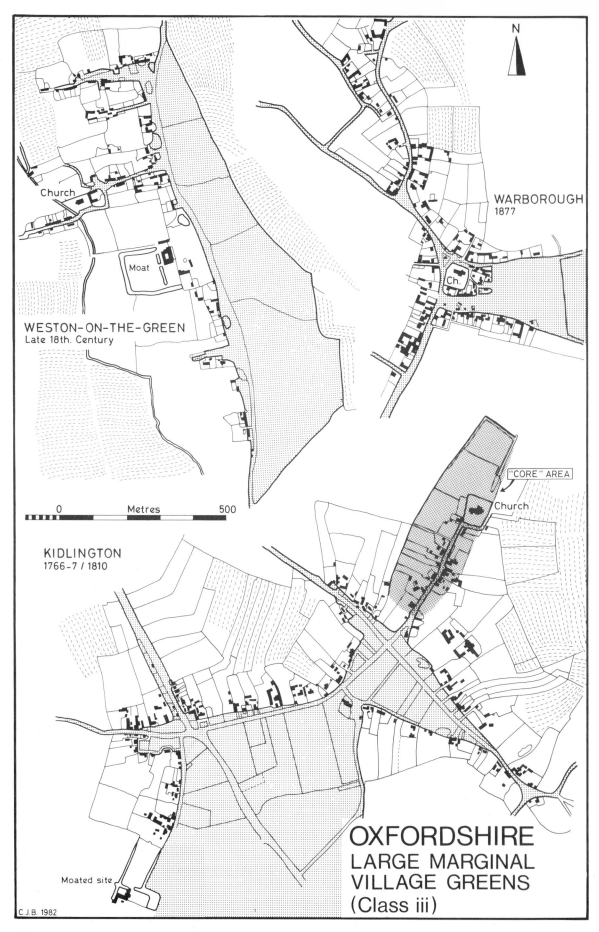

Fig. 9.11   Oxfordshire: large marginal village greens (class iii)

immediately in front of the surviving houses. Some of the earthworks on the green seem to represent former buildings, yards and croft boundaries, which would imply that the church is the last survivor of a whole run of buildings originally lining the eastern side of this street (M.V.R.G. 1975, 6–8). Stub ends of ridge and furrow in one area indicate that the green has also encroached over some land formerly under cultivation. Some of the ditches interpreted as croft boundaries have been over-deepened at a later period, presumably for drainage purposes—a similar occurrence can be seen amongst the earthworks of the deserted village of Wretchwick near Bicester. Although the evidence at Baulking is not entirely unambiguous, it does appear likely on balance that the green is a comparative late-comer created by the clearance of an area previously settled. What is not clear is why such a basic reorganization of the settlement form was necessary. One possible explanation is the presence here of a market in the thirteenth century, which might have produced a need for additional open space; but this cannot account for the apparently similar clearances on the green at Goosey nearby, and the problem remains at present unresolved.

There are several instances where a 'green' settlement appears to have superseded an earlier nucleus elsewhere in the parish. The evidence at Launton for an apparent migration from the vicinity of the church towards the Town Green and Launton Common has already been mentioned. An association between regular greens and crofts which seem to have been laid down over open-field land is also evident at Fringford and Blackthorn. At Tackley the triangular green forming the centrepiece of the present village is surrounded by stone cottages, none of which are obviously earlier than the seventeenth century. The parish church stands isolated on rising ground some 300 m to the south-west. A field just below the church which contained indistinct earthworks was ploughed for the first time in 1974 to reveal a series of buildings accompanied by quantities of early medieval pottery. At Kidlington medieval material has been recorded from within a long sub-rectangular enclosure containing the church, one of the 'core' elements mentioned earlier; but by the sixteenth century, from the evidence of existing buildings, the centre of the village had shifted to the long, funnel-ended green between Mill Street and the Moors, where some of the property boundaries suggest yet another encroachment over open field. At a later stage again, during the eighteenth century, there was a further expansion along the northern margin of the much larger common called Kidlington Green, where the present High Street now runs.

A significant proportion of greens appear to be associated with the colonization of woodland and forest landscapes, and other secondary phases of settlement. Greens at Leafield, Finstock and Delly End belong to new hamlets which came into existence as a result of assarting in Wychwood Forest. The rectangular green in the present hilltop village of Combe can only have become the focal point of the settlement since about 1350, when the previous nucleus down in the Evenlode valley is known to have been deserted. The former rectangular green at Blackthorn, now enclosed, belongs to a secondary settlement which was a daughter-hamlet of Ambrosden. One of the finest regular green villages in Oxfordshire, Marsh Baldon, appears to be a product of a planned colonization of low-lying ground, perhaps the last uncultivated land in the parish which was available for buildings to accomodate an increasing population. Two of the seven Domesday estates called *Baldendone* can be identified from their subsequent manorial history with estates at Marsh Baldon, but it would be unwise to assume from this that the green village was itself in existence by the late eleventh century. There are clearly signs of an earlier nucleus some 300 m to the south-west, where St Peter's church had been built before 1163. Settlement forms produced by assarting or other types of secondary medieval colonization were not, however, entirely dominated by greens; there are many examples of linear and other forms. Hailey, a new settlement unrecorded before 1240 and comprised in 1279 mostly of assart holdings which had been carved out of the woodland portion of the Bishop of Winchester's manor of Witney, contains three nuclei, of which Middle Town and Poffley End are strongly linear in plan; only Delly End has a small rectangular green.[2]

Conclusions and Acknowledgements

The elucidation of the origins and development of over 600 nucleated settlements which had come into existence by the end of the Middle Ages is by any standards a formidable task. It has only been possible here to sketch a fairly tentative outline of a few of the aspects which have come under reassessment recently. Indisputably much more work remains to be done, and the views expressed here can themselves only be regarded as provisional. Further detailed field survey, along with archival investigation and morphological analysis, will continue to illuminate the unique peculiarities of individual settlements. From the patient accumulation and sifting of local material it can confidently be anticipated that new significant common characteristics will also continue to emerge, and will continue to modify our present perspectives for many years to come. One of the perennial drawbacks of publishing papers originally presented at conferences is that, by their very nature, they deal with work in progress and often far from complete; but equally, it would be a very brave man who ever claimed he had 'finished' work on this topic.

In addition to the published works specifically listed in the references, I have borrowed extensively from the research of many friends and colleagues caried out over a number of years, particularly Michael Aston, Don Benson, Richard Chambers, Trevor Rowley and John Steane. I should like to acknowledge their contribution to my own thoughts, without necessarily implying that they would be in agreement with all the views put forward here. Outside Oxfordshire, I have profited greatly from the lines of investigation pioneered by Christopher Taylor and Brian Roberts. I am grateful to Mary Acheson-Gray for allowing me to read her unpublished B.A. dissertation on the morphology of the villages of Bloxham Hundred submitted at the University of Durham in 1980. Locally, I owe an enormous debt to the many people who have contributed information or discussed their own villages with me; amongst them, Louise Armstrong, Evelyn Brown-Grant, Reg Dand, the late Reg Edginton, Percy Hackling, Jasmine and Violet Howse, Gordon Miles,

Ernest Pocock, Margaret Rogers, Pat Tucker and Jill Wishart have supplied material and ideas used directly or indirectly here. Finally, my thanks go to Ival Hornbrook and Elizabeth Leggatt for all their hard work in processing information through the county Sites and Monuments Record; without their interest and commitment the basis for this paper would not exist.

Note on the maps

With the exception of Figs. 9.2, 9.4 and 9.8, all village plans have been drawn to the same scale to facilitate comparison. The basis of the plans dated 1875–81 is the first edition of the Ordnance Survey 1:2,500. Those dated to the 1840s are based upon the Tithe maps, and those with earlier dates are derived from enclosure or estate maps. Areas of greens and commons have generally been superimposed on to larger-scale later maps from Jefferys' county survey of 1766–7, where no adequate alternative source was to hand.

Notes

1. Since this was written the Ordnance Survey's location of a nineteenth-century discovery of Roman material near Kidlington church has been called into question, and there are now some grounds for suspecting that this site may have lain *c*. 750 m away to the north-west.

2. Some of the suggestions contained in this paragraph now require

modification in the light of Beryl Schumer's recently-published argument that many of the Wychwood hamlets, traditionally supposed to have their origins in post-Conquest assarting, were already fully established before the late eleventh century (Schumer, B. 1984: *The Evolution of Wychwood to 1400: Pioneers, Frontiers and Forests* (Leicester University Department of English Local History, Occasional Papers, 3rd series, 6).

References

Allison, K. J., Beresford, M. W. and Hurst, J. G. 1965: *The Deserted Villages of Oxfordshire* (Leicester University Department of English Local History. Occasional Paper 17).

Armstrong, L. 1979: Standlake, Oxfordshire. *Council for British Archaeology Group 9 Newsletter* 9, 31–7.

Arthur, B. V. and Jope, E. M. 1962–3: Early Saxon pottery kilns at Purwell Farm, Cassington, Oxfordshire. *Medieval Archaeology* 6/7, 1–14.

Benson, D. and Miles, D. 1974a: Cropmarks near the Sutton Courtenay Saxon site. *Antiquity* 48, No. 191, 223–6.

Benson, D. and Miles, D. 1974b: *The Upper Thames Valley: an Archaeological Survey of the River Gravels* (Oxfordshire Archaeological Unit, survey No. 2).

Beresford, M. W. 1954: *The Lost Villages of England* (London, Lutterworth Press).

Beresford, M. W. and Hurst, J. G. 1979: Wharram Percy; a Case Study in Microtopography. In Sawyer, P. H. (editor) 1979, 52–85.

Biddle, M. 1961–2: The deserted medieval village of Seacourt, Berkshire. *Oxoniensia* 26/27, 70–201.

Blair, J. 1979: Two early cruck houses in south Oxfordshire. *Oxoniensia* 44, 55–61.

Bond, C. J. 1980: Bloxham, Oxfordshire: village survey. *Council for British Archaeology Group 9 Newsletter* 10, 103–23.

Brodribb, A. C. C., Hands, A. R. and Walker, D. R. 1968–78: *Excavations at Shakenoak* 5 Volumes. (Oxford, private publication).

Chambers, R. A. 1979: Excavations at Westcote Barton parish church, Oxfordshire, 1977. *Oxoniensia* 44, 99–101.

Chambers, R. A. 1981: Launton. *Council for British Archaeology Group 9 Newsletter* 11, 128.

Clack, P. A. G. and Gosling, P. F. (editors) 1975: *Archaeology in the North* (Durham, Northern Archaeological Survey).

Crossley, A. (editor) 1972: *The Victoria History of the Counties of England. A History of the County of Oxford*, Vols. 10, 11.

Emden, C. S. 1951: *Combe Church and Village* (Oxford, private publication).

Emery, F. V. 1974: *The Oxfordshire Landscape* (London, Hodder and Stoughton).

Emery, F. V. 1975: Rural places in the early nineteenth century. In Smith, C. G. and Scargill, D. I. (editors) 1975, 37–43.

Finberg, H. P. R. 1959: *Roman and Saxon Withington: a Study in Continuity* (Leicester University Department of English Local History. Occasional Paper 8).

Fowler, P. J. (editor) 1975: *Recent Work in Rural Archaeology* (Bradford on Avon, Moonraker Press).

Gray, M. 1974: The Saxon settlement at New Wintles, Eynsham, Oxfordshire. In Rowley, R. T. (editor) 1974, 51–5.

Harvey, P. D. A. 1965: *A Medieval Oxfordshire Village: Cuxham, 1240–1400* (London, Oxford University Press. Oxford Historical Series, 2nd series).

Havinden, M. A. 1966: *Estate Villages: a Study of the Berkshire Villages of Ardington and Lockinge* (London, Lund Humphries for University of Reading).

Hawkes, S. C. and Gray, M. 1969: Preliminary note on the early Anglo-Saxon settlement at New Wintles Farm, Eynsham. *Oxoniensia* 34, 1–4.

Hinton, D. A. 1973: Excavations at Church Piece, Tetsworth, Oxon. *Oxoniensia* 38, 116–8.

Hoskins, W. G. 1959: *Local History in England* (London, Longmans).

Hoskins, W. G. and Jope, E. M. 1954: The medieval period. In Martin, A. F. and Steel, R. W. (editors) 1954, 103–20.

Jope, E. M. and Threlfall, R. I. 1959: The twelfth-century castle at Ascot Doilly, Oxfordshire: its history and excavation. *Antiquaries Journal* 39, 219–73.

Limbrey, S. and Evans, J. G. (editors) 1978: *The Effect of Man on the*

Landscape: The Lowland Zone (London, Council for British Archaeology Research Report 21).

Lobel, M. D. (editor) 1957, 1959, 1962, 1964: *The Victoria History of the Counties of England. A History of the County of Oxford,* Vols. 5, 6, 7, 8. (The University of London Institute of Historical Research).

Lobel, M. D. and Crossley, A. (editors) 1969: *The Victoria History of the Counties of England. A History of the County of Oxford,* Vol. 9. (The University of London Institute of Historical Research).

Martin, A. F. and Steel, R. W. (editors) 1954: *The Oxford Region: a Scientific and Historical Survey* (London, Oxford University Press).

Medieval Village Research Group 1975: *23rd Annual Report.*

Medieval Village Research Group 1981: *29th Annual Report.*

Miles, D. 1974: Abingdon and region; early Anglo-Saxon settlement evidence. In Rowley, R. T. (editor) 1974, 36–41.

Paget, E. 1954: Settlements. In Martin, A. F. and Steel, R. W. (editors) 1954, 158–64.

Royal Commission on Historical Monuments (England) 1975: *An Inventory of the Historical Monuments in the County of Northampton,* Volume 1: Archaeological sites in north-east Northamptonshire, (London, H.M. Stationery Office).

Royal Commission on Historical Monuments (England) 1979: *An Inventory of the Historical Monuments in the County of Northampton,* Volume 2: Archaeological sites in central Northamptonshire, (London, H.M. Stationery Office).

Royal Commission on Historical Monuments (England) 1982: *An Inventory of the Historical Monuments in the County of Northampton,* Volume 4: Archaeological sites in south-west Northamptonshire, (London, H.M. Stationery Office).

Ravensdale, J. R. 1974: *Liable to Floods: Village Landscape on the Edge of the Fens AD 450–1850* (London, Cambridge University Press).

Roberts, B. K. 1971: The study of village plans. *Local Historian* 9, part 5, 233–41.

Roberts, B. K. 1972: Village plans in County Durham: a preliminary statement. *Medieval Archaeology* 16, 33–56.

Roberts, B. K. 1975: The northern village; an archaeological perspective. In Clack, P. A. G. and Gosling, P. F. (editors) 1975, 255–64.

Roberts, B. K. 1977: *Rural Settlement in Britain* (Folkestone, Dawson).

Roberts, B. K. 1978: The regulated village in northern England: some problems and questions. *Geographia Polonica* 38, 245–52.

Roberts, B. K. 1982: Village forms in Warwickshire; a preliminary discussion. In Slater, T. R. and Jarvis, P. J. (editors) 1982, 125–46.

Robinson, M. 1973: Excavations at Copt Hay, Tetsworth, Oxon. *Oxoniensia* 38, 41–115.

Rowley, R. T. 1974: Early Saxon settlements in Dorchester on Thames. In Rowley, R. T (editor) 1974, 42–50.

Rowley, R. T. (editor) 1974: *Anglo-Saxon Settlement and Landscape* (Oxford, British Archaeological Reports 6).

Sawyer, P. H. (editor) 1979: *Medieval Settlement, Continuity and Change* (London, Edward Arnold).

Sheppard, J. 1974: Metrological analysis of regular village plans in Yorkshire. *Agricultural History Review* 22, 2 118–35.

Sheppard, J. 1976: Medieval village planning in northern England. *Journal of Historical Geography* 2, 3–20.

Slater, T. R. and Jarvis, P. J. (editors) 1982: *Field and Forest: an Historical Geography of Warwickshire and Worcestershire* (Norwich, Geo Books).

Smith, C. G. and Scargill, D. I. (editors) 1975: *Oxford and its Region: Geographical Essays* (Oxford, Oxford University Press).

Stamp, L. D. and Hoskins, W. G. 1963: *The Common Lands of England and Wales* (London, Collins. New Naturalist series No. 45).

Taylor, C. C. 1977: Polyfocal settlement and the English village. *Medieval Archaeology* 21, 189–93.

Taylor, C. C. 1978: Aspects of village mobility in medieval and later times. In Limbrey, S. and Evans, J. G. (editors) 1978, 126–34.

Wade-Martins, P. 1975: The origins of rural settlement in East Anglia. In Fowler, P. J. (editor) 1975, 137–57.

10. Village Development in the West Midlands

D. Hooke

Nucleation of settlement is a more pronounced characteristic of the south-eastern sector of the West Midland region and was already occurring by the early medieval period. It was associated with the intensive development of arable farming, already at that date organized under a form of open-field agriculture. Processes of depopulation and settlement agglomeration were subsequently to intensify the pattern. Outlying settlements beyond manorial nuclei were more in evidence in the west and north of the region. In the latter, a scatter of minor settlements appear to have been characteristic of a more heavily-wooded countryside in which pastoralism may have played a greater role in the economy. This tendency, too, was to be perpetuated by later developments.

The nucleated village is a typical settlement form over much of the West Midland area. It is especially a characteristic of the south-eastern part of the region and strongly nucleated village clusters are found throughout the Gloucestershire Cotswolds, much of the Warwickshire Feldon and south-eastern Worcestershire. There are marked changes as one moves northwards and westwards—while it is still possible to recognize a village nucleus, there is a tendency for the number of outlying hamlets and farms to increase, until, in some areas, the village nucleus is missing altogether. These variations are recognizable throughout England but the reasons for them still provide ample scope for discussion, and, above all, it would be advantageous to be able to comment upon the origins and stability of the pattern.

A study of the village cannot be separated from that of its economic environment. In most cases the reason for the existence and development of the medieval village community was the exploitation of the land, and in normal circumstances the wealth of the village and of its dwellings would reflect the wealth of its fields. It is not over-presumptuous to expect that the distribution of houses in the settlement would reflect the agricultural practices and techniques of rural agriculture. The village must be thought of, therefore, as complementary to its fields, woods, pastures, etc., and a study of a settlement cannot be divorced from an understanding of its surrounding countryside. The present paper touches upon two particular aspects of village development; the first is village origins, the second, the regional variation already observed in settlement patterns, and it will be shown that these are closely interrelated.

The West Midland area: village origins

The West Midlands, here defined as the region comprising the present-day counties of Worcestershire,

Warwickshire and Gloucestershire, is a highly important region for a study of village origins, in spite of the lack of archaeological evidence. The dangers of utilizing Domesday evidence are well known, but this does appear to have been one of the more intensively developed regions of the country in 1086 (Darby 1977, 132). The density of settlement which had been achieved by the medieval period can only really be appreciated since the cumulative evidence of village desertion, obtained over the last 20 years or so, has contributed towards a reconstruction of the earlier settlement pattern. The concentration of Domesday settlement suggested in this area is matched by an equally noticeable concentration of village desertion (Beresford and Hurst 1971, 66), the number of sites known having increased dramatically within recent years (Bond 1982, 147−71).

This area may well have escaped the more devastating effects of the Anglo-Saxon conquest. The fury of the invaders was largely spent by the time they reached these middle regions and here there was time for negotiation and compromise. It has been argued that there are signs of cultural overlap in the pagan cemeteries of south Warwickshire (Ford 1976, 274; Cook 1958, 80) and Smith (1965, 56–64) has suggested that the Anglo-Saxon kingdom of the Hwicce, which was established over the area of much of the later counties of Worcestershire, Gloucestershire and south-west Warwickshire, was of mixed Celtic-Anglo-Saxon origin. This seems to be borne out by the place-name, linguistic and archaeological evidence (Smith *ibid.*; Wilson 1972; Mills 1960). The kingdom owed fealty to the greater kingdom of Mercia established across Central England by the seventh century. The name of this folk means 'people of the march or border', referring to the fact that their heartland in the Midlands represented the furthest reaches of Anglo-Saxon dominance by the late sixth and early seventh century (Stenton 1971, 40).[1]

If any evidence of continuity in the landscape is to be found, it should perhaps be sought in the West Midland area. This was one of the richest areas of Roman Britain, with *Corinium*, modern Cirencester, recognized as the second largest town in the province. In its hinterland, the Gloucestershire Cotswolds, villa development was more pronounced than almost anywhere else in the country (Rivet 1969, 211). Beyond the region of villas, some of which may have been owned by prosperous foreign investors, native farmsteads were thick on the ground, especially in the rich vales of the Severn and its tributary the Avon, and finds of flue-tiles, wall plaster and pottery show the extent to which Roman standards of living had been adopted by the native farmer. Archaeology has yet to provide a full picture of development in the Romano-British period. From present knowledge the most intensive occupation appears to have been in the central and south-east of the area, and while future discoveries may add to the evidence, it seems likely that the regional pattern suggested so far by surface finds and below-ground excavation will continue to portray accurately the degree of prosperity reached within this area in that period (Hooke 1981a, 60). It was the Avon valley area, too, which was to see the first wave of Anglo-Saxon pagan burials, with a secondary group over the Gloucestershire Cotswolds (Pretty 1975).

The central Avon valley and lands to the south and south-east were without doubt the most fertile and productive parts of the West Midlands in the early medieval period. The number of Domesday plough teams recorded reached the highest densities in this area, averaging over 3.5 per square mile in the regions bordering upon the Vale of Evesham in south-east Worcestershire, the central Avon valley with its tributary valley of the River Stour in Warwickshire and the valleys of the east Gloucestershire Cotswolds (Darby 1971, 432). The intensity of arable cultivation seems to have diminished northwards and westwards and although there is little evidence of pastoralism in the Domesday survey, this may have played a greater role in the rural economy of these regions. This pattern was to persist with remarkable clarity in sixteenth- and seventeenth-century Warwickshire when the southern part of the county, known as the Feldon or 'open country' (Dugdale 1656, preface 3b), was described by Leland as 'for the moste parte champion, somewhat barren of wood, but very plentifull of corne' (Toulmin-Smith 1908, 5, 47). To the north-west, however, the upland regions surrounding the Tame-Blythe basin were known as the Arden, a name possibly derived from a Celtic stem *ardu*, 'high' (Gelling 1974, 74), and traditionally, but not legally, known as a Forest. Leland described the region as 'muche enclosyd, plentifull of gres, but no great plenty of corne' (Toulmin-Smith 1908, 5, 47).

It must be considered how far the level of development reached in the prehistoric and Roman periods was influential in producing the patterns of settlement and field systems existing in the medieval period. There is a close correlation between areas of intensive early development and subsequent settlement nucleation but it is not yet possible to elucidate accurately either the sequence of events which occurred or the precise factors which produced them. There can be little doubt that settlement nucleation took place in those areas in which open-field agriculture was also a prominent characteristic and the one seems indeed to reflect the type of social and agrarian system which produced the other.[2] It is in the Anglo-Saxon period that one is first able to detect most clearly the areas of intensive agricultural activity and, particularly, those areas with the most land utilized for arable cultivation.

The evidence for such activity is to be derived largely from pre-Conquest charters, much of the information contained in the boundary clauses which accompany many of the documents. These clearly show arable land extending as far as the boundaries of estates in particular areas, with the central Avon valley and the rich Feldon areas of the south-east noticeably prominent. It cannot be coincidental that it is in those areas in which arable land features most frequently amongst the boundary landmarks that the charters also contain references to features akin to an early open-field system. While references to furlongs, headlands and furrows are found most frequently in the area of the central Avon and north-east Gloucestershire, with another concentration around Worcester in the Severn valley, it is also in the Avon valley that references occur to divided acres at Alveston, *Fachanleah* and Bredon (Hooke 1981a, 39–63; Finberg 1972, 487–96). In the tenth century land held with an estate at Alveston, Warwickshire, was described as lying *on þære gesyndredan hide*, 'in the divided hide', at Upper Stratford, where the lease was of 'every other acre' there and of 'every third acre' of *feld land*, 'open land', at *Fachanleage* (Sawyer 1968, S. 1310; Robertson 1956, 88–9). A lease of the nearby estate of Bishopton in AD 1016 included 'every third acre of bean-land on *Biscopes dūne*, 'the bishop's hill' (Kemble 1839–48, K. 724). At Aston Somerville in the Vale of Evesham in Worcestershire two hides were described in AD 995 as being situated in common land, in AD 1002 held *sorte communes populari*, 'by popular allotment' (Sawyer 1968, S. 886, S. 901; Kemble 1839–48, K. 692, K. 1295). Furthermore, fragmentation of strip holdings may be suggested by the phrase *ge inner ge utter*, 'both central and outlying', noted in a charter of Moreton in Bredon, Worcestershire, in AD 990. Here land is divided between two brothers with the proviso that 'the elder shall always have 3 acres and the younger the fourth, both central and outlying, as pertains to the estate'

(Sawyer 1968, S. 1363; Robertson 1956, 130–3). Such references clearly indicate intermixed acre-strips which appear to have extended over substantial acreages.

Such areas are also characterized by a distinctive estate pattern. The charter clauses confirm the antiquity of township and parish boundaries and these reveal a close patchwork of small, individual estates. In some valley areas the boundaries often form a regular pattern of valley division which has been noted elsewhere in densely populated riverine locations such as the Wylye valley in Wiltshire or parts of Dorset (Bonney 1972, 168–96; Taylor 1970, 51–2). The township pattern which evolved certainly appears to have pre-dated the drawing-up of ecclesiastical parish boundaries in such areas as the Stour valley of Warwickshire near Stratford (Hooke 1982, 236–40). In the Severn valley of Worcestershire, too, the tiny township divisions produced an irregular parish pattern which fossilized their existence in the mid-Anglo-Saxon period.

Township divisions are equally prominent in the Warwickshire Feldon, although the townships are united within large ecclesiastical parishes and the large parish-estate dominates the overall boundary pattern. Parish size in itself, however, is not necessarily indicative of either antiquity or prosperity. Individual townships could remain united within a composite estate under powerful ownership. The large Gloucestershire parish of Withington, for instance, reflects the presence there of an estate based upon an Anglo-Saxon minster in the eight century (Finberg 1955). Similarly, the large parish of Tredington, now in Warwickshire, was part of a holding granted to the Bishop of Worcester by the under-kings of the Hwicce in AD 757, again supporting a minster church (Sawyer 1968, S. 55; Birch 1885–99, B. 183). Conversely, large parishes are also found in areas of underdevelopment, where economic resources were presumably insufficient to maintain smaller, independent communities capable of providing adequate revenue to the Church. It seems, however, that the smaller unit of the township was a prime administrative unit in Anglo-Saxon England (Hooke 1981b, 82–112). The bounds of these townships can frequently be reconstructed from charter evidence even when they have not survived within the parish-unit today.

The evidence of field systems and estate-patterns can to some extent be gathered relatively easily from the charters. It is more difficult to reconstruct early settlement patterns owing to the nature of the documents. In the present paper sample studies from selected regional zones will be presented in order to investigate the evidence of early settlement types in the West Midlands, and the relation of these to administrative and agrarian organization, with a brief account of subsequent settlement development.

South Warwickshire: the Stour valley and the Feldon

Tredington parish lies in the Stour valley of Warwickshire but was included within the Domesday county of Worcestershire, from which it was transferred in 1931. It is a large parish containing a number of individual townships. The boundaries of these can be reconstructed from nineteenth-century estate maps but the antiquity of some of them is confirmed by pre-Conquest charter evidence. Blackwell formed such a township unit within the parish when leased to Ælfnoth in AD 978 (Sawyer 1968, S. 1337; Kemble 1839–48, K. 620) (Fig. 10.1). It lay to the west of the main village of Tredington and the estate comprised gently sloping land drained by headwater streams of the Back Brook, a tributary of the River Stour. The northern boundary of the township followed ðæt riðig, 'the streamlet', and much of its southern boundary followed the *middelriðige*, 'middle streamlet'. Its western boundary marched with that of the main parish across the lower slopes of Ilmington hill and appears to have been demarcated by dykes for most of its course. In the east, the township extended southwards to take in part of the valley of the Back Brook itself and again less clearly defined parts of the boundary appear to have been deliberately dyked by the tenth century.

Longdon formed a second township-estate recognizable in the tenth century (Sawyer 1968, S. 1321; Birch 1885–99, B. 1243). It lay in the south-western corner of Tredington parish and the southern and western boundaries it shared with the main parish followed marked topographical features which were recorded as boundary landmarks (Fig. 10.2a). The township area was drained by other headwater streams of the Back Brook, and the upper portions of one of these flowed along the western part of the southern boundary, referred to in the clause as a *sīc*, 'a watercourse'. A second stream crossed the western boundary further north as þære lace, 'the slow-moving stream', but much of the western boundary followed two prominent hills referred to by the Old English term *dūn*. The eastern boundary of the township followed less prominent features, and landmarks referred to in the clause include a path, 'the broad waggon-way' (which is still represented by the road joining Longdon and Darlingscott), and a furrow. The middle part of the eastern boundary follows a stepped course and the furrow may have separated the ploughed fields of Longdon from those of Darlingscott. The remaining part of the south-eastern boundary followed þam rigcce, a low natural ridge. The impression gained in this instance is that the township divisions were carved out within a pre-existing estate. Significantly, no form of settlement is mentioned in the clauses of Tredington,

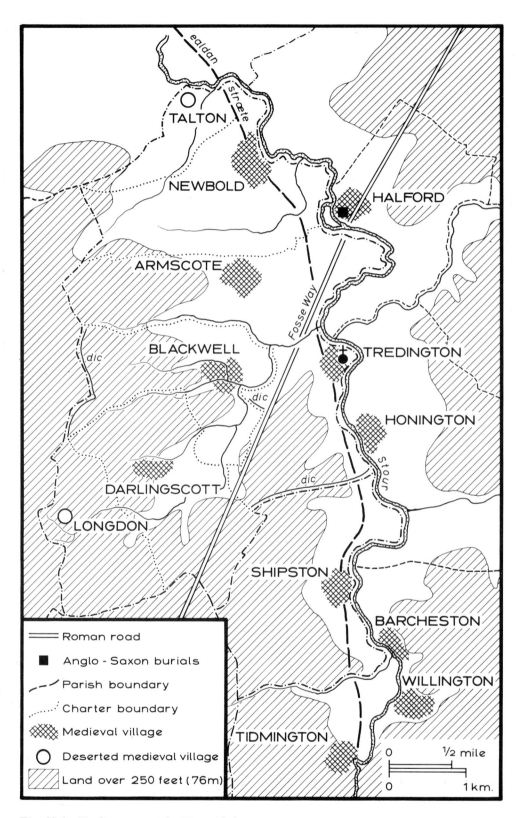

Fig. 10.1   Tredington parish, Warwickshire

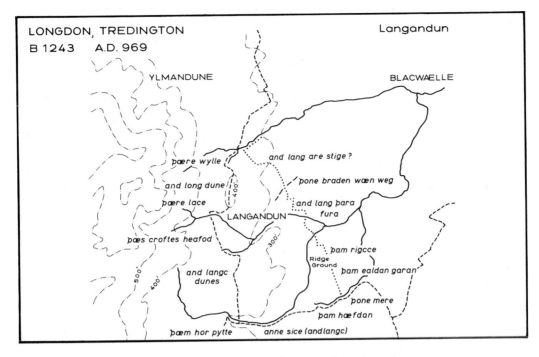

Fig. 10.2 Longdon in Tredington: (a) The 10th-century boundary clause

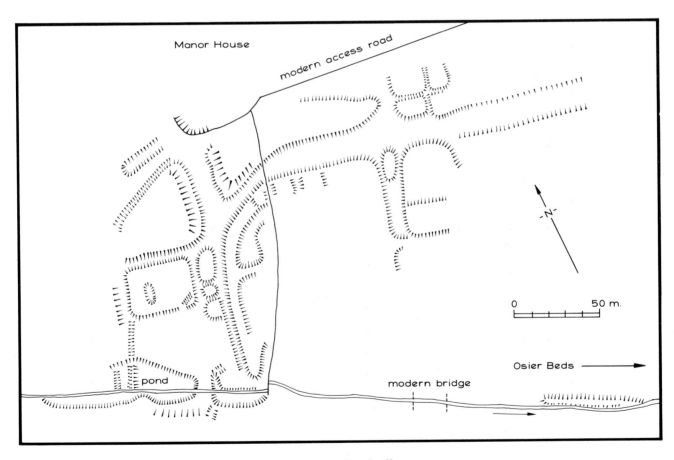

Fig. 10.2 Longdon in Tredington: (b) The deserted medieval village

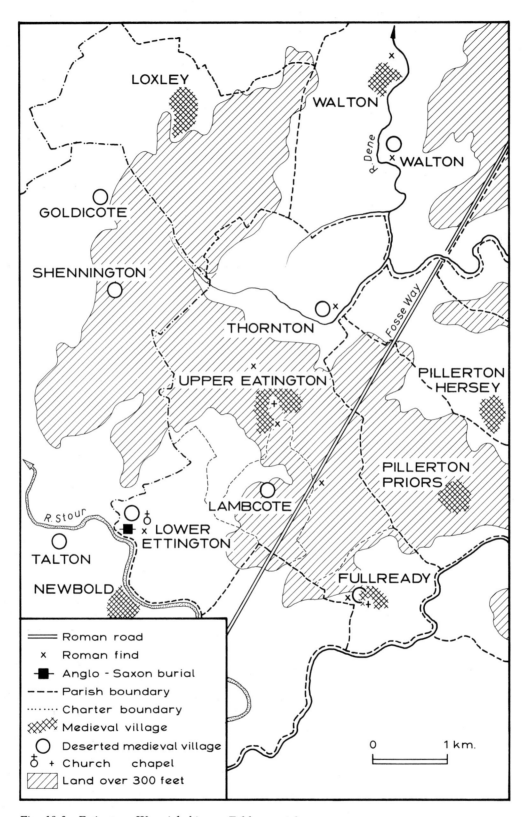

Fig. 10.3 Ettington, Warwickshire: a Feldon parish

and this is typical of the clauses of this region. The absence of settlement references seems to suggest that any centres of habitation lay well within the bounds of even the smaller estates.

The Bishop of Worcester was also to lease out other estates in Tredington parish in the pre-Conquest period. One hide at Newbold and two hides at Talton were leased to the thane Eadric in AD 991 (Sawyer 1968, S. 1366; Robertson 1956, 138) and two further hides at Armscote were leased to the thane Æthelric in 1042 (Sawyer 1968, S. 1394; Robertson 1956, 180). As the chief manor, Tredington lay at the nucleus of an estate said to be assessed at 23 hides in 1086, and only Blackwell and Longdon are mentioned individually in the Domesday survey, the former having been assigned to the support of the monks of St Mary's, Worcester, in the mid-eleventh century (Domesday Book, 1, f. 173c) and the latter being sub-let to Gilbert son of Turold at the time of the survey.

Longdon as a village cannot be identified until the medieval period, and in common with many of the settlements of this area had been abandoned by post-medieval times. It lay in the mid-western sector of the township beside the *lacu/*læce* stream of the Anglo-Saxon charter. The medieval village had comprised a number of blocks of buildings, with side-roads running down to the stream (Fig. 10.2b). While quantities of medieval pottery (including sherds of eleventh- and twelfth-century date) have been found, additional pieces of Samian ware seem to indicate earlier occupation of the site in the Roman period.[3] This is a common characteristic of village sites in this region and although evidence of Anglo-Saxon occupation is still missing in an area which was virtually aceramic in that period, the actual village sites were obviously of ancient origin. There are no records of when desertion occurred at Longdon. This was a four and a half *mansæ* estate when leased to Byrnric in AD 969 and in 1086 the listed inhabitants included eight villeins, two bordars, four slaves and four bondwomen. Eight ploughs were operating on the manor (Domesday Book, 1, f. 173c). Eight tax-payers are still listed in the returns of 1327 (Eld 1895, 22) and this village may have been a victim of deliberate enclosure for grazing, a fate shared with numerous other settlements in this part of Warwickshire. The village street was entirely abandoned and in the sixteenth century a farmhouse was built above the village site with a new access way leading to it.

A few miles to the north-east of Tredington lies the equally large parish of Ettington, straddling the Roman Fosse Way and incorporating a watershed area rising to over 91 m (300 feet) between the valleys of the Stour and Dene, both tributaries of the Avon (Fig. 10.3). Again, it is possible to show that the parish included a number of individual townships, Fullready, Lower and Upper Ettington, Lambcote and Thornton, although no pre-Conquest charters survive to confirm their early existence. Nevertheless, each village site has produced evidence of earlier activity. The main Domesday manor of Lower Ettington lay centred upon a site which produced 'coins of the Lower Empire, brass ornaments, and great quantities of Romano-British pottery', according to a nineteenth-century historian (Shirley 1869, 10). Saxon spearheads found to the south-east of the manor-house probably came from a pagan burial and indicate continued activity in the early Anglo-Saxon period. Pottery finds tended to be ignored until the present century but Roman coins have been recorded on almost every village site in this area and Roman Samian ware has also recently been found at Fullready near the present shrunken village.

At Thornton a fuller picture emerges. Aerial photography reveals the existence of an oval enclosure just above the site of the deserted medieval village. In the field it is possible to identify a spread of stone scatter which probably represents the worn-down remains of an encircling bank or rampart, with suggestions of a second lying outside the first. Worked flints and small quantities of Iron Age pottery have been gathered from the site. Definite evidence of more permanent occupation comes from the Roman period; from concentrations of pottery scatter it has been possible to identify the sites of a number of buildings on and around the later village nucleus dating from this period. So far little evidence of Romano-British occupation has been detected in any of the outer parts of Thornton township or indeed in any of the outlying regions beyond the hamlet nuclei of Ettington[4]. It is too early yet to say whether this is a true picture of the Romano-British settlement pattern but it is possible that the village sites were even then the most important areas of occupation in this region.

The medieval village was a large one and again lay beside a stream, here a tributary of the River Dene. The earthworks of its moated manor are some of the best in the county and the village again consisted of blocks of settlement between streets running down to the stream (Fig. 10.4). When surveyed, part of the site had been destroyed by ploughing but this made it possible to collect both medieval and Roman pottery from that part of the village near the stream. Pottery sherds included the handles of numerous jugs, obviously broken when the villagers collected water. There is no separate entry for Thornton in the Domesday survey, but Ettington then included four separate manors, only Fullready being named. Most of the parish lands were held of Henry de Ferrers by a certain Saswalo, this family changing its name to Shirley in the twelfth century. Thornton was sublet in the thirteenth century when it had some 21 inhabitants, but by 1447 there were only five tenants and again there are few details of how

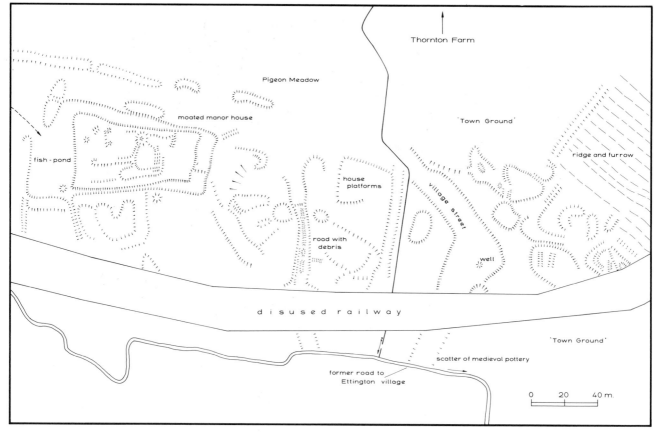

Fig. 10.4   Thornton deserted medieval village

depopulation came about (Dyer 1982, 24). Today, a house of mid-sixteenth-century date stands on higher ground overlooking the village and manor house site. Depopulation affected most of the Ettington hamlets, including the chief manor of Lower Ettington where members of the Shirley family had their home for nearly 900 years. Here they made a deer-park and nothing remains of the village but the ruins of a part-thirteenth-century church and the manor house, which was rebuilt in 1862 and is now a hotel. But the settlement at Upper Ettington, right on top of the watershed ridge, was to grow correspondingly, extending along the roads leading into it from the south-east and south.

A number of features characterize the south-eastern Feldon region of Warwickshire. This appears to have been an area of pre-Conquest prosperity, with a higher proportion of land under cultivation than elsewhere in the county. Such wealth supported a network of individual townships which were more numerous than has usually been appreciated. These were, however, normally grouped into larger parish-estates and by 1086 held tightly together within large manorial units (Fig. 10.5). These were prosperous manors with relatively high population levels, reaching a recorded density of 10–15 per square mile, and a higher than average number of plough teams working, numbers

reaching 4.4 teams per square mile in the Stour valley area, a significant proportion operating on demesne-land. The manorial system was firmly entrenched and there was also a high proportion of slaves in this area of the county.

Until more is known about social organization in the Anglo-Saxon and immediate pre-Norman period, it would be premature to speculate upon how much aspects of estate management owed to those of the Romano-British period (Postan 1972, 1–26), certainly a time when a considerable amount of land lay under the plough and when this region supported a relatively rich rural economy. However, the process which involved the centralization of the manor seems to have been most active in the later years of the Anglo-Saxon period and some explanation must be found which takes into account the obvious concentration of this trend in this particular region. It is important to distinuish between the manor as a form of social organization and the settlement pattern as an expression of the agrarian organization practised within such an administrative unit, but the individual townships of the pre-Conquest period seem to have enjoyed a degree of autonomy at that time. There is clear evidence that open-field methods of agriculture were evolving before the Norman Conquest, apparently associated with each

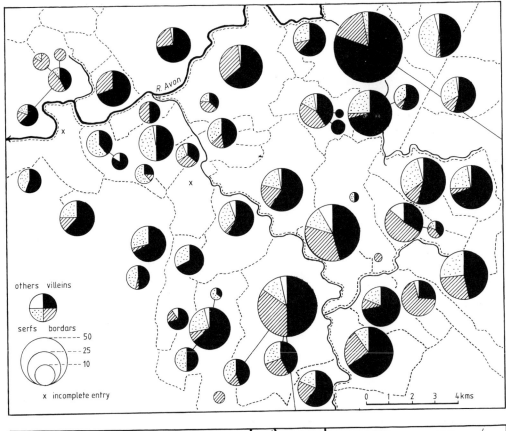

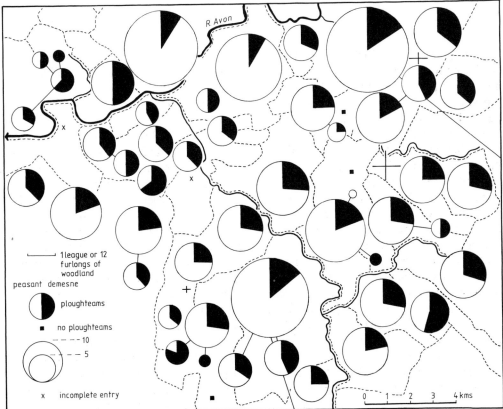

Fig. 10.5   The Warwickshire Feldon: the Domesday evidence

township core. These dependent vills are barely mentioned in the Domesday record and it seems likely that the process of centralization was effected most readily and most decisively in these Feldon areas.

In this region it is still not possible to suggest a firm date for the achievement of settlement nucleation, which may have been an on-going process. The archaeological record is by no means complete but Romano-British occupation has been noted on village sites and, from present evidence, outlying settlements appear to have been few in number. Again, this may indicate a form of villa-type estate organization in the Roman period, with the process of settlement agglomeration already foreshadowed. At Thornton, Romano-British dwellings appear from the evidence of surface pottery finds to have been loosely clustered in the vicinity of the later medieval village but to have extended beyond its confines. Certainly, the dearth of boundary settlements noted in the pre-Conquest charter clauses of the Feldon region suggests that settlement nucleation had largely taken place by the later Anglo-Saxon period.

This seems to be confirmed by information contained within a tenth-century charter of Daylesford, an estate located in the Evenlode valley of north-east Gloucestershire. This is accompanied by a boundary clause in which the bounds run round the estate, starting *be westan tūne*, 'to the west of the tūn', and after continuing along more distant landmarks return to the River Evenlode *be Suðantūne*, 'to the south of the *tūn*' (Sawyer 1968, S. 1340; Kemble 1839–48, K. 623). It has become customary to exercise caution when interpreting the Old English word *tūn* and to translate it as 'estate', but here, as in several other charters, it is clear that the term was being applied to the present village site and to the later Anglo-Saxon settlement. It is interesting to note that *tūn* as a name-term was being applied to settlements throughout the mid to late Anglo-Saxon period, but was not often used before AD 730 (Cox 1975–6, 63; Gelling 1974, 65–9). It was, in other words, fashionable in the period suggested for village formation. The fields of these Gloucestershire settlements are shown by the charter evidence to have occupied well-drained sloping land above the villages, where the slope helped to alleviate the heavy nature of the clay soils. Above these, woodland seems to have survived near parish margins. A few miles to the west, arable fields lay to the west of Donnington in a similar arrangement, but heathland occupied a major section of the parish to the east (Hooke 1981a, 50–2).

Village nucleation, associated with a form of open field agriculture, seems, then, to have been a relatively early feature of settlement history in these areas, developing even before waste and woodland had been removed from the landscape. It seems to have been closely related to an agricultural system the origins of

which are still subject for debate. Communal ownership of land by certain sections of the community may in itself be an ancient feature and seems to have been present in association with some forms of bond tenure in the Celtic West (Jones 1972, 334–58; 1981, 202–25). It may be argued that the changes noted in the Anglo-Saxon documents merely represent an extension of an old-established pattern involving the centralization of the village economy to a marked degree and involving the reorganization of much of the available arable land. Alternatively, an entirely new system may have been introduced into the area from elsewhere. The dramatic field layouts currently being suggested for parts of eastern England (Harvey 1981, 184–201; Hall 1981, 22–38) are of considerable interest and similar processes may have influenced the organization of field layout in the south and east of the West Midland area. Thus, the system could be regarded as either inherently an ancient one responding to a changing social and economic situation or a new type of organization which was receiving active encouragement from the leaders of society at this time. It would be premature, upon the basis of the evidence available so far, to attempt to arrive at any decisive conclusions for this area. The crucial period for change, however, seems to have been the mid to late Anglo-Saxon period, and in time resulted in the nucleated settlement, eventually to be associated with the total reallocation of all of the available land in the township. Whether such a system evolved in order to meet the demands of an increasing population or to increase the revenue of the individual estate is not clear. Harley (1960) has shown that population had reached high levels in south-east Warwickshire by the time of the Norman Conquest, probably reaching saturation point for the system of agriculture then in practise. However, other factors of a political and social nature may also have been influential. Peasant economies are notoriously averse to the acceptance of large-scale alterations in methods of agrarian management and life-style, and it is difficult to envisage major organizational change without powerful leadership. The centralization process reflected in the Domesday manors of the area suggests social and political motivation but the process seems first to have occurred at a lower administrative level within the township unit. At the time that changes were beginning to occur, individual estates were often attaining greater independence as they were being leased or granted to minor lords, each under pressure to increase both its self-sufficiency and its surplus revenue.

Pre-Conquest reorganization of both fields and settlement, whether it developed gradually or as a result of deliberate seigneurial control, seems to have taken place on a large scale, however, only in areas where there was already a high population density, a large amount of cleared land and powerful leadership. These factors were present in the south and east of the West Midland area by the late Anglo-Saxon period and in part may reflect the special historical background of this area.

Similar patterns and processes can be identified throughout England and paralleled on the continent. In Lower Franconia, in Germany, it has been shown how villages which originally appear to have been made up of loose groupings of farmhouses, lying amidst block fields which were subsequently divided into simple strip divisions, could develop into *häufendorfer*, or large densely built-up villages, associated with more sophisticated open field patterns (Mayhew 1973, 39–42).[5] An element of deliberate planning noted in many continental village-settlements can now also be paralleled in this country (Roberts 1977, 117–58). The difficulty is to isolate those changes which took place here in a pre-Conquest contest and were directly due to the social or economic conditions then prevailing.

There is some evidence to suggest that the township fields had not reached their maximum extent in the later Anglo-Saxon period, for at Longdon an area beyond the village stream was termed a *croft* or 'enclosed field' in the tenth-century charter. On the eastern boundary, however, the cultivated fields already extended as far as the township margins. Environmental factors may be called upon to explain the sophisticated adjustments which were later to give rise to the characteristic Midland system of open-field agriculture. This entailed the setting aside of one field annually as fallow for stock-pasture, a system which seems to have developed as the amount of available pasture-land diminished (Fox 1981). The loss of pasture had resulted from a continued expansion of the amount of land under arable, itself a response to the need for increased yields of production. Although Tredington township was still supported by a two-field system in 1299 (Hollings 1939, 279), by the later medieval period a four-field system was frequently in operation and waste had long since ceased to be a significant component of the rural scene in much of the Feldon. Meadowland at Tredington was restricted to locations alongside streams and the bulk of the township area lay under arable cultivation.

Where depopulation took place, whether as a deliberate policy or as the result of a slow decay in the village community, enclosure normally followed rapidly. Where village communities remained intact, however, the open-field system was to survive into the eighteenth and nineteenth centuries, the fields extending throughout most of the parish around a strongly nucleated village settlement. At that date townships which were entirely enclosed lay side by side with others, like Crimscote in Whitchurch which remained open in 1844. The ridge and furrow of Crimscote, now rapidly disappearing from the landscape, shows that at

one time arable cultivation had covered almost every inch of the township area, leaving very little land available for pasture (Roberts 1973, 196). In Tredington, the townships of Talton and Longdon, both deserted village sites, had been fully enclosed before the final steps of parliamentary enclosure completed the procedure in this area in the nineteenth century. However, the open fields of south-western Warwickshire were some of the last to disappear and nineteenth-century maps of Newbold, Armscote, Blackwell and Tredington depict a regular pattern of linear strips grouped into furlongs, matched on the ground by ridge and furrow cultivation with furrows draining down-slope.[6] Although the single farmstead usually replaced the deserted village, the nucleated village was the dominant settlement form in this area throughout the later medieval period. It remained so until outlying farms could be established upon former open-field land in relatively modern times.

Pre-Conquest settlement: charter evidence

In the southern and eastern regions of the West Midlands, where there were extensive areas of arable land, settlement nucleation appears to have been initiated before the Conquest, together with reorganization of much of the arable land. These changes took place in association with minor township communities which were shortly to lose their autonomy under the impact of feudal organization. Because arable land was extensive, it appears frequently in the boundary landmarks of these minor communities and the charters confirm that it was indeed being cultivated under an early type of open-field system. Boundary settlements, on the other hand, are scarce in such areas, but whether any outlying farmsteads had to be deserted, or whether any cottagers living beyond the village nucleus had to be brought into a more centralized system, is not clear from the Feldon evidence alone. It was with this problem unresolved that the study was extended to those areas in which nucleation never fully occurred or failed to become a dominant settlement form.

Charter boundary clauses are more numerous for the area of the modern county of Worcestershire than for Warwickshire (Fig. 10.6) (Hooke 1981b, 26). The most densely populated zone of Worcestershire in the Conquest period was the Vale of Evesham in the south-east of the county, where recorded population figures reached 9.9 per square mile, on a par with the central Avon valley of Warwickshire (Monkhouse 1971, 242). Settlement sites near boundaries are few but have been noted in Strensham, Bengeworth, Elmley Castle and South Littleton. That at Elmley Caste Castle was described as *Byrdingcwīcan*, a *wīc* or 'dairy farm', that at Littleton as *bunewyrðe*, a *worð* or 'enclosure', while

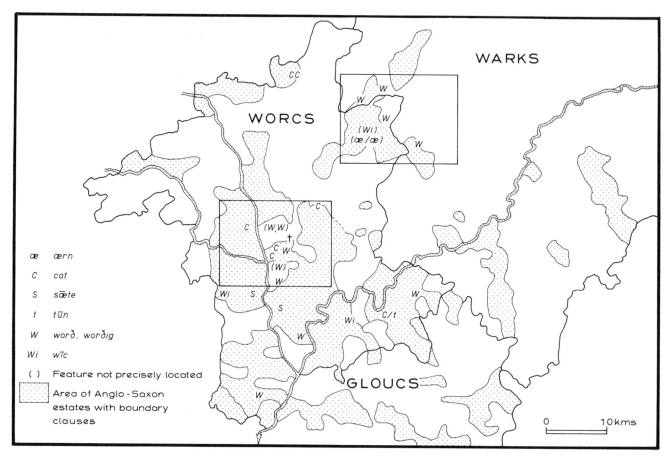

Fig. 10.6   Charter boundary clauses and boundary settlement

that at Bengeworth was variously named as *Potintun*, *poticot* or *potingdūn*, suggesting that it was seen as a *cot*, 'cottage(s)' or *tūn*, the latter possibly implying something grander (Hooke 1981b, 280 – 99). This lay in the extreme southern part of the parish, with a reference to a furlong perhaps denoting its own arable land (Sawyer 1968, S. 1599; Kemble 1839–48, K. 1368), while the boundary seems to make a deliberate attempt to include it within the parish (Fig. 10.7a). This site lay beside a recently identified Roman road but unfortunately woodland cover prevents any real knowledge of its nature. This is an area in which Roman farmsteads were particularly numerous and it is tempting to believe that one of them may have given rise to later settlement. In any case, nucleation does not seem to have progressed as far in this area as in the Warwickshire Feldon. By the late medieval period, however, these minor settlements had disappeared from the landscape and the large nucleated village had become characteristic of the area.

Worcester lay at the heart of a developed area but one in which woodland still remained plentiful in 1086. Both *cot* and *worð* settlements (and those described by the related terms *weorð*, *worðig*, *weorðig*, etc.) have been noted near boundaries and can on occasions be

precisely located (Fig. 10.8). *Cinilde wyrðe/cynelde weorþe*, 'the enclosure of *Cynehild*', for instance, lay upon the boundary of Whittington and Cudley, and is noted as a boudary landmark in both clauses (Sawyer 1968, S. 1329; Kemble 1839–48, K. 670; Birch 1885–99, B. 1298). There are several *worðig* features appended to grants of estates in this area, as at Salwarpe and Battenhall. From the wording of the charters there seems little doubt that these were farms. Those included with the grant of Salwarpe lay *æt Hunigburnan* as *twegen weorðias. 7 twegen aceres earðlandes*, 'two enclosures and two acres or strips of ploughland' (Sawyer 1968, S. 1596; Birch, 1885–99, B. 362), and that at Battenhall in AD 969 as *þone worþig to þære burnan 7 þone croft be suþan þære burnan*, 'the enclosure (?homestead) by the bourne and the croft to the south of the bourne' (Sawyer 1968, S. 1327; Birch 1885–99, B. 1240). The mention of associated land in both of these cases seems to imply that a *worðig* here was some form of farm enclosure and the word appears in many place-names.

Worð and the associated terms *worðig*, *worðign*, etc., do not occur in the earliest Old English documents (Cox 1975–6, 66). They occur in place-names throughout most of England but are particularly prominent in the

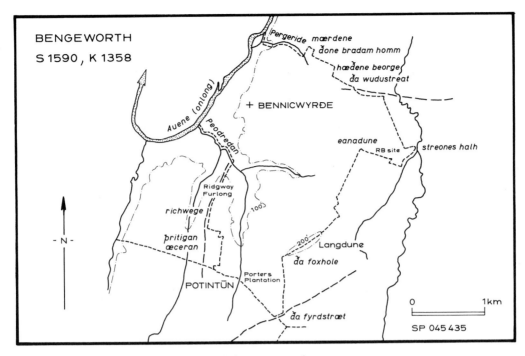

Fig. 10.7 Charter boundary clauses: (a) Bengeworth

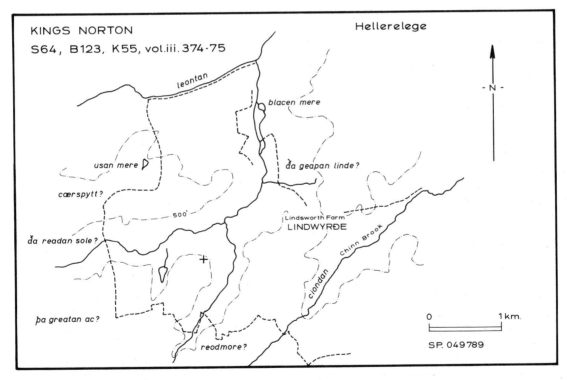

Fig. 10.7 Charter boundary clauses: (b) Hellerelege, King's Norton

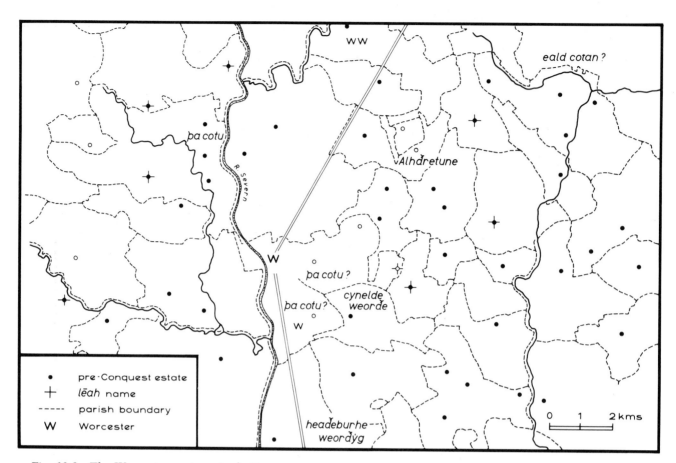

Fig. 10.8   The Worcester region: Anglo-Saxon estates

charters of the south-western part of the country. Here individual farmsteads scattered throughout the countryside were an early and continuing characteristic of the settlement pattern of much of the region, which was itself 'an active frontier for colonisation towards the west' (Fox 1981, 87). The terms seem to have been applied on many occasions to isolated farms and frequent association with a personal name may indicate some form of individual ownership. They may not necessarily have been reserved for late-established secondary settlement, for the possibility of the renaming of existing settlements must always be considered in the interpretation of place-name evidence and the isolated farm may be a very ancient type of settlement form. However, the terms are frequently encountered in marginal regions which were probably being actively colonized in the Anglo-Saxon period.

A third concentration of boundary settlements occurs in the north-east of Worcestershire, running across into north-west Warwickshire (Fig. 10.6). This region, straddling the later county boundary, is known to have been well wooded, at least in the early Anglo-Saxon period. It lay near the boundary of the kingdom of the Hwicce and was an underdeveloped region in which settlement of any kind was relatively sparse. There can be little better way of examining the nature of

these regions in the pre-Conquest period than by looking at the early-recorded place-names of the area. In particular, the farming communities of the south-east and central Avon valley are characterized by a concentration of *tūn* and topographical names, with such settlements extending northwards along the valleys of the Arrow and its tributary the Alne. The watershed between the Alne and the Avon appears to have been wooded in the pre-Conquest period, with *lēah* names indicative of woodland present (Fig. 10.9). Beyond the Alne one passes into an area in which names of any kind become sparser but where woodland names increase in relative frequency.

The Arden area

The place-name indication of woodland in north-west Warwickshire is borne out by the charter and Domesday evidence. Even the woodland entered for the Domesday manor of Brailes in southern Warwickshire lay in Tanworth in the heart of Arden. Charters show, too, that an estate at Shottery was linked with woodland at Nuthurst in Arden and with a wooded place at *Hellerelege*, which lay in King's Norton parish (Sawyer 1968, S. 64; Birch 1885–99, B. 123). Medieval records reveal more of these links and Ford (1976, 280–2) has postulated that they stem from a system of

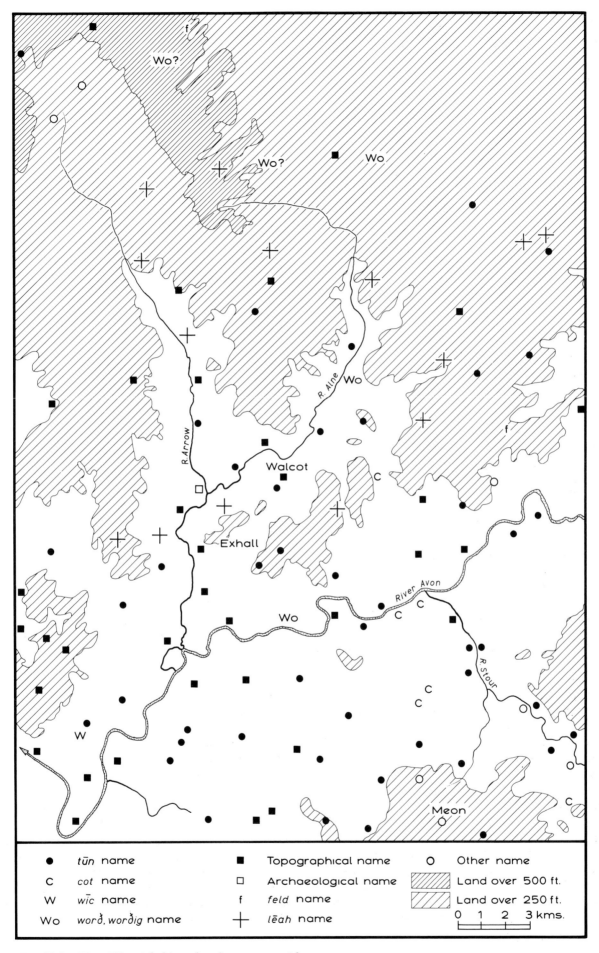

Fig. 10.9   West Warwickshire: the place-name evidence

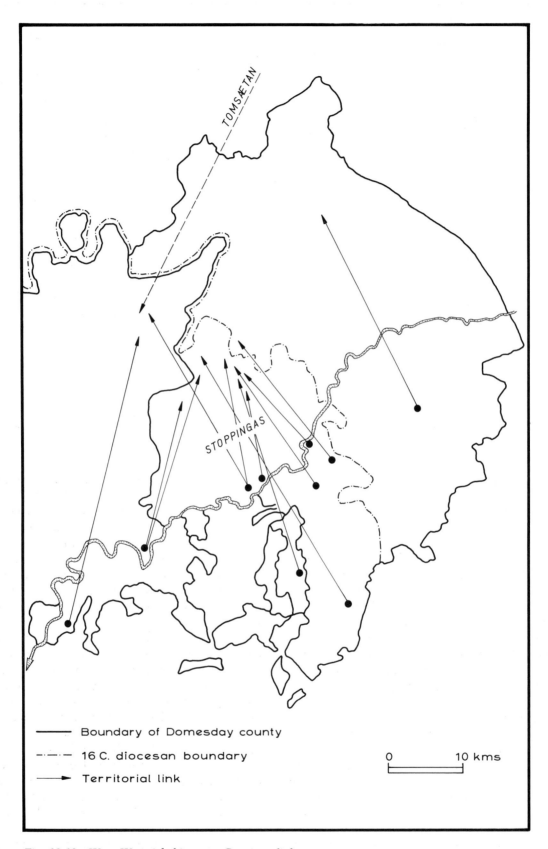

Fig. 10.10   West Warwickshire: pre-Conquest links

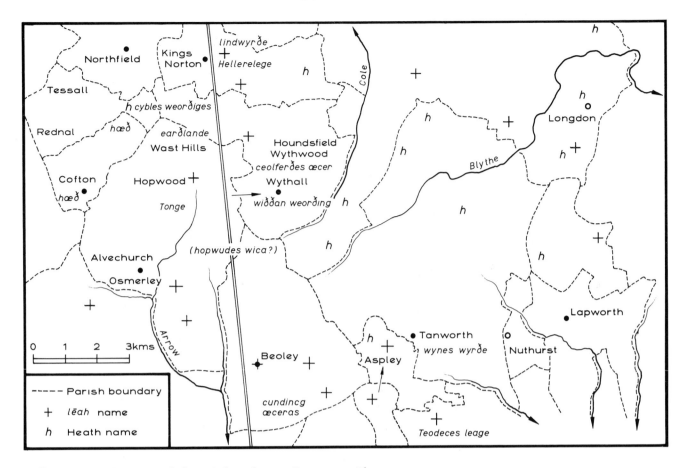

Fig. 10.11 The Warwickshire Arden: the pre-Conquest evidence

transhumance activity such as that practised in the Weald of south-eastern England, with stock being transferred from the developed estates of the Feldon to seasonal pastures in the woodland. Some of the more positive links are indicated on Fig. 10.10 and it can be seen how such an arrangement may have taken place within early folk-areas. In the eastern sector of the Hwiccan kingdom an early eight-century charter (Sawyer 1968, S. 94; Birch 1885–99, B. 157) refers to Wootton Wawen lying in the *regione* of the *Stoppingas*.

The Arden/north-east Worcestershire end of these links coincides with the area of boundary settlement noted in the charters. A further complication arises, however, from the fact that very few of the early boundaries in this area remain unchanged, unlike the situation prevailing over most of the region . The estate at Cofton granted to the church of St Peter, Bredon, in the eight century (Sawyer 1968, S. 117, S. 428, S. 1272; Birch 1885–99, B. 234, B. 847, B. 701, B. 455(1))[7] seems to have extended across the parish of Alvechurch into Wythall. The boundaries of *Teodecesleage* and Beoley were not those of modern parishes and the estate at Oldberrow claimed by Evesham Abbey certainly included an extension to the north of the present parish (Sawyer 1968, S. 1307, S. 786, S. 79; Birch 1885–99, B. 1111, B. 1282, B. 124).[8] This is characteristic of heavily

wooded areas where boundaries were not necessarily stabilized until a relatively late date. The boundary settlements are often *worð, weorðig* settlements, and include Tamworth, '*Tanna*'s ?farmstead', located at the parish margin, and *wynes wyrðe*, '*Wynn*'s ? farmstead', located upon the boundary of the pre-Conquest Oldberrow estate (Fig. 10.11).[9] The evidence from the Worcestershire charters noted above suggests that these were farmsteads associated with small plots of arable and enclosed fields referred to as crofts.

Several features may be noted as characteristic of this area in the pre-Conquest period. Firstly, although later parishes were often large, they consisted of numerous smaller parcels of land or minor estates. The grant referring to Cofton, for instance, includes ten *manentes* at *Wærsetfelda*, five *cassati* at Cofton and five at Rednal, and the later charter of the same estate (Sawyer 1968, S. 1272) adds Wast Hills, Hopwood and *Witlafesfeld*. It is noted that the estate at Cofton centred upon a *hām-stall*, 'a homestead'. In addition, the bounds mention other settlements. *Wiððan weorðing* is Wythall and *cybles weorðiges* lay near West Heath, but Hopwood's *wīc* is also recorded (not Hopwood itself) and there are two references to an *ærn*, 'a house, a building', in *eamban erne*, '*Amba*'s house', and *Wermundes erne*, '*Wermund*'s house'.[10] On the

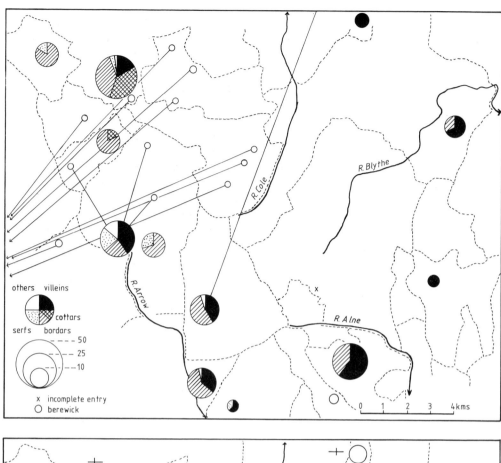

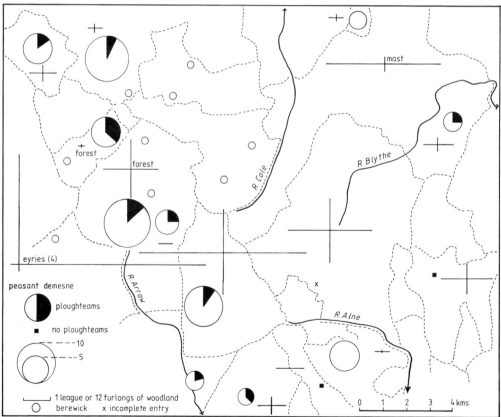

Fig. 10.12 *The Warwickshire Arden: the Domesday evidence (a & b)*

boundary of *Hellerelege*, shown by its bounds to have been the north-western part of King's Norton parish, *lindwyrðe*, 'enclosure by the lime-trees', survived as Lindsworth Farm (Fig. 10.7b). This has been regarded as the earliest occurrence of the term *worð* in England but the boundary clause may well post-date the original charter grant (Cox 1975–6, 66).[11]

In the Domesday evidence numerous other names appear as berewicks of either Alvechurch or the royal estate of Bromsgrove (Fig. 10.12). In Alvechurch these add *Tonge* and an unlocated *Ovretone*, while the berewicks of Bromsgrove were scattered widely throughout the area. Unfortunately, the details of the individual estates are never recorded, but from the vast quantities of woodland entered for the manor of Bromsgrove it is obvious that they contained large acreages of uncleared land. This is confirmed by thirteenth- and fourteenth-century records of assarts in the area (Dyer 1980, 90–7). It is important to note that patches of arable land are also mentioned in the Cofton charter, including *ceolferðes æcer*, '*Ceolferð*'s acre or arable', and *earðlande*, 'ploughland', near Wast Hills. There is one of the earliest references to *gemænan lande*, 'common land', found anywhere in charters. The patches of arable must have been the forerunners of the numerous small but scattered open fields mentioned in the thirteenth- and fourteenth-century extents (Hollings 1934, 208–42), although there is little evidence to show how they were organized in the Anglo-Saxon period. The dispersed nature of settlement and related cultivation in this period must account for the subsequent irregularity of the Midland Forest field system, the medieval fields originating as scattered plots of arable which developed around numerous minor settlements. The lack of development in the heart of Arden is confirmed by the Domesday entry for Oldberrow, recording only 12 acres of arable and no other inhabitants other than two swineherds (Domesday Bk., 1, f. 175c).

As an appendant of the manor of Brailes, there is no separate entry for the manor of Tanworth, but Roberts (1968, 101–13)[12] has shown how the demesne lands to the south-east of the village seem to represent land cleared before 1180. There may have been an Anglo-Saxon cemetery in this area and the name *Oldburi* is recorded by the early thirteenth century. The demesne lands were to focus upon a unit called Bickerscote, while a nucleus of open-field land also lay to the north-east of Tanworth village. There is some evidence to suggest that the earliest arable had been deliberately sited on patches of warmer, lighter soils in the Arden area. The work of Roberts and Skipp (Skipp 1981, 162–83) has shown that the relatively small areas of common field arable associated with village nuclei seem to have been one of the earliest features of the landscape of Arden, the size of the medieval nucleus closely linked

to the extent of the open-field arable. In these areas, however, the church-hamlets and small nucleations with their restricted areas of common arable were a settlement form which was arrested by social and economic change soon after the Norman Conquest.

There were large areas of woodland and waste surviving in Arden and colonization proceeded vigorously, in contrast to the period of stagnation encountered in the heavily populated areas of the Feldon. After about 1180 the lord of Tanworth, the Earl of Warwick, is found granting charters to free colonists to initiate a determined attack upon the waste and woodland. In this way new farm units were established away from the initial nucleus, giving rise to a pattern of dispersed farmsteads by the thirteenth century, and consolidation had also begun in the open-field core. There is ample evidence to show that enterprising colonists from the Avon valley area were being attracted to the opportunities available in Arden with the active encouragement of manorial lords, who were offering land free of labour services at reasonable rents. Some of the family names associated with colonization are of interest. Simon de Charlecote, for instance, may have come from Charlecote in the central Avon valley, and Henry de Wystanecroft, a tenant holding land recovered from the waste in the east of the parish, may have been connected with a family originally established in Bishopton near Stratford, where the tenth-century charter records an acre of land known as 'the croft which Wynstan built' (Sawyer 1968, S. 1388; Kemble 1839–48, K. 724). Colonization was to give rise to a pattern of isolated farmsteads, many of which were moated, and also to land-units like Monkspath, one-third of Tanworth parish sub-infeudated in about 1180. This included an area of land known as Betlesworth, '*Betel's* enclosure', which, to judge from its name, was of Anglo-Saxon foundation and may have been similar to the *worð* settlements of the charter bounds. Cheswick, 'the cheese-producing farm', may also have been a settlement of earlier origin, lying a short distance to the north-east.

The evidence from Arden, therefore, suggests that outlying stock farms and arable holdings were already present beyond the hamlet nuclei before the Norman Conquest. The reference to *ceolferðes æcer* near Cofton is an unusual association of the term *æcer* with an individual and may indicate arable land held in severalty, but hamlet development, often associated with a manorial nucleus, appears to have been closely linked with divided arable holdings of limited dimensions at a relatively early date and the hamlet was socially the dominant component of the settlement pattern. The limited extent of land under arable cultivation in Arden might suggest that the area of open-field arable was directly proportional to population size.

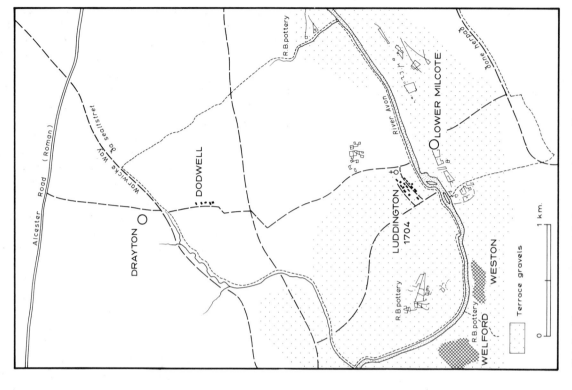

(b) Luddington, Warwickshire: an Avon-valley parish

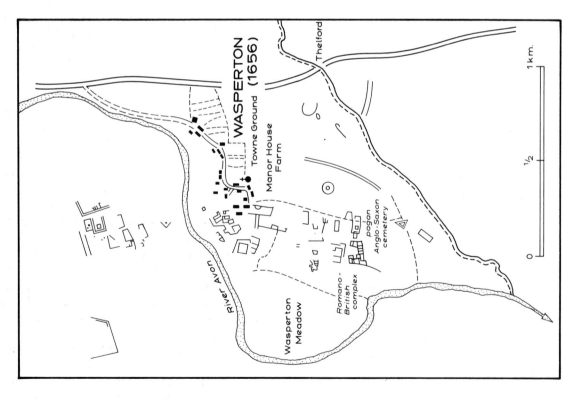

Fig. 10.13 (a) Wasperton, Warwickshire.

Communal farming in some limited form does not, therefore, appear to have been restricted to the replanned and reorganized Feldon areas, but the date of its introduction into the Arden area must remain undecided for the present. It may, indeed, be necessary to distinguish between small-scale communal systems of land ownership on the one hand, detectable at an early stage throughout the region, and the fully centralized open-field system characteristic of the south and east. The settlement pattern of the Arden region is again paralleled on the continent where 'the small irregular hamlet settlement and the *Einzelhof* (from which the former sometimes developed through the division of holdings) were ... characteristic forms of many areas of colonial settlement' (Mayhew 1973, 60).[13] In Germany, as here, this normally entailed movement into woodland.

There is a further element to add to the settlement pattern observed so far. Not all of the Arden peasants were to become substantial landholders and there remained a group of peasants, both free and servile, who held little land or worked for others. They tended to congregate around patches of wasteland and their homes gave rise to the numerous 'End' and 'Green' settlements of the area. While some are recorded as early as the late thirteenth century many of these settlements seem to be of post-medieval date—post-1500. Such settlements normally occupy roadside locations where a narrow patch of land could be taken in to provide a small garden. Those beside larger patches of waste could benefit from a larger area which could be used as pasture. Later 'greens' were often squatter communities established largely illegally upon the waste.

The two regions of Warwickshire examined above represent contrasting areas, the one typified by a pattern of dispersed settlement from very early times which was to be intensified as time went on, the other marked by a tendency towards increasing settlement-nucleation initiated before the Norman Conquest. The environmental background must be considered amongst the various causal factors examined, for settlement dispersal seems to have been strongly associated with less developed regions in which farms and hamlets were separated from each other by extensive areas of woodland and waste. Arable land was present but was limited in extent. Settlement nucleation, on the other hand, seems to have been characteristic of intensively developed areas where large areas lay under arable cultivation. There remains, however, an intermediate type of area which may be worthy of closer examination.

Central Warwickshire: the Avon valley and the Arden foothills

Central Warwickshire comprises two bands of settlement. The central Avon valley represents a zone of early occupation and development which shares many of the characteristics of the Feldon, while development spread northwards along the valleys of the Alne and Arrow but thinned out rapidly on the higher lands of the Alne-Avon watershed and the Arden foothills. Romano-British farmsteads can be shown from cropmark and archaeological evidence to have been numerous along the gravel terraces of the Avon and its tributaries. These were frequently strung out at intervals above the flood plain but there is some evidence of settlement clustering in a number of localities. Such a tendency is apparent from the archaeological and cropmark evidence so far available for Wasperton, in the Avon valley near Warwick. This presents a picture of a loose cluster of Romano-British farmsteads, some possibly of Iron Age origin, lying around the area of the later medieval village (Fig. 10.13a). At the only site to have been partially excavated, a pagan Anglo-Saxon cemetery adjacent to the Roman complex begins to fill the gap in the archaeological record (Crawford 1981). The manorial nucleus was to develop within the band of earlier occupation and by medieval times, at least, the village cluster was concentrated in one locality. At Luddington, too, on the north bank of the Avon near Stratford, outlying farmsteads appear to have been abandoned in post-Roman times as settlement nucleation progressed (Fig. 10.13b). The process, however, never seems to have been carried out as thoroughly as in the Feldon areas and recent work in this region has drawn attention to the number of hamlet nuclei which were present in the medieval period.[14] From the evidence of the Domesday survey it can be seen that numerous small manorial centres were a feature of the central Avon valley area and of the Alne-Avon watershed zone (Fig. 10.14), their lords often enjoying a marked degree of freedom. The large dominant manorial centre characteristic of the south-eastern Feldon is less conspicuous, despite the fact that the individual communities were often less well-endowed than those of the Feldon. Furthermore, manorial subdivision can, on occasions, be directly linked to the greater number of hamlet nuclei in evidence in this area when documentary and field evidence becomes available.

Some of the parishes to the north of the Avon were divided between even more tenants prior to 1086. Luddington had been held by four thanes as two manors and although these were united in 1086, two settlement nuclei can be identified in the medieval period. There are a number of abandoned Roman sites

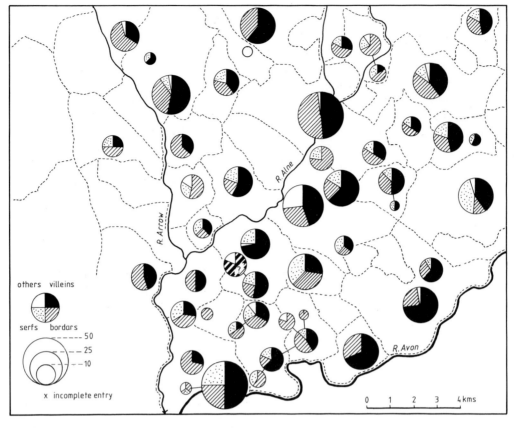

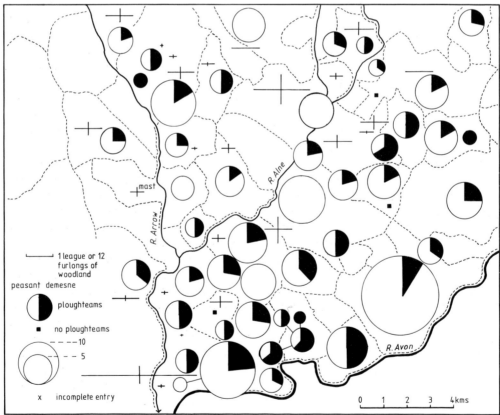

Fig. 10.14   The Arrow valley: the Domesday evidence (a & b)

but the village nuclei comprised the deliberately planned settlement of Luddington lying parallel to the River Avon and a second, more irregular, settlement called Dodwell situated on the heavier clay-lands to the north (Fig. 10.13b). This is now represented by only one farm but, in common with many of the deserted sites of this area, was not completely abandoned as a village until after the early eighteenth century.[15] Sometimes manorial divisions can be detected within a polyfocal village settlement and in this area there is also the interesting phenomena of dual settlement, where hamlets which appear to have been present at an early date remain closely associated with each other (Fig. 10.15a). One of the more interesting is perhaps that of Haselor, which formed three manors in 1086, and where the parish church is planted midway between the hamlet of Upton and that of Walcot, the latter name meaning 'cottage(s) of the British'. The interrelationship between settlement forms and social organization, here exemplified by the number of small manorial nuclei which can be recognized, coupled with the degree of freedom these appeared to enjoy, is obviously a significant factor to be taken into account in a consideration of the settlement history of the county.

In this region parishes with a great deal of arable land were giving way to others with a higher proportion of woodland and waste and the settlement pattern observed seems to be of a type intermediate between that of the Arden and Feldon. Most parishes can be shown to contain at least two settlement nuclei. In Spernall parish, for instance, situated in the Arrow valley, there was a main village beside the river which was according to bishops' registers (Salzman *V.C.H. Warks.*, 1945, 3, 172),[16] largely depopulated by pestilence between 1195 and 1361, but which revived as a hamlet of tenant farmers, working small holdings, and lasted until the eighteenth century. There was also a second hamlet of tenant farmers at Upper Spernall one mile to the east until the same date (Fig. 10.15b).[17] By 1695 the open fields of the parish had been largely enclosed but consolidation of holdings was still taking place.[18] A number of outlying farms had been established but many of these, like the main hamlets, were to disappear as further amalgamation of farm units progressed in the eighteenth and nineteenth centuries. A similar picture emerges in the parish of Coughton to the south. Here a village nucleus has been identified on the east bank of the River Arrow, apparently replacing a linear arrangement of Romano-British farmsteads located on the river gravels. This village, already on the way towards depopulation by the late seventeenth century, lay within a system of open fields which survived into the early part of the following century (Fig. 10.16a).[19] A second earthwork site shows that the surviving village of Coughton, further to the west beside the Ryknield Street, was also once more extensive (Fig. 10.16b). An element of

deliberate planning is apparent from the earthworks of the two deserted sites, each toft measuring approximately one chain or four poles in width. The house sites and gardens may have been laid out as proportions of an acre-strip. A third settlement nucleus in Coughton appears by the thirteenth century, known as Wike, from OE *wīc*, 'dairy-farm'. This lay in the western sector of the parish, in an area which formed part of the Forest of Feckenham in 1300, but it was also associated with 'acres' of open-field arable in the thirteenth century.[20]

A similar pattern exists throughout the Arrow valley area, although manorial nuclei are situated further apart as one moves into less developed regions. The outlying hamlets also become smaller and more difficult to recognize. On the far northern boundary of Studley, Gorcott was one such hamlet, with selions and furlongs of arable recorded near in the thirteenth century.[21] There are also a number of other *wīc* settlements in the area, and a farm-name Gattax in Studley can be traced back to a holding called *Gatwykes* in the fifteenth century, possibly 'the goat-rearing farm'.[22] Hardwick, in the same parish, was 'the herdsman's farm'. These seem to have begun as herding establishments, yet patches of open field survived in the vicinity of most of them in the medieval period, patches which often lay beyond the main open-field systems.

The outlying farmstead can be readily identified by the thirteenth century. Some originated as, or developed into, sub-manors and many lay upon the margins of newly assarted ground. Netherstead, a moated site in Morton Bagot, lay upon the southern margins of the medieval open fields and another in Studley lay beside the marshy land on the western boundary. Some of the more remote areas were donated by manorial lords to religious communities and land near the parish boundary of Spernall was given in this way to a group of nuns by 1198 (Knowles and Hadcock 1971, 273), who later moved to a more accessible site in another parish. Much of western and northern Studley was given to an Augustinian priory established here in the twelfth century and the northern part of the parish was farmed as a monastic grange.[23] As this land became available after the Dissolution, it passed into private hands and the estate deeds of the area show landholders making determined efforts to consolidate their individual estates. Once enclosed, the value of the land increased considerably and a survey of the small manor of St John of Jerusalem in Studley in 1540 shows that land in the common field was worth only 4d an acre, even when the poorest enclosed land, described as 'barreyn ground growing with gosts and briars', was valued at one shilling.[24] Parcels of open land changed hands regularly but the old manorial estates were still holding groups of dispersed strips in the eighteenth century, when each estate was actually farmed as a number of separate units.

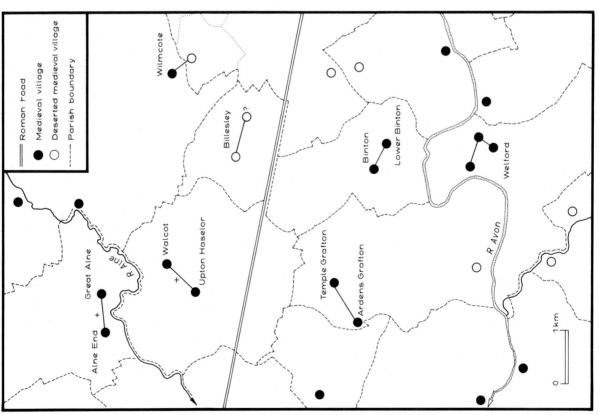

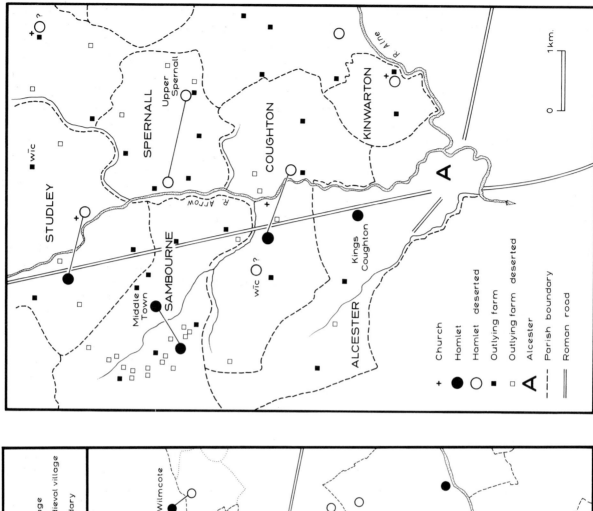

Fig. 10.15 (a) 'Dual settlements' in mid-Warwickshire

(b) Settlement patterns in the Arrow valley of Warwickshire

Map (b) labels

STUDLEY

SPERNALL

Upper Spernall

COUGHTON

KINWARTON

R. Alne

wīc

R. Arrow

SAMBOURNE

Middle Town

wīc ?

wīc ?

Kings Coughton

ALCESTER

A

1 km.

0

Legend (b)

Church +
Hamlet ●
Hamlet deserted ○
Outlying farm ■
Outlying farm deserted □
Alcester A
Parish boundary
Roman road

Map (a) labels

Roman road
Medieval village ●
Deserted medieval village ○
Parish boundary

Wilmcote

Billesley ?

Binton

Lower Binton

Welford

Great Alne

R. Alne

Aln End

Walcot

Upton Haselor

Temple Grafton

Ardens Grafton

R. Avon

1 km

0

Farmsteads were erected as estate consolidation progressed and date from many different periods. In the more northerly parishes of the region, open-field arable had never extended over all the parish area and enclosure began early, linked with further assarting of the undeveloped land. Nevertheless, scattered areas of open field, typical of a woodland system, can be identified in the medieval period and seem to be an early feature in the landscape. Further south the open fields were more strongly established and outlying farm-steads were a later feature of the landscape, established only as holdings in former open-field land could be consolidated. In the extreme south this was not possible before the nineteenth century.[25] The rate of enclosure was obviously affected by manorial attitudes but in general was to take place earlier in the northern parishes where arable land had always formed a smaller proportion of the parish area.

In spite of active assarting in the early medieval period, considerable areas of waste and woodland were to survive in the north and along the western and eastern watershed of the Arrow valley. As at Tanworth, these supported substantial squatter communities which were augmented by the construction of hovels by the overseers of the poor to house the really destitute.[26] Roadside sites were commonly chosen for this type of settlement. Depopulation occurred throughout the area. Even the manorial centres of the northern parishes are represented in the post-medieval period by only one or two farms and a handful of cottages, although the villages of the southern part of the area have left more substantial earthworks. While the village of Spernall was said to have been largely depopulated by the fourteenth century, village communities normally survived while farming was strictly controlled under a manorial system. Although outlying farms were established the village usually lingered on into the eighteenth century. Not all were to shrink and, in particular, settlements beside major roads were to increase in size. In their turn, the smaller farm-units which feature prominently in seventeenth- and eighteenth-century records were to be deserted as amalgamation of units took place and have been located in most of the parishes of the area and especially in Sambourne, Morton Bagot and Spernall. Equally affected by depopulation were the squatter hamlets, especially those occupied predominantly by farm labourers and rural craftsmen, who were increasingly affected in the early nineteenth century by changes in the rural economy and who lost their free pasture on the commons after enclosure of the remaining waste.[27] Depopulated sites are scattered widely throughout the Arrow valley area.

A new development occurred in this area which inevitably encouraged rural depopulation, for here one is able to witness the effect of the industrial revolution upon a predominantly rural community. The needle industry had long been established in the area, due, perhaps, to monastic influence, and had been carried out largely as a cottage industry, helping to sustain the poorer members of the community. Corn-mills were converted as water-power began to be used for the finishing processes of needle manufacture but it was the application of steam-power which initiated rapid industrial growth, with the establishment of James Pardow's mill at Studley in 1800. Artisan communities were to develop in Studley and Alcester, often developing around the settlements already established on the commons in the west of the area. Within 50 years the population of Studley had doubled from just over 1,000 inhabitants to over 2,000, and the needle-making industry and allied trades were to prosper until the present day. Today, the area is one of settlement contrasts. In the west, part of Studley parish has been taken into Redditch New Town and is completely covered with either new housing estates or industrial buildings. The town of Alcester is expanding to the south. To the east, at the moment, there is still a predominantly rural landscape which is probably emptier of settlement now than for many hundreds of years previously, but which is unlikely to remain that way much longer.

Conclusions

The changing patterns observed across the county of Warwickshire present an impression of a natural progression in settlement form. The strongly nucleated villages of the Feldon, which may be recognized from the later medieval and post-medieval documents and surviving field evidence, give way northwards to smaller hamlet nuclei which are often united within a single parish. As formerly less-developed, more heavily wooded country is approached, the hamlet nuclei lie further and further apart, interspersed with single farms of varying dates of origin. It can be shown that this is based upon a settlement pattern which was already established by the early medieval period. The picture is not always so clear, and in Worcestershire a zone of large, nucleated villages appears to lie to the north of the Avon valley region, which is characterized by numerous settlement clusters. The Warwickshire pattern is illustrated diagramatically in Fig. 10.17. The arrow certainly represents development into woodland but it may also represent processes of manorial control, degrees of settlement nucleation and the sophistication of the open field system. The figure as it stands is impressionistic and the problems confronting statistical analysis are immense. The settlement pattern must be examined in relation to estate organization but this in turn requires an understanding of the complex interrelationships between township (or vill), manor

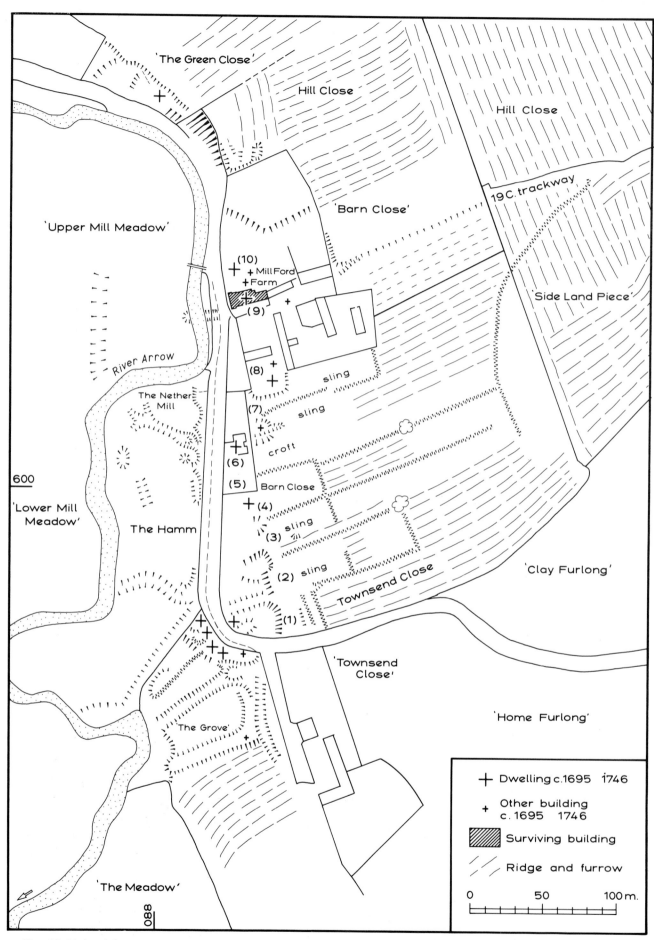

'The Green Close'

Hill Close

Hill Close

'Barn Close'

19 C. trackway

'Upper Mill Meadow'

(10)
Mill Ford
Farm
(9)

'Side Land Piece'

River Arrow

(8) sling

The Nether Mill

(7) sling

600

croft

(6)

'Lower Mill Meadow'

(5) Barn Close

The Hamm

(4)

(3) sling

(2) sling

'Clay Furlong'

Townsend Close

(1)

'Townsend Close'

'Home Furlong'

The Grove

+ Dwelling c.1695 1746

∙ Other building c.1695 1746

Surviving building

Ridge and furrow

0   50   100 m.

'The Meadow'

088

Fig. 10.16 (and facing page) Deserted medieval sites in Coughton

'Tims Close'

former road

Homestall

'Darbys Mead'

'Darbys Green'

mill

pound

The Mill Holmes'

River Arrow

'Westminster Pool'

dam

drained pool

Coughton Court

church

church R.C.

Cain Brook

dove house

barn

'Cane Close'

Hands Homestall

Parkers Homestall

Arnolds

Dixon's Orchard

cross ×

vicarage c.1695

Ryknield Street

604

100 m

0   50   100 m

Dwellings c.1695 1746 deserted   +

Other buildings c.1695 1746 deserted   +

Ridge and furrow

17C. settlement surviving

17C. settlement rebuilt

Fig. 10.16 (and facing page)   Deserted medieval village sites in Coughton

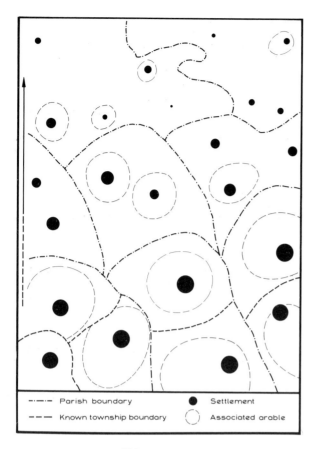

Fig. 10.17   Warwickshire: a settlement model

are more apparent in western regions. Settlements picked up in boundary surveys suggest that similar dispersed settlements were common within the parish unit in these regions in the Anglo-Saxon period. The question must be posed as to whether the hamlet represents an older element in the settlement pattern of the West Midlands or whether such a pattern merely reflects an alternative response to a different environment, one in which woodland and waste remained plentiful. Obviously there is an interplay in this region between ecological and cultural factors. In this region, western areas in particular may be expected to reveal a substantial pre-Anglo-Saxon element in systems of organization. The south and east of the region may have been more open to innovative measures and it is here that nucleation first appears to have taken place and to have developed to its fullest extent. The charter evidence for the Vale of Evesham may even disclose a stage in the progress of change across the region. Studies in the Midland region alone cannot yet provide satisfactory answers to the questions posed but they can help to clarify the situation found to be prevailing when documentary evidence first becomes available and to indicate those problems concerning village origins which remain unsolved at the present time. Above all, the processes which were to result in the settlement pattern familiar to medieval historians must be seen against their geographical setting, for different patterns were to emerge in different regions of England and specifically in different parts of those regions. The present paper has attempted to explore these patterns and the changes which were to take place but makes no attempt to weigh the factors of change, be these historical or environmental, or both. It can, however, be shown that present-day variation in settlement patterns stems from processes which were underway over one thousand years ago, themselves influenced by many hundreds of years of previous agrarian activity.

and parish. In particular, much more evidence is required about the settlements and their field systems. If there is a close association between population size and the amount of land under arable cultivation, how far does this relate to the hamlet and its associated open field? How, in turn, does this relate to the area of the individual township? In the West Midland region we are only just at the stage of identifying early township communities and the nature and extent of their field systems can only be guessed at. In the Domesday survey these communities are often hidden within compound manorial assessments which makes a study of population figures and related data highly problematical. Nevertheless, this is undoubtedly a field for further research.

It is also apparent from the West Midland evidence that minor settlements, often situated near boundaries,

Acknowledgements

I am grateful to Professor David Thomas of the Department of Geography, University of Birmingham, for making available the facilities of the department and, in particular, to Mrs Jean Dowling for the fair tracing of the maps.

Notes

1. The name incorporates Old English *mearc*, 'march, boundary'.
2. For a fuller discussion of the possible origins of open-field agriculture see Rowley, T. (editor): 1981 *The Origins of Open Field Agriculture*. (London, Croom Helm).
3. I am indebted to members of my University of Birmingham Extramural classes for the contribution made by their field survey work to much of the information contained within this paper.

4. The Roman find-spot indicated beside the Fosse Way in Fig. 10.3 represents a coin-hoard beside the Roman road and not a settlement. Warwickshire Sites and Monuments Record, Warwick County Museum.
5. Mayhew cites the work of Krenzlin, A. 1961: Zur genese der gewannflur in Deutschland. *Geografiska Annaler*, 43, 195.
6. Warwick County Record Office (WCRO): Newbold & Armscote (1840) CR 569/176 A & B; Blackwell (1843) CR 569/245; Tredington (1843) CR 569/244B.

7. For a partial solution of this boundary clause, see Hooke, D. 1983: *The Landscape of Anglo-Saxon Staffordshire: the charter evidence*. Keele, University of Keele.

8. For partial solutions of the first and last of these, see Hooke, D. 1978: The Oldberrow charter and boundary clause; *Teodeces leage* boundary. *West Midlands Archaeological News Sheet*, 21, 81–3.

9. Near Bickers Court Farm in Tanworth parish fields known in the nineteenth century as Hither, Middle and Further Wazor may derive their names from a small parcel of land referred to as *Wertheswrthe c.* 1290 in a charter of the Archer family (inf. B.K. Roberts). This seems to be derived from the charter landmark *wynes wyrðe*, which lay upon the boundary of an enclave of land beyond the present parish of Oldberrow.

10. The term *ærn* may indicate some form of storehouse.

11. The boundary clause appears to date from the ninth century, more probably s. ix 2 (inf. P. Kitson).

12. Much of the following information concerning the parish of Tanworth is more fully discussed in Roberts' paper and I am grateful to be able to repeat its contents here.

13. Mayhew cites the work of Krenzlin, A. 1952: Dorf, feld and wirtschaft im gebiet der grossen tatler und platten ostlich der Elbe. *Forschungen zur Deutschen Landeskunde*, 70, 38–47; and Kotzschke, R. 1953: Landliche seidlung und agrarwesen in Sachsen. *Forschungen zur Deutschen Landeskunde*, 77, 191f.

14. Again I draw upon the work I have carried out with Extramural classes. Interim reports may be found in *West Midlands Archaeological News Sheet, now West Midlands Archaeology*: Hooke, D. 1980: 23, 108–11; 1981: 24, 25–33, 64–7; and in *Medieval Village Research Group, 29th Annual Report*: Hooke, D. 1981: 12–13.

15. Conway estate map, WCRO, CR 114 Rag. 111/6.

16. Bond, D. M. 1945, Spernall. *V.C.H. Warks.* 3, 172 cites the Registers of Bishop Brian (Worcester).

17. *Survey of the Manour of Spernall and also several lands in Great Aulne belonging to Sir Robert Throckmorton Bart. by Thomas Thorp, 1746*, WCRO, CR 1998/map 10.

18. Survey of Throckmorton Estates *c.* 1695, WCRO, CR 1998/15.

19. Survey of Throckmorton Estates *c.* 1695, WCRO, Z 328/2 (U); Manor rolls, Throckmorton Mss. The Shakespeare Birthplace Trust Record Office, Stratford-Upon-Avon (S/A) DR5, 2191–2243; *Plan of the Parish and Manor of Coughton Court belonging to Sir Robert Throckmorton surveyed by Th. Thorp in the year 1746*, WCRO Z 123 (U).

20. Saunders Mss. S/A, ER1/62, 186.

21. Saunders Mss. S/A, ER1/61, 19, 19b.

22. Deed, Birmingham Reference Library, 167471.

23. Foundation charter and lands granted to the priory in *Cal. Charter Rolls, 4. AD 1327–41*, 1912, 60–2.

24. Land Rev. Misc. Bks. 361, f. 60–61. PRO London.

25. *A Plan of the Parish of Kinwarton in the County of Warwick by Robert Smith (c. 1800)*, WCRO CR 1886 M485; Ordnance survey 1:10560 1886; these maps are conveniently reproduced in Slater, T.R., and Bartley, G. (editors) 1981: *Rural Settlements in Warwickshire*. Birmingham Branch of the Geographical Association, 6–7.

26. E.g. Sessions Order Book, 1665–74. *Warwick County Records* 1939, 5, 87, in which it is ordered that 'a convenient habitation be forthwith built upon the waste' at Morton Bagot for a poor inhabitant, William Hands, he being 'destitute of an habitation'.

27. 15 houses fringing the common at Morton Bagot have disappeared since 1807: Morton Bagot Inclosure Award WCRO, DR 274/18.

References

Baker, A. R. H. and Butlin, R. A. (editors) 1973: *Studies of Field Systems in the British Isles* (Cambridge, Cambridge University Press).

Beresford, M. and Hurst, J. G. (editors) 1971: *Deserted Medieval Villages: Studies* (London, Lutterworth Press).

Bessinger, J. B. and Creed, R. G. (editors) 1965: *Franciplegius: Medieval and Linguistic Studies of Francis Peabody Magoun Jr.* (New York and London, George Allen and Unwin).

Birch, W. de Gray 1885–99: *Cartularium Saxonicum* (London).

Bond, C. J. 1982: Deserted medieval villages in Warwickshire and Worcestershire. In Slater, T. R. and Jarvis, P. J. (editors) 1982, 147–71.

Bonney, D. 1972: Early boundaries in Wessex. In Fowler, P. J. (editor) 1972, 168–86.

Cox, B. 1975–6: The Place-names of the earliest English records. *Journal of the English Place-Name Society* 8, 12–66.

Cook, J. M. 1958: Anglo-Saxon cemetery at Broadway Hill. *Antiquaries Journal* 38, 58–84.

Crawford, G. 1981: Excavations at Wasperton: 2nd interim report. *West Midlands Archaeology* 25, 31–44.

Darby, H. C. and Terret, I. B. (editors) 1971. *The Domesday Geography of Midland England* 2nd edition (Cambridge, Cambridge University Press).

Darby, H. C. 1977: *Domesday England* (Cambridge, Cambridge University Press).

Domesday Book, Record Commission 1783.

Dugdale, W. 1656: *The Antiquities of Warwickshire* (London).

Dyer, C. C. 1980: *Lords and Peasants in a Changing Society. The Estates of the Bishopric of Worcester 680–1540* (Cambridge, Cambridge University Press).

Dyer, C. C. 1982: Deserted medieval villages in the West Midlands. *Economic History Review* 35, 19–34.

Eld, F. J. (editor) 1895: *Lay Subsidy Roll for the County of Worcester, 1 Edward III*. Worcestershire Historical Society.

Finberg, H. P. R. 1955: *Roman and Saxon Withington: a study in continuity*. (University of Leicester Department of English Local Hisory, Occasional Paper 8, Leicester University Press).

Finberg, H. P. R. (editor) 1972: *The Agrarian History of England I, II AD 43–1042*. (Cambridge, Cambridge University Press).

Finberg, H. P. R. 1972: Anglo-Saxon England to 1042. In Finberg, H. P. R. (editor) 1972, 385–525.

Ford, W. J. 1976: Some settlement patterns in the central region of the Warwickshire Avon. In Sawyer, P. H. (editor) 1976, 274–94.

Fox, H. 1981: Approaches to the Midland System. In Rowley, T. (editor) 1981, 64–111.

Fowler, P. J. (editor) 1972: *Archaeology and the Landscape, Essays for L. V. Grinsell* (London, John Baker).

Gelling, M. 1974: Some notes on Warwickshire place-names. *Transactions of the Birmingham and Warwickshire Archaeological Society* 86, 59–84.

Hall, D. 1981: The origins of open-field agriculture—the archaeological fieldwork evidence. In Rowley, T. (editor) 1981, 22–38.

Harley, J. B. 1960: *Population and Land-utilisation in the Warwickshire Hundreds of Stoneleigh and Kineton, 1086–1300* (Unpublished PhD thesis, University of Birmingham).

Harvey, M. 1981: The origin of planned field systems in Holderness, Yorkshire. In Rowley, T. (editor) 1981, 184–201.

Hollings, M. (editor) 1934: *The Red Book of Worcester* (Worcestershire Historical Society).

Hooke, D. 1981a: Open-field agriculture—the evidence from the pre-Conquest charters of the West Midlands. In Rowley, T. (editor) 1981, 39–63.

Hooke, D. 1981b: *Anglo-Saxon Landscapes of the West Midlands: the Charter Evidence* (Oxford, British Archaeological Reports 95).

Hooke, D. 1982: Pre-Conquest estates in the West Midlands: preliminary thoughts. *Journal of Historical Geography* 8, 227–44.

Hooke, D. 1983: *The Landscape of Anglo-Saxon Staffordshire: the charter evidence* (Keele, University of Keele).

Jones, G. R. J. 1972: Post-Roman Wales. In Finberg, H.P.R. (editor) 1972, 283–328.

Jones, G. R. J. 1981: Early customary tenures in Wales and open-field agriculture. In Rowley, T. (editor) 1981, 202–25.

Kemble, J. M. 1839–48: *Codex Diplomaticus Aevi Saxonici* (London)

Knowles, D. and Hadcock, R. N. 1971: *Medieval Religious Houses, England and Wales* (London, Longman).

Mayhew, A. 1973: *Rural Settlement and Farming in Germany* (London, Batsford).

Mills, D. 1960: *A Linguistic Study of Gloucestershire Place-Names* (Unpublished MA thesis, University of London).

Monkhouse, F. J. 1971: Worcestershire. In Darby, H. C. and Terrett, I. B. (editors) 1971, 217–72.

Postan, M. M. 1972: *The Medieval Economy and Society* (London, Wiedenfeld and Nicolson).

Pretty, K. 1975: *The Welsh Border and the Severn and Avon Valleys in the Fifth and Sixth Centuries AD, an Archaeological Survey* (Unpublished PhD thesis, University of Cambridge).

Rivet, A. L. F. (editor) 1969: *The Roman Villa in Britain* (London, Routledge and Kegan Paul).

Roberts, B. K. 1968: A study of medieval colonzation in the Forest of Arden, Warwickshire. *Agricultural History Review* 16, 101–13.

Roberts, B. K. 1973: Field systems of the West Midlands. In Baker, A. R. H. and Butlin, R. A. (editors) 1973, 188–231.

Roberts, B. K. 1977: *Rural Settlement in Britain* (Folkestone, Dawson).

Robertson, A. J. 1956: *Anglo-Saxon Charters* 2nd edition (Cambridge, Cambridge University Press).

Rowley, T. (editor) 1981: *The Origins of Open Field Agriculture* (London, Croom Helm).

Salzman, L. F. and Styles, P. (editors) 1945: *The Victoria County History of the Counties of England, A History of the County of Warwick*, Vol. 3 (The University of London Institute of Historical Research).

Sawyer, P. H. 1968: *Anglo-Saxon Charters, An Annotated List and Bibliography* (London, Royal Historical Society).

Sawyer, P. H. (editor) 1976: *Medieval Settlement, Continuity and Change* (London, Edward Arnold).

Shirley, E. P. 1869: *Lower Eatington, its Manor House and Church* (London).

Skipp, V. 1981: The evolution of settlement and open-field topography in north Arden down to 1300. In Rowley, T. (editor) 1981, 162–83.

Slater, T. R. and Jarvis, P. J. (editors) 1982: *Field and Forest, an Historical Geography of Warwickshire and Worcestershire* (Norwich, Geobooks).

Smith, A. H. 1965: The Hwicce. In Bessinger, J.B. and Creed, R.P. (editors) 1965, 56–65.

Stenton, F. M. 1971: *Anglo-Saxon England* 3rd edition (Oxford, Oxford University Press).

Taylor, C. 1970: *Dorset* (London, Hodder and Stoughton).

Toulmin-Smith, L. (editor) 1908: *The Itinerary of John Leland in or about the years 1535–1543* Vol. 5, Part 11 (London, George Bell and Sons).

Wilson, M. 1972: *Archaeological Evidence of the Hwiccan Area* (Unpublished PhD thesis, University of Durham).

11. Forms and Patterns of Medieval Settlement in Welsh Wales

G. R. J. Jones

According to some observers, like Archbishop Pecham, settlement in medieval Wales was scattered, but the statements of contemporary jurists imply the presence of a variety of settlement forms ranging from dispersed homesteads to hamlets or even villages. On the most widespread of the customary tenures, hereditary land, freemen held substantial homesteads which were sometimes located in patrilocal clusters but more frequently were disposed in loose girdle patterns around the edges of open-field arable sharelands. The bond under-tenants of such freemen occupied hereditary land and resided in hamlets. So too the king's bondmen, who occupied reckoned land, dwelt in hamlets. The king's court in every commote was adjoined by one such hamlet but near by the king's officers were also accommodated so that this settlement was usually a multi-focal village. Aberffraw (Anglesey), Hendre-Gaerwys (Clwyd) and Llan-non (Dyfed) are examined in detail as specific examples of these main types of medieval settlement.

Giraldus Cambrensis, writing at the close of the twelfth century, observed that the Welsh 'do not live in towns, villages or castles (*non urbe, non vico, non castris cohabitant*), but lead a solitary existence, deep in the woods'. Moreover, they do not build 'great palaces or vast and towering structures of stone and cement' but content themselves with wattled huts on the edges of the woods, 'put up with little labour or expense, but strong enough to last a year or so' (Dimock 1868, 200–1; Thorpe 1978, 251–2). Here Giraldus was clearly referring to Welsh Wales, the territories which had retained their independence of Norman and English rule, principally Gwynedd, the uplands of central Wales and the lowlands of West Wales. For the border area of Powys he presented a different picture, albeit in an incidental statement, by referring to 'Welsh churches with their villages and churchyards (*cum villis et coemeteriis*)' which had been burnt down by the English (Dimock 1868, 203; Thorpe 1978, 202). Nevertheless the main impression that Giraldus created has persisted. Nor is this surprising, for Archbishop Pecham, in a report to Edward I in 1284 after the conquest of Gwynedd, wrote of the Welsh that 'they do not dwell together but each far from the other (*il ne habitent pas en semble eins meint chescun loinz de autre*)'. Pecham even considered that the savageness of the Welsh arose chiefly from this (Martin 1885, 776–7, 981–2); and thus he advocated, for their reform, that they should be commanded to dwell together in '*viles*' (towns or villages).

The presence of scattered dwellings in Welsh Wales (*Pura Wallia*) is also confirmed by some of the statements made in the Welsh lawbooks, the handbooks of practising jurists. The oldest extant texts of these lawbooks were compiled only after the early thirteenth century, but these incorporate some archaic material. Although only incidentally concerned with settlement, and then mainly in a generalized way, the lawbooks can yield an insight into settlement forms and patterns, provided care is taken not to accept literally the over-schematic statements of the jurists. As a law-text of the fifteenth century records: 'Every habitation ought to have two footpaths: one to its church; and one to its watering place'; and again: 'Every habitation ought to have a bye-road (*hwylfa*) to the common waste of the vill or township (*tref*)' (Owen, 1841, 270–1). Such precise statements are hardly likely to have been made by jurists unless many, if not most, homesteads were scattered. Paradoxically, however, another fifteenth-century law text records the complement of a legal *trefgordd*, which appears to have been a hamlet with a communal organization. This complement was: 'nine houses, and one plough, and one kiln, and one churn, and one cat, and one cock, and one bull, and one herdsman' (Owen 1841, 692–3). The nine houses were closely grouped as is indicated by the rules given in earlier law-texts, including the oldest, governing compensation for fire damage. In order to prevent fire damage, a kiln was not to be sited nearer the hamlet than a stipulated distance which ranged in different lawbooks from nine paces to seven fathoms. Some lawbooks, including the oldest, refer to a public bath instead of a kiln, probably because the kiln used to dry corn was also used to provide heat for bathing. The fire precautions applied to a kiln or bath-house were also applied to a smithy which, moreover, had to be roofed with shingles, tiles, broom or turf. If, despite fire precautions, a house in a hamlet (*trefgordd*) caught fire through the owner's negligence, he had to pay compensation. The rules differ slightly from lawbook to lawbook but usually compensation was paid for the nearest houses, or for one on each side, except where there was sufficient space for the wind to go between the houses. Such fire precautions would have been very necessary where houses were huddled close together. Clearly therefore, just as a reference to an outbreak of fire in the oldest Life of St Cuthbert provides one of the few pieces of literary evidence for the plan of the early English village (Stenton 1943, 283–4), so the evidence of fire precautions in medieval Welsh law can be invoked as testimony for the presence of at least some nucleated settlements, if only hamlets, in Welsh Wales during the Middle Ages.

Settlement Forms and Patterns as envisaged for Hereditary Land

Further evidence for the physical form and distributional pattern of settlement is provided in those sections of the lawbooks which deal with customary tenures of land. Of these by far the most widespread was that known as hereditary land. The essential feature of this tenure was that rights to land passed to male descendants in equal shares and each heir was a trustee on behalf of his own descendants (Jenkins 1967, 241–7). Originally, rights to land were shared equally among the surviving male members of four-generation inheritance groups or kindreds. These were the descendants of a common great-grandfather extending outwards to, and including, second-cousins (Charles-Edwards 1972, 17–26). Indeed, it was continued occupation of land by members of a kindred over a prescription period of four generations which ensured the conversion of bare possession into legal proprietorship. Rights to land were re-shared with the passage of each generation but an attempt appears to have been made to provide each heir with a standard holding. The lawbooks which reflect conditions in South Wales deem such a holding to have been a shareland of 312 acres. These acres were used for different purposes and thus the *Book of Blegywryd* (Williams and Powell 1961, 71; Richards 1954, 75) refers to the owner of a shareland having 'in the three hundred acres, arable, pasture and fuel wood, and space for building on the twelve acres'. Since the acres cited in different lawbooks differed from each other, the area of the complete shareland varied. The smallest acres were those recorded in the *Book of Blegywryd* so that the 300 acres of the Blegywryd shareland used for arable, pasture and fire wood amounted to only thirty-one and three quarter acres by statute measure and the 12 acres for building to some one and a quarter statute acres. The largest acres in the South Welsh texts were those of Latin Redaction A, so that the 300 acres amounted to sixty-seven and a half

statute acres and the area for 'buildings' (*domicilia*) to almost two and three quarter statute acres (Emanuel 1967, 136).

The lawbooks which reflect conditions in Gwynedd, known collectively as the *Book of Iorwerth*, refer to a smaller holding which was further subdivided, in the jurists' schematic models, into four sharelands. The holding comprised 64 acres with seemingly four acres for the homestead (*tyddyn*), or dwelling site, and the remaining 60 for regularly cultivated land; but since the Iorwerth acre was relatively large, the regularly cultivated land amounted to about 18 statute acres (William 1960, 60).

The contrast envisaged between the shareland of North Wales and that of South Wales may well reflect a change in inheritance customs on hereditary land. After about AD 1100 in Gwynedd, and in some districts there probably long before, sharing by the members of the four-generation kindred had come to be replaced as the normal inheritance custom by equal division *per stirpes* among brothers. Subsequently a kindred did not split, as before, with the passage of each generation but only as circumstances demanded. With each new generation now a kindred would normally have increased and, from starting as a nuclear family, would grow into a much larger entity, a patrilineal descent group (*progenies*) which was also known as a *gwely (lectus)*. The same term *gwely* (plural *gwelyau*) was also used later for the holding of the descent group. Within the typical *gwely (lectus)*, by the thirteenth century, a hereditary proprietor's share of his patrimony would normally have consisted of a personal holding of appropriated land and an undivided share of joint land. The former would have comprised a homestead (*tyddyn*), some parcels of 'scattered land' lying in a number of arable sharelands and some plots of meadowland. The joint land, within which the proprietor exercised proportional appurtenant rights, would probably have embraced an expanse of common pasture, waste and wood. On these appurtenances a proprietor could erect a summer dwelling (*hafod*) for use in time of common pasture. When Giraldus referred to wattled huts on the edges of the woods which lasted a year or so he probably meant such summer buildings, and not the much more substantial permanent dwellings.

Clearly the size of the homestead used for the permanent dwelling would have an important bearing on the form and pattern of more permanent settlements; for, in places, the North Welsh lawbooks record that the four acres were 'by (*wrth*)', rather than 'in' the homestead (*tyddyn*). They even envisage that there could be eight or as many as 12 acres in a homestead but also state that the *tyddyn* was normally of four acres; and certainly in some parts of Gwynedd, homesteads corresponding closely in size to the legal *tyddyn* of four acres, which contained 5,760 statute square yards, were recorded in 1334 (Jones 1972, 328). These appear to have been compact units but this need not have been the case with the larger area of 12 acres devoted to buildings in the South Welsh shareland. These larger areas could well have accommodated not only the proprietor but also undertenants, and the latter need not have resided near the proprietor.

Even on the relatively small area of the four-acre *tyddyn* envisaged for North Wales, if on immediately adjacent homesteads each dwelling were placed in the midst of its homestead, then the dwellings would have been as much as 75 yards apart. By the thirteenth century freemen undoubtedly made up a majority of the population and, despite the earlier observations of Giraldus Cambrensis, the dwellings of these freemen were not mere wattle huts. According to the lawbooks the hall of the freeman was a substantial cruck-built structure adjoined by a number of outhouses including a barn, a cowhouse, a pigsty, a kiln, and at the front of the hall, a chamber. The hall could no doubt be placed towards the corner of the homestead, thereby affording better opportunities for the accommodation of heirs who wished to establish their dwellings near the parental homestead, the 'old settlement' (*hendref*). Many heirs would have wished to live there, possibly for reasons of sentiment, but perhaps also because the 'old settlement' was usually sited near the best available land for cultivation. The result would have been the emergence of a loose patrilocal cluster of dwellings and buildings; but manifestly there would have been limits to this process of settlement growth. With inheritance by four-generation groups such clusters are particularly likely to have developed. Thus, one South Welsh lawbook, which envisaged a free vill or township (*tref*) as containing three sharelands each of 312 acres for occupancy and a fourth as pasturage for the three, also hints at the subdivision of such a shareland into thirds (Wade-Evans 1909, 53). The resulting nine homesteads per vill might well have been grouped together in a loose cluster. With partible inheritance by brothers, however, this kind of settlement growth appears to have been obviated. Various readings of the Iowerth manuscripts suggest that there was a tendency in thirteenth-century Gwynedd for the youngest son to inherit his father's homestead and the structures on it. These according to a later text would have included 'the buildings between which the wind does not blow' (Owen 1841, 582–3, 666–7).

Whereas lands were divided by the youngest son and chosen in order of seniority by all the brothers, it was the youngest son but one who divided any remaining homesteads; and these were then chosen in order of seniority by all save the youngest of the brothers. In practice, just as the youngest son remained in his father's homestead, so his other brothers are likely to have remained in the dwellings they had already made for themselves on the hereditary land in their father's lifetime, for it appears that a scion of free stock, after attaining the age of 14, could establish his own homestead on some part of the family land. Hence the rule that if one brother built before another the first was not to depart from the place where he had built but was to give to the other a side and an end of the land on which he was seated; and if this were not available they were to share (Jenkins 1973, 17). Even if, after normal division among brothers, there was a re-sharing, as was permitted among heirs up to and including second cousins, no one was to move from his homestead (*tyddyn*) for it was claimed that the size of the homestead made sharing unnecessary (Owen 1841, 868–9). Yet, many brothers, save the youngest in any family, appear to have established their dwellings away from the 'old settlement (*hendref*)' and near outlying patches of arable land. There, in order to economize on the limited areas of arable land usually available, they tended to site their dwellings on the peripheries of the arable patches; hence the development, with hereditary land tenure, of what have been described for convenience as 'girdle-patterns' of homesteads, flexibly adapted as it were to the contour (Jones 1955, 33).

The statements of the jurists about the inheritance of hereditary land and homesteads refer principally to freemen but there were also bondmen who held hereditary land inherited in broadly the same way. The ensuing settlements appear to have been similar to those of the freemen, including clusters and girdles of homesteads. The lawbooks refer in particular to aliens who could become proprietors in the fourth generation after they had been settled on the waste of the king or on that of notables. Henceforward the aliens were tied to the soil in bondage. According to the *Book of Iorwerth* such aliens, after they had become proprietors, were to have 'their homesteads (*tyddynod*) on the land, and land to them also; and their land, excepting such, to be land of plough-share and coulter between them' (Wiliam 1960, 58–9). In other words aliens, after becoming bond proprietors, had the same rights to homesteads as freemen, and the same rights to share arable land (Jenkins 1963, 38, 158–9). These rules suggest that such undertenants acquired their own homesteads for the first time only in the fourth generation, and by so doing also provide a pointer to the process whereby sometimes the girdle-patterns of homesteads associated with hereditary land could be established. They certainly imply that aliens, before becoming proprietors, must have lived in other kinds of dwellings. Some indication of what these were is provided by reference in the *Book of Iorwerth* to a second kind of land: *tir corddlan*.

Settlement Forms and Patterns as envisaged for Nucleal Land

According to the *Book of Iorwerth* the land (*tir*) known as *tir corddlan* appears to have been a variant of hereditary land. It was however, 'not to be shared as homesteads (*tyddynod*) but as gardens (*gerddi*)'; and if there were 'houses (*tai*) on it' the youngest son was no more entitled to them than the eldest, but instead they were 'to be shared as chambers (*ystefyll*)' (Wiliam 1960, 58; Jenkins 1963, 38, 155-6). The word *corddlan* appears to have come to mean an enclosure (*llan*) held by, or at least associated with, a kindred (*cordd*). Since a nucleus of some kind was implied, the term *tir corddlan* may be rendered as nucleal land.

To judge from variant forms of the name *corddlan* this nucleus or enclosure could have been used for different purposes: for the folding of animals in a pen (*corlan*); or for the disposal of the dead as in a graveyard, literally a corpse enclosure (*corfflan*). Hence the statement that 'the measure of a *corflan (sic)* was a legal acre in length with its end to the graveyard (*mynwent*)'; and 'that circling the graveyard, its compass' (Wiliam 1960, 44). It appears therefore that the gardens, or long narrow strips of land, into which *tir corddlan* was shared, were disposed in radial fashion around the nucleus which was generally, though not invariably, a churchyard. On their outer limits these gardens were apparently encompassed by a strong fence so that they could not be entered by grazing animals. The houses on nucleal land appear to have been located usually at the inner limits of these gardens, but were sometimes placed at the outer edges. As befits the proximity of the houses to the gardens the latter were heavily manured and cultivated year in, year out, like an infield.

The *Book of Iorwerth* provides an indication of the relationships between nucleal land and the sites of churches. Thus the rule about 'the measure of a *corflan*' is given in a section dealing with church land and the right of sanctuary (Wiliam 1960, 44). The church (*eglwys*) envisaged in this context was a mother church belonging to a community of canons (*clas*) which included at least one priest. The title of the chief officer, known as the abbot, and the way in which the community shared the church revenues, afford strong evidence that the *clas* was originally a monastery. By the time when the extant texts of the Welsh laws were written the *clas* had become an hereditary ecclesiastical corporation consisting usually of one or more kindreds in possession of the church and its lands. Nevertheless such churches continued to offer sanctuary so that: 'Whoever took protection was, to walk about within the *mynwent* (graveyard) and the *corfflan* without relics upon him'; and his cattle were to be 'with the cattle of the *clas* and the abbots' to the furthest limit to which they went and afterwards were 'to return to their cattle-pen' (Wiliam 1960, 44).

In the lawbooks which deal with nucleal land the rules about sharing it are preceded by the statements that 'a mill, a weir and an orchard' were the 'three ornaments of a kindred (*cenedl*); and these three were not to be shared nor removed, but their produce was to be shared between those with a right to it' (Wiliam, 1960, 58; Jenkins 1963, 38). Since the office of the head of a kindred (*pecenedl*) persisted until the fourteenth century it is not surprising that a thirteenth-century *Book of Case-law*, probably incorporating much contemporary material, should cite the same three ornaments in the same order (Jenkins 1973, 10). Nevertheless, when sharing and re-sharing of hereditary land among members of the four-generation inheritance group came to be supplanted by equal division among brothers, the changed inheritance custom was apparently applied to the ornaments of a kindred. In one post-conquest text therefore 'an orchard, a mill and a weir' (Owen 1841, 688-9), designated as 'buildings', were said to be in common among brothers. Earlier in a Latin law-text of the mid-thirteenth century the 'three buildings (*tria edificia*)' said to be common among brothers are, however, listed as 'a church, a fishery and a mill', and a text of the later thirteenth century records these buildings, in Latin and Welsh, as 'a church, a mill and a fishery, that is a weir' (Emanuel 1967, 231, 289). It appears likely therefore that, at an earlier stage, a church could also have been an ornament of a kindred. Just as the heirs of a *gwely (lectus)* could have under-tenants who held small parcels of nucleal land adjoining buildings 'in common among brothers', so too in an earlier period the members of a four-generation inheritance group are likely to have had under-tenants whose chambers on nucleal land adjoined the 'ornaments of a kindred'.

Settlement Forms and Patterns as envisaged for Reckoned Land

A third kind of land recorded in the Welsh lawbooks was that known as *tir cyfrif* (reckoned land) or *tir cyllidus* (taxable land). This was held by villeins, men without pedigree, the most servile of bondmen and bound to the soil. Even their shares of land were determined by the king's officers. Thus, according to the *Book of Iowerth* '*Tir cyllidus* it is not right to share according to brothers, but it is right for reeve and bailiff to share it and to give to everyone in the vill (*tref*) as good as to each other; and on that account it is called *tir cyfrif*' (Wiliam 1960, 54; Jenkins 1963, 36). A re-sharing took place when a bondman died or when any of his sons, save the youngest, came of age at 14. Hence the term *cyfrif*, which means 'to count' or 'to reckon', for a counting of adult male heads necessarily preceded the re-sharing. Occasionally in the lawbooks the expression used was *tref gyfrif* (reckoned vill), thus implying that the land of the whole vill or township was shared equally among all the bondmen save the youngest son in every bond family. The youngest son, however, had to await the death of his father since it was in his father's 'place (*lle*)' that he was to sit (Jenkins 1973, 30). Despite such re-sharing a right to a particular house plot was recognized, as is implied by the statement that 'No one is to move from his legal homestead (*tyddyn cyfreithiol*) if an equivalent can be obtained for it of other land' (Wiliam 1960, 54); or by the statement that 'It is right to maintain every man of a reckoned vill in his homestead (*tyddyn*) if it can be done without exiling another' (Jenkins 1963, 36). Nevertheless, the qualifications in both statements reveal that, when there was no other means of accommodating additional bondmen, a shifting of homesteads would take place.

There was one reckoned vill of especial importance, that known as the reeve's vill (*maerdref*) which adjoined the king's court. In the same way that the greater reeve and the king's bailiff allocated shares of land to the bondmen of the ordinary reckoned vill, so the lesser reeve shared the land of the reeve's vill among the men of the *maerdref* and, if it were feasible, the lesser reeve also was to allow each of these men to keep his existing homestead.

The characteristic settlement of bondmen on reckoned land, or in a reckoned vill, was probably a hamlet. This was the *trefgordd* whose notional complement was recorded in a fifteenth-century text as nine houses, and, to judge from the one kiln, the one plough, the one bull, and the one herdsman, a communal organization (Owen 1841, 576–7). A hamlet however was quite unlikely to have remained of exactly this size. Nor would its ground plan remain immutable, for changes in the form of settlement on reckoned land are clearly anticipated given the provision that a homestead would be vacated if an equivalent area of other land were not available.

Notionally in the lawbooks, however, a contrast appears to be envisaged between the hamlet of the bondmen on reckoned land which had but one kiln and the settlements occupied by bondmen holding hereditary land. It was almost certainly among the ranks of the latter that was to be found the kind of bondman said to have a substantial cruck-built house which, though only half the value of the freeman's hall, was adjoined by outhouses including its own kiln. Such bond homesteads would have been accommodated more readily as part of a girdle of homesteads than in a clustered hamlet.

Settlement Forms and Patterns as envisaged for the King's Vills

According to the *Book of Iorwerth* there were to be two vills for the use of the king in each of the administrative districts known as a commote. One was the king's waste and summer pasture land; the other was to be the land of the *maerdref* (reeve's vill).

The summer pasture was usually in the uplands and there bondmen tended the royal herds of horses, cattle and swine. These bondmen, probably holding reckoned land, appear to have resided in hamlets. The linking of waste with the summer pasture suggests that settlement on waste by aliens, or even by servile bondmen, was countenanced, so that these in the fourth generation would have acquired rights of proprietorship over hereditary bond land. Although their settlements probably began as hamlets they are likely to have developed into girdles of homesteads. Such hereditary bondmen no less than freemen exercised grazing rights over common pastures during the summer months. The lawbooks imply, however, that they grazed their stock independently of their neighbours and thus, like the freemen, did so from their widely scattered summer dwellings (Wiliam 1960, 22).

At the other extreme was the settlement in the lowland vill which contained the king's court. A much larger settlement, its layout was clearly influenced by the physical form of the court itself. This was made up of a group of separate buildings which stood within the court enclosure. According to a revised version of the *Book of Iorwerth* (Jenkins 1963, 40) there were seven buildings 'within the court (*ofewn y llys*)', namely the king's hall, the sleeping chamber, the refectory, the kitchen, the brew-house, the stable and the privy. All seven were to be built by the king's bondmen, seemingly those from outlying reckoned vills (Wiliam 1960, 62). Of these buildings by far the most important was the hall (*neuadd*), a substantial timber structure, probably of a basilical character with a nave and side aisles; moreover, a number of out-houses adjoined this hall. Incidental statements in sections of the lawbooks dealing with the Laws of the Court reveal that there were yet more buildings within the court enclosure. Among them were the porter's lodge which also served as a prison, the mead-chamber; and the sleeping chamber of the queen. Reference to the queen's priest and to the priest of the household implies the presence of a chapel within the court; and certainly in the South Welsh lawbooks a chapel takes the place of a refectory in the list of buildings said to be erected for the king by the bondmen (Wade-Evans 1909, 57; Williams and Powell 1961, 57). The court enclosure which encompassed these buildings was normally entered or left by means of the great gateway which was flanked by

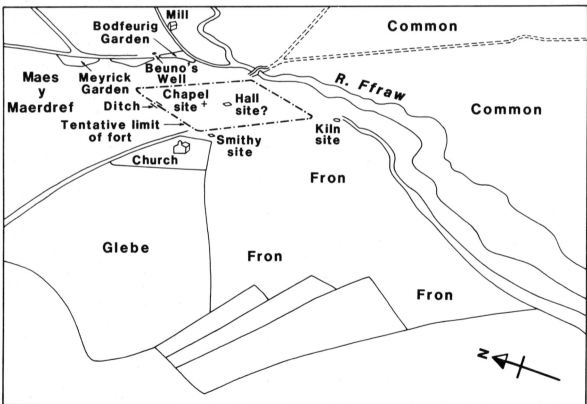

Fig. 11.1   The village of Aberffraw (Cambridge University Collection, copyright reserved)

the porter's lodge but, in addition, there could be ingress or egress via a postern.

Outside the court enclosure were the king's barn and his kiln which, according to the *Book of Iorwerth*, were to be erected 'on the *maerdref* by the bondmen of the same reeve's vill. These presumably lived in a hamlet which adjoined the court enclosure. No specific details of their hamlet are given in the lawbooks but, for the remainder of the settlement near the court, some information is provided by those Laws of the Court which deal with the lodgings of a few of the king's officers and servants. Since these sections of the lawbooks contain archaic material the conditions which they describe are likely to have been old-established. The steward was to share the lodgings: 'to himself the nearest to the court and all of the officers with him'. The lodging of the head of the household troop of warriors was to be 'in the largest and most central house (*tŷ*) in the *tref* (vill)' for, apart from those of the troop he chose to be with him, the remainder were to stay around his lodging. With the head of the household dwelt the bard of the troop and the physician; but the priest of the troop, with the king's clerks and the queen's priest, lodged in the house (*tŷ*) of the chaplain. By contrast the head huntsman lodged in the king's kiln, probably the kiln-house, which was sited in the *maerdref* (reeve's vill). In the *maerdref* too, but probably at some distance from the kiln, was the king's barn, for it was here that the head falconer lodged 'in case his birds should catch the smoke' (Wiliam 1960, 5–16, 20). The head groom lodged in the house (*tŷ*) nearest to this barn for it was his duty to distribute the fodder; and with him lodged the groom of the queen.

If the house next to the barn housed only two officers, there were at least two other houses in the settlement adjoining the court which were large enough to house numbers of officers and servants. Yet this same settlement also embraced the reeve's vill which contained the humbler dwellings of those of the king's local bondmen who cultivated the mensal land for the provisioning, in part, of the king's table. The settlement which contained the king's court and which thus served as a commote capital, was inhabited by members of all social groups from the highest to the lowest. It is likely therefore to have been a village.

Medieval Settlements as recorded in practice

The jurists of medieval Wales envisaged that settlement forms and patterns in *Pura Wallia* were far more complex and varied than the observations of Giraldus Cambrensis and Archbishop Pecham would suggest. That the statements of the jurists were not too far divorced from reality can be demonstrated by reference to well-authenticated examples of settlements where vestiges of medieval dispositions have survived.

Aberffraw

Pride of place can be accorded to the vill of Aberffraw in south-west Anglesey for this was the site of the 'principal seat' of Gwynedd (Williams and Powell 1942, 3; Wiliam 1960, 2; Emanuel 1967, 277). To this day the most striking feature of the landscape in this locality is the nucleated village on the west bank of the River Ffraw, close to the limit of ordinary tides and near a convenient crossing point (Fig. 11.1). It was thus placed midway between common pasture to the east of the river and the formerly extensive arable open fields to the west. The common pasture on the sandy wastes of Tywyn Aberffraw still survives but the arable open fields have long since vanished. Thus there remain no visible traces of Maes y Maerdref (Open Field of the Reeve's Vill) where once the arable quillets or strips of the king lay intermingled with those of his tenants and the glebe quillets of the Church. Yet, to the south of the village, in at least part of the area called Fron (Breast), there still remain, as vestiges of the former open fields, some long narrow strip-like fields (Jones 1966, 211–15).

The medieval settlement of Aberffraw proper was a composite unit which, besides the royal court, contained the two bond hamlets of Maerdref (Reeve's vill) and Garddau (Gardens), as well as the holdings of a number of freemen. The precise area embraced within the court enclosure is not known but it was large enough to have included the king's hall, his chamber and his privy. This hall and chamber were recorded even in 1352 as being constructed in part by means of the labour services of freemen living in outlying vills of the Hundred of Aberffraw. On the other hand the bondmen of one outlying vill were responsible for making 'part of each house of the lord prince's manor of Aberffraw'. The bondmen of another outlying vill were to 'make and clean the lord's privy there'; and these were also to make good against the rain the roof of the chamber of the *rhaglaw*, the king's chief official in the Hundred (Ellis 1838, 45–8, 54). Other records reveal the presence within the court enclosure of a chapel, and at the entrance to the enclosure a gatehouse which doubled as a prison. The chapel known at a later date as Eglwys y Beili (Church of the Enclosure), and then as the Eagles, was the venue of the court baron and court leet of the Manor of Aberffraw even as late as 1939. The medieval court within which this chapel undoubtedly stood was enclosed by means of a stone wall. The task of constructing this perimeter wall was still recorded in 1352 as an obligation on the bondmen who made the king's privy; but, in addition, the heirs of the free *Gwely Porthorion* (Gwely of the Porters), all of whom resided in the vill of Aberffraw, were responsible for making and repairing a length of wall on either side of the gate of the manor. Recent excavation, which was prompted by the discovery of carved medieval masonry on the western edge of the settlement, has revealed a

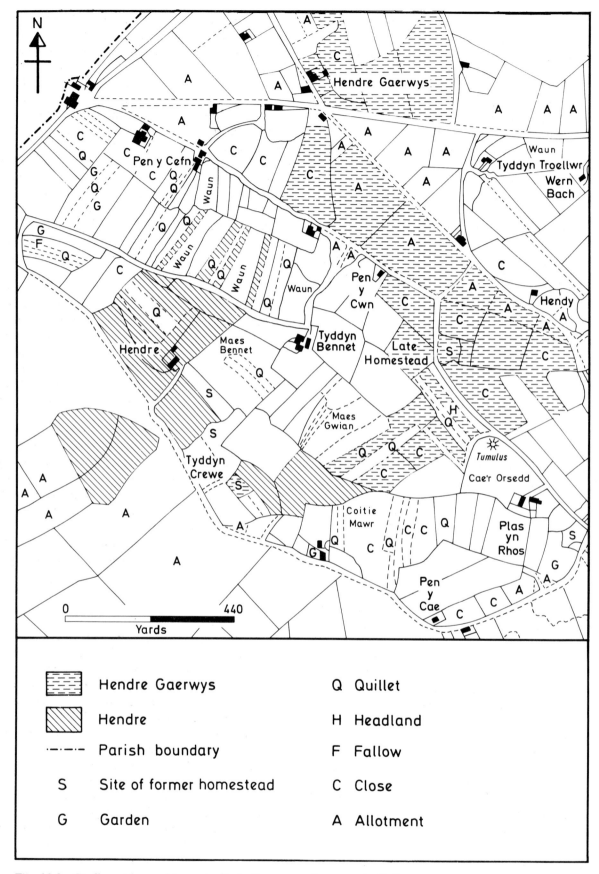

Fig. 11.2 *Girdle patterns of homesteads in Bryngwyn Caerwys, in 1848*

substantial ditch of three phases, apparently forming part of a rectangular enclosure lying beneath the present village. The profile of the primary ditch is very reminiscent of Roman work and accordingly the enclosure has been tentatively interpreted as a Roman fort; but the two re-cuts are much more irregular and the stone rampart which went with at least one of them was of rough rubble construction and arguably belongs to the post-Roman period (White 1977, 140–5; 1979, 319–42). Using traces of what could have been other defences in the village area, and taking the dimensions of the Roman fort at Segontium (Caernarfon) as a guide, the excavator has suggested that this enclosure would have occupied a central position in relation to the present village. If, as is likely, the medieval walled enclosure had a similar perimeter it would have included within its bounds the chapel and the king's hall, the latter probably to the east of the chapel (Fig. 11.1). In 1317 however no less than 148 pieces of assorted timber were taken 'from the hall and other buildings of the late prince at Aberffraw (*de aula et aliis domibus quondam principis apud Aberfrau*) and re-used in Caernarfon Castle (Peers 1915, 17; Taylor 1963, 386). Nevertheless, in 1337–8 a new tiled roof was provided for the king's chamber so that part of the court complex there was still standing, and in use at that time (Carr 1982, 123, 152). In 1346 the prison in the gatehouse of Aberffraw was still used as a prison for, in that year, a Welshman who had disturbed the peace at Aberffraw fair escaped from the prison, but it was the porter (*portarius*) and the *rhaglaw* who were held culpable (Seebohm 1904, Appendix Ad). By 1608, however, the capital messuage of the Manor of Aberffraw could be described in a survey as being totally ruined from a time beyond which the memory of man did not run.[1]

The area immediately to the north of the medieval court enclosure was probably inhabited by some of the freemen of Aberffraw vill, among them the heirs of the Gwely of the Porters and possibly also those of the Carpenter's Holding (*Gafael Saer*). Thus in 1608 part of the free land of the Manor of Aberffraw lay at the northern end of the village where Sir Hugh Owen, the most substantial freeholder, held the water mill with its adjacent curtilage of one acre. He also held a capital messuage, with 14 other houses, six other buildings with 12 gardens 'lying together' in an area of some three acres, in other words about half the area of the fort enclosure. Thus it is likely that this cluster of properties lay to the north of the court, where it appears to have included, among other lands, Bodfeurig garden, one of the gardens radiating from the 'watering place' of Beuno's well. Since Bodfeurig was a free hamlet one mile to the west of Aberffraw and occupied by the freemen of Gwely Bodfeurig, this particular garden probably formed part of the nucleal land (*tir corddlan*) held by an under-tenant of the *gwely*. A short distance

to the north-west was Meyrick garden, the only garden in the village held in 1608 by Sir Richard Meyrick. This, however, was part of the bond land of the two hamlets of Maerdref and Garddau which were surveyed together in 1608; but, as Garddau contained only 14 gardens, each allegedly of only one acre or so, the whole of Garddau with its cottages and gardens could well have been at the northern end of the village. The more substantial houses of the freemen in the Middle Ages, and certainly those of the heirs of the Gwely of the Porters, would have been located near the main gateway into the court and thus towards the centre of the village. In this event the bond hamlet of Maerdref, which was inhabited by at least nine bondmen in 1294, would have been at the southern edge of the village, probably in the vicinity of the kiln as recorded in the late eighteenth century. As the lawbooks indicate, the king's kiln and barn were erected by the men of the reeve's vill, outside the court, probably in the Maerdref; and although this specific obligation was not recorded for medieval Aberffraw, there was a not dissimilar obligation on the prince's bondmen of Aberffraw proper to work on the animal house of the said manor (Ellis 1838, 49). Nor should the presence of the parish church at the south-western corner of the village belie this interpretation, for the church appears to have been a late intrusion whose oldest surviving features can be ascribed to the twelfth century, the very period when Gruffydd ap Cynan, ruler of Gwynedd, was building lime-washed churches, constructing courts, and making great churches for himself in his chief courts (Jones 1913, 64–7). But be that as it may, medieval Aberffraw was evidently a relatively large multi-focal settlement whose morphological complexity matched the very diverse social composition of its inhabitants.

Hendre Gaerwys

The forms and patterns of settlement associated in Welsh Wales with hereditary land, whether clusters of homesteads or girdle-patterns, have rarely survived. Among the exceptions are some of the vills which were formerly part of the estates of the Welsh bishops and where the bishops had prevented the replacement of increasingly fragmented *gwely* holdings by consolidated estates. The same is true of areas where the lands of a bishop were formerly intermingled with those of laymen, even when the bishop's estate was but one *gwely* among a number of *gwelyau*, or merely a lesser subdivision of a *gwely* known as a *gafael* (holding) among a number of such holdings (*gafaelion*). One good example of the latter situation where a number of girdle-patterns have survived down to the present day is the vill of Bryngwyn Caerwys in north-east Wales (Fig. 11.2). Here, according to an account of 1357, the Bishop of St Asaph held one *gafael* (holding) known as

'*Gafael Esgob* in Hendre Gaerwys (*Gauelescop in Hondrecayrus*)', whose lands were intermingled with those of a number of lay holdings[2] (Evans 1929, xxix–xxx).

At Bryngwyn Caerwys the largest of the original sharelands was that which included Maes Gwian (Gwian's Open Field) and a large number of other quillets or strips as well as one headland. Even in 1848 this shareland was almost encompassed by a girdle of homesteads including the former site of Hendre Gaerwys (Old Settlement of Caerwys), then known as Late Homestead, and among other homestead sites those of Pen y Cwn, Plas yn Rhos, Pen y Cae and Tyddyn Bennet (Bennet's Homestead). Save in the area to the south of Tyddyn Bennet, the shareland was surrounded by a roadway to permit easy access (Fig. 11.2). This shareland, closely associated with Hendre Gaerwys, was probably the oldest shareland, for its lands, which overlay limestone with but a thin covering of drift, were more readily cultivable than those of adjacent areas. Moreover, adjoining Plas yn Rhos was Cae'r Orsedd (Close of the Assembly), the venue of a law-court whose proceedings probably took place on the southern flank of the tumulus in the corner of the same field; while nearby, in the middle of this field, an early Christian memorial stone of the sixth century, bearing the upright Latin inscription '*Hic iacit mulier Bona Nobilis* (Here lies Bona, the wife of Nobilis)', stood until the early nineteenth century (Royal Commission 1912, 10–11; Nash-Williams 1950, 116).

Alongside this evidently old-established shareland newer ones were added with the growth of population. Hence the emergence of the shareland immediately to the south-west which included Maes Bennet (Bennet's Open Field) and was flanked on its outer edge by Hendre (Old Settlement), and a number of other former homestead sites including that of Tyddyn Crewe (Crewe's Homestead). To the north-west was added yet another shareland, more rectangular in shape but completely encompassed by a road, and flanked on its north-eastern edge by a string of homesteads including Pen y Cefn. This shareland was on much less well-drained land, hence the frequent occurrence of the field name Waun (Meadow, Pasture). The same was true of the shareland which was flanked by Hendy (Old House), Tyddyn Troellwr (Spinner's Homestead) and Wern Bach (Little Alder-Marsh), and bounded on its south-western and western edge by a curvilinear road (Fig. 11.2).

As might be expected, the arable quillets in the oldest and most desirable shareland, as for example at Maes Gwian, were smaller than those of the newer sharelands, but in due course even the latter tended to become morcellated with the continued operation of the inheritance custom of equal division by brothers on hereditary land. Nor could this be countered by the creation of new sharelands for there were both physical and juridical limits to the continued expansion of the arable lands of any *gafael* or *gwely*. Thus in the vill or township of Bryngwyn Caerwys the greater part of the lands surrounding the arable sharelands near Hendre Gaerwys remained as common pastures (Fig. 11.2). In this vicinity most of the fields known as allotments were newly carved from the common pastures of the township after the execution of the enclosure act of 1809.[3] Some of these allotments, particularly those in the area between the Hendre Gaerwys and Hendy sharelands, were still in process of being enclosed by means of hedges as late as 1848.[4] Divided from each other by straight hedges, and often roughly square or angular in shape, these recent enclosures can be readily distinguished from the older closes of pasture and, in particular, from the oldest closes of arable land. The latter had been created in the main by the amalgamation of separate quillets, hitherto divided from each other only by 'the usual greensward boundaries' or by mere-stones, and later their enclosure within quickset hedges. Such was the case with the four parcels of land said in a deed of exchange of 1588 to 'lie dispersed in one clausure of lande called Quetkae Mawr', for the same enclosure was later known as Coitie Mawr, a name which reveals that it was a close surrounded by a quickset hedge; and characteristically, even in 1848 it still contained within its outer limits a number of quillets belonging to different owners.[5]

As part of this process of amalgamation and enclosure of arable quillets, which was far from being completed in Bryngwyn Caerwys by 1848, the forms and patterns of settlement had only recently been modified. Thus the site of the former homestead to the south-east of Plas yn Rhos could still be described in that year as the 'site of a house now down' (Fig. 11.2). Further west near Hendre there were a number of such sites. Among these, Tyddyn Crewe had not long been incorporated within Hendre Gaerwys which, with 66 acres, was the largest farm in the vicinity; and following the execution of the enclosure act of 1809 even the original homestead of Hendre Gaerwys was abandoned in favour of a new homestead better placed in relation to the larger area of new allotments recently enclosed out of the former common pastures.

These changes which were taking place at an unusually late date in Bryngwyn Caerwys were very similar to those which elsewhere in Welsh Wales had been initiated in the fourteenth century and had led over the greater part of the country to the disappearance of former arable sharelands and the blurring, if not the complete elimination, of the girdle patterns of homesteads frequently associated with them.

Llan-non in Llansanffraid

Nowhere in Wales is it possible to gain a better impression of the form and pattern of Welsh medieval hamlet settlement than in the area known as Morfa Esgob (Bishop's Sea-place?) in Llansanffraid parish on a low coastal shelf overlooking Cardigan Bay (Fig. 11.3). There to this day, within the limits of the ancient administrative unit formerly known as Rhandir yr Esgob (Shareland or Hamlet of the Bishop) are three hamlets of apparently medieval origin. All three were sited on the edges of Morfa Esgob, an expanse of former open-field arable land covering some 108 statute acres. One hamlet was at Llan-non proper where at an early date there was, probably near the Clydan crossing, a chapel dedicated to Non, allegedly the mother of St David, who ministered in the sixth century (Bowen 1969, 80–3, 183). A second hamlet was some 550 yards to the east of Llan-non between Cae Gwastad (Level Field) and the River Peris; in this vicinity, at the north-eastern limit of the hamlet, where it overlooked the Peris, was the venue of the medieval law-court of Llan-non. The third hamlet, some 660 yards north-east of Llan-non, was virtually on the river boundary separating Rhandir yr Esgob (Shareland of the Bishop) from the Vicar's hamlet which included the site of the parish church of Llansanffraid. Originally the three hamlets in Rhandir yr Esgob had been physically quite distinct but their separateness had been obscured by the time the aerial photogaph was taken in 1946, and to a lesser extent even before 1841, by the spread of houses along the roads linking the hamlets and especially also along the turnpike road running north-north-east from Llan-non (Fig. 11.3). By the mid-nineteenth century the two westernmost hamlets were larger than at an earlier date, partly because of the development of maritime activities at the mouths of the Peris and the Clydan, but above all because of the presence of numerous craftsmen (Thomas 1957, 6–10; 1963, 412–4).

At present, as in earlier centuries, the occupants of the three hamlets hold long narrow strips or 'slangs' of arable land on Morfa Esgob. The strips are usually separated from each other by turf balks and, save near the hamlets where they are now down to pasture, have remained unfenced like the roads. Earlier in 1841 there were no less than 70 owner-occupiers or owners of land in Morfa Esgob, the majority holding strips or slangs which lay scattered through one or more furlong-like divisions of the open field (Davies 1973, 526–7). Such was the case with Evan Jones, the mason, who occupied some four and a half acres made up of Llain Hir (Long Strip), one slang near his homestead in Llan-non and four other slangs in two furlongs (Fig. 11.3). Most of Morfa Esgob was cultivated in 1841, especially for cereals but, significantly, the only relics of common pasture at that date were the two small areas of common on the eastern edge of Morfa Esgob.[6]

That the open-field arable land and the common pasture were traditional features of the agrarian economy in this locality is abundantly clear from earlier sources but by the seventeenth century the slangs were renowned, above all, as barley land (Green 1927). Still earlier in 1326, the *Black Book of St David's*, an extent of the lands of Bishop David Martin (Willis-Bund 1902, 210–11), records that there was at that date in the vill of Llan-non 'one *lectus* which is called *gwely (qui dicitur gwely)*'. Of this *gwely* there were three named freemen, the three jurors for the Llan-non extent, 'with the following and the descendants from them (*cum sequela et descendentibus ab eisdem)*'. The *sequela* and their descendants could possibly have been the heirs and descendants of the three named freemen but they were much more likely to have been the bond under-tenants of these three freemen. Thus the extant records that there was in Llan-non in 1326 'a small piece of land (*una porcuncula terre)*' which was in the land of the lord by escheat, or forfeiture, because of the felony of the former occupant; and since there could be no escheat in reckoned land according to Welsh law, this 'small piece' must have been hereditary land, probably the bond holding of an under-tenant. If each of these three freemen in the one *gwely* had his own under-tenants then each is likely to have occupied his own hamlet. In other words, there is a strong possibility that in Rhandir yr Esgob by 1326, besides the church hamlet of Llan-non proper, and the court hamlet, the third hamlet, on the west bank of the Peris near Llansanffraid, was already in being. Nevertheless the pleas and perquisites of the law-court at Llan-non in 1326, and for a considerable time thereafter, went with those of the court of Llanddewi Aber-arth, some four miles to the south-west,[7] and in this vill, as in Llan-non but nowhere else on the lands of the bishop, the members of the *lecti* are recorded as named individuals, 'with the *sequela* and the descendants from them'.

For the lands of the one *gwely* in Llan-non the occupants paid the bishop 6s 8d per annum, and they all gave a cow as *commorth* (animal tribute) in the Kalends of May every third year. They performed the same services and customs as the bishop's tenants at Llanddewibrefi, some 12 miles distant and the site of the celebrated *clas* church dedicated to St David. Their obligations included transport and building services for the bishop's hall, chamber, kitchen, stable and grange at his manor of Llandygwydd, some 22 miles to the south-west, as well as transport and building services for the bishop's mill. In addition they, along with the occupants of a number of other vills including Llanddewi Aber-arth, were to make enclosures in the customary places at the important and prosperous fair of Llanddewibrefi. Nevertheless the Lord Bishop had

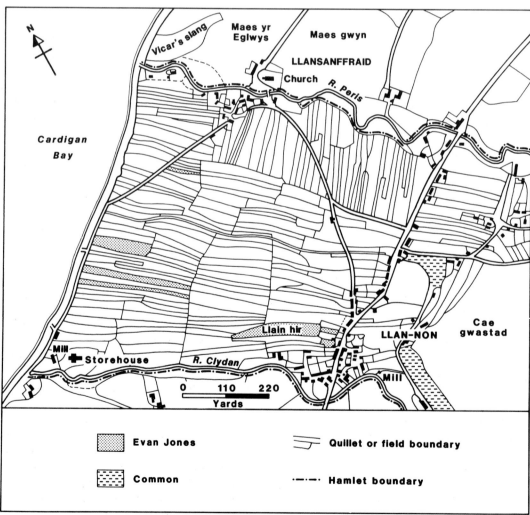

Fig. 11.3   Llan-non in Llansanffraid, in 1841 and 1946 (Crown copyright reserved)

his own fair at Llan-non, albeit a small one, and a weekly market. These trading activities probably took place at Llan-non proper (Willis-Bund 1902, 197–211).

Although the hamlets in Rhandir yr Esgob have survived, such was not the case in the immediately adjoining vicar's hamlet of Llansanffraid. By 1841 the only vestiges of the hamlet that formerly existed here were a small garden adjoining the churchyard on its north-eastern side, the farmhouse immediately to the north-west of the churchyard and, at a distance of over 110 yards, the vicar's slang (Fig. 11.3). The latter, the last surviving parcel of vicarial glebe land, was on the edge of a large enclosed field whose name, Maes yr Eglwys (Open Field of the Church), indicates that it had once lain open. Like the adjoining Maes Gwyn (White Open Field) it contained the same kind of excellent land for barley as that in Morfa Esgob. The curious curvilinear shape of part of the inner edge of the vicar's slang suggests that the area between this slang and the churchyard had once formed a segment of an expanse of nucleal land centred on the church but confined to the area north-east of the River Peris. Faint traces of the outer boundary of this semicircle of nucleal land can be discerned on the aerial photograph of 1946, particularly in Maes gwyn.

A large expanse of nucleal land is only to be expected here, for the church of Llansanffraid with five carucates—probably 300 statute acres—of arable land in demesne had been granted to the Knights Hospitallers of St John of Jerusalem in the twelfth century. The grant was confirmed, if not made, by the Norman Roger de Clare, Earl of Hertford, during his occupation of Ceredigion from 1158–64 but it was subsequently confirmed by the Welsh ruler, Rhys ap Gruffydd, after 1165, as a grant of the church and all the land that belonged to the vill of Llansanffraid (Rees 1897, 102, 204; Rees 1947, 28, 113; Charles 1948, 182, 194). As a Hospitaller church, Llansanffraid would have exercised one of the most valued privileges of the Order, the right of sanctuary. Like a *clas* church it could provide those who sought protection from the rigours of the law with refuge within the sacred precincts, and the sanctuary would probably have included the semicircular expanse of nucleal land. The Order in England was suppressed in 1540 but already its particular needs had no doubt brought about changes in the settlement pattern at Llansanffraid proper. Given the needs of the Hospitallers for ready money, their lands tended to be assessed at fixed standard rents, and in cash rather than in kind, with the result that there was frequently an early breakdown in the traditional agrarian economy on Hospitaller estates (Rees 1947, 19). Consequently their lands were often enclosed and consolidated into large farms at an early date. Small wonder therefore that by 1841 some 345 acres, out of the 380 or so acres in the vicar's hamlet, were owned by

one large landowner and that few traces of the old hamlet of Llansanffraid proper remained. The contrast with Morfa Esgob, where by 1841 there were no less than 62 lay owners of some 108 acres, could not have been greater.

Changes in Settlement Forms and Patterns

Changes in settlement patterns if not in settlement forms were inherent in the expansion of any *gwely* or *gafael* to its maximum extent. Once this stage was attained further changes usually ensued; for thereafter, given the continued operation of equal division among brothers, any subsequent growth of the descent group would have resulted in the reduction of the arable lands of some heirs beyond the economic minimum. Thus opportunities were opened up for some individuals, particularly those whose forbears had not been too fecund, or those who commanded extraneous resources, to acquire the increasingly morcellated arable quillets of the penurious. Although the Welsh proprietor had no more than a life interest in his land, and was thus prohibited from disposing of that land to the detriment of his successors, there were in practice various methods of circumventing this prohibition. Even before the conquest a Welsh proprietor could convey his land to another by Welsh mortgage arrangements (*prid*) and, after the conquest, this device was supplemented by the conveyancing methods of English law (Beverley Smith 1977, 263–77; Davies 1978, 402–13). By means of successive small adjustments the fortunate could enlarge their holdings by securing the fragmented arable quillets of less fortunate neighbours, and thereby could also acquire appurtenant rights to meadow and common pasture. These acquisitions were then usually consolidated into larger parcels of land and enclosed along with fringing allotments of meadow as well as hitherto undivided parts of the common pasture. In due course the ensuing engrossed holdings were incorporated into expanding estates whose perpetuation was facilitated by the adoption of the practice of land inheritance by the eldest son only, and by resort to entail to prevent any would-be irresponsible heir from disposing of his estate (Jones Pierce 1972, 195–247). In place of the former hereditary lands there emerged large estates, which were divided in turn into tenant farms usually larger and more compact than the small patrimonies they had displaced. Over time therefore the number of homesteads decreased and, in place of the medieval cluster or girdle patterns of homesteads associated with Welsh hereditary land, there emerged a pattern of more widely dispersed farmsteads. In any vill where such changes had been initiated at an early date there might well be only one estate by the nineteenth century, with the mansion house alone bearing the name of the medieval township and with all the lands divided into large compact farms. Only where exceptional conditions obtained, as for example on the episcopal lands of Morfa Esgob and Hendre Gaerwys, did forms and patterns of settlement akin to those of the Middle Ages survive.

Change also supervened alike in the ordinary reckoned vill and in the *maerdref* (reeve's vill) where, characteristically, mensal or demesne land adjoined the royal court. In the reckoned vill, as in the reeve's vill, obligations as well as rights to land were shared equally among adult bondmen. Thus, if but one bondman survived he was to have the whole vill, but would then be responsible for all the rents and services normally levied on that vill. When bond communities declined in size during the fourteenth century the burdens on the surviving bondmen were such that many fled when any opportunity arose during the fourteenth and fifteenth centuries (Jones Pierce 1972, 39–57; Carr 1982, 327–30). As a result many bond lands and even demesne lands fell into decay. Such decayed lands provided further opportunities for estate builders who, by means of Crown leases or even illegal encroachments from adjoining estates on former hereditary land, acquired bond and demesne lands and, in due course, converted them into compact holdings. Consequently, most of the hamlets on former reckoned land disappeared and their place was usually taken by single large farms.

Where a *maerdref* (reeve's vill), besides serving as a commote capital, had acquired additional functions as a trading centre before the conquest, it often became the site of an English borough. In such cases the village associated with the Welsh royal court would be lost because of subsequent urban growth. On the other hand, where a former reeve's vill was not granted burghal status it would usually have been subject to the same process of change as an ordinary reckoned vill and often became a single large farm. Only exceptionally, where there were opportunities to practise supplementary activities, or where the rivalries of major landowners delayed estate consolidation, did villages survive; and of the survivors, Aberffraw, where there were rivalries between landowners and where too there were opportunities to practise trade as well as maritime callings, provides a supreme example. In the main, however, most of the hamlets and villages of medieval origin in Welsh Wales have been drastically modified or even completely replaced by large farms.

Over the centuries after the Middle Ages there was in the rural districts of Welsh Wales an increasing convergence of settlement forms and patterns alike on hereditary land and reckoned land. Yet, during the twelfth and thirteenth centuries to which the oversimplified observations of both Giraldus Cambrensis and Archbishop Peckham relate, most districts of Welsh Wales were characterized by a marked variety of settlement forms and patterns. These settlements were already very old-established but nevertheless they were not immutable. Hence the comments of a jurist concerning various 'defunct testimonies' which stood well in a man's pleas about hereditary land, as recorded in a South Welsh lawbook of the thirteenth century (Wade-Evans 1909, 136–7, 278–9). Among them was the visible evidence on the ground of 'the hearth-stone of a father, or a grandfather, or a great-grandfather, or one of the kindred of the same title as himself; and the tofts of the houses and their barns, and the furrows of the land ploughed, and the acres, every one of which affords testimony to a man's title'.

Notes

1. Public Record Office, LR2/205.
2. Public Record Office, SC6/114/23.
3. University College of North Wales, Mostyn Mss. 2138, 8583.
4. National Library of Wales, Tithe Apportionment and Map, Caerwys Parish, 1848.
5. University College of North Wales, Mostyn Ms. 2024.
6. National Library of Wales, Tithe Apportionment and Map, Llansanffraid Parish, 1841.
7. British Library, Harleian Ms 6696 f. 35.

References

Baker, A. R. H. and Butlin, R. A. (editors) 1973: *Studies of Field Systems in the British Isles* (Cambridge, Cambridge University Press).
Beverley Smith, L. 1977: *Tir prid*: deeds of gages of land in late-medieval Wales. *Bulletin of the Board of Celtic Studies* 27, 263–77.
Bowen, E. G. 1969: *Saints, Seaways and Settlements in the Celtic Lands* (Cardiff, University of Wales Press) 80–3, 183.
Carr, A. D. 1982: *Medieval Anglesey*, Llangefni. *Studies in Anglesey History* 6, (Anglesey Antiquarian Society) 123, 152, 327–30.
Charles, B. G. 1948: The records of Slebech. *National Library of Wales Journal* 5, 179–98.
Charles-Edwards, T. M. 1972: Kinship, status and the origins of the hide. *Past and Present* 56, 3–33.
Colvin, H. M. (editor) *The History of the King's Works, Vol 1: The Middle Ages* (London, Her Majesty's Stationery Office).
Davies, M. 1973: Field systems of South Wales. In Baker, A. R. H. and Butlin, R. A. (editors) 1973, 480–529.
Davies, R. R. 1978: *Lordship and Society in the March of Wales, 1282–1400* (Oxford, Clarendon Press).

Dimock, J. F. (editor) 1868: *Giraldi Cambrensis Opera VI* (London, Longmans, Green, Reader and Dyer. Rolls Series 21).
Ellis, H. (editor) 1838: *The Record of Caernarvon* (London, Record Commission).
Emanuel, H. D. (editor) 1967: *The Latin Texts of the Welsh Laws* (Cardiff, University of Wales Press).
Evans D. L. (editor) 1929: *Flintshire Ministers' Accounts, 1328–1353* (Hawarden, Flintshire Historical Society Record Series No. 2) xxix–xxx.
Eyre, S. R. and Jones, G. R. J. (editors) 1966: *Geography as Human Ecology* (London, Edward Arnold).
Finberg, H. P. R. (editor) 1972: *The Agrarian History of England and Wales, I, II, AD 43–1042* (Cambridge, Cambridge University Press).
Green, F. (editor) 1927: *The Crosswood Deeds* (Aberystwyth, National Library of Wales Calendars of Deeds and Documents) 2.
Jenkins, D. (editor) 1963: *Llyfr Colan* (Cardiff, University of Wales Press).
Jenkins, D. 1967: A lawyer looks at Welsh land law. *Transactions of the Honourable Society of Cymmrodorion* 220–48.

Jenkins, D. (editor) 1973: *Damweiniau Colan* (Aberystwyth, Cymdeithas Llyfrau Ceredigion Gyf).

Jones, A. (editor) 1913: *The History of Gruffydd ap Cynan* (Manchester, Manchester University Press, University of Manchester Publications 30, Historical series 9) 64–7.

Jones, G. R. J. 1955: The distribution of medieval settlement in Anglesey. *Transactions of the Anglesey Antiquarian Society and Field Club* 27–96.

Jones, G. R. J. 1966: Rural settlement in Anglesey. In Eyre, S. R. and Jones, G. R. J. (editors) 1967, 198–230.

Jones, G. R. J. 1972: Post-Roman Wales. In Finberg, H. P. R. (editor) 1972, 283–328.

Jones Pierce, T. 1972: *Medieval Welsh Society* (Cardiff, University of Wales Press) 39–57, 195–249.

Martin, C. T. (editor) 1885: *Registrum Epistolarum Fratris Johannis Peckham Archiepiscopi Cantuariensis Vol. 3* (London, Rolls Series) 776–7, 991–2.

Nash-Williams, V. E. 1950: *The Early Christian Monuments of Wales* (Cardiff, University of Wales Press) 116.

Owen, A. (editor) 1841: *Ancient Laws and Institutes of Wales 2* (London, Record Commission).

Peers, C. R. 1915–16: Caernarvon Castle. *Transactions of the Honourable Society of Cymmrodorion* 17, 1–74.

Rees, J. R. 1897: Slebech Commandery and the Knights of St John. *Archaeologia Cambrensis* 14, 5th series, 85–107, 181–228.

Rees, W. 1947: *A History of the Order of St John of Jerusalem in Wales and on the Welsh Border* (Cardiff, Western Mail and Echo Ltd.).

Richards, M. (editor) 1954: *The Laws of Hywel Dda* (Liverpool, Liverpool University Press).

Royal Commission On Ancient and Historical Monuments in Wales and Monmouthshire (1912) *County of Flint* (London, His Majesty's Stationery Office) 10–11.

Seebohm, F. 1904: *The Tribal System in Wales* (London, Longmans Green).

Stenton, F. M. 1943: *Anglo-Saxon England* 1st edition (London, Oxford University Press) 283–4.

Taylor, A. J. 1963: The King's Works in Wales, 1277–1330. In Colvin, H. M. (editor) 1963, 293–1040.

Thomas, S. 1963: The enumerators' returns as a source for a period picture of the parish of Llansantffaid. *Ceredigion* 4, 408–21.

Thomas, S. 1963: The Enumerators' Returns as a Source for a Period Picture of the Parish of Llansantffraid. *Ceredigion* 4, 408–21.

Thorpe, L. (editor) 1978: *Gerald of Wales: The Journey through Wales: The Description of Wales* (Harmondsworth, Penguin Classics).

Wade-Evans, A. W. (editor) 1909: *Welsh Medieval Law* (Oxford, Clarendon Press).

White, R. B. 1977: Sculptured stones from Aberffraw, Anglesey. *Archaeologia Cambrensis* 78, 140–5.

White, R. B. 1979: Excavations at Aberffraw, Anglesey, 1973 and 1974. *Bulletin of the Board of Celtic Studies* 28, 319–42.

Wiliam, A. R. (editor) 1960: *Llyfr Iorwerth* (Cardiff, University of Wales Press).

Willis-Bund, J. W. (editor) 1902: *The Black Book of St David's* (London, Cymmrodorion Record Series 5) 97–211.

Williams, S. J. and Powell, J. E. (editors) 1961: *Llyfr Blegywryd* (Cardiff, University of Wales Press).

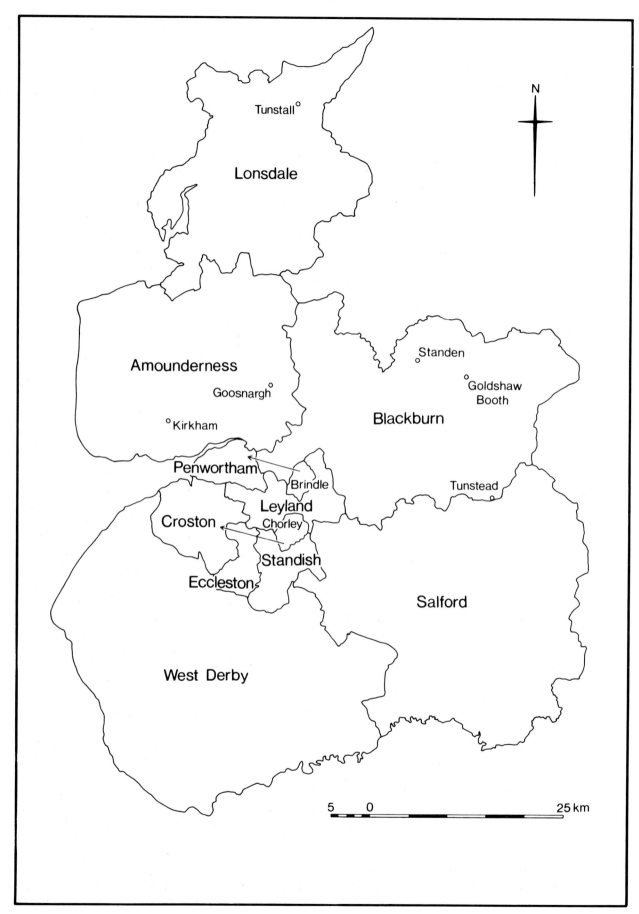

Fig. 12.1 The hundreds of Lancashire (excluding Furness and Cartmel), the ancient ecclesiastical parishes of Leyland Hundred, and places mentioned in the text.

12. Some Settlement Patterns in Lancashire

M. A. Atkin

This paper examines some dispersed patterns of settlement in an area of Northern England which exhibits a high degree of continuity of both landscape and landownership. Several examples of large primary double-oval enclosures are described, and also the settlements associated with them, many of which have names ending in 'ley'. The patterns of ownership and tenancy in their internal subdivision into fields is examined, and their possible origin and evolution is discussed. They are associated with a network of tracks which form broad swathes along township boundaries. The place-names 'green' and 'moor' recur along these stock tracks. A possible distinction between these two place-name elements is explored. Their relationship with the 'ley' names of the double-oval enclosures is considered in the context of pastoral farming usages thought to be integral features of multiple estates by J.E.A. Jolliffe and G.R.J. Jones.

The student of medieval settlement newly arrived in the Lancashire[1] countryside will find evidence that few of the vills listed in 1334 (Glasscock 1975, 149–56) consisted of the familiar single nucleated village with recognizable common arable fields. Although this settlement and field pattern is not wholly absent (Elliot 1973, 41–9), scarcely a vill is without a record of small hamlets and isolated halls or farms in existence before 1400. These were sometimes additional to a central village but some vills appear to have been composed entirely of scattered hamlets and dispersed farms. This emphasis towards dispersion is evident in all hundreds of the county at that time. This paper will largely be confined to examining some examples of these settlement patterns, notably those associated with large oval enclosures and with a network of drove roads in the hundred of Leyland.

Although the county of Lancaster was established relatively late in history (Jewell 1972, 44), the administrative units of which it was composed had much greater antiquity, and, furthermore, exhibit a high degree of continuity. This continuity was owed in part to the fact that these administrative and tenurial units were royal hundredal estates, many of them recorded in Domesday Book in abbreviated form under the entry of the principal royal vill in each hundred. South of the Ribble the six royal hundreds, later amalgamated into four by the absorption of the two smallest into West Derby hundred (Fig. 12.1), were held in 1066 by Edward the Confessor. This district 'between Ribble and Mersey' had the nature of a debatable land between Northumbria and Mercia, having been incorporated at various times during the Anglo-Saxon period with one or the other (Ekwall 1922, 227–33). North of the Ribble the two hundreds or wapentakes of Amounderness and Lonsdale were, prior to the Norman Conquest, held by Count Tostig

and had formed part of Northumbria. Jolliffe (1926) noted in all these hundreds, both north and south of the Ribble, customs which he regarded as Northumbrian in character, particularly the 'shire' structure of the manorial units. The essential nature of the shire lay in the fact that its administrative, judicial and economic functions extended over many vills, and that the pasture rights of the individual vills were intermingled in an intercommoned shire moor. The rights in these pastures lying beyond the bounds of the individual vill were paid for by forinsec pasture-rents. The more familiar equation of a manor with a single vill was largely absent in all these areas, and instead the manor incorporated a caput to which a number of dependent vills was attached. Thus in Lancashire, administrative, judicial and economic functions were centralized on the royal caput of the hundred. Here was sited the hundredal manorial court, the bailiff's office and the central demesne farm to which were owed the labour services and agricultural dues from the bondmen of the dependent vills. The terms 'shire' and 'hundred' were apparently used as synonyms in medieval Lancashire deeds. These shires or hundreds continued after the Norman Conquest in royal or quasi-royal hands, and they remained largely intact until the nineteenth century.

Like the hundreds, the ancient ecclesiastical parishes of Lancashire continued in largely unchanged form until the eighteenth or nineteenth centuries, each parish in the majority of cases comprising several townships (civil parishes). The same degree of longevity may be claimed for the townships themselves. There is little difference between the list of vills in 1334 and the townships of the nineteenth century; a few have been divided, others have become a single unit by amalgamation, but the great majority were the same as the units of 500 years before. As far as can be

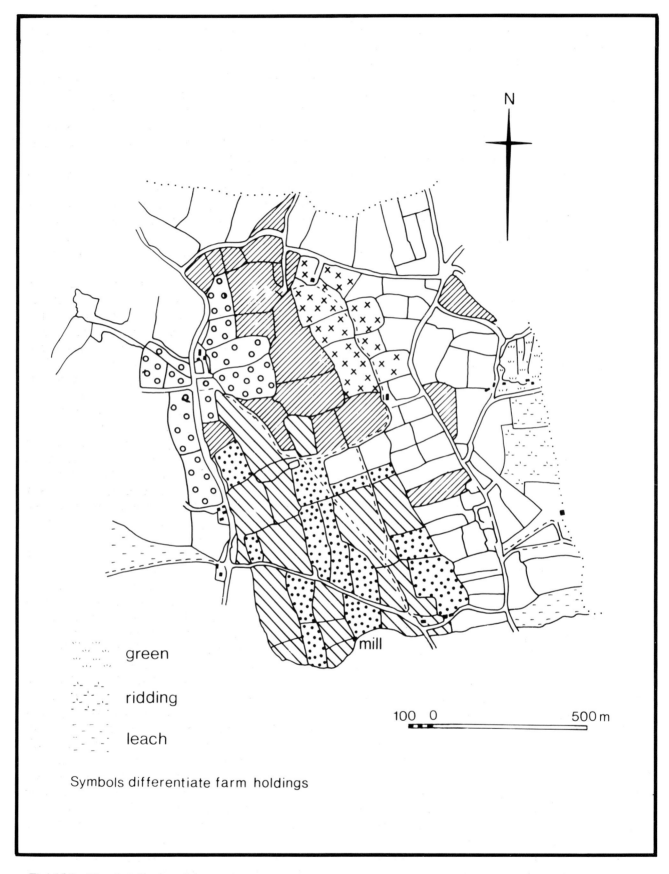

green

ridding

leach

Symbols differentiate farm holdings

100 0   500 m

mill

N

Fig. 12.2   The distribution of farm holdings in 1841 at Tunley in Wrightington, Leyland Hundred

ascertained, even township boundaries changed very little, and those portrayed in the 1840s on the Ordnance Survey's first edition six-inch maps provide an acceptable framework for the medieval villar units.

Similarly, there has been in the county a high degree of continuity of land holding. Many of the larger estates 'have remained in the same families for six, seven and even eight hundred years' (Sharpe France 1962, 79). Family tenancies, though less well documented, field-names and even the fields themselves have been established with little change over long periods. Enclosure of the common arable fields was largely completed by the Tudor period, often by piecemeal enclosure and exchange, with the result that the form of the ancient selions is still part of the agrarian landscape. Enclosure by Parliamentary Act was confined to the common pastures and wastes, and even these were mostly effected during the eighteenth century. The Lancashire landscape therefore is one which admirably fits Rackham's description of an 'Ancient Countryside' (Rackham 1976, 17), 'A land of hamlets, of medieval farms in the hollows of the hills, of lonely moats in the claylands, of immense mileages of quiet minor roads, hollow-ways and intricate footpaths; of irregularly shaped groves and thick hedges....'. It is therefore a county which despite the paucity of documentary evidence until the early thirteenth century offers to the historical geographer an unusual degree of continuity, both in its land tenures and its landscape features.

Much of this paper arises from a presently continuing study of the field and settlement patterns of the hundred of Leyland which, of the hundreds of Lancashire between the Ribble and the Mersey, was that least affected by eighteenth- and nineteenth-century industrialization. The hundred was one of the smallest, being about 21 km (13 miles) from north to south, and 26 km (16 miles) from east to west. The coast facing the Ribble estuary is backed by a coastal plain where low hills barely rise above peat mosses and coastal marshes. Behind the coastal plain are foothills at 90–150 m (300–500 feet) rising to part of the Rossendale upland which, within the hundred, reaches 370 m (1200 feet). The 40 townships of the hundred were recorded in 1341 as being grouped into five ecclesiastical parishes (Farrer and Brownbill, *V.C.H. Lancaster*, 1911, 6, 55–9). Each ecclesiastical parish included townships which were lowland in character, and at least one which was wholly in the upland. This is most conspicuous in the cases of Croston parish, which included in its 11 townships the detached township of Chorley in the upland, and Penwortham parish which comprised six townships including the detached upland township of Brindle. Leyland parish included nine townships, three of which were in the upland. These three together formed the ancient area of Gunnolfsmores, whose bounds were described in a twelfth-century charter (Farrer 1902,

375–6). Eccleston parish contained four townships, of which Wrightington and Parbold were largely upland; and Standish parish, with ten townships, included Heath Charnock which at its highest point reaches 200 m (682 feet) and Coppull which means 'hilltop', though the altitude is relatively low at 90 m (300 feet).

Rural settlement patterns of the past are compounded firstly of the individual farmstead with its fields, and secondly of each farm with its neighbours. Since the hundred of Leyland in the period 1837–47 has a complete set of Tithe Award surveys, it is possible to map the individual farm holdings for the whole hundred at that time; then following Bloch's precept of using 'evidence from periods close to our own to shed light on the very remote past', to work back to earlier settlement patterns with the help of earlier maps and documents (Bloch 1966 edn.)

Among the landscape features of the hundred are several oval enclosures, 800 m (half a mile) or more in diameter, and subdivided within into smaller fields. Many of these enclosures, as at Tunley in Wrightington (Figs. 12.2, 12.3 and 12.4h) occur in pairs, the two ovals usually being interlocked. They are defined by lanes and footpaths, sometimes by township boundaries, by discontinuity of field patterns on the boundaries of the oval enclosures, and in several cases by the existence on the perimeter of the oval of huge banks surmounted by hedges with a high count of hardwood species which suggests that the hedges at least date back to the early post-Conquest period (Pollard 1974). The two ovals typically have different field and settlement patterns. There is evidence that one of them may be interpreted as an arable oval and the other as a pasture oval.

The arable oval is associated with several farms usually sited round the perimeter, and often sharing the same name, but sometimes grouped in a small hamlet. These farms share the land of this oval and may also have land outside it, but it is rare for any other farm to have fields within the oval. The pattern of fields and holdings associated with the arable oval is reminiscent of that described as a girdle pattern by Jones (1955, 27–96; 1966, 207–11; 1977, 88–9). The holdings are organized in a manner which resembles Fox's interpretation of the laws of Ine (Fox 1981, 87). Each farm holding forms a coherent block which interlocks with other holdings in the centre of the oval, but which places a continuous length of perimeter fence into the care of each individual farm. Typically the fields are small and show signs of aratral curves but these arable strips were evidently short in length. Field-names common to several of the farms suggest that some of the land within this oval may have been held and used in common. This oval has been interpreted as primarily an arable oval, but it might include some pasture or convertible land.

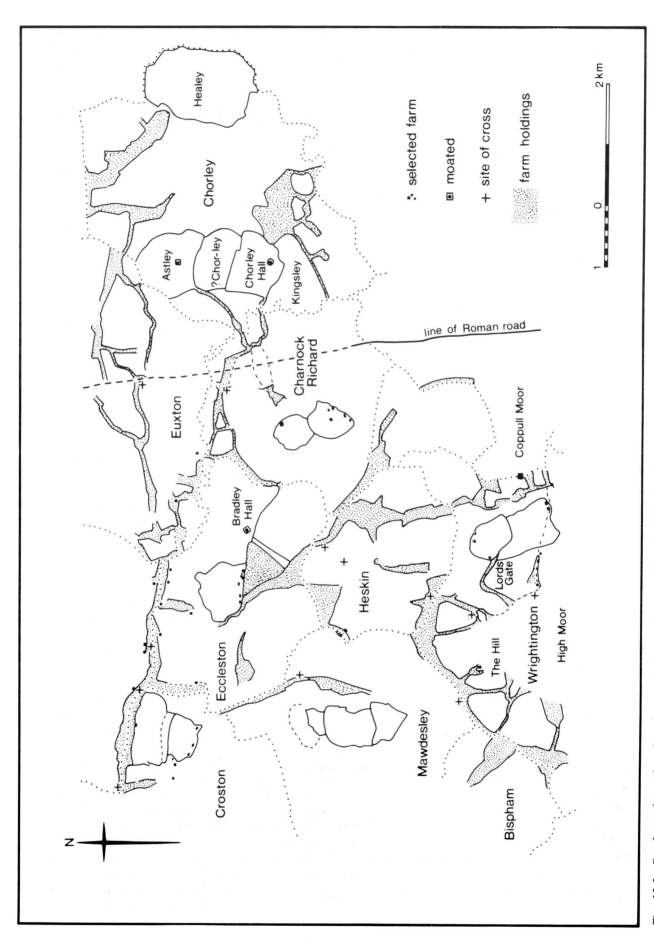

Fig. 12.3   Stock tracks and oval enclosures in the south part of Leyland Hundred

The pasture oval, by contrast, is normally held by one significant farm, often called a hall, and several examples are moated. It is usually larger than the arable oval, and is associated with one or more stock funnels which lead from the oval directly to open or one-time open grazings, or into drove roads or driftways (Adams 1976, 95, 131) which form a network of tracks across the landscape. The stock funnels, several of them bearing the name 'leach' (Atkin 1982–3), occur where a fenced lane from a settlement widens out steadily until it debouches on the open common. These funnels facilitate the ingathering of animals, for as they descend from the open land, the narrowing walls or hedges herd them into an easily managed group. Presumably *leach*, meaning a bog, refers to the muddy, trampled nature of the ground in the stock funnel. *Tong* and *rake* (Smith 1956, 2, 181 and 80) may also occur as field-names associated with stock funnels, though the latter may more strictly refer to the whole stock track. Commonly in the funnel there is a spring or well for watering the stock, and sometimes a pinfold on the lane between the funnel and the settlement. A farm is frequently sited by the narrow throat of the funnel, and so-placed would be in a position to control or regulate the numbers of stock being taken to the open grazing. These farms sometimes include the word leach in their names. Where a stock funnel opens directly on to the moor from a settlement, the farm on the funnel is often called Moor Gate. In a damp climate such as that of Lancashire, low hills of naturally well-drained soil offered advantages to arable and pastoral farming in the past, and the oval enclosures often include land of this type. Small streams often form part of the boundary, and not infrequently the pasture oval is crossed by a stream, useful for the watering of stock. Most of the double-oval enclosures incorporate a water-mill site.

The double-oval enclosure at Tunley in Wrightington (Fig. 12.3) is defined by lanes on the north, west and south, and the two ovals are separated from each other by footpaths which, with the lanes, completely encircle the northern, arable oval. The eastern boundaries of both ovals are characterized by massive hedgebanks which in many places follow a break of slope, and frequently are marked by a ditch as well. The hedges which crest these banks contain a fairly high number of hardwood species. The arable oval was shared in 1841[2] by three farms, one of which is North Tunley Hall, the only one of the three lying within the perimeter of the oval. Each farm held some land outside the oval as well. Two of the farms held adjoining fields which shared the name High Field. Aratral curves, and butt ends of strips showing in the field boundaries, ran both east-west and north-south, suggesting an interlocking pattern of arable strips of rather short length. One of these fields is called Short Shoots.

The southern oval was in 1841 held by two farms, one being South Tunley Hall, which stand together at the southern end of this, the larger oval. The field pattern here is more regular and runs from north to south. The holdings of the two farms interlocked in echelon formation, and some field-names were common to both farms. The internal pattern of this oval would best be explained by a division of the whole oval into two moieties, possibly in the fifteenth century when a lease naming some of the fields belonging to the farm holding marked with large dots on Fig. 12.2 described them as being part of 'Tonley demesne'.[3] This oval was evidently once a single undivided area, and from its association with stock funnels leading from it on to the Hill of Wrightington may be interpreted as having once been a huge demesne pasture, controlled by or belonging to the single predecessor of the two South Tunley farms. One of these stock tracks leads westward out of the oval by way of a stock funnel in which stands a farm called Stone Leach Farm at the narrow end of a field also called Stone Leach. Another funnel, which is unnamed, opens out between the two ovals of North and South Tunley; it leads through a series of long, narrow fields before turning into one significantly called Lord's Gate, which leads upwards to the Hill of Wrightington (see Fig. 12.3). A third funnel, east of the two South Tunley farms, leads through Dig Leach to Coppull Moor. Close to the Hall there was a mill,[4] now vanished, though its leat can still be recognized, and the field in front of the Hall is called Fish Pond. Tunley was held by Cockersand Abbey prior to 1540[5] and the holders of Tunley appear as witnesses of deeds frequently from 1332.

Similar double-oval enclosures occur in other parts of the hundred, as in Charnock Richard, and less clearly demarcated at Mawdesley (Fig. 12.3). There are further examples in other parts of the county (Fig. 12.1). At Tunstall in Lonsdale Hundred (Fig. 12.4a), the double-oval lies across two townships, the pasture oval being held by the moated hall now called Thurland Castle in Cantsfield township. The arable oval was held in 1846[6] by seven farms, including Tunstall Hall and the Glebe Farm. The farms were loosely clustered at the south end of the oval, which is defined on the west by a lane leading to a ford over the River Lune. The name *tūn-stall* may imply a cattle farm or vaccary (Smith 1961, 3, 125). The double-oval of Tunstead in Rossendale (Fig. 12.4b), in Blackburn hundred, is defined on the Ordnance Survey first edition six-inch map because it was an extra-parochial area, and its boundaries were therefore shown. The smaller, arable oval was held by a series of small farms which shared the name of Tunstead: Far Tunstead, Higher Tunstead, Lower Tunstead, Waggoner Tunstead and Tunstead Mill. The pasture oval extended on to the Rossendale upland and no doubt its size is the

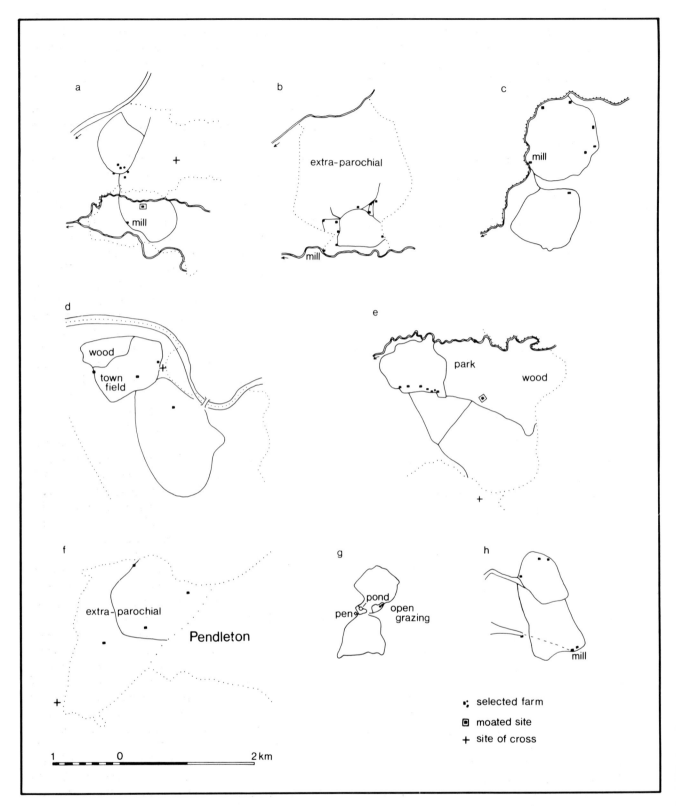

Fig. 12.4 Some examples of double-oval enclosures, drawn at the same scale: a) Tunstall in Lonsdale, b) Tunstead in Rossendale, in Blackburn Hundred, c) Lickhurst and White Lee in Goosnargh in Amounderness, d) Penwortham in Leyland Hundred, e) Bradley in Eccleston, in Leyland Hundred, f) Standen in Pendleton, Blackburn Hundred, g) Roystone Grange in Derbyshire, h) Tunley in Wrightington, Leyland Hundred

consequence of the poor quality of the terrain, for it reaches 300 m (1100 feet). Tunstead was one of the medieval vaccaries of the Forest of Rossendale.

In Goosnargh township (Fig. 12.4c) (Calderbank 1978) the northern oval was held in 1849 by five farms lying on the perimeter of the oval. The largest one, called Lickhurst, named an estate held by the Hospitallers, and the mill was Lickhurst Mill in 1662. Some of the land in this oval is not of arable quality, and may represent intake at some early period. The southern oval was held by the single farm of White Lee. The two ovals here do not interlock and between them lies a wide funnel leading out on to Beacon Fell, still partly unenclosed today. This funnel is approached by a bridge over the River Brook. Since the latter is the township boundary, it suggests that the grazing on the fell was used by other townships, and that stock could gain access to the hill grazings without encroaching on the enclosed ovals. The position of White Lee farmhouse at the side of the funnel would give the owner supervision and control of passing stock. Goosnargh was an outlying and detached member of the very large ecclesiastical parish of Kirkham and is another example of an upland township attached to a largely lowland parish.

In all these examples the field patterns in the area beyond the ovals terminate against their boundaries. It is clear, therefore, that these 'double-ovals' are primary field enclosures, and it is probable that their enclosure from the waste took place at a very early period. They show a close resemblance to two large enclosures at Roystone Grange in Derbyshire (Hodges and Wildgoose 1980, 48–53), assigned to the Roman-British period (Fig. 12.4g). These enclosures were enclosed by double-orthostat walls. The arable enclosure contained 'ladder-like' field systems: 'perhaps five hectares of land was cultivated'. The second enclosure was thought to be a winter pasture. It incorporated a pond; and a settlement which occupies one side of the pasture enclosure contained datable material. In the angle between the two enclosures was a stock pen. Surrounding the enclosures was unenclosed summer grazing.

In Goldshaw Booth, a medieval vaccary in the Forest of Pendle in Lancashire, there is another example of a double-oval enclosure. One oval is surrounded by a group of farms named Sabden Great Hall, Sabden Fold, Lower Hall and Old House which held the land within the oval. The holdings interdigitated, and the zig-zag fencing at the ends of some fields indicated that some of the land had once been held in strips of rather short length. Excavations in the fields of Old House suggest that earthworks evidently representing a bank and ditch enclosure of a low hill could be assigned to the Romano-British period (Higham 1968). The second oval (Higham, pers. comm.) is rather larger than the

first, and formed a pasture which at some point had been subdivided by now degraded field banks. It was apparently associated with Sabden Hall. The hill above the double-oval enclosure was open grazing until it was assigned to individual farms in the complex at a relatively recent date.

Returns rendered at Michaelmas for the medieval vaccaries in the Forest of Pendle provide evidence (Lyons 1884) of a farming system which might have given rise to the field and settlement patterns of these double-ovals. Each vaccary had a breeding herd of about 40 cows, which with their progeny of several years would make a total on each vaccary of perhaps twice the breeding herd. These animals constituted the demesne stock, and the vaccary was run by a vaccary keeper for his lord. No doubt the vaccarius could also run stock of his own with the demesne herd. The full size of the unit was therefore considerable, even by comparison with modern stock farms. Each autumn the stock in each of the 11 vaccaries of Pendle was accounted for to the bailiff in charge of the whole estate, and old and barren cows were replaced from a central pool of young animals. The returns indicated the products of the vaccaries. In Pendle they were concentrating on the production of plough oxen for the nearby granges, of which Standen in Pendleton (*vide infra*) was one, but some of the oxen were despatched to more distant de Lacy estates in South Yorkshire, Lincolnshire and Norfolk. In vaccaries in other parts of Lancashire, dairy products, called lactage or 'white', were more significant. Such large enterprises required a considerable body of herdsmen, and we can safely infer a number of small farms additional to the vaccary keeper's farmstead and sufficient land under the plough to provide subsistence for the vaccary unit.

The establishment of vaccaries and studs was a recognized method of exploitation in the medieval forests of Brittany (du Halgouet 1921) and they are recorded in forests, parks and monastic holdings in Britain. Most of these can be shown to have been demesne lands of the king or great lords at some time, and it may be that the association of the demesnes with vaccaries is to be ascribed to the fossilizing of institutions under demesne management. Vaccaries are recorded in Domesday Book in the Vale of White Horse and in Yorkshire (Darby 1977, 144), and the 'hardvices' of Monmouthshire have been interpreted as dairy farms (Moore 1982, 162a); pre-Conquest vaccaries are recorded near Harewood, Yorkshire (Faull and Moorhouse 1981, 3, 194) and at Wadborough, near Pershore in Worcestershire (Darby 1977, 148). In Leyland Hundred the royal demesnes appear to have been dispersed soon after the Conquest, if not before, and although it was clearly a heavily wooded area in 1086, no forest is recorded there in Domesday Book. Nevertheless, residual traces of erstwhile forest remain.

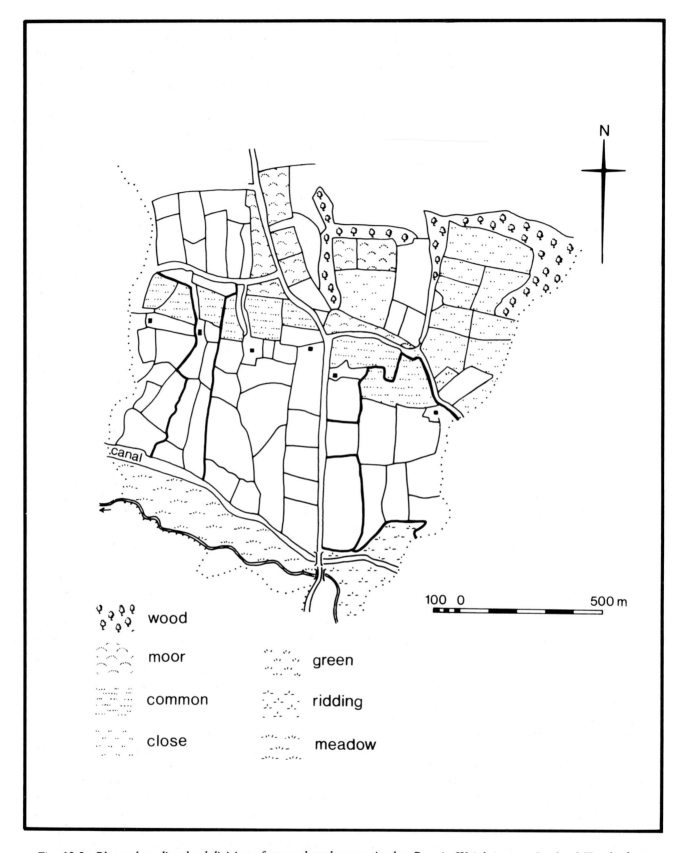

N

canal

100 0   500 m

wood

moor   green

common   ridding

close   meadow

Fig. 12.5 Planned medieval subdivision of an oval enclosure: Appley Row in Wrightington, Leyland Hundred

The chief forester of Lancashire had a holding of the Forest Fee in the hundred, Healey Park still had tenuous links with the royal demesnes, and 'forest of Mawdesley' is mentioned in a thirteenth-century grant (Farrer and Brownbill *V.C.H. Lancaster*, 1911, 6, 92).

Such a farming organization need not have its origin in the Middle Ages. Evidence of the Irish laws shows that cattle could be given by a lord to his vassal as a fief which would be returned to the lord on the death of the vassal (Howells 1972/3, 48–67). Howells has identified in the early Welsh laws a similar cattle fief known as *daered* which he dates back at least to the pre-Norman period, and perhaps, as in Ireland, to the seventh century or even earlier. Higham (1978a, 7–15) has argued that a Celtic stock-leasing system was associated with *erg* place-names, and suggested that a similar organization might have existed within the Roman imperial estates. A system of daered would not imply that all such cattle fiefs were necessarily demesne farms of a lord. The relationship of lord and client was that of a lord with his trusted man and less hierarchical than that of the medieval lord with his demesne tenant.

It may well be that the vaccary was a fossilized form of the earlier system, and that the earlier system itself preserved and developed the economic exploitation of double-ovals which had been enclosed from the waste at a far earlier date. The first requirements of the prehistoric farmer were a protected enclosure for his stock and a separate enclosure for his crops. His first concern would be to clear and enclose these two essential units of land from the waste. Later periods might see addition to, or enlargement of, these units before they became embedded in the pattern of subsequent external enclosure. Two fields of the western farm in the arable oval of Tunley in Wrightington hint at a small irregular circle within the larger oval which might date back to the prehistoric period (Fig. 12.2).

Some such early farming system might have laid its mark upon the ground many hundreds of years ago and still be recognizable. 'If agrarian customs appear to remain static over several centuries it is because they in fact altered very little, and because what small advances were made usually took place without commotion' (Bloch 1966). Bloch linked that remark with a warning that changes did occur. In Tunley, the pasture oval was split into moieties, in Eccleston (see Fig. 12.3) the 'broad ley' became in part a severalty of Bradley Hall and in part an addition to Eccleston Green (*vide infra*). Some of the pasture ovals had by the nineteenth century become ornamental parks. In Appley in Wrightington there is an example of an oval or double-oval which underwent a planned redevelopment in the medieval period.

Appley (Fig. 12.5) is south of the High Moor of Wrightington and just off the southern edge of

Fig. 12.3. In 1841[7] the settlement comprised six farms known as Appley Row. The pattern of these farms and their fields is sufficiently distinctive to mark off this oval area as a unit on its own. It was physically isolated from the rest of Wrightington by the presence on its northern side of Appley Moor, Appley Common and the demesne of Wrightington Hall, which probably included the now vanished Appley Wood. The other three sides are all administrative boundaries; Parbold and Shevington on the west and east respectively, and the hundred boundary on the south along the river Douglas. Like Tunley, its name appears from the thirteenth century in Cockersand charters; the name Appley is applied to the whole unit, its Common, its Moor, its Wood and the bridge over the Douglas. It was, in effect, a 'sub-township' of Wrightington. In medieval deeds such units were often described as 'a hamlet in x', and the term implies for such a settlement a degree of autonomy, economic at least, if not administrative.

The six farms of Appley Row stand well spaced out, facing on to Appley Common which was enclosed shortly before 1759.[8] South of each farm lay a roughly rectangular block of land extending to the valley floor, where each farm had a share of Douglas Meadow. This pattern of fields and farms must arise from a systematic and planned subdivision, and a deed of 1393[9] is clearly describing as 'intake' the holding of one farm created by that division:

'A place called the Intak in Appeley in Wrightington lying between the land of Edward of Lathum and the land of Sir Richard of Kyrkeby with one end extending to the Doglas the other to the Comyn of Appeley'.

This may have been the division of a pasture oval, the arable oval of which is no longer identifiable. Alternatively, the area might have included both an arable and pasture oval. The existence at the western end of Oven House Field and a number of others called Acre and Shoot may suggest that this end had constituted an arable oval. The pasture oval would in that case have been at the eastern end, where most field-names are Hey, Close and Earth, and the eastern farm of the Row the one controlling the pasture.

The oval enclosures discussed thus far have all been in upland townships where the vaccary model is not inapplicable, and where it is possible to envisage, in the remoter past, islands of enclosed and organized land use in a sea of undeveloped though not unexploited waste. There are, however, very similar, often considerably larger, oval enclosures in lowland areas where such a model seems inappropriate. 'Similar forms need not mean similar origins' (Roberts 1981, 148) and it is necessary to consider not only the form but also the economic and social context which might have produced these similar but larger double-oval

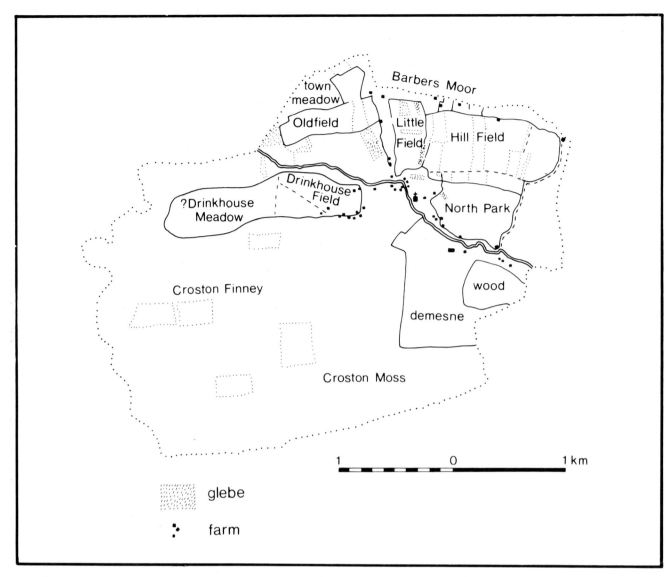

Fig. 12.6 (and facing page)   Croston township, Leyland Hundred: a) Settlement and field patterns

enclosures. The moated Bradley Hall in Eccleston in Leyland Hundred (see Figs. 12.3 and 12.4e) was associated in the medieval period with a deer-park and warren. In the post-Conquest period, it was held of the Forest Fee by the hereditary Chief Forester of Lancashire. To the south of the hall is a very large enclosure almost 2 km in length. A funnel, described as Waste in the Tithe schedule, opens into this enclosure at its eastern corner. This suggests that this huge area was a large enclosed pasture. Its boundaries are marked by lanes, those on the south and west being coincident with township boundaries. The oval is divided by a very straight road, to the north-west of which are rectangular fields, many of them called Green. The fields of this Green are shared by the farms of the village. It seems that the villagers had some rights of pasture here which were recognized by the addition of part of the oval to the less regular area of Eccleston

Green which fringed the oval on the western side. The rest of the oval seems to have been attached to Bradley Hall until the nineteenth century. Since it is clearly a very early enclosure, the suspicion must arise that this was the original Bradley, 'the broad ley'.

To the north of the Green is an arable oval held by the seven farms which face on to the Green. A distinction can be made between the eastern farms, which are clustered as a tiny hamlet on a bend in the lane, and a western group, probably later in date, which are spread out along a building line lying back from the lane. The fields run back behind these farms in irregular north-south blocks, but the individual farm holdings within these blocks are fragmented. The pattern also suggests that an earlier enclosure had been added to: as at Tunley there is a small circular enclosure within the larger oval, shared by four farms.

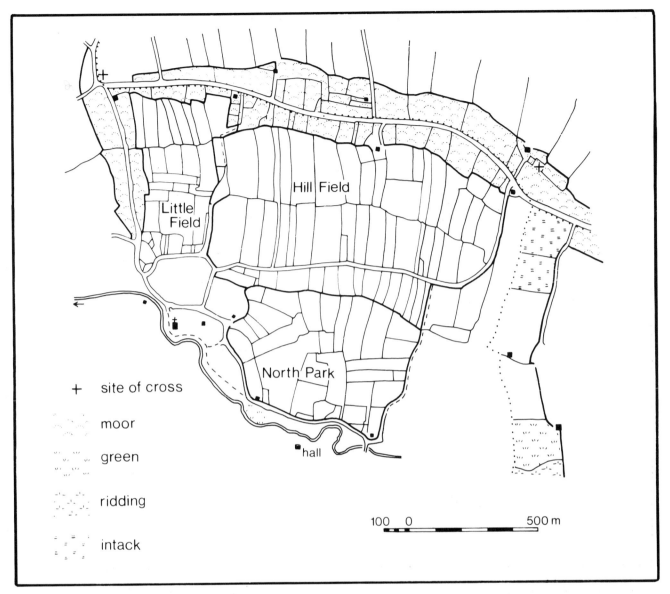

b) Field patterns in the North Park, Hill Field, the stock funnel of Cannel Leach, and Barber's Moor; and relevant farms

Similar large double-oval enclosures are found at Penwortham in Leyland hundred (see Fig. 12.4d), and at Standen in Pendleton in Blackburn hundred (see Fig. 12.4f). Both these vills were royal holdings in 1066. By 1086 the former was a borough and had a castle, and in the high Middle Ages became the caput of the barony of Penwortham, usurping the functions of the erstwhile hundredal caput of Leyland. Standen was one of the capital manors of the great de Lacy estates in the Middle Ages and, as Standen Grange, was the centre at which the peasants of neighbouring villages performed labour services at seeding and harvest. The accounts rendered at Michaelmas to the bailiff of the whole estate show that both arable and pastoral activities were taking place at Standen Grange. It is and was part of the township of Pendleton but its boundaries within the township were recorded on the Ordnance Survey first

edition six-inch map because it was an extra-parochial area. These boundaries define two 'ovals', a north-eastern one shared by three farms and a southern one held by the single farm of Standen Hey. The larger size of these three units, Bradley Hall, Penwortham and Standen Grange, may be related to their important status from before the Norman Conquest as administrative centres or as holdings of leading administrators; and a comparison may be drawn between them and the central caputs of Jolliffe's shires or the maerdrefi of Jones' commotes (Jones 1976, 15).

Croston (Figs. 12.6a and 12.6b) offers an example of what appears to be the evolution of a double-oval enclosure resulting from the establishment of a medieval borough. The village lies at the end of a low ridge projecting into the mosslands called Croston Finney fringing the lower River Douglas. It contained the leading church of the hundred, which was first mentioned in 1094,[10] and was the caput of a mesne tenant of the Hornby fee whose holding comprised five of the vills of the ecclesiatical parish. The arable oval, which later became the North Park of Croston Hall, was shown in the Tithe Award survey of 1837[11] to be an area of small, narrow, curving fields which inter-digitated in an irregular pattern. The fields bore names like Two Acre, Three Butts, Wood Butts, Farrier's Acre. The seven farms which held the land were round the perimeter of the oval and included the Rectory farm, the Hall farm, and one across the river to the west of the church.

The identification of the pasture oval is less secure. It was most probably associated with the Hall and its demesne lying south of the North Park. Field-names like Hall Field and Old Hey suggest ancient enclosure, but field shapes are regular and there is no hint of a large oval primary enclosure. An alternative possibility is the markedly oval area north of North Park, called the Hill Field. The layout of the fields within this area is very regular; all of them are long and narrow, with curving boundaries, and aligned from north to south. Under certain conditions of light, frost or plant growth these fields show clear signs of ridge and furrow, running parallel to the field boundaries. Holdings here by both tenants and landowners are scattered and intermixed, and this is especially marked in the case of the Glebeland. The whole pattern closely resembles the *esch* of a *drubbel* of north-west Germany (Mayhew 1973, 18; Fig. 2, 21 and Plate 3). The area is divided by a shallow ditch running from east to west and only rarely do the lines of field boundaries cross the ditch. North of this ditch, field-names characteristically end in -hey. The southern part, crossed by Highfield Lane, has field-names which mostly end in -hill. There are documentary references to 'the Common Hill or High Field', and to selions in the Hill Field,[12] and it is evident that the south part, at least, was one of the common arable fields of the township. The northern part of the oval may also have functioned as common arable, as its field shapes suggest, or it may have been outfield, convertable sometimes to meadow or pasture. In 1519/20 there was a grant of 'land in a close called Croston Hey, i.e. (*sic*) 2 acres of meadow',[13] which may be a reference to this area. That this part, at least, was once pasture is implied by the Out Lane which leads from it to the village, by the stock funnel at the entrance to the field, and by the presence of the pinfold and a pond in Out Lane. There is no immediately apparent farm which might have held Hill Field as a pasture oval. The large farm on its northern edge or one in the centre of the village might fit this role. However it may be that the Hill Field should be regarded as having been carved out of Barber's Moor.

The very regular layout of this area suggests organized land use planning which may at some early period have converted an erstwhile pasture oval to arable townfield, perhaps in two stages, the Hill Field first and the Heys later. Such a conversion implies a growth in population and a likely period for this would be in the thirteenth century when the lord of Croston established a borough there. References to burgages occur in the thirteenth century.[14] These were sited in Cannel Leach, a large stock funnel leading northwards from the church village on to Barber's Moor, which lies on the northern edge of the township, straddles three township boundaries and was intercommoned. Croston village in 1837 comprised the farms and cottages in the core of the village north of the church, the farms around North Park, the Hall, and the few farms but many houses and cottages in Cannel Leach. West of this was the hamlet of Drinkhouses, with almost a dozen farms, and the distribution of their holdings sharply emphasizes the separate identity of the hamlet from the village. Only four Drinkhouse farmers held fields in the Croston side of the township and in each case these fields were only a small part of the total farm. All the other fields of Drinkhouse were in Drinkhouse Field, so-named in 1461,[15] in the Town Meadow, Oldfield, and in the Finney which had been the common grazing of the town until it was enclosed in 1725.[16] Drinkhouse farmers held most of the meadow shown in Fig. 12.6a as 'Drinkhouse Meadow', though it is not recorded that this name was actually used. Croston presents a picture of a conventional nucleated village with medieval common pasture and common arable fields. Nevertheless, underlying this pattern there appears to be another of the oval enclosures which may have great antiquity.

That traces of this ancient pattern remain in Penwortham and Croston is probably due to the failure of these two medieval boroughs to survive. This is not so in the case of Chorley (see Fig. 12.3). The medieval borough established there before 1257 (Porteus 1931, 15) survived and grew in the industrial era, and the boundaries of the oval enclosures may only be defined tentatively. There appear to be at least four enclosures in the township, associated with Astley Hall, Chorley Hall (now Gillibrand Hall), both moated, Healey Park, a medieval deer park, and Kingsley.

These oval enclosures appear to be associated with a network of drove roads or stock tracks which provided a link between the lowland townships of Croston parish and its detached upland township of Chorley. This type of ecclesiastical association between a core of lowland townships and a detached outlier has already been noted, and is not uncommon in Lancashire. It probably had its origins in some very early economic association between lowland and upland which was reflected in lordship, and therefore in ecclesiastical and administrative organization. The most likely economic link between lowland and upland was that of seasonal stock grazing, combined with exploitation of woodland resources. In the course of plotting Tithe Award data for the hundred of Leyland, township by township, it became apparent that along township boundaries there were often 100 to 400 metre-wide swathes of land which might be interpreted as stock routes or drove roads by which animals could be moved from the lowland villages of Croston parish to the hill grazings which would have been available in the large township of Chorley. These swathes of land form a network followed today by modern roads, lanes and tracks, which not only link Chorley and Croston, but extend into and through neighbouring parishes. Similar stock tracks have been identified in other hundreds, including one in Amounderness which links the mother church township of Kirkham with the outlying township of Goosnargh. It is possible that they form part of much longer transhumance links, such as those by means of which in 1258 120 young oxen and cows were taken from the vaccaries of Amounderness to the king's larder at Westminster (Cunliffe Shaw 1956, 357) or those by which the bondmen of Singleton in Amounderness carried their lord's provisions and food to Richmond, York, Doncaster, Pontefract and Newcastle 'with 12 horses as well in summer as in winter' (Farrer 1907, 2, 132).

On the Ordnance Survey first edition six-inch maps, dating in Lancashire to 1844–77, these stock tracks appear as a wide band of fields, occasionally narrowing to road width, whose outer edges terminate in a line of more or less continuous parallel hedgerows (see Figs. 12.6b and 12.3), as on Barber's Moor, on the northern boundary of Croston. These parallel hedges mark two lines of discontinuity on which hedges both within and without the track terminate and along which farmsteads stand. The township boundary may be in the centre or to one side of the swathe of land, and this is true also of the modern road or lane which follows the track. Enclosure of the tracks as roadside waste, common, moor or green has resulted in a pattern of small fields, often contrasting with larger ones beyond the track boundary. Occasionally the tracks leave the township boundary where the latter follows a narrow river valley. Squatter settlements may have occurred within the wide band of the tracks, for smallholdings and cottages are characteristic here. Field-names like Waste, Intack, Close and Ridding occur within the swathe and some stretches are called Moor, as along the Croston-Ulnes Walton-Eccleston boundaries. This was still unenclosed in 1580.[17]

Several sections of the stock tracks are called Green and almost always are associated with a small hamlet.

These are not central village greens of settlements which are townships, such as the Green villages of County Durham and the Midlands (Thorpe 1949, 153). These are of the type which Thorpe noted as having the word Green as part of the name, and which he regarded as 'squatting settlements of fairly recent date'. That the settlement may be late, however, does not mean that the stock route is also late. At each green the stock track widens along the line of the track, and most were enclosed by the mid-nineteenth century. Many cottages may have originated at that time, but several greens include at least one substantial farm of considerable age. Perhaps these wider portions called Green were enclosed areas where stock in transit could be penned for grazing. If some financial dues were demanded of the drovers, such as the tolls known as payage, for their passage from township to township, the greens would make suitable tally points where stock could be counted. This would explain the presence of a substantial farm for the official responsible for exacting the dues.

The antiquity of these stock tracks is suggested by their association with stone crosses: 'Pedestal of Stone Cross' is marked on Ordnance Survey maps in several places along the routes and a few cross bases are still *in situ*. They are big socketed stones, and in some districts are known as plague stones from a belief that alms for plague-stricken communities were placed in the socket. They seem to mark the route rather than the boundaries, for several occur at places on the routes which are not on boundaries. The Ordnance Survey first edition six-inch map shows wells along these routes, not only along roads and lanes, but also where the tracks pass through fields. Where the route crosses a stream there are fords, and these, too, are usually marked on the map. Many of the fords are paved, some with huge flags of stone, others with setts. Smithies are indicated by field-names along several stock tracks and many survived to be recorded by the Ordnance Survey in the nineteenth century. Counts of hardwood species in the hedgerows along the tracks also point to the antiquity of the routes. Many of these flanking hedgerows grow to considerable size and the lanes which follow the routes and occupy part of the tracks often run in a hollow-way, the consequence of long years of wear. The association of the stock tracks with the township boundaries also underlines their probable antiquity.

Some of the stock tracks lead into the Chorley ovals. The tracks round the northern boundary of Charnock Richard cross the river by fords and climb the eastern bank to enter Astley and Kingsley, while a side branch leads to the oval associated with Chorley Hall. A route further north through Euxton passes round the northern boundary of Chorley and leads to Healey

Park. The existence of so many -ley names in Chorley underlines its importance as a potential upland grazing area for the lowland townships of Croston parish.

The terms associated with these Lancashire stock tracks and enclosures may in the past have had a significance which we have lost sight of. For example, a distinction might be drawn between Greens and Moors. The former were in fact enclosed sections of the stock route: they were separated from the land beyond the track by walls or fences and were probably demarcated from the track itself by having gates or barriers at each end of the Green. Although the greens lie on the boundaries, their individual names appear to be attached to only one of the townships, as in Heskin Green, Eccleston Green, Whittle Green. It is possible, therefore, that the greens were restricted to the animals of that township and to animals in transit which paid dues.

Much of this description would apply to a Moor such as Barber's Moor: by steady encroachment it, too, was enclosed from the lands on either side and it was common land; but it differs from the Greens in that it was intercommoned in being shared by three townships. If a definition of Moor as unenclosed, intercommoned grazing were applied to examples examined in Lancashire, they would conform, provided that allowance was made for the late assignment of once intercommoned moors to the townships on either side. So, for example, Mawdesley Moor and Bispham Moor adjoin across a very straight township boundary but significantly the moors on both sides of the boundary are called Black Moor. Here would seem to be a moor, once intercommoned, which was allocated to the individual townships at a relatively late date, probably in the early Tudor period. A similar example in Blackburnshire is the survival of the name Pendle Moor in the area which now includes Downham Moor, Mearley Moor, Pendleton Moor and Wiswell Moor. Here a large once intercommoned Pendle Moor has been split between the sharing townships.

The Moors of Chorley and Wrightington appear at first sight to be anomalous on the basis of that definition, since these moors are internal to each township and not on the boundary edges. But if these townships did provide the grazing for the lowland townships of their respective parishes then these moors were indeed intercommoned. These two upland townships would provide grazings for the animals of people who came from outside those townships, for those who, in North Country parlance, are termed 'foreigners'. These intercommoned moors were in fact what Jolliffe discussed as forinsec grazings. He saw this common scheme of pasturage as an essential feature of the unity of the Northumbrian shires, 'wide estates from whose central mansio a score of vills may be arrented and administered and which, for purposes of pasture and justice form a unified circumscription' (Jolliffe 1926, 12 and 2).

The townships which received stock from elsewhere on their grazings would need to have protected pastures for their own use. This may offer an explanation of some of the -ley enclosures in Wrightington and Chorley. The king's pasture, the churls' pasture, the tun's pasture: Kingsley, Chorley and Tunley, might well need to be set aside for the stock of the township. Astley, which means east-ley, lies at the west side of Chorley so that the name makes no sense within that township; but Astley does lie to the east of the lowland townships of Croston parish, and perhaps this was a particular enclosed pasture for these 'foreign' cattle.

Some of the -ley names are undoubtedly associated with known vaccaries; other vaccaries are known by terms such as tunstall, hardwick, -ergh, some of which appear to be double-oval enclosures. There is however no chance of establishing a simple connection between these terms and field patterns and vaccaries. Ley is a frequent place-name and was used in Leyland Hundred in a variety of contexts, and Gelling[18] has indicated that it changed its meaning over time. It is likely that this is true of the other terms. Areas elsewhere in the country with similar land use in the past could usefully be examined in the light of the suggestions offered above. The relationship of 'green' to the stock routes may not be unconnected with the term 'green roads' for drove ways. The relationship of 'moor' to fen may be an alternative usage or a later one: there have been shifts in the ways that land was used and we must expect shifts in the way that terms were used. Terms used in other parts of the country could be considered: in Leyland Hundred, perhaps in Lancashire as a whole, the terms 'heath' and 'common' are relatively infrequent; but this is not so elsewhere, and it may be that examination of the context of these terms can shed more light on ancient practice.

Leyland Hundred offers in its topography one of the forms of evidence called for by Fox (1981, 101) which would shed light on the disintegration of a hundredal estate. Sadly, the other type of evidence, pre-Conquest charters, is almost completely lacking. But the last stages of the dismemberment of the royal hundredal estates in Lancashire were sufficiently late to reach into the historical period; the private hundredal estates of the de Lacys in Blackburnshire and West Yorkshire appear to have functioned almost intact into the fourteenth century (Smith 1961; Higham 1978b) and are, for this area, richly documented. Jolliffe's and Jones' models of shires and multiple estates offer us not only a framework for the development of the Midland field system, as Fox has suggested, but also a context in which to examine the field, settlement and land-use patterns which once extended from central caputs over dozens of vills.

Notes

1. Lancashire throughout this text refers to the County of Lancaster as it was prior to its reorganization in 1974. Note, however, that the Furness and Cartmel districts of Lancashire are not considered in this paper.
2. Lancashire Record Office, DRB 1/215.
3. L.R.O. DDSc 63/39.
4. L.R.O. DDK 1411/10 and 11.
5. The chartulary of Cockersand Abbey was compiled in 1267–8: Farrer, W (editor) 1898–1909: *The Chartulary of Cockersand Abbey*, Chetham Society, New series, 38, 39, 40, 43, 56, 57, 64.
6. L.R.O. DRB 1/190.
7. L.R.O. DRB 1/215.
8. L.R.O. DDHe 117/12.
9. L.R.O. DDSc 63/35.
10. Roger of Poitou granted a number of churches including Croston to Lancaster Priory as a cell of the Abbey of St Martin at Sées. (Farrer 1902, 289–90).
11. L.R.O. PR 681.
12. L.R.O. DDHe 11/87, 1580.
13. L.R.O. DDHe 11/51, 1519/20.
14. L.R.O. DDHe 11/2, 1295, and 11/35, 1483.
15. L.R.O. DDHe 11/28, 1461.
16. L.R.O. PR 737, 1725–6.
17. L.R.O. DDHe 11/87.
18. See discussion in Gelling, M. 1976: *The Place-Names of Berkshire, Part 3*, English Place-Name Society Vol. 51, 888 and 935–6. Dr. Gelling has told me that the -ley names of Leyland Hundred are likely to be the late usage, implying pasture.

References

Adams, I. H. 1976: *Agrarian Landscape Terms: a Glossary for Historical Geography* (London, Institute of British Geographers special publications No. 9).

Atkin, M. A. 1982–3: Stock tracks along township boundaries. *Journal of the English Place-Name Society* 15, 24–32.

Baker, A. R. H. and Butlin, R. A. (editors) 1973: *Studies of Field Systems in the British Isles* (Cambridge, Cambridge University Press).

Bloch, M. 1966: *French Rural History: An Essay on its Basic Characteristics. Translated by Janet Sondheimer* (London, Routledge and Kegan Paul).

Branigan, K. (editor) 1980: *Rome and the Brigantes* (Sheffield, University of Sheffield).

Calderbank, P. M. 1978: *An examination of Field and Settlement Patterns in Goosnargh Township in 1849* Unpublished BEd dissertation, University of Lancaster.

Cunliffe Shaw, R. 1956: *The Royal Forest of Lancaster* (Preston, private publication).

Darby, H. C. 1977: *Domesday England* (Cambridge, Cambridge University Press).

Eidt, R. C., Singh, K. N. and Singh, R. P. B. (editors) 1977: *Man, Culture and Settlement, Festschrift to Professor R.L. Singh* (New Delhi, Kalyani).

Eyre, S. J. and Jones, G. R. J. (editors) 1966: *Geography as Human Ecology: Methodology by Example* (London, Edward Arnold).

Farrer, W. 1902: *The Lancashire Pipe Rolls* (Liverpool).

Farrer, W. 1907: Lancashire inquests, extents and feudal aids, part 2. *Record Society of Lancashire and Cheshire* 54.

Farrer, W. and Brownbill, J. (editors) 1906–14: *The Victoria History of the Counties of England. A History of the County of Lancaster.* (The University of London Institute of Historical Research).

Faull, M. L. and Moorhouse, S. A. (editors) 1981: *West Yorkshire: an Archaeological Survey to AD 1500* (Wakefield, West Yorkshire Metropolitan County Council).

Fox, H. S. A. 1981: Approaches to the adoption of the Midland System. In Rowley, T. (editor) 1981, 64–111.

Glasscock, R. E. 1975: *The Lay Subsidy of 1334* (London, British Academy).

Du Halgouet, H. 1921: *La Vicomté de Rohan et ses Seigneurs* (Paris, Saint-Brieuc).

Higham, M. C. 1968: *The Origins of Settlement in Pendleside* (Unpublished Certificate of Education dissertation, Chorley College of Education).

Higham, M. C. 1978a: The 'erg' place-names of northern England. *Journal of The English Place-Name Society* 10, 7–17.

Higham, M. C. 1978b: *The Forest of Bowland: a Study in Continuity* (Unpublished MA thesis, University of Hull).

Hodges, R. and Wildgoose, M. 1980: Roman or native in the White Peak. In Branigan, K. (editor) 1980, 48–53.

Howells, D. 1972–3: The four exclusive possessions of a man. *Studia Celtica* 9, 48–67.

Jewell, H. M. 1972: *English Local Administration in the Middle Ages* (Newton Abbot, David and Charles).

Jolliffe, J. E. A. 1926: Northumbrian Institutions. *English Historical Review* 4, 1–42.

Jones, G. R. J. 1955: The distribution of medieval settlement in Anglesey, *Transactions of the Anglesey Antiquarian Society and Field Club* 27–96.

Jones, G. R. J. 1966: Rural settlement in Anglesey. In Eyre, S.J. and Jones, G.R.J. (editors) 1966, 198–230.

Jones, G. R. J. 1976: Multiple estates and early settlement. In Sawyer, P.H. (editor) 1976, 15–40.

Jones, G. R. J. 1977: Hereditary land: its effects on the evolution of field systems and settlement patterns in the vale of Clwyd. In Eidt, R.C., Singh, K.N. and Singh, R.P.B. (editors) 1977, 82–96.

Lyons, P. A. 1884: Two compoti of the Lancashire and Cheshire manors of Henry de Lacy, Earl of Lincoln. *Chetham Society* Old series, 112.

Mayhew, A. 1973: *Rural Settlement and Farming in Germany* (London, Batsford).

Moore, J. S. (editor) 1982: *Domesday Book 15, Gloucestershire* (Chichester, Phillimore).

Oxford English Dictionary 1979: (London, Oxford University Press).

Pollard, D., Hooper, M. D. and Moore, N. W. 1974: *Hedges* (London, Collins).

Porteus, T. C. 1931: The hundred of Leyland in Lancashire. *Chetham Miscellanies* Vol. 5, *Chetham Society* New series 90, 1–119.

Rackham, O. 1976: *Trees and Woodlands in the British Landscape* (London, Dent).

Roberts, B. K. 1981: Townfield origins; the case of Cockfield, County Durham. In Rowley, T. (editor) 1981, 145–61.

Rowley, T. (editor) 1981: *The Origins of Open Field Agriculture* (London, Croom Helm).

Sawyer, P. H. (editor) 1976: *Medieval Settlement, Continuity and Change* (London, Edward Arnold).

Sharpe France, R. 1962: *Guide to the Lancashire Record Office* (Preston, Lancashire County Council).

Smith, A. H. 1956: *English Place-name Elements. Parts 1 and 2.* English Place-Name Society Vol. 25–26 (Cambridge, Cambridge University Press).

Smith, A. H. 1961: *The Place-names of the West Riding of Yorkshire. Part 1–8.* English Place-Name Society Vol. 30–37 (Cambridge, Cambridge University Press).

Smith, R. B. 1961: *Blackburnshire: a Study in Early Lancashire History.* Department of English Local History Occasional Paper, series No.15 (University of Leicester, Leicester University Press).

Thorpe, H. 1949: The green villages of County Durham. *Transactions of the Institute of British Geographers* 15, 155–80.

13. Some Aspects of the Evolution of Small Towns and Villages in Scotland

D. G. Lockhart

Although the Scottish rural landscape underwent dramatic changes during the eighteenth and nineteenth centuries, when more than 400 planned villages were established, there is nevertheless much surviving documentary and field evidence relating to villages and small burghs founded between medieval times and the late seventeenth century. The paper examines the evolution of nucleated settlement, principally burghs of barony, kirktowns and seatowns, the ground plans and functions of these places, and the changes which have occurred since 1700. Finally, J. B. Caird's assertion tht the rural landscape of Scotland is a product of recent change is shown to be only partly true. While it is certainly applicable to the Highlands and inland plateau of the North East, the survival of older forms of settlement is particularly noticeable along the east coast between Banff (Banffshire) and Kirkcaldy (Fife) and throughout the Border counties.

It has been frequently suggested that the character of the present-day Scottish rural landscape was mainly shaped during the eighteenth and nineteenth centuries. In the context of village studies, writers have stressed the importance of planned villages built between 1725 and 1850. Such villages were associated with the development of the textile and fishing industries (Archiestown, Morayshire; Lybster, Caithness), the replacement of medieval villages and hamlets due to the creation of parks around the houses of landowners (Fochabers, Morayshire; New Scone, Perthshire), and with agricultural improvements such as enclosure (Urquhart, Morayshire) and reclamation (New Pitsligo, Aberdeenshire) (Houston 1948; Caird 1964; Smout 1970; Lockhart 1980). The planned villages are certainly prominent features of the rural landscape of the Highlands, the North East, and Dumfries and Galloway, though in only a very few counties are they the dominant type of village (Caithness, Morayshire, Wigtownshire). Elsewhere, the survival of medieval and early modern villages is more impressive and in the Lothians and Border counties, green villages such as Midlem and Denholm (Roxburghshire) and Direlton (East Lothian) co-exist with irregular nucleated villages dating from before 1700. Furthermore, if burghs created by landowners (burghs of barony) and hamlets situated at parish churches (kirktowns) are included in the analysis, the presence of pre-1700 settlements in today's landscape is considerably greater. A variety of source material for the study of settlements that existed before 1700 is available to researchers and includes rentals and leases in estate papers, topographical descriptions by seventeenth-century writers, Acts of the Scottish Parliaments, poll tax and hearth tax rolls, and eighteenth-century plans which depict the pre-enclosure landscape (Whyte and Whyte 1981). The documentary evidence can be used to study four aspects of Scottish settlement patterns:

i) the evolution of medieval and early modern towns and villages,

ii) morphology,

iii) employment and functions such as markets and fairs, and

iv) processes of change that occurred after 1700 and which profoundly affected earlier settlement patterns.

The Evolution of Medieval Nucleated Settlement

The larger towns of Scotland, like those in England and Wales, originated as early medieval burghs. The major county towns such as Elgin (Morayshire), Linlithgow (West Lothian) and Haddington (East Lothian) were built from the early twelfth century and represented an attempt to consolidate the authority of the monarch and to control domestic and foreign trade (Lockhart 1974, Vol. 1, 7). The trading functions of royal burghs partly explain their coastal and valley-route locations and it was also significant that several inland burghs developed outports, such as Haddington which used Aberlady on the Firth of Forth. Vessels are known to have anchored here as early as 1336 and the settlement which grew up at the head of navigation is shown on Blau's map (1654). A similar kind of partnership evolved between Elgin and Lossiemouth (Morayshire) (Graham 1968–9, 212).[1]

The trading rights of the royal burghs were jealously guarded by the Crown, a Convention of representatives of the burghs and the burgesses, and, as a result, towns

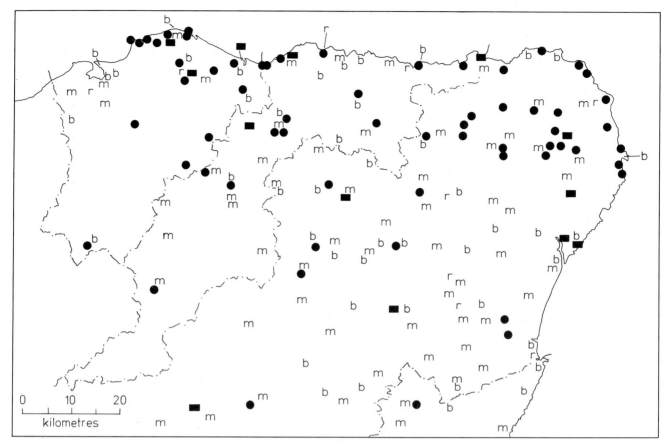

Fig. 13.1   The distribution of royal burghs, burghs of barony, non-burghal markets and planned villages in north-east Scotland. Key: r = royal burgh, b = burgh of barony, m = non-burghal market, ● = planned village, ■ = failed settlement

and villages which had markets and fairs did not multiply, as they had done in England and France, until the late fifteenth century (Keith 1913). The distribution of royal burghs reflected strategic as well as commercial factors. The necessity to provide a safe refuge for craftsmen and trade in less secure times created a pattern of burghal settlement not always related to the realities of population distribution. Extensive areas such as north-east Aberdeenshire and upland Morayshire were left inconveniently distant from a royal burgh (Fig. 13.1).

Three solutions to servicing such areas were possible:
i)   more royal burghs could be created,
ii) an alternative burghal institution, a burgh of barony, might be established, or
iii) markets and fairs could be founded in villages and hamlets that lacked burghal status.

In fact only 32 new royal burghs were founded throughout Scotland after 1450 (Table 13.1), largely because existing royal burghs wished to protect their trading hinterlands (Keith 1913; Pryde 1965). However, burghs of barony and non-burghal settlements, promoted by landowners, were the most common types of market settlement in Scotland until

the Union of Parliaments in 1707 (Tables 13.2 and 13.3).

The inhabitants of burghs of barony were not allowed to participate in foreign trade. They were, however, permitted to engage in domestic trade within the confines of the burgh. Burghs of barony were founded throughout the period between the mid-fourteenth and early eighteenth century but were especially numerous in lowland Scotland during the seventeenth century and reflect the growth of wealth and trade in an era much less tolerant of the monopolistic trading privileges of the royal burghs. Non-burghal markets, too, were intended to facilitate local trade. The church in each parish was usually the focus of the local road network and its associated settlement; the kirktown, which contained the manse, glebe, a farm and several houses occupied by tradesmen, was a popular location for markets and fairs, a status borne out in the writings of estate management: 'the little village which generally attends the kirk tends to promote industry and improvement'.[2]

Royal burghs, burghs of barony and kirktowns were the service centres of medieval and early modern Scotland; however, two further types of nucleated

Table 13.1   The distribution of royal burghs

	Higlands & Islands	North East	West Central	East Central	Borders	Dumfries & Galloway	Total
1100 – 49	–	4	4	4	3	–	16
1150 – 99	1	1	1	4	–	1	14
1200 – 49	1	1	2	–	1	–	4
1250 – 99	1	1	–	–	1	1	4
1300 – 49	1	1	–	1	–	1	5
1350 – 99	–	–	1	–	–	–	1
1400 – 49	1	–	1	2	–	1	5
1450 – 99	1	–	–	1	–	–	2
1500 – 49	–	–	1	3	–	2	6
1500 – 99	3	2	–	6	–	1	12
1600 – 49	2	1	1	4	–	2	10
1650 – 99	–	–	–	–	–	–	0
1700 – 07	1	1	–	–	–	–	2
TOTAL	12	19	11	25	5	9	81

Source: Pryde, G. S. 1965: *The burghs to Scotland: a critical list*. Glasgow.

Table 13.2   The distribution of burghs of barony

	Highlands & Islands	North East	West Central	East Central	Borders	Dumfries & Galloway	Total
1450 – 99	4	13	7	8	2	5	39
1500 – 49	1	23	9	14	3	3	53
1500 – 99	1	10	11	12	5	1	35
1600 – 49	11	18	17	19	10	10	85
1650 – 99	15	30	19	17	6	5	92
1700 – 07	2	5	3	4	–	4	18
TOTAL	34	99	61	74	26	28	322

Source: Pryde, G. S. 1965: *The burghs of Scotland: a critical list*. Glasgow.

*Table 13.3   The distribution of non-burghal markets and
fairs in Scotland*

	1571–1660	1661–1707	Total
Highlands and Islands	0	13	13
North East	6	53	59
West Central	0	26	26
East Central	1	27	28
Borders	2	8	10
Dumfries and Galloway	0	8	8
TOTAL	9	135	144

Source: Ballard, A. 1916: The theory of the Scottish burgh. *Scottish Historical Review*, 13, 16–29; Carstairs A. M. 1950: *The distribution of the population of Scotland, 1450 to 1750*. Unpublished B.Phil. Thesis, University of St Andrews.

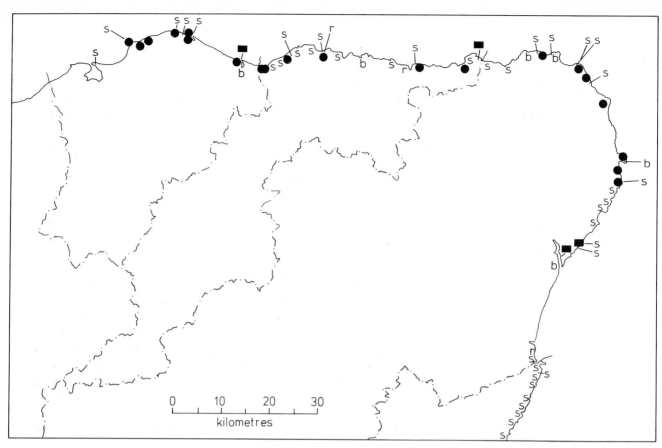

Fig. 13.2 The distribution of maritime settlements in north-east Scotland

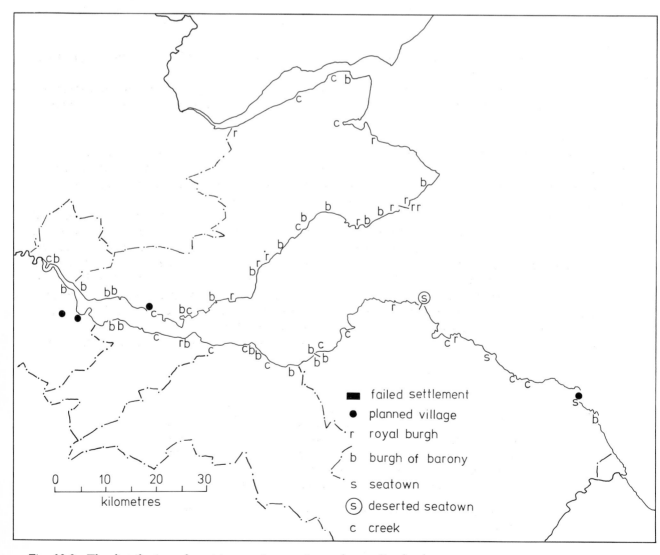

■ failed settlement

● planned village

r royal burgh

b burgh of barony

s seatown

ⓢ deserted seatown

c creek

Fig. 13.3 The distribution of maritime settlements in south-east Scotland

settlement existed, namely, fermtowns, known in the Highlands as clachans, and fishing villages (seatowns). Examples of the former can no longer be seen today since these were removed during enclosure in the eighteenth and early nineteenth centuries. Such settlements were smaller than English medieval villages, housing between three and ten families, and were associated with open-field agriculture organized on an infield-outfield system (Dodgshon 1975). The infield was more or less permanently cultivated while the outfield was used for occasional cultivation and provided pasture for animals, as did extensive areas of uncultivated land known as commonties.

Fishing villages occur widely along the east coast between the Moray Firth and Berwickshire but are concentrated particularly in Banffshire, Aberdeenshire and Kincardineshire (Fig. 13.2). Fewer seatowns are located between Angus and the English border, partly because many of the maritime settlements had burghal status and partly owing to the existence of a large number of minor creeks used by local shipping which did not give rise to nucleated settlement adjacent to them (Fig. 13.3). Unlike fermtouns, few seatowns have been deliberately replaced by another settlement. One example is Burghead (Morayshire), where in 1805 the old town was cleared to make way for a planned village and a large harbour (Lockhart 1974, Vol. 2, 7–9). However, in some areas development pressures on seatowns have been great. The mining industry of the Lothians, for instance, led to the alteration of the fabric of many coastal settlements during the last 250 years. On the other hand, there are many examples of seatowns in Banffshire and Aberdeenshire which have changed little in terms of size and alignment of housing since their foundation (Crovie, Banffshire; Pennan and Pitullie, Aberdeenshire). The founding of seatowns was a result of three major influences:

i) landowners who wished to increase the rentals of their estates and who held out inducements to fishermen to settle,

ii) the migration of fishermen from older settlements, especially coastal burghs, seeking less crowded conditions and better facilities, and

iii) an increase in the demand for fish from the population of the landward area.

Migration distances were generally fairly short and were accomplished by the movement of entire boat crews (Table 13.4).

Village Forms

The source materials available to reconstruct medieval village forms in Scotland are patchy when compared with evidence in England. National atlases such as Blau's are very generalized, while Roy's Map (1747–55), at a scale of one inch to 1,000 yards, only shows house outlines and alignments and does not indicate land use within villages (Moir 1973). Large-scale plans are also very rare before the 1740s, although after the mid-century the production of plans rapidly increased as the pace of agricultural improvement quickened. It was usual for a survey of the 'old' landscape to be made when enclosure was planned. This type of survey is valuable because it shows features of the landscape that were about to disappear.

Alternatively, rentals and title-deeds of property which contain a description of the dimensions of each plot can be used to reconstruct settlement morphology. This approach has been pioneered recently by Whyte in a reconstruction of seventeenth-century Direlton, which he suggests was a three-row green village with rectangular-shaped building plots. Whyte then goes on to compare this plan with a recent Ordnance Survey map (Whyte 1981, 13–14).

Using both kinds of evidence, it is possible to suggest a preliminary classification of village forms. Four broad categories are recognized:

i) irregular,

ii) regular with house gable ends facing at right angles to the coast,

iii) regular linear villages comprising two rows, and

iv) regular, grouped around a central square or green.

(i) Irregular plans

The irregularity of Scottish settlement morphology was heavily criticized by late-eighteenth-century improving landowners who advocated radical change. A typical example noted that:

'The houses were not built according to any general plan but scattered in every direction. The roads and alleys were inconceivably bad, especially in wet weather, as few of them were paved, and what added greatly to their miserable state was the abominable practice of placing the dunghill . . . before their doors'. (Sir John Sinclair, quoted in Caird 1964, 73; Aiton 1812, 125–32).

Fermtouns and the majority of kirktowns lack planned

Table 13.4   Migration to seatowns in Banffshire

Village and National Grid Reference	Origin	Distance (kilometres)	Date
Portknockie (NJ 488686)	Cullen	3.0	1677
Findochty (NJ 464680)	Fraserburgh	55.0	1716
Nether Buckie (NJ 423658)	Gollachy	1.5	1723
Portessie (NJ 439665)	Findhorn	48.0	1727

Source: Sinclair, Sir J. (editor): 1794 *The Statistical Account of Scotland*. Edinburgh, 13, 400–1.

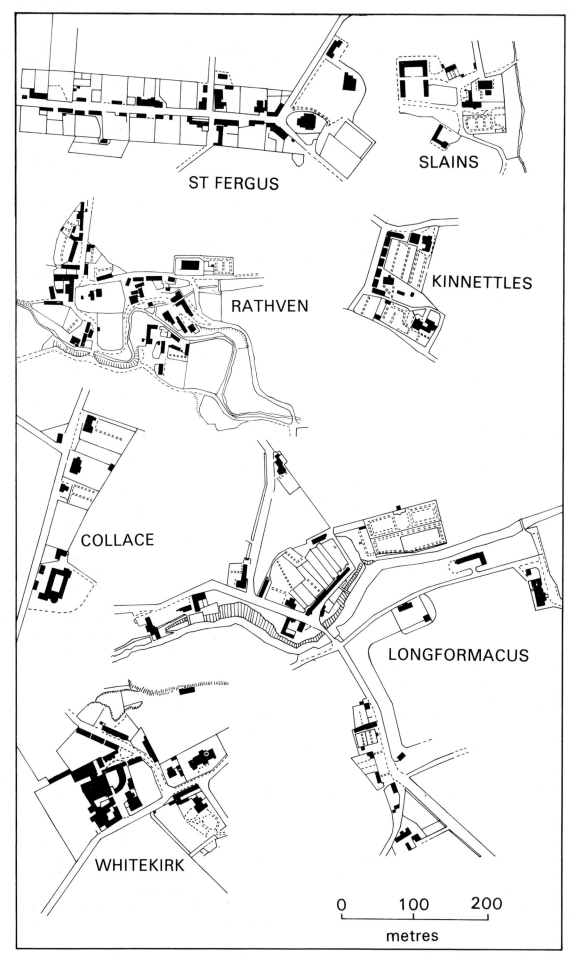

ST FERGUS

SLAINS

RATHVEN

KINNETTLES

COLLACE

LONGFORMACUS

WHITEKIRK

0   100   200

metres

Fig. 13.4 Some kirktown forms (Source: redrawn from the Ordnance Survey, first edition 1858–72, except Whitekirk which is based on the second edition of 1894)

layouts, houses were set down in different directions and land use was extremely chaotic comprising irregular farmyard and garden plots (Fig. 13.4). Large kirktowns, however, were more likely to show some evidence of street development, particularly when the settlement was situated at a road junction. In some, a market stance appears to have occupied an adjacent area of open ground (Fordoun, Kincardineshire) while in others a central area was used for markets (Kettins, Angus).

(ii) Regular plans with house gable ends facing at right-angles to the coast

This type of plan is associated with east coast seatowns. The nature of the site and of the beach or rocky inlet was an important determinant of the size and form of such fishing communities. On very restricted sites such as those on the Buchan coast, one-row settlements have always been the norm (Crovie; Old Castle, Aberdeenshire). Where flat land was available several rows may have developed (Avoch, Ross and Cromarty). In such villages, the earliest housing occupied the area closest to the beach where gable-end housing was particularly common. Behind this area, dwellings were arranged in approximately parallel rows (Fig. 13.5).

The pattern of land use within villages was very similar. The ground between each house was either gravelled or grass surfaced and was used to dry washing or to store boats and fishing equipment. Vegetable gardens have always been uncommon owing to the fisherman's traditional lack of interest in agricultural activities which goes back to the seventeenth century when the majority of seatowns were established.[3] Indeed, it was only after about 1800 that field lots in fishing villages became common and these were usually cultivated by tradesmen and labourers.[4]

(iii) Regular linear villages

Regular settlements with properly developed streets were not uncommon. Most were burghs of barony and the remainder were non-burghal markets. Such settlements were characterized by linear street plans and flanked by rectangular-shaped building plots giving two-row settlements (Kinrossie, Perthshire). There is much evidence of careful planning of burghs of barony among the writings of local historians. It was noted that in Gretna (Dumfriesshire):

> 'The kirk stands at the end of a pleasant and fine village called Gratnay Green where Coll Johnston has a fine house with all regularitys conforme. The whole village with a tolbooth being lately built by him after a new modell.' (Mitchell 1906, 371).

An eighteenth-century description of the founding of Kilmaurs (Ayrshire) in 1577 is equally illuminating. Here 'the five-pound land . . . consisting of 240 acres, was disponed to 40 different persons . . . to be held in

equal proportions by them. It is obvious that the great design . . . was to bring together into one place as many trades people as possible.' (Sinclair 1793, 367–9).

Regular linear plans seem to be derived from the layout of royal burghs. At Kilmaurs the street was widened sufficiently to allow markets to be held, a tradition which was established in burghs as far apart as Elgin (Morayshire) and Lauder (Berwickshire). More elaborate linear plans were rare and occurred mainly among seventeenth-century burghs of barony. Grid-iron plans occur at Stornoway (Inverness-shire) and Fraserburgh (Aberdeenshire). There are also a few examples of settlements built at crossroad locations whose plans comprised a principal street and a lesser street which met approximately at right angles to one another (Huntley, Aberdeenshire; Kippen, Stirling-shire).[5] (Geddes 1947, 57–68).

(iv) Regular plans grouped around a central square or green

Villages of this type are rare in the period before 1700 and most occur in the South East. A few late burghs of barony and non-burghal settlements were laid out with rectangular-shaped squares (Rosehearty, Aberdeenshire; Gifford, East Lothian) while green villages in East Lothian include Direlton and Stenton, and, in the Border counties, Midlem and Denholm (Roxburghshire) and Polwarth (Berwickshire) (Elliot 1863–8, 309–11; Smout 1970, 73).

Among the reasons put forward for the existence of greens have been the diffusion of ideas from northern England and the role of the green as a defensive mechanism to protect communities from cross border raiding. Such measures were rarely very satisfactory and many villages were repeatedly burned and rebuilt during medieval times. Occasionally, too, rebuilding took place on a different site (Greenlaw, Berwickshire) and some green villages may in fact be the product of rebuilding and replanning, such as Denholm (Fig. 13.6) (Gibson 1905, 1, 11–23).

Settlement and Employment

Data on employment is scarce. Occupations are given in leases and feu-charters which survive among estate papers, chartularies in solicitors' offices and in the *Register of Sasines*, a record of transactions involving the sale of land which is housed in the Scottish Record Office. Much time and effort would need to be invested in searching this type of source material, which in any case is patchy before 1700. More readily available information can be found in the Poll Tax returns for 1695–6 which have survived for Aberdeenshire and Renfrewsire (Stuart 1844; Semple 1864).[6] The returns give useful information on settlement size and family structure as well as employment. An excerpt from

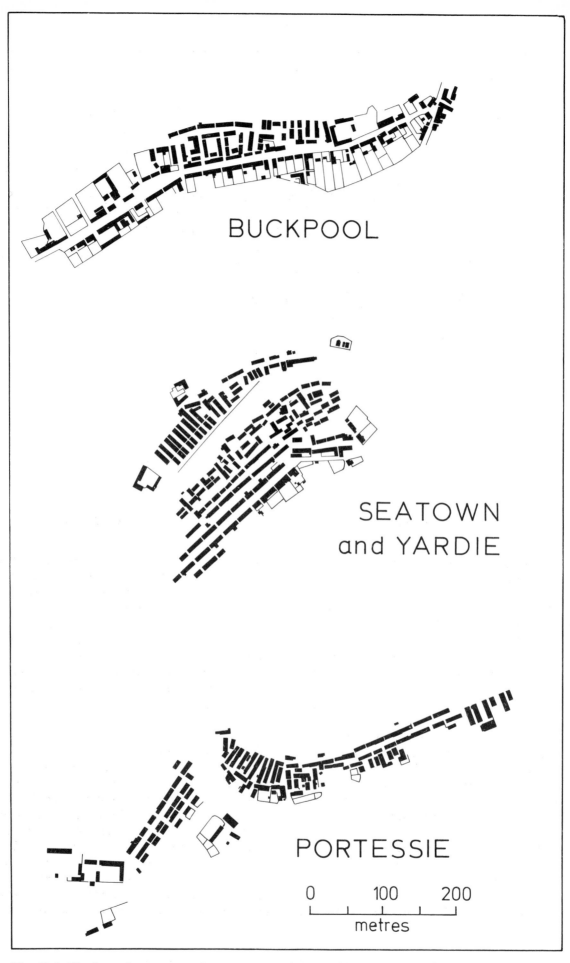

BUCKPOOL

SEATOWN
and YARDIE

PORTESSIE

0   100   200

metres

Fig. 13.5   The form of maritime settlements near Buckie, Banffshire (Source: redrawn from the Ordnance Survey, first edition 1868)

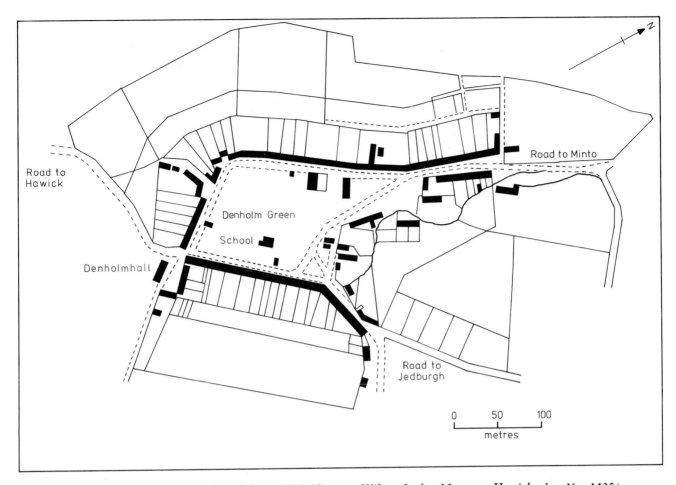

Fig. 13.6   Plan of Denholm, Roxburghshire, 1835 (Source: Wilton Lodge Museum, Hawick plan No. M35)

Strichen parish (Aberdeenshire) illustrates the nature of the source (Table 13.5). It can be shown that the number of household heads in fermtouns varied from about three to nine or ten. Geddes and Forbes have examined a sample of parishes in Highland (Deeside) and Lowland parts of the county and suggest the existence of two patterns. The Highland parishes contained fermtouns which had a high proportion of tenants and few tradesmen, while the Lowland parishes were characterized by fewer tenants and a much greater variety of other occupational types (Table 13.6).

Further examination of the returns for Strichen parish reveals many fermtouns that would fit the Lowland model. Neither Adiell (Adziel, NJ 947532), for example, was inhabited by two tenants, two herdsmen, one servant, one tradesman and one person whose occupation was not stated. Scattered throughout the lowland area of the county were larger hamlets, usually kirktowns, which were peopled by tradesmen such as that of Culsalmond (NJ 650330) which contained 46 household heads, exactly half of whom were tradesmen (Stuart 1844, 265–66). The Renfrewshire returns also highlight the role of kirktowns as

service centres. Eaglesham could offer no less than 11 different crafts that were practised by a total of 41 tradesmen and the professional services of a schoolmaster and a minister (Semple 1864, 10–11). Lastly, the returns also provide information on the size and occupational structure of seatowns, and it is interesting to note that the ratio of fishermen to craftsmen during the seventeenth century was similar to that recorded in various estate papers in the early and mid-nineteenth century.[7]

Markets and Fairs

Markets and fairs were the functions that most distinguished burghs of barony and kirktowns from nucleated settlements that were concerned with farming and fishing. The creation of markets and fairs reflected real or perceived growth of wealth and population and until the mid-fifteenth century the privilege of holding markets was reserved to the royal burghs. It is only after this time that other settlements with market rights emerged, notably burghs of barony. It was not unusual for burghs to be established at the site of kirktowns

Table 13.5   Excerpt from the Aberdeenshire Poll Book, 1696: Whitehill, Strichen Parish (NJ 921566)

Whitehill

Thomas Cruden, tennant ther, and his wife, their general poll	£ 0	12	0
His proportion of valuatione is	0	8	0
Thomas, Alexander, and Christine Crudens, his children *in familia*	0	18	0
Magaret Grant, his servant, her fee per annum is £6, the fortieth pairt whereof is 3s., and generall poll is 6s., both is	0	9	0
Alexander Milne, his herd, his fee per annum £2, the fortieth pairt whereof is 1s., and 6s of generall poll, both is	0	7	0
William Milne, wyver, and his wife	0	18	0
William and Jean Milnes, his children *in familia*	0	12	0
	£ 4	4	0

Source: Stuart, J. (editor) 1844: *List of pollable persons within the shire of Aberdeen 1696*. Spalding Club, Aberdeen, I, 603.

Table 13.6   Mean employment structure of fermtoun populations in two sample areas of Aberdeenshire

	Highland parishes	Lowland parishes
tenants	4.0	1.8
sub-tenants	–	1.0
servants	1.5	1.9
tradesmen	0.13	0.7
cottars/grassmen	–	0.94
no occupation stated	–	0.1
TOTAL	5.63	6.44

Note: Tradesmen would have possessed some land and shared in harvest work.

Source: Geddes, A. and Forbes, J. 1947: Rural communities of fermtoun and baile in the lowlands and highlands of Aberdeenshire, 1696. *Aberdeen University Review*, 32, 98–104.

because the latter were already nodal points of community life. Such burghs are easily identified since they bear the name of the parish in which they were founded, as, for instance, Insch, Huntly and Clatt (Aberdeenshire). Evidence for the establishment of markets in burghs is contained in the charters of erection and in Acts of Parliament which ratified existing market rights (Carstairs 1980, 104). Acts of Parliament are also a valuable source of information for the founding of markets at kirktowns in the period after 1600. The fact that such Acts only begin to be recorded during the late seventeenth century suggests increasing rivalry among burghs of barony and non-burghal settlements and that the latter sought confirmation for trading rights which were already in existence, as at Bowden (Roxburghshire), which had held markets since 1571 according to an Act of Ratification in 1661.[8] In the case of new markets, it is possible to use the Acts to discover the motives of their promoters. The most common argument offered in support of a market between 1661 and the 1680s was distance from an existing market town. Thus Cluny (Aberdeenshire) was authorized in 1681, since there were no weekly markets held between Aberdeen and Kincardine (32 km) and between Aberdeen and Insch (48 km).[9] Another common reason given was related to site factors, particularly if these concerned a location adjacent to a major routeway frequented by travellers, as at Torphichen (West Lothian), which lay on the road between Edinburgh and the west of Scotland.[10] Later Acts are much less useful and were drafted on a standard model which did little more than stress the general desirability of creating markets for the good of the nation and went on to suggest that the settlement was an appropriate place for a market or fair.

The founding of non-burghal markets ended with the Union of Parliaments and few burghs of barony were established after 1707. It would be unwise to suggest that the profound changes in the fabric of settlement in the countryside that occurred during the eighteenth and early nineteenth century had been triggered by the changing political circumstances of the Scottish nation. Evidence from research by Whyte suggests that agricultural improvements which were taking place in the seventeenth century merely quickened after 1700 (Whyte 1980, 117–35). A parallel sequence of events appears to have characterized the evolution of nucleated settlements. Landowners during late medieval and early modern times had, as we have seen, experimented with elementary settlement planning and had encouraged local markets and tradesmen to settle at these places. Although relatively little capital investment was involved, valuable experience was gained in physical planning and the legal aspects of founding new settlements. That experience was to prove invaluable during the eighteenth century when much larger villages and towns were built and endowed with a variety of industrial and commercial enterprises that required a considerable input of capital.

Many landed families have remarkable records of involvement in planning over several centuries. The Cunningham-Grahams, for instance, erected Buchlyvie (Stirlingshire) as a burgh of barony in 1677 and in the mid-1720s founded the planned village of Gartmore (Perthshire) at the entrance of Gartmore House. The Seafield family were even more active and founded a series of burghs of barony and seatowns in the sixteenth and seventeenth centuries, as well as four planned villages on their estates in Banffshire and Morayshire (between 1750 and 1820).

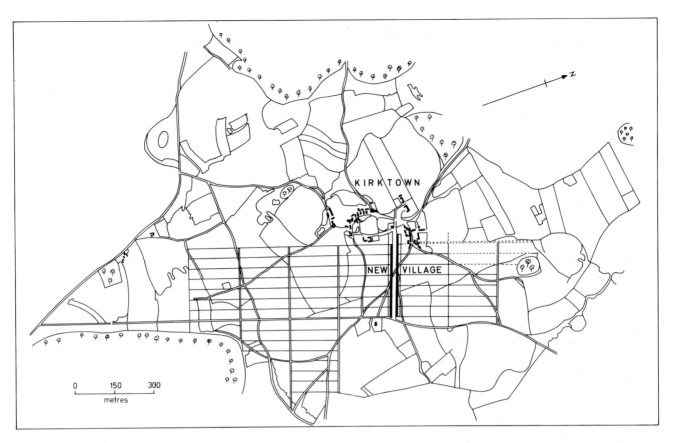

Fig. 13.7 Plan of the lands of Urquhart, Morayshire, 1783 (Source: SRO RHP 31339)

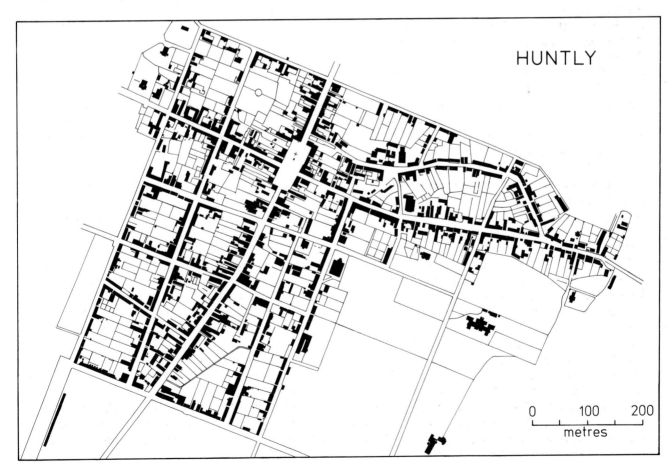

Fig. 13.8 Plan of Huntly, Aberdeenshire (Source: redrawn from the Ordnance Survey, first edition 1872)

Change during the Eighteenth Century

Agricultural change and village planning after 1700 affected existing settlements in a number of ways. This paper contends that four processes may be identified. First, elements of the 'old order' were removed from the landscape. Such a fate affected fermtouns and those kirktowns which were replaced by planned villages (Urquhart, Morayshire (Fig. 13.7); Houston, Renfrewshire) (Crawford 1782, 106–77). Second, there was partial reorganization which led eventually to desertion (Lix, Perthshire). In such cases, fermtouns disappeared in stages; initial replacement by fewer buildings in the eighteenth century was followed by complete clearance in the mid-nineteenth century after the introduction of sheep farming (Fairhurst 1960, 74–6). A third type of change was the replanning of existing nucleated settlement. At Turriff (Aberdeenshire), a large extension was built adjacent to the old town. However, change could be more thorough and at neighbouring Huntly a grid of streets was superimposed upon the old 'crooked cross' morphology, thus converting it into a rigidly planned town (Fig. 13.8). Fourthly, in spite of the wide-ranging changes that took place during the eighteenth century, the ground plans of certain medieval and early modern settlements have survived with a minimum of modification. Examples are fairly common among seatowns (Pennan and Cairnbulg, Aberdeenshire), while the street plans of a number of small burghs of barony have also been little affected by development (Tarland, Aberdeenshire; Thornhill, Dumfriesshire).

Caird's contention that the present-day Scottish rural landscape is one that has been shaped by revolutionary rather than evolutionary processes, is, in terms of the evidence presented here, only partly true (Caird 1964, 72). Goemetric field patterns and rigid settlement planning are certainly prominent throughout the length and breadth of the country but among small burghs and seatowns much has survived. Indeed, it is one of the paradoxes of Scottish settlement development that counties such as Aberdeenshire and Dumfriesshire, which can boast very large numbers of planned villages, have also a rich heritage of baronial burghs, kirktowns and seatowns.

Notes

1. Feu Contract Between James Brodie of that Ilk and the Magistrates of Elgin, 9 March 1698. Elgin City Chambers—Town Clerk's Department, Attic Store B 7/1; Elgin Town Council Minutes 1/1/5, 123, 10 May 1725.
2. NLS Saltoun Mss Acc 2933, box 329, Hints about the improvement of the Highlands, May 1757.
3. SRO British Fishery Society Papers GD 9/366/2, Hints and observations regarding fishers and fishing villages . . . March 1808.
4. Garden of Troup Papers NRA (Scot) 1314 bundle 34, Rental of lands and estate of Troup Crop 1813; Skateraw, Kincardineshire: BM 7330 (151) 104, Plan of the lands of Gillybrands and Newtonhill. By Messrs Robertson and Noble 1859; Downies, Kincardineshire: BM 7330 (151) 23, Plan of the lands of Clashfarquhar. By James Forbes Beattie 1870; BM Add Mss 6897 Population Act 1811, Enumeration Abstract f.136; British Fishery Society Papers, *op.cit.*
5. Wood, J. 1818–1825: *Atlas of Scottish Towns*; NLS Gartmore Papers Acc 7282/1 Plan book of the estate of Gartmore: Plan of the Town of Kippen *c.* 1792; SRO Draft plan of new town of Huntly showing existing houses and new street plan. By Thomas Milne. 1770. RHP 2145.
6. In addition to these printed works, some manuscript returns for Berwickshire are in the Scottish Record Office (Series E70), while the returns for part of the parish of Stow (Mid Lothian) are summarized in *NSA* I, p.431 and the tax rolls for part of Banffshire are printed in *Trans. Banff Field Club*, 1903–4, 24, 3–18.
7. A ratio of approximately two fishermen to every tradesman is apparent in the Aberdeenshire poll tax returns. A similar ratio existed in many Moray Firth fishing settlements in the nineteenth century, for instance at Gardenstown, Portgordon and Hopeman (Lockhart 1974, 190–91); Hopeman Estate Book No.1, Wink and Mackenzie, Solicitors, Elgin.
8. APS 1661 c156.
9. APS 1669 c120.
10. APS 1669 c32.

References

Aiton, W. 1812: *General View of the Agriculture of Ayr* (Glasgow).
Caird, J. B. 1964: The making of the Scottish rural landscape. *Scottish Geographical Magazine* 80, 72–80.
Carstairs, A. M. 1950: *The Distribution of the Population of Scotland 1450 to 1750* (Unpublished B Phil thesis, University of St. Andrews).
Crawford, G. 1782: *The History of the Shire of Renfrew . . . continued to the present day by William Semple* (Paisley) Part 2.
Dodgshon, R. A. 1975: Farming in Roxburghshire and Berwickshire on the eve of Improvement. *Scottish Historical Review* 54, 140–54.
Elliot, Sir, W. 1863–8: Denholm and its vicinity, *History of the Berwick Naturalists' Club* 5.
Fairhurst, H. 1960: Scottish Clachans. *Scottish Geographical Magazine* 76, 74–6.
Geddes, A. 1974: The development of Stornoway, *Scottish Geographical Magazine* 63, 57–63.
Gibson, R. 1905: *An Old Berwickshire Town: History of the Town and Parish of Greenlaw from the Earliest Times to the Present Day* (Edinburgh).
Graham, A. 1968–9: Archaeological notes on some harbours in eastern Scotland. *Proceedings of the Society of Antiquaries of Scotland* 101, 200–85.
Houston, J. M. 1948: Village planning in Scotland, 1745–1845. *Advancement of Science* 5, 129–32.
Keith, T. 1913: The trading privileges of the royal burghs of Scotland. *English Historical Review* 28, 454–71, 678–90.
Lockhart, D. G. 1974: *The Evolution of the Planned Villages of North-East Scotland* (Unpublished PhD thesis, University of Dundee, 2 Vols.).
Lockhart, D. G. 1980: Scottish village plans: a preliminary analysis. *Scottish Geographical Magazine* 96, 149–53.
Mitchell, Sir, A. (editor) 1906: Geographical collections relating to Scotland. *Scottish History Society* 51. Made by Walter MacFarlane, Vol. 1.

Moir, D. G. (editor) 1973: *The Early Maps of Scotland to 1850* 3rd edition (Edinburgh, Royal Scottish Geographical Society).

Parry, M. L. and Slater, T. R. (editors) 1980: *The Making of the Scottish Countryside* (London, Croom Helm).

Phillipson, N. T. and Mitchinson, R. (editors) 1970: *Scotland in the Age of Improvement* (Edinburgh, Edinburgh University Press).

Pryde, G. S. 1965: *The Burghs of Scotland: a Critical List* (London, Glasgow University Publications).

Semple, D. (editor) 1864: *The Poll Tax Rolls of the Parishes in Renfrewshire for the year 1695* (Paisley).

Sinclair, Sir J. (editor) 1791–99: *The Statistical Account of Scotland.* (Edinburgh) 21 Vols.

Smout, T. C. 1970: The landowner and the planned village in Scotland 1730–1830. In Phillipson, N. T. and Mitchison, R. (editors) 1970, 73–106.

Stuart, J. (editor) 1844: *List of Pollable Persons Within the Shire of Aberdeen, 1696* (Aberdeen).

Whyte, I. D. 1980: The emergence of the new estate structures. In Parry, M. L. and Slater, T. R. (editors) 1980, 117–35.

Whyte, I. D. 1981: The evolution of rural settlement in lowland Scotland in medieval and early modern times: an exploration. *Scottish Geographical Magazine* 97, 4–15.

Whyte, I. D. and Whyte, K. A. 1981: *Sources for Scottish Historical Geography, an Introductory Guide.* Historical Geography Res.Ser. No.6, Inst. of British Geographers. (Geo Abstracts).

Wood, J. 1818–1825: *Atlas of Scottish Towns* (Edinburgh).

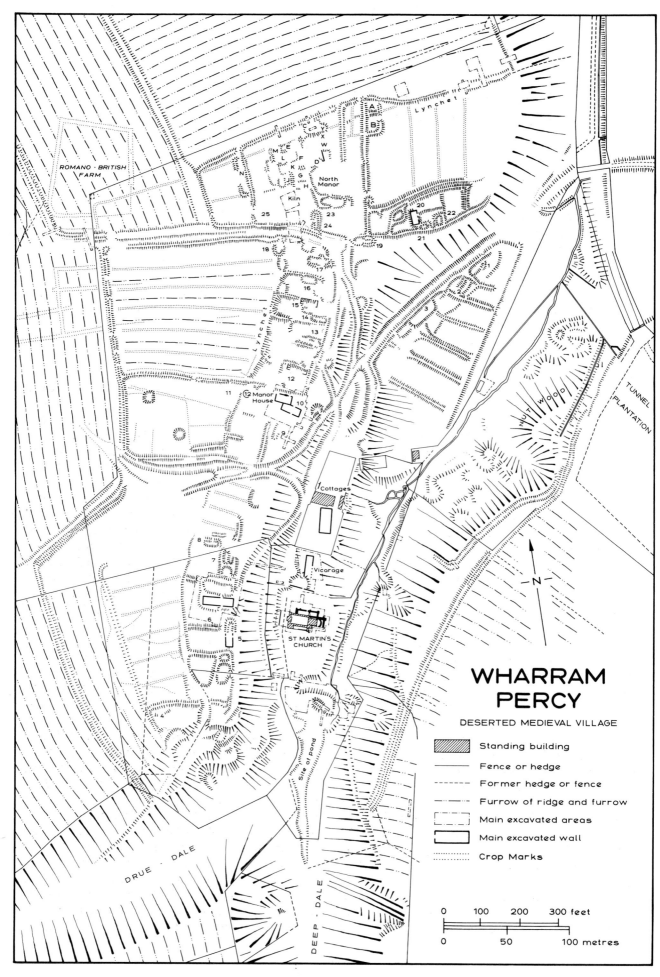

Fig. 14.1 *Wharram Percy deserted medieval village*

14. The Wharram Research Project: Problem Orientation and Strategy 1950-1990

J. G. Hurst

Early references to Wharram Percy are summarized, and the history of the excavation is described. Work in the 1950s and 1960s was restricted but included excavation of two tofts with their peasant houses, of the camera of a Norman manor house, and of the whole of the parish church. A wider ranging programme of research, leading up to the display of the site to the public, has been possible since it was placed in Guardianship in 1972-4. The eighteenth-century Improvement Farmstead near the church, the vicarage, changing graveyard boundaries, and a sequence of dams, have been excavated, the latter providing palaeoecological evidence from Saxon times onwards. Trenches across earthworks have shown that the topography of the medieval village was set in a prehistoric or Roman framework. This work is being put in a larger context by study of the whole parish. Priorities for future work are indicated.

The deserted medieval village (DMV) of Wharram Percy was finally depopulated *c.* 1500 as a result of the change-over from arable farming, requiring many villagers, to sheep farming needing only a single shepherd. It is likely, however, that knowledge of its site survived locally throughout the post-medieval period. The parish church of St Martin, serving until the nineteenth century the inhabitants of Thixendale township and the other farms in the parish, clearly marked the location of the site, with its complex pattern of earthworks fossilized under grass. A survey of the village was made in 1851 for the first edition of the Ordnance Survey six-inch map (published 1854). The site has subsequently appeared on all Ordnance Survey large- and medium-scale maps, down to the resurvey shown on the latest edition (1981) of the National Grid 1:2,500 sheet SE 8564.

In most areas of the country DMV sites were ignored by the nineteenth-century Ordnance Survey, but here in the East Riding of Yorkshire the surveyor (Capt. Bayly, RE) clearly had an interest and recorded a number of these sites. Various notes and articles on the isolated church and its contents appeared in the late nineteenth and early twentieth centuries but the first academic interest in the DMV arose in 1948: first, M. W. Beresford visited the site in late June as part of his programme of examining Yorkshire DMVs, then, a month later—on 22nd July 1948, (as part of his programme of photographing DMVs which had started that year)—J. K. S. St. Joseph flew over the site to take the first oblique air photographs. (The site in fact showed up well from the air on the 1946 RAF vertical cover but this was not examined until later). It is of considerable interest that the two pioneers of medieval landscape archaeology who were to collaborate in a seminal work on the subject ten years later

(Beresford and St. Joseph 1958) should both unwittingly have visited Wharram Percy at this time to produce the first known academic input to the site.

M. W. Beresford had been carrying out limited DMV excavations in the Midlands and the north since 1947, with the restricted aims of confirming that the earthworks did cover houses and of establishing archaeologically the date of desertion to compare with the historical evidence. Work at Wharram Percy started in 1950 following an invitation from the local schoolmaster, Mr Winstanley of Settrington, who had heard a 1949 BBC broadcast by Beresford on the occasion of the six-hundredth anniversary of the Black Death. Excavations continued on a number of house sites and the north manor for a number of weekends in 1950, 1951 and 1952. It was in 1952 that J. Golson and I, then both postgraduate students at Cambridge, contacted Beresford with a view to combining archaeological and historical work on DMVs. In April 1952 I joined Beresford's excavation on house 5 at Wharram Percy; in a single weekend, by extending the limited area opened up, we established the possible complexity of the site by finding an earlier wall on a different alignment under the latest building, with both of these overlying a stone quarry. At least three stone building phases in this toft were thus demonstrated, while near by a post-hole cut into the solid chalk suggested a still earlier timber phase. (Beresford and Hurst 1971, pl. 5.1). The Deserted Medieval Village Research Group (DMVRG) was founded at Wharram Percy in August 1952, with the object of co-ordinating work on DMVs by archaeologists, architects, geographers, historians and others interested in this subject. In addition to its fieldwork and work on documents, the DMVRG decided to continue the excavation at Wharram Percy in an attempt to study the life of the medieval peasant. The site was thus chosen largely by chance. In addition Wharram Percy was a site where there was a sympathetic landowner (the eleventh Baron Middleton) and the presence of nineteenth century cottages offered possible accommodation for the project, which was essential in view of the isolated nature of the site.

Although the excavation was a multidisciplinary team project from the first, it started off with very limited objectives because no research funds were available; it was therefore mainly voluntary, and in fact remained so for 20 years. The only financial help was a grant for equipment from the Society of Antiquaries, and Leeds University and University College London both paid for their contingents' keep. The site was used for grazing so it was possible to fence off only one area at a time for excavation, so even if funds and time had been available it is unlikely that permission would have been given to open up extra areas. The policy in the 1950s was, therefore, to excavate completely a single peasant house. Area 10 was chosen in December 1952 quite arbitrarily as it was nearest to the cottages. It must be confessed that the topography of the site had not been fully studied when the choice of site was made. The fact that Area 10 was different from the other tofts was not apparent until the first full plan of the site, produced in 1952 by the Ordnance Survey through the good offices of C. W. Phillips, was redrawn and compared with the site earthworks while work on Area 10 was in progress. In view of the promising nature of the first two major seasons on Area 10 in 1953 and 1954 it was decided to continue the excavation and extend the area. This work was completed in eight seasons between 1953 and 1960, each lasting for about three weeks, and amounting to 176 days or nearly six months; in the early years there were 15 to 20 volunteers, rising to an average of 35 during 1960.

This excavation clearly demonstrated the complexity of the site, with a series of peasant houses frequently rebuilt in different positions and on varying alignments. This was expected from earlier work, but the discovery of a Norman manor house underneath the later peasant houses destroyed the idea that the village had always had the same internal plan and encouraged the excavation of a second house site (Area 6). In 1960 a second ten-year programme was initiated to excavate this and also to expand the aims of the excavation by attempting a complete excavation of the parish church. The DMVRG felt that, in view of the promising results, the Wharram project should be continued, since other people were by this time both sampling individual peasant houses and carrying out larger research excavations on a wide range of different sites all over the country. It was therefore in 1960 that the conscious decision was taken for the DMVRG to concentrate effort on one site at Wharram Percy. There were,

however, at this time still no research funds and it was still possible to open up only one site in the main village area, which was grazed. On the other hand, interest in the project had grown and it was possible to attract up to 50 volunteers at a time, many of whom were still willing to pay for their keep. It was therefore felt practical to start the complete excavation of the church concurrently with Area 6 during the 1960s. This was practical as it was in a separate field not affected by grazing. A further catalyst to the church excavation was provided by the collapse of the tower in 1959.

Area 6 was chosen as it was at the southern end of the village west of the church and it was hoped that here there would be a longer sequence of peasant houses and, because of the Norman manor house, not only late ones as in Area 10. Excavation took 11 seasons between 1960 and 1970 for a total period of 36 weeks, but with between 30 and 50 volunteers to excavate a larger area. The excavation produced similar results for the fourteenth and fifteenth centuries, as in Area 10, with a complex sequence of chalk-built peasant houses in different positions and varying alignments. Underneath were a series of post-holes and slots from earlier timber buildings but there had been so much later disturbance that it was not possible to determine the plan of any of them. Nevertheless it was possible to demonstrate a considerable amount of information about the medieval peasant house, its plan, construction, complex rebuilding and resiting; all these were subjects about which almost nothing was known before. These results, together with excavations on DMVs elsewhere, have built up a considerable picture of this previously much neglected subject (Hurst 1971). In addition, the material finds have added considerably to our knowledge of the daily life of the peasants, both in the fields and in the home, and have provided insights into local industry and local and long distance trade. The results of this first 20 years work on the two peasant house sites (Area 10 and 6) were published as a monograph of the Society for Medieval Archaeology (Andrews and Milne 1979).

The parish church of St Martin had been kept in repair until the late nineteenth century, when the only other major surviving settlement in the parish, Thixendale, acquired its own church in 1870. After that date the fabric steadily declined, and was last restored in 1923. After the Second World War, with the last service being held in 1949, the decay was rapid. The fittings were removed and the gradual collapse of the roof in the 1950s and the fall of the west face of the tower in 1959 reduced the church to a ruin. A church on a DMV is an ideal subject for study if it is no longer in use, as it is possible not only to completely excavate the site but also to examine the standing fabric. It was, therefore, decided to carry out this work to extend our information about other aspects of the DMV, together with selective excavation of the churchyard to provide a sample of medieval rural skeletons. Work took place between 1962 and 1974 and for the first time in Britain a rural medieval parish church was completely excavated, demonstrating its development from a small proprietary church of the tenth century to the large parish church of the thirteenth century, with aisles and chapels, which then contracted in the post-medieval period with the desertion of the surrounding settlements. A sequence of 1,000 burials from the church and areas to the north and west has produced important evidence for the physical anthropology of the villagers, their diet, diseases and mortality rates. An interim report was published shortly after the excavation was completed (Hurst 1976) and the full publication will go to press in the autumn of 1984 as the second monograph in the Wharram series, also to be published by the Society for Medieval Archaeology.

After the first 20 years, therefore, a considerable amount had been achieved, considering that most of the work was voluntary and the areas which could be excavated were severely limited. The situation changed fundamentally at this time due to the involvement of the then Ministry of Public Building and Works. In 1965 the DMVRG had submitted a Memorandum to the Ministry recommending the preservation of the 50 best DMVs in the country and suggesting that the best six should be taken into guardianship (Beresford and Hurst 1971, 303–9). In 1967 the Ancient Monuments Board visited Wharram Percy and commended the proposals. In 1972 the church was placed in guardianship of the MOPBW by the Church Commissioners and, by the generosity of the eleventh Baron Middleton, the whole 30-acre village site was placed in guardianship in 1974. It was now possible to plan for further work on other aspects of the village without restrictions as to where excavation could take place. At the same time public funds were available: first of all to consolidate the standing remains of the church and mark out the various periods on the ground; and second, limited help became available to excavate and lay out, for the information of the general public, those features of village life which so far had not been examined.

A ten-year programme was therefore drawn up for the 1970s with the aim of examining the dams which retained the millpond and fishpond south of the church, the sequence of medieval and post-medieval parsonages north of the church, the post-medieval farm on the site of the cottages and the earthworks of boundaries and roads, to determine their date and the general development of the topography of the village. Department of the Environment (as the MOPBW then became) funds were used mainly to pay for archaeological supervisors, which enabled several different projects to be mounted at once, more

equipment to be bought and subsidized food to be provided for the volunteers.

It has not yet been possible to excavate the medieval parsonage, as it is under an access road which is at present in constant use, but it is hoped it will be possible to move this and excavate later in the 1980s. The yard of the medieval parsonage has been excavated, showing that in the fourteenth century it was built over the graveyard which previously extended much further north. The eighteenth century vicarage has been excavated, producing important correlations between the archaeological remains and the glebe terriers which recorded its dimensions and details of its construction. This work also extended the sequence of material remains into the post-medieval period after the desertion of the village. To the south and north of the present cottages, the foundations of the eighteenth-century Wharram Percy Farmhouse and its out-buildings around a courtyard have been excavated. As the site here on the terrace was restricted, the farm was moved to its present position on the plateau nearly a mile to the south-west in the 1840s. It is hoped to erect an open-fronted building on the lines of the east range of the courtyard to house a series of panels explaining the site to the general public. The foundations of the parsonage and farm will then be marked out.

The twelve-year excavation of the dam area between 1971 and 1982 has produced a very complex sequence of clay dams related to late Saxon and medieval mills which were then covered by a large chalk thirteenth-century dam to retain a fishpond. The main chalk areas of the DMV are quite unsuitable for the survival of environmental evidence, so the waterlogged conditions of the dam area have been crucial in extending the range of information available. The examination of the pollen, seeds, beetles, and wood will provide important evidence for the palaeoecology of the site. Along the stream to the north of the dam, to the east of the church and the cottages, a nature reserve has been established to preserve the flora and fauna of the area and to compare this with those of earlier times. The dam will be recreated in its thirteenth-century form and the pond refilled and stocked with fish to show the visitor another dimension of the village.

On the western plateau, a ten-year programme of trenches across the various earthworks at selected intervals from the southern to the northern limits of the DMV has thrown remarkable light on the origins and development of the village. Many of the major and minor boundaries have been demonstrated to be prehistoric or Roman, thus providing a basic framework in which the topography of the Saxon and medieval village developed. The earliest features seem to be a series of Bronze Age or Iron Age linear earthworks and droveways on the plateau, with settlement on the terrace north and south of the church.

In Romano-British times there was a farm on the terrace and at least two others, plus a possible Roman villa, on the plateau (Hurst 1981). These discoveries immediately demolished the simplistic view of the 1950s and 1960s that there was an original early Saxon settlement on the terrace which later expanded up on to the plateau (Hurst 1972). It is now likely that, at two of the Romano-British farm sites on the plateau, there may have been continuity through the Saxon period to the twelfth-century manor houses. There still seems to be a gap in the settlement of the terrace, which one would expect to be a preferred settlement site. The practicability of excavating all over the village in a series of selected trenches has therefore made it possible to suggest a chronology of development from prehistoric times to the medieval nucleated village.

Since 1974 a survey of the two ecclesiastical parishes of Wharram Percy and Wharram le Street using aerial photography, fieldwalking, geophysical survey and the study of maps and documents has enabled Wharram Percy village to be put into its wider context. For the prehistoric period, the barrows and linear earthworks have been plotted, suggesting a cleared landscape organized primarily for grazing (Hurst 1980). The importance of this part of the Wolds has been confirmed by the large Neolithic ceremonial centre recently discovered at Duggleby (Riley 1980). By the Romano-British period (if not a millennium before) the area was fully settled, with farms every half-mile and a Roman villa at both Wharram le Street and Wharram Grange (Hurst 1981). There is not so much evidence for Anglo-Saxon settlement but it appears that scattered settlement continued until the late Saxon period when the various centres, including those at Wharram Percy itself, were formed into nucleated villages about a mile apart. In addition the medieval field systems have been plotted and fieldwalked, showing a remarkable regular series of long selions up to 1,000 m long, together with evidence for manuring in those parts of the fields nearest to the village.

For the 1980s, following an assessment of the results of the first 30 years' work, it is suggested that the priorities should be to examine the nature of the possible continuity on the two manor house sites on the plateau (Hurst 1981), to do more work on the terrace to check if there really is a hiatus in the Saxon period, and to extend the parish survey with a series of limited excavations to check significant points. Initial work alongside the Area 10 manor house has already produced large quantities of Anglo-Saxon pottery and the bonus of the first medieval smithy so far found at Wharram; previously only loose slag had been found. In the north manor several phases of timber building have been identified, together with Saxon pottery, while the hollow-way to the south is being excavated and linked with a survey of the system of through roads and access tracks: an important sequence from prehistoric through Roman and Saxon times is now being investigated. On the terrace, when work is complete on the post-medieval parsonage and farm, it is hoped to excavate the supposed late medieval parsonage with the aim also of looking at earlier levels over a wider area of the terrace where the apparent lack of Anglo-Saxon occupation is so puzzling.

By 1990, therefore, it is hoped that most of the major aspects of Wharram Percy medieval village will have been subject to some investigation: parish church, two manor houses, parsonages, mills and fishponds, smithy and peasant houses: all set in their context both in space and time. As the prime site in the country where this can be achieved this should result in a medieval village site marked out and displayed to the public, giving a detailed view of medieval rural life in all its aspects, and also show how this is merely one episode in a settlement history extending over at least 4,000 years.

A full duplicated interim report is issued each year. Shorter reports appear in the *Annual Reports of the (Deserted) Medieval Village Research Group*, and the *Medieval Britain* section of *Medieval Archaeology*.

References

Addyman, P. and Morris, R. (editors) 1976: *The Archaeological Study of Churches* (Council for British Archaeology Report 12, 36–39).

Andrews, D. D. and Milne, G. (editors) 1979: Domestic settlement 1: Areas 10 and 6. In Hurst, J. G. (editor) 1979.

Beresford, M. and Hurst, J. G. (editors) 1971: *Deserted Medieval Villages: Studies* (London, Lutterworth Press).

Beresford, M. and Hurst, J. G. 1976: Wharram Percy: a Case Study in Microtopography. In Sawyer, P. H. (editor) 1976, 114–44 and Sawyer, P. H. (editor) 1979, 52–82, with supplement 83–5.

Beresford, M. and St. Joseph, J. K. S. 1958: *Medieval England: An Aerial Survey* (Cambridge, Cambridge University Press 2nd edition 1979).

Evison, V. I. (editor) 1981: *Angles, Saxons and Jutes: Essays presented to J. N. L. Myres* (Oxford, Clarendon Press).

Hurst, J. G. 1971: A review of archaeological research (to 1968). In Beresford, M. and Hurst, J. G. (editors) 1971, 76–144.

Hurst, J. G. 1972: The changing medieval village in England. In

Ucko, P. J. Tringham, R. and Dimbleby, G. W. (editors) 1972, 531–40.

Hurst, J. G. 1976: Wharram Percy: St Martin's Church. In Addyman, P. and Morris, R. (editors) 1976, 36–9.

Hurst, J. G. (editor) 1979: *Wharram: a Study of Settlement on the Yorkshire Wolds* Vol. 1. (Society for Medieval Archaeology Monograph Series, No. 8.)

Hurst, J. G. 1980: Archäologische forschungen in der siedlungskammer Wharram, England. *Offa* 37, 301–8.

Hurst, J. G. 1981: Wharram: Roman to Medieval. In Evison, V. I. (editor) 1981, 241–55.

Riley, D. N. 1980: Recent air photographs of Duggleby Howe and the Ferrybridge henge. *Yorkshire Archaeological Journal* 52, 174–8.

Sawyer, P. H. (editor) 1976: *Medieval Settlement, Continuity and Change* (London, Edward Arnold).

Sawyer, P. H. (editor) 1979: *English Medieval Settlement* (London, Edward Arnold).

Ucko, P. J., Tringham, R. and Dimbleby, G. W. (editors) 1972: *Man, Settlement and Urbanism* (London, Duckworth).

15. Wharram Percy Research Strategies

P. A. Rahtz

Wharram Percy is now a multi-period site, rather than a deserted village. It can best be studied within a systemic framework, which will assist the understanding of change through time. Its academic aims must run parallel with its social ones: the explanation of a complex settlement site to a public used to castles and abbeys. Progress in both has been impressive in 30 years but still only five per cent has been dug. Is there any scope for sampling at Wharram? The North Manor provides an appropriate case-study. Wharram of 1984 is very different from the austerity and innocence of the Beresford and Hurst pioneers.

I became involved with John Hurst in the Wharram Project when we founded the Department of Archaeology at York in 1978. We were interested in the prospect of a training excavation not too far from York and in one with a massive data base (accumulated by Hurst over three decades), and an organization by Maurice Beresford which is one of the saga-epics of British archaeology. The data base, although large, is still by no means big enough to enable us to have more than a limited understanding of the history of Wharram. The excavated sample is still less than five per cent even of the site itself, and a minute part of what Hurst and I would now regard as the minimum study area—the two parishes of Wharram Percy and Wharram le Street. It has been our experience that the accumulation of more data from each season's excavation does not in itself solve problems; it (a) creates new ones, (b) refutes any hypotheses that may have been evolved in earlier years, (c) exposes new horizons of ever-increasing interest. At the end of each season the siren of truth leads us stumbling further into what seems sometimes like a hypothetico-deductive peat-bog; we have to have faith that one day she will lead us (or more probably our successors) on to firmer ground.

The archaeology of any separate period lacks the very essence of our discipline—the change through time. It is this that distinguishes our approaches from the narrower ones of the sociologist, social anthropologist or economist, who are content to see the last three minutes of a long play without wondering what happened in the first three acts. To confine ourselves within a limited period of 1,000 years, and recent ones at that, has been to fall into the same trap as medieval historians, who think the only important things that happened were those that happened after writing was invented. I have, I hope, found a way out of that overcrowded cage into the pleasures of diachronic, trans-spatial and cross-cultural archaeology, though at my age necessarily as a dilettante (Rahtz 1981a).

Wharram offered such opportunities as it became increasingly apparent that the bumpy surface which used to be called the earthworks of the deserted medieval village was like a crumpled duvet over a bedrock on which the world had been struggling for thousands of years. The plan may now be seen to have been determined originally by topographic constraints and opportunities, by the changing locations of resource exploitations, and by the linear movement zones resulting from home-to-work travel, social intermixing, and the ever-expanding network of surplus disposal and exchange with neighbouring and distant communities. The process probably began in the later Mesolithic, accelerated during the Neolithic and Bronze Ages, and arrived at a complex pattern by the eve of the Roman Conquest. We are not yet certain how drastic, if at all, were the results of Roman reorganization or exploitation, but we would feel confident that the basic layout of the boundaries, living areas, and routeways, as we see them today, owes little to the Saxon and medieval settlements.

To make the Wharram data more manageable to York students, and to emphasize the diachronic and dynamic aspects of the study, I have attempted to order them into a thematic framework (Fig. 15.1). This is based on eight principal themes or topics, all of which can potentially be studied over some 10,000 years (Rahtz 1981b). As a neo-Higgsian determinist, I have a vertical axis linking Environment to Settlement History, all other hominid activities being derived ultimately from the interaction of man with the changing Wolds landscape. None of these topics can however be studied in isolation; each is closely related to the others in positive or negative ways, hence the feedback element within the basic nucleus. Each principal theme is subdivided into a series of subsidiary topics. There are here many dissertation or thesis topics which we believe the Wharram project should now generate.

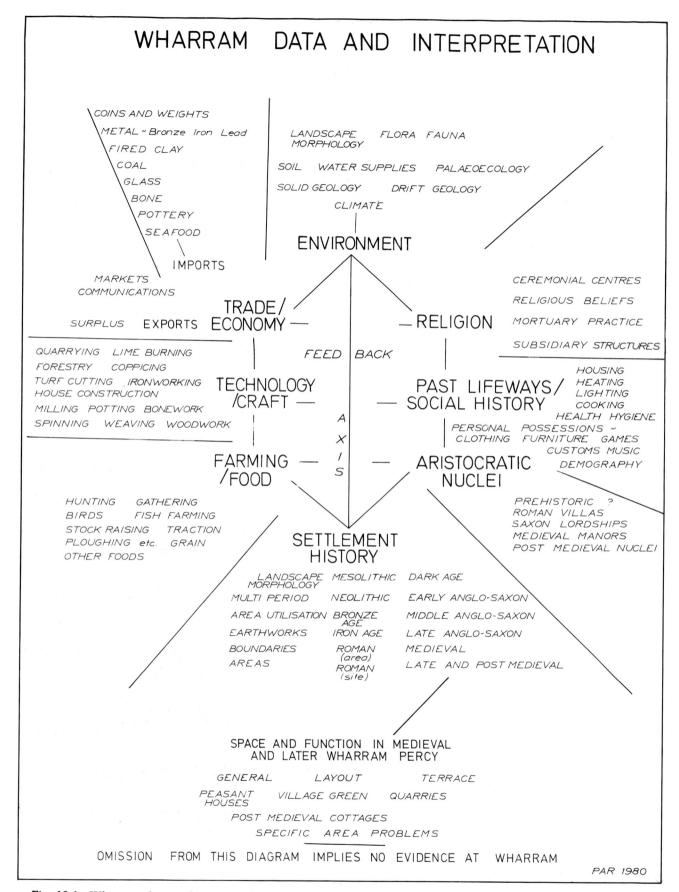

Fig. 15.1 *Wharram data and interpretation*

Table 15.1

WHARRAM

RELIGION

Subdivisions	Sources	Data published	Data unpublished	Problems	Research modes
Ceremonial centres	Duggleby Henge (cf Rudston); barrows; graveyards; churches (at WP & WLS)	Hurst 1976a Andrews and Milne ed 1979 ch II Taylor and Taylor 1965	church and grave-yard data; former in prep	serving who or which area? barrow concentrations: re great group to W at Aldro; fewer around WP except on ridgeway; why?	analysis of grave memorials in area for recent times and registers further survey of WLS
	cross? WP church, WLS church special prob-lems	church monograph in prep; see biblio for interim state-ments and plans and older accounts		freestanding? dating timber church and first stone church does XI C14 date of graves under slabs make sequence post-Scandi? when was large early Norman church built? Norman prestige = population, should be after North harrowing, but not too much because of Saxo-Norman tower added S aisle 1180's with apse and S manor, was this Chamberlains? if XII dump in pond what was occasion of final expansion of N aisle (XIII) & NE chapel? occasion of shrinkage after desertion? relation of expansion/contraction to settlement/aristo sequence	cf develop-ment in 5 town-ships, to study
Mortuary practice	structures and graves within and unassociated (barrows, odd graves, grave-yards, and within church)	Beresford 1980-1	graveyard data and more in current excavations	relationship of barrows to settlement-see above; significance of Roman boundary? problem of crouch burial in graveyard (80bc); significance of sceattas of VIII and IX	collation of published data; further C14? dig areas to W & S of croucher (small scale)
	church graveyard special problems			pre-church origins? association with cross? or market? dating, how and when did graveyard develop? linear? polyfocal, radial etc, constraints by paths, boundaries? true that 4x used? if so, what deter-mined each time? gradual? sudden markets pre-memorial stage? mounds, post, curbs, memory? reasons for limits and their aban-donment for expansion and contrac-tion to N? S limit inviolable? (cf XVIII/XIX & Roman) all usual re sex, age, burial posi-tion, etc., orientation, by area, eg. N different from S? paupers, suicides, females etc to N? extent of destruction eg late Saxon burials cut away for Norman, and medieval slabs built into fabric	further C14? detailed research on pot among graves much collation needed of grave plans cf demography above any info? computerisation
Religious beliefs	data in above section; memorials; folklore; ?artefacts		1979 data + earlier medieval and Saxon	attitudes to deity, death, after-life, etc (see Rahtz in 1979 Int. Rep) expansion and decline in Christianity VII-XX; extent of pagan practice pre-VII & VII & later	collation ethnographic; local study
Subsidiary structures associated with religion	priests' houses; ?other structures, eg mortuary houses; well-houses; doc. sources	ch by Beresford in Andrews and Milne ed 1979	current, parsonage excavation	why encroachment by parsonage of XIII? (cf timber building under N extension graveyard); stone wall and parsonage ?XIV; vicarage/rectory/priest's house: location at all times; cf major ashl r building W of glebe; move to cottage garden after XIV fire?	

Analysis needed of interrelationships between main and sub-topics, both direct and as feedback;
dynamic elements to be constantly borne in mind; these tend to be obscured by topic and period
fragmentation

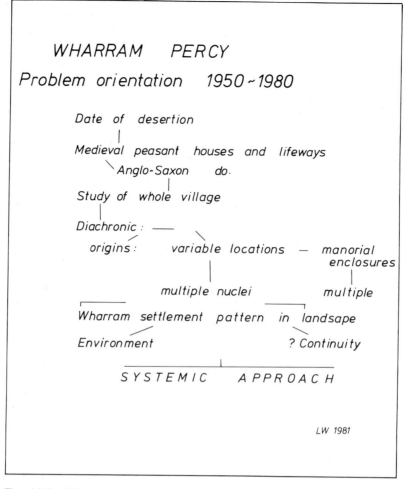

Fig. 15.2   Wharram Percy: problem orientation 1950—1980

It is remarkable that there is evidence from Wharram for every one of the sub-topics shown on this diagram, even if in some cases, like music, the evidence would not occupy more than a line or two. This will perhaps be some comfort to those who believe that 30 years excavation *should* have added to knowledge. There are indeed many 'facts' implied in the small print of the diagram, derived from archaeological and other sources. These can be described and talked about, but in themselves do not answer the important 'why' questions of culture process. Hopefully, however, showing them as part of an integrated network of interdisciplinary and interacting themes may encourage attempts to incorporate particularizing enquiry within a framework of full systemic approach. This is far from being achieved, and awaits the attentions of some brilliant young archaeologists. All that I have tried to do here is to sketch the notes for an agenda.

Some of the subdivisions, as for instance those of technology and craft, can to some extent be considered discretely. In others, such as aristocratic nuclei, we are viewing the theme through time, in its well-known

period manifestations. In the case of Settlement History, we have again a chronological sequence related to morphological and functional sub-topics. One of these is the surface of our duvet, the space utilization and function in the medieval and later periods at Wharram. This section of the diagram is perhaps one which has been overemphasized in medieval rural nucleated settlement studies.

For the convenience of students, I have compiled a 'text' or a series of notes that expand the diagram (e.g. Table 15.1) (from Rahtz 1981b). For each subdivision I have listed, horizontally across the page, the sources of evidence which may be considered, which may or may not have been exploited by archaeologists or historians; the data concerning each which has been published; and (rather greater in volume) that which is at present unpublished; the micro-questions which may be asked of extant and future evidence (some of major importance in the big themes of culture process); and finally, the modes of research which could, if resources permitted, be brought to bear.

The Wharram Data Sheets as they exist in their second edition need much more ordering and amplification, and incorporation into a research design. Hurst has discussed (this volume, Chapter 14) changing problem orientations (Fig. 15.2) research designs and results over the years, and we hope that these will continue to develop and expand in the dynamic and flexible way that has been one of the best-known aspects of the Wharram Research Project under his guidance.

At Wharram we are fortunate not only in our devoted excavation team, some extending into a third generation, and in our site supervisors, but also in the extent to which the project has attracted specialist researchers and advisers from many fields.

The welding of all these efforts together is a function of Maurice Beresford's management, and operates within a singularly favourable research environment created by the long-term and generous support of the Department of the Environment (not to be confused with John Hurst), and by the generosity of Lord Middleton in giving the site into Guardianship.

Wharram does not exist just for research and training. Archaeology is doomed if it is not socially relevant. Increasingly therefore, the research designs and directions and their ultimate synthesis must be closely allied to publication, conservation, display and explication on site and in lectures. The combination of Research and Management is well defined in the diagram contributed by Martin Carver (Fig. 15.3).

The argument is best illustrated by looking at one major theme, that of Religion, as seen in a diachronic and cross-cultural approach to Wharram (Table 15.1). The first subdivision here is ceremonial centres. If one is to look at religious institutions through time in a certain area, or compare ones in different areas, such as Europe and Central America, it is necessary to find a neutral and all-embracing term such as ceremonial centre. So that when, at Wharram, we consider the role that the possible henge of Duggleby Howe played in the area, and compare it with that of the medieval church, we are more likely to consider this in a wider anthropological framework if we refer to them both as ceremonial centres, rather than divorce them totally by merely thinking of one as a prehistoric henge and the other as a Christian Church.

The sequence of ceremonial centres is closely allied to that of *mortuary practice* or body disposal facility locations, from Neolithic and Bronze Age barrows to Roman burials and pagan Saxon graves; and to the much-discussed question of whether a Saxon cemetery preceded any church in the valley bottom terrace of Wharram Percy. Of these topics, it is of course the Christian Church and its graveyard that have received a disproportionate share of research, for obvious reasons. A new source material for this topic is seen in the post-medieval period, in the change to the epigraphic evidence for mortuary practice on the gravestones (Chapter 16 this volume). The associated graves are for this period inviolate, because of the constraints of our own culture.

Within this broad diachronic and thematic background of religion, seen in ceremonial centres and mortuary practice, there are many details to fill—the re-evaluation of nineteenth-century barrow-digging, the boundaries and markers of graveyards, the details of church alterations, expansion and decline in tune with the secular, social and economic background, the detailed data on skeletons and memorial stones, and the complicated relationships of the medieval and later church to its subsidiary structures of vicarages, rectories and parsonages.

It is one thing to pose research problems and strategies, another to carry them out. Constraints of time, money, expertise, and free access to land, effectively prohibit implementation of most research designs; to the point indeed when the grandiose research framework of Wharram deserves something more akin to a full-time staffed research institute than to the annual three-week gathering of up to 100 people. In these circumstances, should we give up? I don't believe that we should. Progress is slow but impressive, and I am a subscriber to the old adage, 'If a thing is worth doing at all, it's worth doing badly'. Wharram has many problems of methodology but each year John Hurst and I solve some.

If we cannot work on a large enough scale, is there any future in sampling? I will conclude with a brief summary of the choice of area and method of digging in York's own patch of the Wharram site, the North Manor.

The north part of the site (Fig. 15.4) contains within its 1.43 ha (= 143 10 × 10 m squares), we believe, a prehistoric lynchet and linear movement zone, successive aristocratic or economic nuclei of a Roman villa, an Anglo-Saxon 'lordship' nucleus and a medieval manor (Fig. 15.5). At the present rate of excavation, the elucidation of all these relationships in this area would take about 500 years.

On the assumption that we knew quite a lot about medieval manors, and should therefore devote our efforts to the earlier aristocratic or economic nuclei, one possibility was that we might bulldoze off all the medieval levels and start from there; this did not meet with general approval. Another possibility was a sample transect from north to south, 10 m wide, through the medieval manor area, in the hope of determining stratigraphically, if not in plan or detail, the relationship between villa, manor, and linear movement zone. This transect was to be dug in 10 × 10 m squares (incorporating earlier excavations in this area—1961, 1975, and 1977–80 in Fig. 15.4), and

WHARRAM – Research and Management

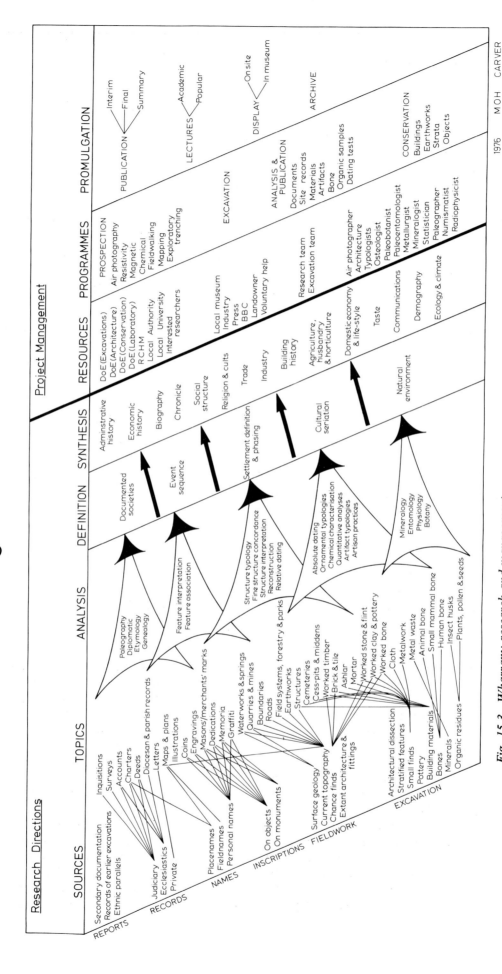

Fig. 15.3 Wharram: research and management

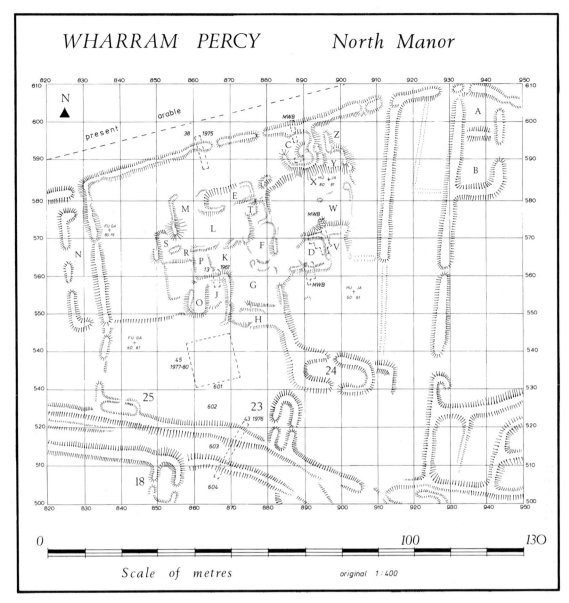

Fig. 15.4   Wharram Percy: North Manor

would take ten years or more. This scheme also was not greeted with roars of rapturous applause in some quarters, but John Hurst and I thought it was rather a good strategy. In 1980, accordingly, we began at the south end with two 10 m squares (602 and 603 in Fig. 15.4). The results of this work in 1980 and 1981 were, however, so promising in detail that we decided to abandon the transect and concentrate on an area excavation around our 1980 square (602–604 in Fig. 15.4). Thus do the best-laid schemes of sampling come to grief when faced with the temptation offered by the recovery of a limited area of first class data, however small and however unrepresentative of the whole area of the North Manor, or the site, or the parish, or the study area, or the vast diachronic, transpatial and cross-cultural themes with which I began this paper.

The important thing is, however, to demonstrate, in a small area, but one of high density of prime archaeological data, the *kinds of evidence* (i.e. in terms of post-depositional theory), the *methods of data recovery*, and the *modes of analysis*, which would, if multiplied over a wide area in the next half-millennium of the Wharram Project, give some big answers to my big questions.

Lawrence Butler, in a recent review (Butler 1981) of the first Wharram monograph, compared the Wharram pioneers with those other stalwarts of the Yorkshire landscape, the early Cistercians—'they would go they knew not where by a road they knew not of'—in the Wharram case, the railway line and the track from Bella Farm. In Butler's model the cottages were the Rievaulx of the mid-twentieth century, the source and inspiration

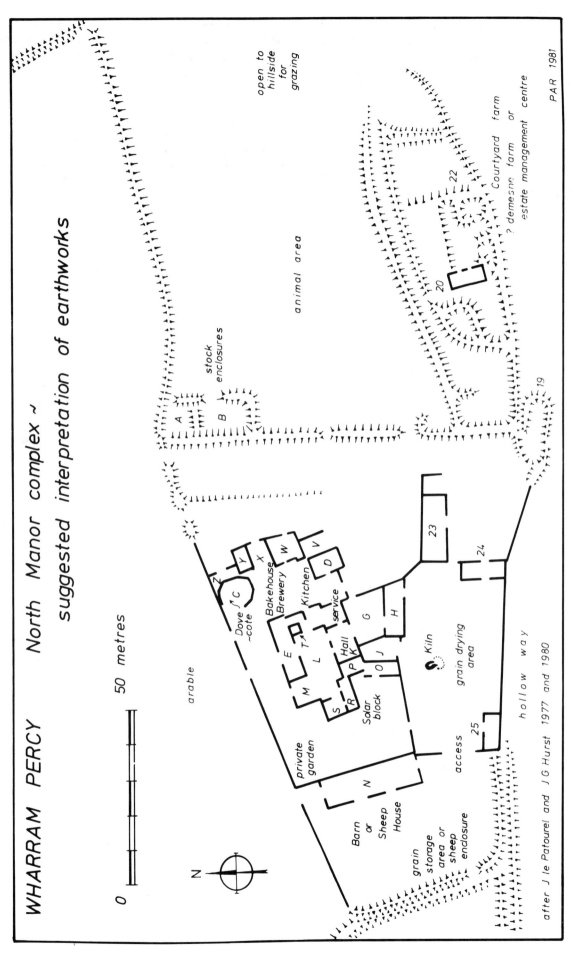

Fig. 15.5 Wharram Percy: North Manor complex, suggested interpretation of earthworks

of medieval rural archaeology in many countries. The innocence of the 1950s is perhaps now past. Systems theory may be seen by some as the decline of the Order into corruption, leading eventually to the Dissolution of the Project. This is not my view, however, and I end with the closing sentence of Lawrence's review 'Now they glimpse a vision of a new promised land. When the present excavations and surveys are published, what new visions will float before us? Will Wharram still be a rural El Dorado?'

References

Butler, L. 1981: Review of Andrews, D. D. and Milne, G. Domestic settlement 1: Areas 10 and 6. In Hurst, J. G. (editor) 1979. Review in *Yorkshire Archaeological Journal* 53, 153.

Hurst, J. G. (editor) 1979: *Wharram: A Study of Settlement in the Yorkshire Wolds* Vol. 1. (Society for Medieval Archaeology Monograph Series No. 8).

Rahtz, P. A. 1981a: *The New Medieval Archaeology*. Inaugural lecture, University of York.

Rahtz, P. A. 1981b: *Wharram Data Sheets* 2nd edition. Medieval Village Research Group and Department of Archaeology, University of York.

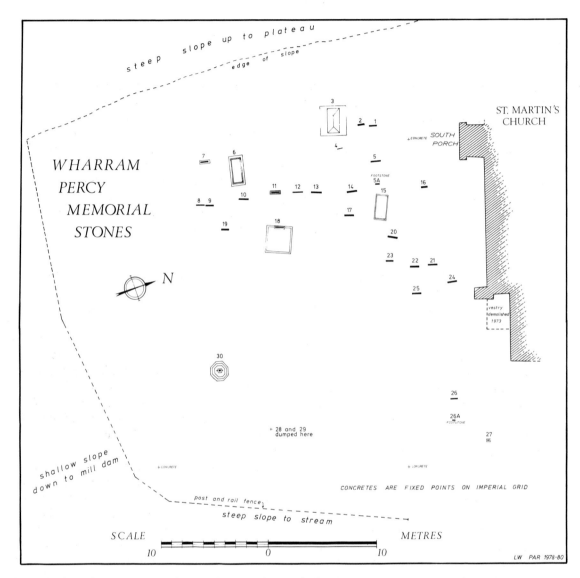

Fig. 16.1 Wharram Percy memorial stones (general plan)

16. Wharram Percy Memorial Stones: an Anthropological View from Mars

Rilip Phahtz

The memorial stones at Wharram Percy offered a unique opportunity to the Martian expedition to Planet Earth. Their inscriptions inform us of the beliefs of Earthpersons concerning death and the afterlife. The stones appear to be closely associated with inhumation burial in the area, which has provided our physical anthropologists with a rich haul of the bony parts of these bipeds. Boris Meresford, a leading expert on English, has found useful complementary written material in the ruins of nearby Eboracum. It has enabled a ruined building close to the stones to be identified as a 'church'. The stones are informative too for economic and social studies of Earthpersons, class-structure being clearly evident in terms of spatial distribution and resource expenditure. Certain designs on the stones have affinities with details on ruins around the Mediterranean Sea. The result of the work has been to increase yet further our high opinion of Earthperson culture, these beings far removed from their traditional image in Martian eyes as green bug-eyed monsters.

Among the many aims of the Martian expedition to the planet Earth settlement at Wharram Percy was an examination of 31 memorial stones, upright stone slabs and three stone box-like structures. These all stood in an open space south of a large ruined stone building (Fig. 16.1), interpreted as a centre of public ritual, partly because there was no evidence of hearths or domestic features and partly because under and around it were hundreds of skeletons of Earthpersons. These have provided our physical anthropologists with a very rich haul of material.

There was thus a strong *prima facie* case to be made for the stones themselves having a ritual rather than a secular purpose, and also that they too were associated with Earthperson burials, a possibility that could be checked in further excavations. They are mostly inscribed in various styles of cut or inlaid lettering, and one of these indeed does say 'Here Rest in Peace the remains of Mathew the son of John Leppington'—it seems very likely that these 'remains' are the skeleton of this person, buried somewhere in the vicinity. In no other case, however, is this relationship between stone and Earthperson burial made explicit. In many others the stone is clearly principally a memorial to the dead person: 'In memory of . . .', 'Sacred to the memory of . . .', 'In loving memory of . . .', 'In affectionate Remembrance of . . .' etc. The use of the word 'Sacred' in several cases confirms the ritual and serious nature of the memorials.

The inscriptions have all been studied by one of our expedition staff, Boris Meresford, who has confirmed that they are in the language of English, of which evidence has been found by many of our expeditions.

Boris Meresford has been digging in the ruins of a building some 30 English miles away, in a town whose name we know from an inscription to be *Eboracum*. This building seems to have been called the Borthwick Institute, and he was fortunate enough to find among the fused rubble a document, well-preserved in a metal box, which gave lists of names of Earthpersons who had undergone a ritual initiation called 'baptism', and also a list of those who had died, and when they had been buried. One can imagine his pleasure in finding that the Earthpersons named included those on our stones, and this list also gave us the name of Wharram Percy. It is clear, however, that only a small number of those who died and were buried had a memorial stone, 47 out of 318 between earth-years 1770–1878.[1] This is a conclusion we had come to independently from the density of skeletons in the adjacent areas. Apart from those named in the Borthwick document who are not named on a stone, a slab found in the ruins of the nearby ritual building tells us of George Wrangham, who died in 1791, aged 49 earth-years, and 'now sleeps among his kindred in the adjoining churchyard'. This gave us the very valuable information concerning the direct equation between sleep and death in the minds of these people. We may, therefore, anticipate finding the skeleton of George Wrangham, who is not named on any stone, though his kindred are. The name 'churchyard' is interpreted as the yard or space of the 'church', and the hypothesis that this name 'church' was that of the ruined building was fortunately confirmed by another document unearthed by Meresford, a message written by one John Richardson before his death that he wanted to be buried 'in ye

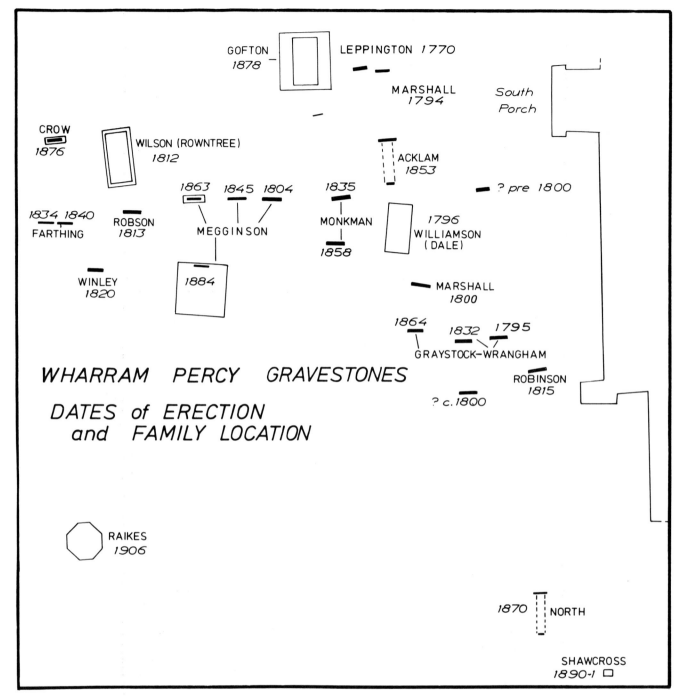

Fig. 16.2 Wharram Percy gravestones: dates of erection and family location

churche of Wharram Percy neere unto the place weere my wiefe was buried'—the desire presumably to sleep near his wife in death as he had in life.

Some stones commemorate one person, others whole families, 53 Earthpersons being named on the 31 stones. A further connection with what we may now safely call the 'church' is the direct spatial relationship between the stones and the doorway to this building; the earliest stones lie closest to it, the latest are furthest away. The simplest explanation here is that the stones

were meant to be seen by those entering and leaving the church, thus securing maximum commemoration in the minds of the living. There is, however, evidence not only of linear or radial development in the plan, but also of kin grouping (Fig. 16.2). Apart from the box-like memorials which have several names of one kin-group, there is also kin-grouping of adjacent stones—four Megginson stones lie close together, and two of several other families, together with relationships worked out by Meresford to be the result of pair

217

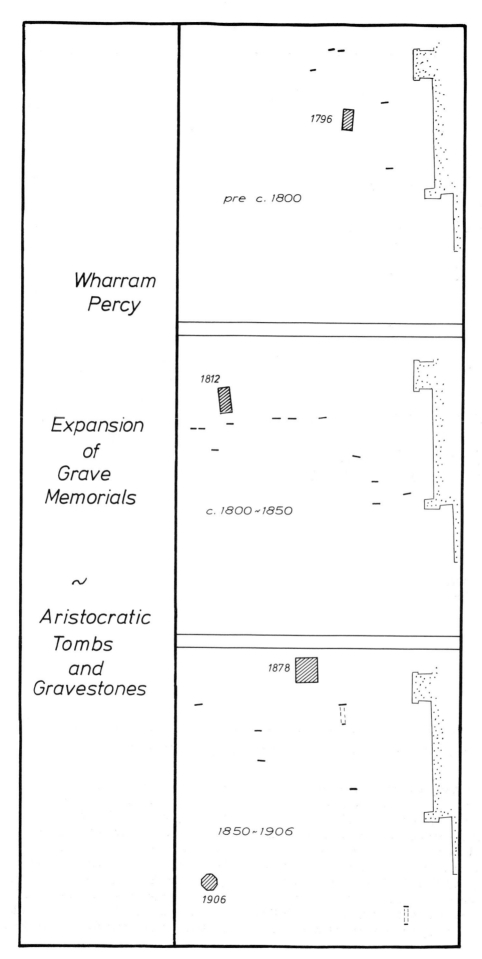

Fig. 16.3 Wharram Percy: expansion of grave memorials, aristocratic tombs and gravestones

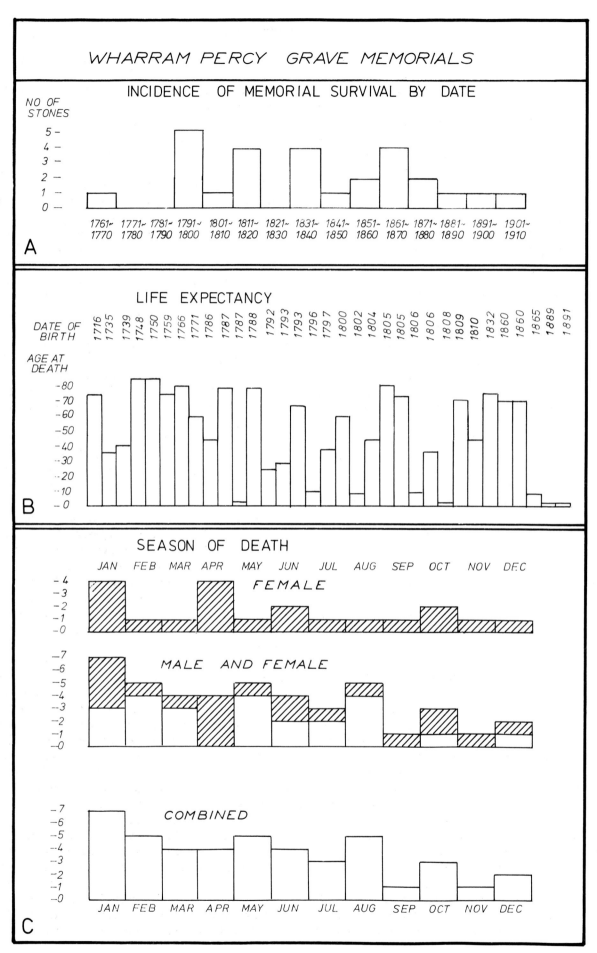

Fig. 16.4 Wharram Percy memorials: incidence of memorial survival by date

bonding in patrilinear descent. The box memorials clearly represent greater resource expenditure, presumably by surviving relatives; their aristocratic nature is perhaps underlined by their isolated positions away from those of lower status (Fig. 16.3). This is a social separation in contrast to aristocratic graves lying as the nuclei of groups in a multi-nuclear body disposal area. We shall return to social status in discussing occupations.

As already indicated, a further social or economic separation is shown by the small minority commemorated on stones in 1770–1878. It is uncertain whether such social separation will be seen in earlier periods of burial at this site. Archaeologically, from the density of skeletons in excavated areas and the extent of the burial area, we estimate a total of several 1,000 dead over *c.* 1,200 earth-years. It is clear, therefore, that the stones represent only layer one of the archaeological cemetery, and it would be unsafe to extrapolate anthropological conclusions from these back into earlier periods. Wharram Percy is being developed as an 'ancient monument' where Martian tourists may see, laid out and displayed, the living places and other features of this Earthpersons' community. The churchyard itself is maintained as cut grass with a few thorn bushes. Small mammals and birds frequent the area, and a wild bees' nest caused some concern to our stone recorders. The principal living organisms using the stones as hosts are, however, what our botanists have identified as a lichen, a non-malignant form unlikely to be such a menace as the recently-exterminated Triffids. The extent of the lichen colonization may, it seems, be a means of dating stones in the absence of epigraphic evidence.

Most stones refer only to a single generation, often a pair-bond of husband and wife. Male superiority, implied by patrilinear descent, is confirmed in several cases by the placing of the male name first, even where this was not the first death. Other stones extend to two or even three generations; on the one hand parents, indicating ancestral antecedents; on the other hand children. In either case, lineage was clearly an important feature to be commemorated on stones.

Both the Borthwick document and also the epigraphic evidence give us a representative selection of forenames in this period prefixed as one or two names before that of the family. Some show popularity over a long period, such as Elizabeth, John or William. Others, such as Newlove or Rosehannah, are restricted to the years in the later 1800s.

What did these people do in their society? Only three occupations are named on the stones. Thomas Farthing was a farmer—a cultivator of land. John Robinson was in the Royal Navy, which Meresford tells me was a warlike body of persons under the command of a king, who fought from boats on the sea, though the nearest sea to Wharram is 30 miles away. Francis Raikes was a Judge of the County Court. As a law-dispenser, his important position in society is reflected in his grandiose and isolated memorial stone in the shape of a 'plus' sign on top of a column (Fig. 16.7). Occupation was obviously not an important thing to commemorate compared to lineage, age, place and sentiment. Meresford's researches in the ruins of the Borthwick have shown that (although not so-mentioned on the stones) most of the males named were in fact farmers of some substance, hence the resource-expenditure on their stones. There are exceptions; firstly, Joseph Crow, who was only an agricultural labourer. His widow, however, outlived him for 30 years and it was only at her death that a stone commemorated them both. She must in this period have acquired wealth by other means. Secondly, John Winley was only a servant and can hardly by the time of his death at 27 years old have acquired wealth. We can only guess that he was well-loved enough by his employers for them to provide a stone in his memory.

The average age at death of those named on stones is 46 earth-years, though ten lived to be over 70. The sample of population represented is however demographically quite unrepresentative (Fig. 16.4). The archaeological evidence of skeletons shows a life expectancy at birth of no more than 18–19. The stones are clearly of those who lived long enough to attain status or accumulate wealth sufficient to be commemorated in stone.

One obvious aim of the expedition was to recover evidence from the stones of the religious beliefs of those commemorated at Wharram Percy; but this proved, as so often the case in archaeology, very elusive.

I have already indicated that disposal of the dead was by extended inhumation, as shown in excavation; one inscription however, to Ann Marshall, as 'sleeping in thy Urn', may imply cremation or a very compressed inhumation.

Excavated skeletons were all orientated east-west, heads to west facing east, and it is probably no coincidence that the stones also face east, or are aligned on this orientation. The connection with the church is also emphasized by the similar orientation of this building, its narrower (but not its highest) end pointing east. On Earth, the sun rises in the east, and we may well see some connection here between the dead facing the place from which light was to come after darkness and belief in some life after death, when new life came from the same direction as new light.

The inscriptions themselves do have passages or words which presumably refer to religious beliefs, but their meaning eludes even that great student of earth beliefs, Tarles Chomas. A certain 'Christ' is named on a stone as 'joining in love'; perhaps he was a priest who joined male and female in a pair-bond sanctified by society. 'Jesus' is named: someone or somewhere in

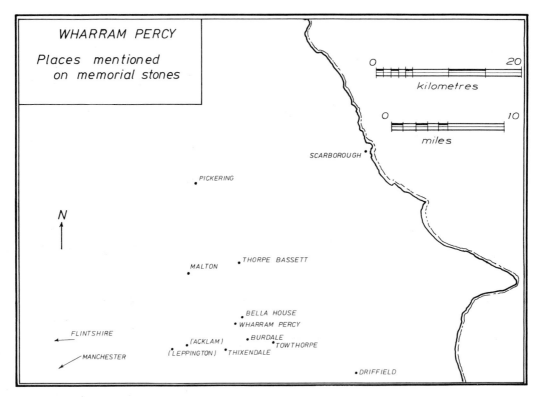

Fig. 16.5   Wharram Percy: places mentioned on memorial stones

whom or where one sleeps, a metaphor whose meaning we can only boggle at. There is a quotation from something called 'Matt. 24 chap. 44 verse': 'Therefore be ye also ready: for in such an hour as ye think the Son of Man cometh.' This is presumably a literary source that was familiar to everybody at the time; Meresford tells me the language style is of a period some 200 years earlier than the stone, so this 'Matt.' appears to be from some venerable and well-known book. The implication of the quote sounds like a warning of some kind to be in a certain state of readiness, otherwise there will be a disaster when this 'Son of Man' arrives. Who he was, or is expected to be, is ambiguous, except that he is clearly human rather than divine.

Belief in a life beyond death is implicit in the Marshall stone:

'Sleep on thou Blessed in thy Urn,
My tears can not awake thee,
I must stay here until my Turn,
and then with Joy, I'll o'ertake thee'—

this implies that the surviving partner might, on his death, 'overtake' his wife, in the sense of being rejoined, rather than in the sense of how we use this word today in our inter-planet 125 shuttle service.

On the Wilson box tomb, similar ideas are expressed:

'Death cant disjoin whom Christ hast joined in love
Life leads to Death, and Death to Life above
In Heaven's a happier place . . .
Live Well to gain in future life the prize'

Here the power of death to separate is denied, and another 'Life' in a place called 'Heaven' is envisaged 'above' (perhaps in Mars?); and here we also have the important though seemingly élitist idea that life after death is not for everyone, but only as a reward, a 'prize' for those who 'live well'.

Belief in a specific occasion when life returns for all those who deserve it by earthly conduct is seen in one stone, with circumstantial detail, the 'trump of doom that rends the tombe, and bids the dead arise, shall only raise her heart with praise, and call her to the skies'.

Other quotations are less hopeful. Earthpersons were, as we have seen, warned to be constantly ready for inevitable death, which might come unexpectedly. 'In the midst of Life, we are in death'; 'Boast not thyself of to-morrow; for thou Knowest not what a day may bring forth'. Death is seen as a malignant if impotent force: 'which fatal stroke caused many a friendly tear'; or as a deliverer of pain: 'her pains are past, she sleeps and all is well', and (death here equated with God) 'Afflictions sore, long time I bore, physicians strove in vain; Till God did please to give me ease, and ease me from my pain'. This mention of a (?single) god is only on one or two of the stones. Here the deity seems to be a beneficent death-god who brings release. The god is also named on the stone in which Jesus is also mentioned: 'Them also which sleep in Jesus, will God bring with him'.

By no means all those commemorated in the stones lived at Wharram Percy; it appears to have been a

Fig. 16.6 Wharram Percy gravestones 1

MONKMAN
1835

14

FARTHING
1840

HICKSON DRIFFIELD

9

MEGGINSON
1845

HICKSON   DRIFFIELD

12

ACKLAM
1853

HOLMES NORTON

5

MONKMAN
1858

17

MEGGINSON
1863

11

DAWSON
1863-4

T L SMITH   28

GRAYSTOCK
1866

HICKSON DRIFFIELD

23

3   GOFTON   1878

NORTH
1870

26

CROW
1875

HICKSON DRIFFIELD

7

MEGGINSON
1884

COATES SCARBRO

18

RAIKES
1906

27

SHAWCROSS
1890-1

100 cm   0   1 m

30

WHARRAM PERCY GRAVESTONES II

Fig. 16.7 Wharram Percy gravestones 2